Bibliography of Canadian bibliographies

Bibliographie des bibliographies canadiennes

# Bibliography of Canadian bibliographies

SECOND EDITION
REVISED AND ENLARGED

Compiled by
DOUGLAS LOCHHEAD
Index compiled by
Peter E. Greig

Published in association with the
Bibliographical Society of Canada by
University of Toronto Press

# Bibliographie des bibliographies canadiennes

DEUXIEME EDITION
REVUE ET AUGMENTEE

Compilée par
DOUGLAS LOCHHEAD
Index préparé par
Peter E. Greig

Publié sous les auspices de la
Société bibliographique du Canada par
University of Toronto Press

First edition 1960
© University of Toronto Press 1960
Second edition revised and enlarged 1972
© University of Toronto Press 1972
Printed in Canada by
University of Toronto Press
Toronto and Buffalo
ISBN 0-8020-1865-3
Microfiche ISBN 0-8020-0195-5
LC 76-166933

# Preface to the second edition

Since the publication of the first edition in 1960, three supplements, embracing the years 1961-65, have been published by the Bibliographical Society of Canada. This new edition incorporates the contents of the supplements as well as information gathered about bibliographies compiled since that time, up to June 1970.

Many individuals have assisted in the compilation of this new, revised edition. Miss Madeleine Pellerin of the National Library of Canada compiled the supplements thereby continuing her very considerable contribution to the first edition prepared under the direction of the late Raymond Tanghe. Librarians from many parts of Canada and elsewhere provided assistance, information and useful suggestions. Among these special thanks are extended to: Mr Laurie M. Allison, Chief Librarian, Bishop's University Library; Mr Roland-M. Charland, Les Editions Fides, Montreal; Professor Edith Jarvi, School of Library Science, University of Toronto; Mr Helmut Kallmann, Chief of the Music Division, National Library, Ottawa; Miss Jean R. Kerfoot. Librarian, Legislative Library, Parliament Buildings, Toronto; Mr Paul Kitchen, Chief, Bibliography Division, National Library, Ottawa; Dr Gerhard R. Lomer, University of Ottawa (Library School); Mr Peter F. McNally, Librarian, Reference Department, McGill University Library; Mr Alan D. Marsh, Librarian, Library School, University of Ottawa; Mr William F.E. Morley, Curator of Special Collections, Douglas Library, Queen's University; Professor Florence B. Murray, School of Library Science, University of Toronto; Miss M. Ruth Murray, Head of Reference and Canadiana, Library, University of Saskatchewan; Mr Jacques Paradis, Librarian, Ecole de Bibliothéconomie, Université de Montréal; Dr A. Robert Rogers, Director, Bowling Green State University Library, Ohio; Dr Samuel Rothstein, Director, School of Librarianship, The University of British Columbia; Miss Margaret Slater, Reference Department, University of Toronto Library; Miss Katherine Wales, Head, Reference Department, University of Toronto Library.

For assistance provided in the actual work of compiling, editing and indexing I am grateful to Sara Lochhead, and, in particular, to Patricia Kennedy and Peter E. Greig of Massey College and to Dr David M. Hayne, University College, University of Toronto.

This book has been published with the help of a grant from the Humanities Research Council of Canada and the Social Science Research Council of Canada, using funds provided by the Canada Council. On behalf of the Bibliographical Society of Canada I thank these organizations for making possible the appearance of this second edition of the *Bibliography of Canadian Bibliographies.*

Massey College
University of Toronto
July 1, 1971

Douglas Lochhead
Chairman
Publications Committee
Bibliographical Society of Canada

## Préface de la deuxième édition

A la suite de la publication en 1960 de l'édition originale de la *Bibliographie des bibliographies canadiennes,* la Société bibliographique du Canada l'a complétée par trois suppléments consacrés aux ouvrages parus entre 1961 et 1965. La deuxième édition que voici contient, en plus des titres cités dans les trois suppléments, ceux de tous les ouvrages bibliographiques publiés au Canada entre 1965 et le mois de juin 1970.

Un grand nombre de personnes ont collaboré à la préparation de cette édition augmentée. Mlle Madeleine Pellerin de la Bibliothèque nationale du Canada a préparé les trois suppléments, continuant ainsi la lourde tâche dont elle s'était chargée au moment de la compilation de l'édition originale sous la direction du regretté Raymond Tanghe. Des bibliothécaires canadiens et étrangers ont fourni de partout des renseignements, des suggestions utiles et une aide en somme précieuse. Je tiens à remercier surtout M. Laurie M. Allison, Chief Librarian, Bishop's University Library; M. Roland-M. Charland, Les Editions Fides, Montreal; Professor Edith Jarvi, School of Library Science, University of Toronto; M. Helmut Kallmann, Chief of the Music Division, National Library, Ottawa; Mlle Jean R. Kerfoot, Librarian, Legislative Library, Parliament Buildings, Toronto; M. Paul Kitchen, Chief, Bibliography Division, National Library, Ottawa; M. Gerhard R. Lomer, University of Ottawa (Library School); M. Peter F. McNally, Librarian, Reference Department, McGill University Library; M. Alan D. Marsh, Librarian; Library School, University of Ottawa; M. William F.E. Morley, Curator of Special Collections, Douglas Library, Queen's University; Professor Florence B. Murray, School of Library Science, University of Toronto; Mlle M. Ruth Murray, Head of Reference and Canadiana, Library, University of Saskatchewan; M. Jacques Paradis, bibliothécaire de l'Ecole de bibliothéconomie de l'Université de Montréal; M.A. Robert Rogers, Director, Bowling Green State University Library, Ohio; M. Samuel Rothstein, Director, School of Librarianship, The University of British Columbia; Mlle Margaret Slater, Reference Department, University of Toronto Library; Mlle Katherine Wales, Head, Reference Department, University of Toronto Library.

A ceux qui m'ont aidé à compiler cette bibliographie, à en préparer le manuscrit et à en dresser l'index, notamment à Mlle Sara Lochhead, à Mlle Patricia Kennedy, à M. Peter E. Greig de Massey College et à M. David M. Hayne de University College, j'exprime ma reconnaissance la plus sincère.

Ce volume voit le jour grâce à la bienveillance du Conseil canadien de recherches sur les humanités et du Conseil canadien de recherches en sciences sociales du Canada, qui lui ont accordé un octroi à même les fonds destinés par le Conseil canadien des Arts à encourager la publication d'ouvrages. Au nom de la Société bibliographique du Canada je remercie les deux Conseils d'avoir ainsi rendu possible la publication de cette deuxième édition de la *Bibliographie des bibliographies canadiennes.*

Massey College
University of Toronto
le 1$^{er}$ juillet 1971

Douglas Lochhead
Président du comité de publication
Société bibliographique du Canada

# Preface to the first edition

In 1930, a pamphlet entitled *A Bibliography of Canadian Bibliographies* was published in Montreal. It was compiled by the students in bibliography at McGill University Library School, under the direction of Miss Marion Higgins, Instructor in Bibliography. As Dr Gerhard Lomer, Director of the School, pointed out in an introductory note, 'the compilers felt that most appropriate beginning for a Library School contribution to the subject would be a classified and indexed bibliography of Canadian Bibliography.'

This bibliography has proved valuable, but with the tremendous development in the fields of research and publishing during the past thirty years, it was obviously desirable that it should be brought up to date. A motion to this end was endorsed at the 1958 meeting of the Bibliographical Society. Several members agreed to form a committee to collect information on bibliographies of local interest or 'in progress.' The library schools supplied a list of works prepared by their students.

The staff of the National Library has assisted in the compilation of this new edition. Miss Madeleine Pellerin, who has considerable experience in bibliographical work, has contributed largely to bringing the project to completion.

The Humanities Research Council of Canada and the Social Science Research Council of Canada made a joint grant to the Bibliographical Society of Canada towards the publication of the present volume, using funds provided by the Canada Council for aid to publication.

On behalf of the Society, I thank the three Councils and the contributors to this work. I hope that the new version of the *Bibliography of Canadian Bibliographies* will be useful.

Raymond Tanghe

## Préface de la première édition

En 1930, paraissait à Montréal *A Bibliography of Canadian Bibliographies* réunie, sous la direction de Mlle Marion Higgins, par les étudiants de l'Ecole de bibliothécaires de l'Université McGill. M. Gerhard Lomer, directeur de l'Ecole, soulignait dans l'introduction combien il était judicieux que la première publication des étudiants en bibliothéconomie fût une liste classifiée des bibliographies canadiennes.

Cette brochure a rendu de réels services, mais depuis trente ans, les recherches et les publications se sont multipliées au Canada: il devenait nécessaire de la reprendre et de la mettre à jour. En juin 1958, un projet dans ce sens fut approuvé par l'assemblée annuelle de la Société bibliographique du Canada. Plusieurs membres acceptèrent de faire partie d'un comité chargé de recueillir des renseignements sur les bibliographies d'intérêt local ou sur celles en préparation. Les écoles de bibliothécaires fournirent une liste de travaux soumis par leurs étudiants.

Le personnel de la Bibliothèque nationale du Canada a contribué à la compilation. Mlle Madeleine Pellerin, qui a une grande expérience en bibliographie, a fait sa large part pour mener le travail à bonne fin.

Pour pouvoir imprimer le présent volume, la Société bibliographique du Canada a reçu du Conseil canadien de recherches sur les Humanités et du Conseil de recherche en Sciences sociales du Canada un octroi à même les fonds destinés par le Conseil canadien des Arts à encourager la publication d'ouvrages.

Au nom de la Société et en mon propre nom, je tiens à remercier ces trois institutions ainsi que toutes les personnes qui ont contribué à la réalisation de ce projet, et j'espère que la *Bibliographie des bibliographies canadiennes* rendra service.

Raymond Tanghe

# Introduction

The major changes introduced in this second edition are an alphabetical arrangement of entries regardless of subject and a consolidation of indexes. As a result of the use of an alphabetical list and the consequent renumbering of all items included, it should be pointed out that entry numbers *do not* correspond with those in the first edition. Furthermore all new numbers for entries in this second edition are preceded by '2:.' Such a major alteration in the scheme of the work has made frequent consultation of the index indispensable. The index has been expanded and consolidated and, it is hoped, will enable the reader to locate information with a minimum of consultation. The index locates the bibliographies by subject (in most cases by several entries), and by compiler.

As in the first edition the nature of the bibliographies listed here has some Canadian connection, either by the subject, compiler, geographical location, etc. The following definition of what constitutes a bibliography has been agreed upon:

> A bibliography is a list of books, brochures, newspapers, periodicals, maps, or their reproductions, with information for their identification (author, title, place, date, publisher).

The following categories have been omitted with a few exceptions:
(a) bibliographies or catalogues on cards, unless a list is expected to be made available for circulation;
(b) bibliographies included in a monograph, a thesis or in a periodical article;
(c) catalogues and price lists of publishers, booksellers and second-hand book-dealers;
(d) analytical writings on bibliography or on source material;
(e) subject or name indexes;
(f) directories, trade lists, biographical dictionaries, even though they include cursory bibliographies.

Items in category (b) are so numerous that it has been impossible to list them all. We regret the omission of such useful material but it is hoped that steps will be taken to correct this limitation in future editions. In any event, some items of this type have been included for the convenience of the general reader.

Lists submitted by students for library school requirements can often be useful, and we have listed all those brought to our attention. The library school to which they were submitted is listed after the collation.

It has not been possible to examine the great majority of bibliographies described. Future editions might well endeavour to correct and to expand entries as well as to provide annotations to increase the usefulness of the work.

It should be pointed out once again to users of this edition of the *Bibliography of Canadian Bibliographies* that all entries are listed in a straight alphabetical arrangement. The greatly expanded bilingual index provides an increased number of references both by subject and compiler. When in doubt, please consult the index.

*Index.* The index includes subjects and names of compilers. Emphasis has also been placed on geographical classification where applicable. Numbers refer to the entry in the book. All numbers are new to this second edition:

eg: 2:1 – the '2' denotes edition, the number following
designates the order of the entry in the list.

# Introduction

Cette deuxième édition diffère principalement de la première par le fait de suivre un ordre rigoureusement alphabétique, quel qu'en soit le sujet, et d'être munie d'un index cumulatif. Pour respecter le nouvel ordre alphabétique, il a fallu donner de nouveaux numéros aux titres d'ouvrages; par conséquent ces numéros, précédés du chiffre 2, ne correspondent point à ceux de l'édition originale. Ce remaniement complet de l'ouvrage rend indispensable la consultation fréquente de l'index cumulatif, lequel a été considérablement augmenté en vue de fournir rapidement les renseignements voulus. L'index permet de repérer les ouvrages bibliographiques selon le nom du compilateur ou bien selon le ou les sujets traités.

Comme c'était le cas dans l'édition originale, tous les ouvrages recensés ici se rapportent de près ou de loin au Canada, que ce soit par le sujet, par la nationalité du compilateur, par le lieu de publication, ou autrement. Une bibliographie est, selon nous:

≪une liste de livres, de brochures, de journaux, de périodiques, de cartes ou de plans, ou de reproductions de ces derniers, avec les précisions nécessaires pour les identifier (nom d'auteur, titre, lieu de publication, date, éditeur)≫

Nous avons cependant cru devoir omettre, à peu d'exceptions près, les catégories suivantes:
(a) les bibliographies, catalogues et répertoires sur fiches, sauf dans les cas où une publication éventuelle est annoncée.
(b) les listes d'ouvrages consultés au cours de la préparation d'une thèse, d'une monographie ou d'un article de revue.
(c) les listes d'ouvrages et catalogues de vente distribués par un libraire-éditeur ou un libraire d'occasion.
(d) les études de sources ou de méthode bibliographique.
(e) les index analytiques ou onomastiques.
(f) les annuaires, listes de publications ou dictionnaires biographiques, même pourvus de bibliographies sommaires.

Les titres de la catégorie (b) sont si nombreux qu'il nous a été impossible de les inclure tous. Nous regrettons l'absence de ces informations utiles, et nous espérons qu'il sera possible de combler cette lacune dans une autre édition. De toute façon nous avons retenu un certain nombre de titres avec l'espoir de rendre service au lecteur non-spécialiste.

Les listes bibliographiques présentées aux écoles de bibliothécaires par leurs étudiants en vue de l'obtention d'un grade en bibliothéconomie ont souvent une grande utilité; nous avons pris note de celles qui avaient été portées à notre attention, en indiquant, après la pagination, le nom de l'école.

Nous nous sommes trouvé dans l'impossibilité d'examiner un exemplaire de la plupart des bibliographies que nous signalons. Nos successeurs auront la tâche de corriger et d'amplifier nos mentions et d'ajouter à notre compilation les commentaires qui s'imposent.

Nous nous permettons de rappeler au lecteur que tous les titres inclus dans cette nouvelle édition de la *Bibliographie des bibliographies canadiennes* sont arrangés par ordre alphabétique sans exception. L'index bilingue, très augmenté, contient un grand nombre de renvois aux sujets et aux compilateurs. Prière de consulter l'index en cas de doute.

*Index.* L'index contient les titres, les sujets et les compilateurs des bibliographies; dans la mesure du possible, nous proposons aussi une classification géographique. Les numéros, entièrement nouveaux dans cette deuxième édition, renvoient aux titres, selon l'example que voici:

2:1 Le chiffre 2 indique la deuxième édition; le numéro
1 qui suit renvoie au premier titre de la liste alphabétique
numérotée.

# Contents / Table des matières

Bibliography of Canadian bibliographies

Bibliographie des bibliographies canadiennes

2:1  **Abbott, Maude Elizabeth Seymour**
Classified and annotated bibliography of Sir William Osler's publications (based on the chronological bibliography by Minnie Wright Blogg), edited by Maude E. Abbott ... 2d ed., rev. and indexed. Montreal, Medical Museum, McGill University, 1939. 163 p.
'Reprinted, with additions, from the Sir William Osler memorial volume of the International Association of Medical Museums (Bulletin no. IX) 1926, p. 473-605.'

2:2  **Abbott, Maude Elizabeth Seymour**
Publications of ... 1899-1940. [N.p.n.d.] 2 v.

2:3  **Abernethy, George L.**
Pakistan; a selected, annotated bibliography compiled by George L. Abernethy. 3d ed., rev. and enl. Vancouver, Distributed by the Publications Centre, University of British Columbia, 1968.
iii, 56 p.
First ed. 1957, and 2d ed. 1960, New York American Institute of Pacific Relations.

2:4  **L'Académie canadienne-française**
L'Académie canadienne-française. Montréal, 1955. 58, [3] p.
Bio-bibliographie [des membres] : p. [23]-49.

2:5  **Acadia University**, Wolfville, N.S. Library
Catalogue of books, manuscripts, maps and documents in the William Inglis Morse collection, 1926-1931. London, Curwen, 1931. vi p., 1 *l.*, 85 p.

2:6  **Acadia University**, Wolfville, N.S. Library
A catalogue of the Eric R. Dennis collection of Canadiana in the library of Acadia University, by Helen D. Beals, prepared under the direction of Mary Kinley Ingraham. Wolfville, N.S., The University, 1938. vi, 212 p.

2:7  **Acadia University**, Wolfville, N.S. Library
A catalogue of the Maritime Baptist historical collection in the Library of Acadia University. Kentville, N.S., Kentville Pub. Co., 1955. 41 p.

2:8  **Achille, frère**
Thèse A: Répertoire des sources manuscrites de l'histoire religieuse canadienne en Europe, surtout à Paris, à Rome et à Londres, de 1608

à 1860. Thèse B: Chronologie de l'histoire religieuse canadienne, 1608 à 1860. [Par] Frère Achille Gingras, i.e. (Guy Laviolette) Saint-Romuald d'Etchemin, Québec, Frères de l'Instruction chrétienne, 1958-59.

25 f.

2:9 **Adam, Margaret Isabella**
Guide to the principal parliamentary papers relating to the Dominions, 1812-1911, prepared by Margaret I. Adam, John Ewing, and James Munro. Edinburgh, Oliver and Boyd, 1913. 190 p.

List of parliamentary papers relating to Canada is given on p. 3-34.

2:10 **Adams, Charles Joseph**
A reader's guide to the great religions. New York, Free Press; London, Collier-Macmillan [c1965]

xv, 364 p.

2:11 **Adams, Dorothy S.**
Bibliography of Canadian artists; [material in the Hamilton Public Library]. [Toronto, 1930] [1], 19 *l.* (Ms. Toronto Univ. Libr. School)

2:12 **Adams, Ethel M.**
Bibliography of Sir Gilbert Parker ... [Toronto, 1933] [1], 6 *l.* (Ms. Toronto Univ. Libr. School)

2:13 **Adams, Margaret B.**
A bibliography of the works of George Bryce. [Toronto] 1938. [10] *l.* (Ms. Toronto Univ. Libr. School)

2:14 **Adams, R.D.**
Index of selected articles from Canadian journals pertaining to the forest products industries, 1965-1967, by R.D. Adams, M.L. El-Osta and R.W. Wellwood. Vancouver, Faculty of Forestry, University of British Columbia, 1968.

iv, 23 *l.*

2:15 **Adelmus, frère**
Bibliographie analytique de l'oeuvre de Mgr Léonce Boivin. Préface de Mgr Victor Tremblay. Champigny, 1961. 38 p. (Ms. Ecole de Bibl., U.L.)

2:16 **Aedy, Lenora Gladys**
A bibliography of Thunder Bay district arranged chronologically by imprint date. [Toronto, 1957] 17 *l.* (Ms. Toronto Univ. Libr. School)

2:17 **Agnès-de-Marie, soeur**
Essai de bio-bibliographie: Mgr Pierre-Avila Sabourin, p.d. 1953. 26 p.
(Ms. Ecole de Bibl., U. de M.)

2:18 **Aitken, Barbara Boyd**
Local histories of Ontario municipalities published in the years 1958-
1968, compiled by Barbara B. Aitken. Rev. ed. [Kingston, Ont.,
Kingston Public Library, 1968]
[12] *l.*

2:19 **Alarie, Maurice**
Canadian archaeology and prehistory. 1963. viii, 5 l. (Ms. U. of O.
Libr. School)

2:20 **Albert, Thérèse**
Bio-bibliographie de Monsieur Gérard Morisset. 1950. 80 p. (Mf.
Ecole de Bibl., U. de M.)

2:21 **Alberta. Department of Agriculture**
Publication list. [Edmonton, 1964] 11 p.

2:22 **Alberta. Department of Education**
List of publications. 19—?— [Edmonton, 19—?—] folder. annual.

2:23 **Alberta. Oil and Gas Conservation Board**
Catalogue of publications, services and maps. Aug. 1964— Calgary
[1964—  ]. annual.
Title varies: 1959?-1963, Publications, services and maps.

2:24 **Alberta. Queen's Printer**
Catalogue of Alberta government publications. v. 1, no. 1. March
1954. Edmonton, 1954. [2] , 5-32 p. form.

2:25 **Alberta. University.** Library
Bibliographies (national and trade) used by the Order Department,
Cameron Library, University of Alberta, compiled by G. J. MacInnis,
1964. [Edmonton, University of Alberta, 1965]
iv, 65 *l.*
Supplement I, compiled by G.J. MacInnis. [Edmonton, University of Alberta,
1965]
iii, 26 *l.*

2:26 **Alberta. University.** Library. Periodicals Dept.
Newspaper holdings catalog, compiled by Gillian Banbury and Eugene
G. Olson. [Edmonton] 1967.
27 *l.*

2:27  **Alberta Library Association**
A suggested buying guide to Canadian books for small Alberta
libraries. Rev. ed., Edmonton, 1963.

1 v.

First ed. 1956, another ed. in 1958

1965 supplement. Edmonton [1965]
17 *l.*

1966 supplement. Edmonton [1966]
16 *l.*

1967 supplement. Edmonton [1967]
16 *l.*

1968 supplement. Edmonton [1969?]
33 *l.* annual

2:28  **Alberta-Marie, soeur**
Bibliographie analytique de l'oeuvre de M. le curé L. Boisseau.
Préface du chanoine J. B. Carignan. Trois-Rivières, 1961. 50 p. (Ms.
Ecole de Bibl., U.L.)

2:29  **Alberta Society of Petroleum Geologists**
Annotated bibliography of geology of the sedimentary basin of
Alberta and of adjacent part of British Columbia and Northwest
Territories, 1845-1955. Compiled and edited by R. G. McCrossan
[and others] . Calgary, Alberta Society of Petroleum Geologists, 1958.
xv, 499 p.

2:30  **Alberta Weekly Newspapers Association**
Data, Alberta weekly newspapers; a quick reference book published
for your convenience listing member papers of Alberta Weekly Newspapers' Association. 1960– [N.p., 1960–  ] annual.

2:31  **Allaire, Violette**
Notes bio-bibliographiques sur Louis Guzon. 1953. xi, 99 p. (Ms.
Ecole de Bibl., U. de M.)

2:32  **Allan, Charlotte E.**
Bibliography of books and monographs printed and published in
Nova Scotia, 1895-1920 ... Toronto, 1939. [3] , 36 *l.* (Ms. Toronto
Univ. Libr. School)

2:33  **Allan, Charlotte S.**
Alexander Mackenzie, fur trader and explorer. [Toronto, 1932] 5 *l.*
(Ms. Toronto Univ. Libr. School)

2:34  **Allard, Lucienne, soeur**
Notes bio-bibliographiques sur le R. P. Adélard Dugré, s.j. 1953. 48 p.
(Ms. Ecole de Bibl., U. de M.)

2:35 **Allard, Marguerite**
[Bibliographie de l'histoire du Canada, 1837-1838]. 1940. [30] p.
(Ms. Ecole de Bibl., U. de M.)

2:36 **Allard, Thérèse**
Bio-bibliographie de M. Ernest Bilodeau, chevalier du St-Sépulcre,
bibliothécaire-adjoint du Parlement fédéral. 1945. xxv, 179 p. (Mf.
Ecole de Bibl., U. de M.)

2:37 **Allary, Marguerite**
Bio-bibliographie de Madame Hélène-B. Beauséjour. Trois-Rivières,
1946. 50 p. (Mf. Ecole de Bibl., U. de M.)

2:38 **Allen, David E.**
Business books translated from English: 1950-1965, compiled by
David E. Allen. Reading, Mass., Addison-Wesley Pub. Co.; Don Mills,
Ont., Addison-Wesley (Canada) [c1966]
xiv, 414 p.
Includes industries of Canada.

2:39 **America: history and life** v. 1— July 1964—
Santa Barbara, Calif., Clio Press.
v. 4 no. a year.
'A guide to periodical literature.'
Includes abstracts of articles about Canadian history and Canadian life. Annual
Index issued each year as no. 4.

2:40 **American Foundation for the Blind**
Periodicals of special interest to blind persons in the United States
and Canada. [New ed. New York] 1960. [5], 48, 4 p.
'Canada': p. 45-48.

2:41 **American Geophysical Union**
Annotated bibliography on hydrology, 1941-1950, United States
and Canada. Prepared by the American Geophysical Union, National
Research Council of the National Academy of Science, in co-opera-
tion with the Subcommittee, Federal Interagency River Basin Com-
mittee ... [Washington, G.P.O., 1952] [5], 408 p. (Subcommittee on
Hydrology, Notes on hydrologic activities, Bulletin no. 5)
Continues, for the period 1941-50, the annual *Bibliography of hydrology,
United States of America,* published by the American Geophysical Union for
the years 1935-40.

2:42 **American Geophysical Union**
Annotated bibliography on hydrology (1951-54) and sedimentation
(1950-54), United States and Canada. [Washington, G.P.O., 1956]

[4] , 207 p. ([U.S.] Inter-Agency Committee on Water Resources, Joint hydrology-sedimentation bulletin no. 7)

'Supplement to the *Annotated bibliography on hydrology* (Notes on hydrologic activities, Bull. no. 5) and *Annotated bibliography on sedimentation* (U.S. Soil Conservation Service, Sedimentation bulletin no. 2).'

2:43  **Ami, Henri Marc**

Bibliographical sketch of George Mercer Dawson. Ottawa, Ottawa Printing Co., 1901. 31 p.

Bibliography, geology and paleontology (principally Canadian), 1870-1901, p. 21-31.
(Reprinted with addition of bibliography from the *Ottawa naturalist,* v. 15, no. 2, p. 43-52, May 1901)

2:44  **Ami, Henri Marc**

Bibliography of Dr George M. Dawson. (In B.J. Harrington. *George Mercer Dawson.* Minneapolis, Geological Pub. Co., n.d., p. 67-86.) (Reprint from *American geologist,* v. 28, Aug. 1901)

Bibliography of Canadian paleontology.
Also in Royal Society of Canada, *Transactions,* 1902, sec. IV, p. 192-201.

2:45  **Ami, Henri Marc**

... Canada & Newfoundland. 2d ed., rev. London, Stanford, 1915. 1069 p. (Half-title: Stanford's compendium of geography and travel (new issue) [North America, v. 1] )

Supersedes Dawson's edition, London, 1897.
Bibliography: p. 1025-1054.

2:46  **Ami, Henri Marc**

Progress of geological work in Canada during 1899. 'Reprinted from the *Canadian record of science,* vol. VIII, no. 4, for July, 1900.' [Ottawa? 1900] 15 p.

2:47  **Ami, Henri Marc**

Sir John William Dawson. A brief biographical sketch. [Minneapolis? 1900] 57 p.

From the *American geologist,* v. 26, no. 1, p. 1-48, July, 1900, with corrections and additions to bibliography.
The bibliography is also in Royal Society of Canada, *Transactions,* 1901, sec. IV, p. 15-44.
Reprinted with additions and corrections from the *American geologist* (*supra*) Minneapolis, American geologist, 1900. 64 p.

2:48  **Ami, Henri Marc**

Sketch of the life and work of the late Dr Alfred R.C. Selwyn ... Director of Geological Survey of Canada from 1869 to 1894. (Extracted from the *American geologist,* January, 1903.) [N.p., 1903?] 24 p.

Bibliography: p. 16-23.
Also in Royal Society of Canada, *Transactions,* 1904, sec. IV, p. 173-205.
(Bibliography: p. 191-205)

2:49   **Amyot, Michel**
Bibliographie analytique de l'Ile-aux-Coudres, province de Québec.
Québec, 1952. 34 p. (Ms. Ecole de Bibl., U.L.)

2:50   **Anastase, frère**
Essai de bio-bibliographie: R.F. Théodule, s.c. 1953. 40 p. (Ms. Ecole
de Bibl., U. de M.)

2:51   **Anderson, Ann Christine**
Canadian spinning and weaving, yesterday and today. [Toronto]
1966. ii, 8 *l.* (Ms. Toronto Univ. Libr. School)

2:52   **Anderson, Beryl Lapham**
Basic cataloguing tools for use in Canadian libraries. Rev. ed. Ottawa
[Canadian Library Association] 1968.

28 *l.* (Canadian Library Association. Occasional paper, no. 59)
First ed. 1966.

2:53   **Anderson, William**
Bibliography of world literature on the strawberry, 1920-1962.
[n.p.] 1966.

2 v. (645, [170] p.)
Thesis submitted for Fellowship of the Library Association.
Includes Canadian material.

2:54   **André-Marie, frère**
Bibliographie de Mgr Henri Têtu. 1945. 22 p. (Ms. Ecole de Bibl.,
U. de M.)

2:55   **Annual Bibliography of Commonwealth Literature**:
In *The journal of commonwealth literature,* University of Leeds,
Heinemann Educational Books Ltd.

Annual section on Canada since 1964, comps. C.F. Klinck and Mary M.S. Brown.
No. 1 (September, 1965), pp. 27-43
No. 2 (December, 1966), pp. 39-55
No. 4 (December, 1967), pp. 46-62.

2:56   **Arcand, Césaire, père**
Bio-bibliographie du R.P. Adrien-Marie Malo, o.f.m. 1940. [24] p.
(Ms. Ecole de Bibl., U. de M.)

2:57   **Archer, John H.**
A bibliographical essay on sources for the writing of local history with
particular reference to Saskatchewan. Montreal, 1949. 33 *l.* (Ms.
McGill Univ. Libr. School)

2:58 **Archibald, Raymond Clare**
... Bibliography of the life and works of Simon Newcomb. Ottawa, Hope, 1905. 110 p.
'From *Transactions of the Royal Society of Canada,* 2d series, 1905-1906, v. XI, Section III, Mathematical, physical and chemical sciences.'

2:59 **Arctic Institute of North America**
Arctic bibliography. Montreal, McGill University Press, 1953–
v. fold. col. maps.
Editor: 1953–  Marie Tremaine.
Imprint varies: 1953-1965, Washington, Dept. of Defense.

2:60 **Arctic Institute of North America**
A selected reading list of books about the Arctic. Montreal, 1965.
6 *l.*

2:61 **Arctic Institute of North America. Library**
Catalogue of the Library of the Arctic Institute of North America, Montreal. Boston, Mass., G.K. Hall, 1968.
4 v.
To be kept up to date by supplements.

2:62 **Ariano, Alphonse**
Bio-bibliographie de l'abbé Léon Provancher. 1949. 10 p. (Ms. Ecole de Bibl., U. de M.)

2:63 **Armour, Milly**
The growth of Canadian national consciousness. 1964. iv [2] 6 1. (Ms. U. of O. Libr. School)

2:64 **Arteau, Jean-Marie**
Bio-bibliographie de monsieur Carl Faessler, professeur à la faculté des sciences de Laval. Québec, 1948. 28 p. (Ms. Ecole de Bibl., U.L.)

2:65 **Arthurs, H.W.**
Bibliographies on the legal profession and legal education in Canada [by] H.W. Arthurs [and] Brian D. Bucknall. [Toronto, York University Law Library, 1969]
viii, 95 p.

2:66 **Ashcroft, Edith**
Bibliography of Edward Blake, including both publications by and publications about him. [Toronto, 1933] [2], 10 *l.* (Toronto Univ. Libr. School)

2:67 **Ashman, Stanley**
The development of technical vocational education in Ontario, 1945-1964. 1965. vi, 5 1. (Ms. U. of O. Libr. School)

2:68 **Association canadienne des éducateurs de langue française**
Bibliographie analytique de la littérature pédagogique canadienne-française [par Alice Ratté et Gilberte Gagnon]. [Montréal, Centre de Psychologie et de Pédagogie, pour] L'Association canadienne des éducateurs de langue française, 1952. 108 p.

2:69 **Association canadienne des éducateurs de langue française**
Projet du relevé de la documentation reçue au secrétariat. [Québec, 1966]
13 f.

2:70 **Association des éditeurs canadiens**
Catalogue collectif de l'édition canadienne. Août 1958. [Montréal, 1958] 64 p.
Deuxième édition: Mars 1962. [Montréal, 1962] 103 p.
La première édition a été publiée par l'Association sous son nom antérieur, Société des éditeurs canadiens du livre français.

2:71 **L'Assomption, Québec. Collège. Bibliothèque**
Bibliographie des oeuvres des anciens du Collège de L'Assomption, compilée par Réjean Olivier. L'Assomption [Québec] 1967.
52 p.

2:72 **L'Assomption, Québec. Collège. Bibliothèque**
Guide méthodique et alphabétique des périodiques en cours reçus par la bibliothèque en 1965-1966, rédigé par André Contant. Ed. provisoire. L'Assomption [Québec] 1966.
ix, 67 f.

2:73 **Atlantic Provinces checklist**; a guide to current information in books, pamphlets, government publications, magazine articles and documentary films relating to the four Atlantic Provinces ... [Halifax, N.S.] Atlantic Provinces Library Association in co-operation with Atlantic Provinces Economic Council.
Editors: Shirley B. Elliott and D.G. Lochhead. v. 1-9, 1958-1965

2:74 **Atlantic Provinces Economic Council**
Bibliography of research projects. Oct. 1965. Fredericton, N.B., Atlantic Provinces Research Board, 1965.
iii, 102 *l.* annual.
addendum. 2d; Feb. 1967. [Fredericton, N.B.] Atlantic Provinces Research Board, 1967.
64 *l.* annual.

2:75 **Atomic Energy of Canada limited. Technical Information Branch**
List of publications. 2: Sept. 1959-Oct. 1963. Chalk River, Ont., 1963. 2 p. *l.,* 70 p.

Replaces the 4 supplements to the 1952-59 list and covers more recent publications.– Cf. Introd.

Supplement I. Nov. 1963 to June 1964. Chalk River, Ont., 1964. 2 p. *l.*, 18 p.

2:76 **Audet, Claire**
Bio-bibliographie du T.R.P. Louis Lachance, o.p. Préface de M.
Raymond Tanghe. 1944. 49 p. (Ms. Ecole de Bibl., U. de M.)

2:77 **Audet, Mme M.-R.**
Bibliographie analytique du Dr Emile Gaumond, professeur à la
faculté de médecine de Laval. Préf. du Dr Sylvio Leblond. Québec,
1953. 65 p. (Ms. Ecole de Bibl., U.L.)

2:78 **Auger, Pauline**
Essai de bio-bibliographie de Mr Léon Trépanier. Préf. de Victor
Morin. Montréal, 1954. xv, 157 p. (Ms. Ecole de Bibl., U. de M.)

2:79 **Auger, Roland**
Brève bio-bibliographie de M. Esdras Minville. 1947. 9 p. (Ms. Ecole
de Bibl., U. de M.)

2:80 **Auger, Roland**
Essai de bio-bibliographie sur Ludger Duvernay, imprimeur, journaliste
et fondateur de la Société Saint-Jean-Baptiste. Préface de M. Jules
Bazin. 1953. 114 p. (Mf. Ecole de Bibl., U. de M.)

2:81 **Augustin-Marie, soeur**
Bio-bibliographie de M. l'abbé Albert Gravel. Préface de Soeur
Thérèse-Marie. Sherbrooke, 1946. 56 p. (Ms. Ecole de Bibl., U. de M.)

2:82 **Avignon, Marguerite-Marie d'**
Notes bio-bibliographiques sur Gérard Malchelosse. 1948. 20 p.
(Mf. Ecole de Bibl., U. de M.)

2:83 **Avis, Walter Spencer**
A bibliography of writings on Canadian English (1857-1965) Toronto,
W.J. Gage [c1965]

17 p.
Much of ... [the bibliography] has already been published cumulatively each
year since 1955 in the *Canadian journal of linguistics* (formerly the *Journal of
the Canadian linguistic association.* –p. [2]

2:84 **Ayer, firm**
N.W. Ayer & Son's Directory of newspapers and periodicals; a guide
to publications printed in the United States and possessions, the
Dominion of Canada, Bermuda, Cuba and the West Indies; including ...

maps; descriptions of the publications; the states, cities and towns in which they are published; complete classified lists. Philadelphia, Ayer, 1880?—.

Title varies: 1880-1909, American newspaper annual; 1910-1929, American newspaper annual and directory; 1930— Directory of newspapers and periodicals.

2:85 **BMI Canada Limited**
Biographies and lists of works of many Canadian composers available on request.

2:86 **Babin, B.J.**
Bibliographie analytique des évêques et de quelques Pères eudistes au Canada. Préf. du R.P. Bernier. Québec, 1949. 164 p. (Ms. Ecole de Bibl., U.L.)

2:87 **Baboyant, Marie**
Bio-bibliographie du R.P. Joseph-Henri Ledit, s.j. Préface de Mlle Marie-Claire Daveluy. 1946. 75 p. (Ms. Ecole de Bibl., U. de M.)

2:88 **Baillargeon, Constantin-M., père**
Bio-bibliographie du R.P. Laval Laurent, o.f.m. Les Trois-Rivières, 1946. xviii, 56 p. (Ms. Ecole de Bibl., U. de M.)

2:89 **Ball, John L.**
'Theater in Canada' in *Canadian literature* 14:85-100, August 1962.

2:90 **Ball, Katharine L.**
Canadian biographical material in the University of Toronto Library. [Toronto, 1947] [1], 10 *l*. (Ms. Toronto Univ. Libr. School)

2:91 **Barath, Tibor**
Les publications du Comité paritaire de l'industrie de l'imprimerie de Montréal et du district, 1945-1961. Montréal, 1961. 65 p. (Ms. Ecole de Bibl., U. de M.)

2:92 **Barbeau, Victor**
L'Académie canadienne-française. Montréal [Académie canadienne-française] 1960. 84 p. ill., portr.

Contient la bio-bibliographie des membres et la liste des publications de l'Académie.
Deuxième édition: *1963*. 84 p. ill., portr.

2:93 **Barbeau, Victor**
La Société des écrivains canadiens; ses règlements, son action; bio-bibliographie de ses membres. Montréal, Editions de la Société des écrivains canadiens, 1944. 117 p.

2:94  **Bardyn, Michael**
Pulp industry in Canada. 1964. x, 8 1. (Ms. U. of O. Libr. School)

2:95  **Bareil, Catherine**
Essai de bio-bibliographie de Rina Lasnier, membre de l'Académie
canadienne-française. 1948. vii, 16 p. (Mf. Ecole de Bibl., U. de M.)

2:96  **Barnabé, Michèle**
Bibliographie de l'île d'Anticosti. Québec, 1959. 41 p. (Ms. Ecole de
Bibl., U.L.)

2:97  **Barnes, Sandra**
Education for librarianship in Canada. 1964. viii, 12 1. (Ms. U. of O.
Libr. School)

2:98  **Barnett, John Davis**
The books of the political prisoners and exiles of 1838. (Reprinted
from *Papers and records,* v. XVI, Ontario Historical Society) 8 p.

2:99  **Barry, Catherine, soeur**
Essai de bibliographie canadienne: la Vén. Mère d'Youville et les
Soeurs de la Charité de Montréal (Soeurs Grises) 1938. 38 p. (Ms.
Ecole de Bibl., U. de M.)

2:100  **Barsalo, Andrée**
Bio-bibliographie du R.P. Ferdinand Coiteux, o.f.m. 1947. 48 p.
(Ms. Ecole de Bibl., U. de M.)

2:101  **Bealey, Margaret E.**
French Canadian folk-songs; a list of sources in the libraries of
Toronto ... [Toronto] 1938. [1], 16 *l.* (Ms. Toronto Univ. Libr.
School)

2:102  **Béatrice-du-Saint-Sacrement, soeur**
Bibliographie analytique de l'oeuvre de l'Abbé Pierre Gravel, curé de
Boischâtel. 1ère partie (1917-1941) Préface de M. Robert Rumilly.
Sherbrooke, 1961. 108 p. (Ms. Ecole de Bibl., U.L.)

2:103  **Beauchemin, Louise**
Notes bio-bibliographiques sur M. l'abbé Auguste Lapalme. 1948. 11 p.
(Ms. Ecole de Bibl., U. de M.)

2:104  **[Beaudé, Henri]**
Louis Fréchette [par] Henri d'Arles [pseud.] Toronto, Ryerson
[1924]. 127 p. (Makers of Canadian literature ...)
Bibliographie: p. 117-121.

2:105   **Beaudet, Jeanne**
Essai de bio-bibliographie sur la personne et l'œuvre littéraire, oratoire
et politique de M. Joseph-Napoléon-Henri Bourassa. 1937-1938. 42 p.
(Mf. Ecole de Bibl., U. de M.)

2:106   **Beaudet, Suzanne**
Bio-bibliographie de M. Napoléon Bourassa. 1944. 28 p. (Mf. Ecole
de Bibl., U. de M.)

2:107   **Beaudoin, Gabriel**
Notes bio-bibliographiques sur Marcel Trudel. Lettre-préface de M.
l'abbé Albert Tessier. 1949. ix, 53 p. (Ms. Ecole de Bibl., U. de M.)

2:108   **Beaudoin, Gilles**
Rév. P. Gonzalve Poulin, o.f.m.; bibliographie analytique. Québec,
1955. 85 p. (Ms. Ecole de Bibl., U.L.)

2:109   **Beaudoin, Hélène-C.**
Essai de bibliographie sur M. Victor Morin. 1938-39. 25 p. (Mf.
Ecole de Bibl., U. de M.)

2:110   **Beaudoin, Juliette**
Bio-bibliographie de Vieux Doc [Dr Edmond Grignon]. Préface de
Madame Germaine Guèvremont. 1946. 40 p. (Mf. Ecole de Bibl.,
U. de M.)

2:111   **Beaudoin, Léopold**
Bio-bibliographie de Mgr Ignace Bourget. Préf. de M. le chanoine
Raoul Drouin, 1950. xv, 173 p. (Ms. Ecole de Bibl., U. de M.)

2:112   **Beaudoin, Yolande**
Notes bio-bibliographiques sur M. Raymond Tanghe. 1947. 6 p.
(Ms. Ecole de Bibl., U. de M.)

2:113   **Beaudry, Pauline**
Bibliographie analytique de Baie-Comeau, sur la côte nord du Saint-
Laurent. Préface de Paul Provencher, i.f. Québec, 1959. 57 p. (Ms.
Ecole de Bibl., U.L.)

2:114   **Beaugrand, Paul**
Le Collège militaire royal de Saint-Jean. 1964. (Ms. Ecole de Bibl.,
U.L.)

2:115   **Beaulieu, André**
Guide d'histoire du Canada [par] André Beaulieu, Jean Hamelin [et]
Benoît Bernier. Québec, Presses de l'Université Laval, 1969.
xvi, 540 p. (Les Cahiers de l'Institut d'histoire, 13)

2:116  **Beaulieu, Désiré, père**
Bio-bibliographie du R.P. Ange-Marie Portelance, o.f.m. 1946. ix, 78 p.
(Ms. Ecole de Bibl., U. de M.)

2:117  **Beaulne, Renée**
Bio-bibliographie du R.P. A.-G. Morice, o.m.i. Préface du R.P. L.-R.
Lafleur, o.m.i. 1945. 46 p. (Mf. Ecole de Bibl., U. de M.)

2:118  **Beauregard, Denise**
P. Jean Laramée, s.j.; essai de bio-bibliographie. 1953. 28 p. (Mf.
Ecole de Bibl., U. de M.)

2:119  **Beauregard, Thérèse**
Bibliographie de Jacques Rousseau, précédée de notes biographiques.
1943. 44 p. (Ms. Ecole de Bibl., U. de M.)

2:120  **Beauregard, Thérèse**
Bio-bibliographie de Monsieur Pierre Benoit. Préface de Mlle Marie-
Claire Daveluy. 1947. 35 p. (Mf. Ecole de Bibl., U. de M.)

2:121  **Beauregard, Yvonne**
Bio-bibliographie de Sir James MacPherson Lemoine. 1939-40. 95 p.
(Mf. Ecole de Bibl., U. de M.)

2:122  **Bédard, Berthe**
Essai de bibliographie analytique des brochurettes sur la santé et
l'hygiène publiées par la Metropolitan Life Insurance Company,
depuis juillet 1909. 1939. 53 p. (Ms. Ecole de Bibl., U. de M.)

2:123  **Bédard, Denyse**
Bio-bibliographie de Jules-S. Lesage. Québec, 1948. 28 p. (Ms. Ecole
de Bibl., U.L.)

2:124  **Bédard, Francine**
Les livres de recettes publiés au Québec ainsi que quelques articles sur
la cuisine québécoise. 1967. iv, 12 l. (Ms. U. of O. Libr. School)

2:125  **Bédard, Raymond-Pierre, frère**
Bio-bibliographie de M. Damase Potvin. Québec, 1956. 111 p. (Ms.
Ecole de Bibl., U.L.)

2:126  **Bédard, Suzanne**
Bibliographie analytique de l'œuvre de Charlotte Savary. Québec,
1951. 75 p. (Ms. Ecole de Bibl., U.L.)

2:127  **Beers, Henry Putney**
The French & British in the old Northwest; a bibliographical guide to

archive and manuscript sources. Detroit, Wayne State University Press, 1964. 297 p.
'Bibliographical Sources': p. 195-225.

2:128 **Beers, Henry Putney**
The French in North America; a bibliographical guide to French archives, reproductions and research missions. Baton Rouge, Louisiana State University Press [1957]. 413 p.
Bibliography: p. 279-350.

2:129 **Bekker-Nielsen, Hans**
Old Norse-Icelandic studies; a select bibliography. [Toronto] University of Toronto Press [c1967]
94 p. (Toronto medieval bibliographies, 1)

2:130 **Bélair, Andrée**
Bio-bibliographie de Claude Aubry. Préface de M. Pierre Ricour. 1947. xiv, 47 p. (Mf. Ecole de Bibl., U. de M.)

2:131 **Bélanger, Juliette**
Bio-bibliographie du R.P. Eugène Nadeau, o.m.i. 1952. 71 p. (Ms. Ecole de Bibl., U. de M.)

2:132 **Bélanger, Léonie**
Bio-bibliographie de Mère M.-Catherine-de-Suède. 1948. 39 p. (Mf. Ecole de Bibl., U. de M.)

2:133 **Bélanger, Lucile**
Notes bio-bibliographiques sur Maxine [Mme Taschereau-Fortier]. 1953. 24 p. (Mf. Ecole de Bibl., U. de M.)

2:134 **Bélanger, Marguerite**
Bibliographie de Mme Blanche Lamontagne-Beauregard. 1938. 30 p. (Mf. Ecole de Bibl., U. de M.)

2:135 **Bélanger, Pauline**
Les notices nécrologiques des ministères de la Couronne du Québec. Québec. 1965. (Ms. Ecole de Bibl., U.L.)

2:136 **Bélanger, Pierrette**
Bibliographie analytique de l'œuvre de monsieur Auguste Viatte, docteur ès lettres, professeur à l'Université Laval. Québec, 1948. 80 p. (Ms. Ecole de Bibl., U.L.)

2:137 **Belec, Thérèse**
Bibliographie de M. René Desrochers, ptre. Préface de M. l'abbé G.-Etienne Boileau. 1947. 24 p. (Ms. Ecole de Bibl., U. de M.)

2:138  **Bélisle, Alvine**
Bibliographie; liste de chroniques et récits de voyages dans la province de Québec, publiés en français et en anglais de 1800 à date, 'Collection Gagnon.' 1938. 21 p. (Ms. Ecole de Bibl., U. de M.)

2:139  **Bélisle, Alvine**
Notre héritage française; choix de livres sur le Canada français.
[Ottawa, Association canadienne des bibliothèques, 1963?] [4] p.

2:140  **Bélisle, Germain**
Le Révérend Père Henri Morisseau, o.m.i. Biographie et bibliographie choisie. Ottawa, Université d'Ottawa, Ecole de Bibliothécaires, 1953. 30 p. (Ms. U. d'O. Ecole de Bibl.)

2:141  **Béliveau, Madeleine**
Bio-bibliographie de Maxine [Mme Taschereau-Fortier] 1943. 26 p. (Ms. Ecole de Bibl., U. de M.)

2:142  **Bell, Inglis Freeman**
Canadian literature 1959–  A checklist. (In *Canadian literature,* Winter 1960–  ) annual.
Issued as supplement to Winter issue 1960–
In two parts: English-Canadian literature, comp. by Inglis F. Bell;–Littérature canadienne-française, liste établie par A.E. Ford [et Geoffrey P. Selth]

2:143  **Bell, Inglis Freeman**
Canadian literature, Littérature canadienne, 1959-1963. A checklist of creative and critical writings. Bibliographie de la critique et des oeuvres d'imagination. Edited by Inglis F. Bell and Susan W. Port. [Vancouver] Publications Centre, University of British Columbia, 1966.
140 p. illus.
'Amended cumulation of the annual lists from *Canadian literature'.*–Pref.

2:144  **Bell, James Ford**
Jesuit relations and other Americana in the library of James F. Bell; a catalogue compiled by Frank K. Walter and Virginia Doneghy. Minneapolis, University of Minnesota Press; London, Oxford University Press [1950]. 419 p. facsims.

2:145  **Bell, Marion R.**
A bibliography of Toronto newspapers. [Toronto] 1933. [24] *l.* (Ms. Toronto Univ. Libr. School)

2:146  **Bell, Sheila M.**
A bibliography of material relating to the history of Kent County, to the year 1900. [Toronto, 1936] [5], 27 *l.* (Ms. Toronto Univ. Libr. School)

2:147 **Bellavance, B., sœur**
Bibliographie des œuvres de Monsieur Léon Gérin. 1938-39. 24 p.
(Mf. Ecole de Bibl., U. de M.)

2:148 **Bellemare, Gertrude**
Bio-bibliographie de l'abbé Joseph-G. Gélinas. Préface de M. Gélinas.
1947. 149 p. (Ms. Ecole de Bibl., U. de M.)

2:149 **Bellerive, Georges**
Nos auteurs dramatiques, anciens et contemporains; répertoire
analytique. Québec, Garneau; Montréal, Beauchemin, 1933. 162 p.

2:150 **Belley, David**
Liberté de presse et périodiques canadiens. 1966. vi, 7 1. (Ms. U. of O.
Libr. School)

2:151 **Belzile, Françoise**
Bio-bibliographie de Emile Benoist. 1947. 9 p. (Ms. Ecole de Bibl.,
U. de M.)

2:152 **Belzile, Marie-Paule**
Bio-bibliographie du docteur Philippe Hamel. Préf. du R.P. Francis
Goyer, s.s.s. Québec, 1949. 85 p. (Ms. Ecole de Bibl., U.L.)

2:153 **Belzile, Rachel**
S.E. Mgr Georges Courchesne, archevêque de Rimouski. Essai de bio-
bibliographie. 1951. 14, [4] p. (Ms. Ecole de Bibl., U. de M.)

2:154 **Bender, Louise**
Bio-bibliographie de Mgr Louis Paquet. 1948. vii, 32 p. (Ms. Ecole de
Bibl., U. de M.)

2:155 **Benigna-Marie, sœur**
Bibliographie du R.P. Eugène Nadeau, o.m.i. Lettre-préface de Sœur
Marie-Saint-Edgar. 1946. 52 p. (Ms. Ecole de Bibl., U. de M.)

2:156 **Benoît, Ignace-Marie, père**
Bio-bibliographie du R.P. Paul-Eugène Trudel, o.f.m. 1943. 38 p.
(Ms. Ecole de Bibl., U. de M.)

2:157 **Bérard, Andrée**
Bio-bibliographie de Renée Des Ormes [Marie Ferland-Turgeon].
1947. iv, 24 p. (Mf. Ecole de Bibl., U. de M.)

2:158 **Bérard, Berthe**
Bio-bibliographie de Monsieur l'abbé Emile Lambert. 1945. 63 p.
(Mf. Ecole de Bibl., U. de M.)

2:159   **Bérard, Fernande**
Bio-bibliographie du R.P. J.-F. Bérubé. 1952. 16 p. (Ms. Ecole de Bibl., U. de M.)

2:160   **Bergeron, Gilles**
Une bibliographie annotée de M. Vincent Massey. 1967. vii, 9 1. (Ms. U. of O. Libr. School)

2:161   **Bergeron, Hélène**
Bibliographie de René Ouvrard. Québec, 1957. 32 p. (Ms. Ecole de Bibl., U.L.)

2:162   **Bergeron, Juliana**
Bio-bibliographie du chanoine Jean Bergeron (1868-1956). Préface de Mgr Félix-Antoine Savard, p.d. Québec, 1958. 85 p. (Ms. Ecole de Bibl. U.L.)

2:163   **Bergeron, Laure**
Bio-bibliographie de Guy Boulizon, commissaire scout de France. Préface de M.J. Salet. Granby, 1946. 32 p. (Mf. Ecole de Bibl., U. de M.)

2:164   **Bergevin, André**
Henri Bourassa [par] André Bergevin, Cameron Nish [et] Anne Bourassa. [Montréal] Editions de l'Action nationale, 1966.
lxii, 150 p.
Index des écrits, par A. Bergevin.–Index de la correspondance publique 1895-1924, par C. Nish.

2:165   **Bernad, Marcel**
Bibliographie des missionnaires oblats de Marie Immaculée ... Liège, Dessain, 1922–
Sommaire.–1. Ecrits des missionnaires oblats, 1816-1915.
Pour la suite, voir Carrière, G. Bibliographie des Oblats de langue française au Canada.

2:166   **Bernard, Edgar**
Bio-bibliographie de Gérard Morisset. Préface par Jean-Marie Gauvreau. 1947. 123 p. (Ms. Ecole de Bibl., U. de M.)

2:167   **Bernard-de-Notre-Dame, sœur**
Notes bio-bibliographiques du R.F. Pierre Langevin, s.s.p. 1953. 30 p. (Ms. Ecole de Bibl., U. de M.)

2:168   **Bernier, Anne-Marie**
Essai de bio-bibliographie. Biographie du R.P. Joseph-Papin Archambault, s.j., et bibliographie de son œuvre littéraire. 1939. 40 p. (Mf. Ecole de Bibl., U. de M.)

2:169   **Berthiaume, Jacques**
Bio-bibliographie du R.F. Léopold Taillon, c.s.c. 1953. 47 p. (Ms.
Ecole de Bibl., U. de M.)

2:170   **Berton, Pierre Francis deMarigny**
A Klondike bibliography. [Toronto? 1958] 23 *l.*

2:171   **Bertrand, Madeleine**
Bibliographie de l'œuvre d'Anne Hébert, précédée de sa biographie.
Préface de Théophile Bertrand. 1946. 23 p. (Mf. Ecole de Bibl.,
U. de M.)

2:172   **Bérubé, Pierrette**
Bio-bibliographie de Mme A[rthur] Saint-Pierre. Introduction de
P.-E. Bérubé, ptre. 1944. 17 p. (Ms. Ecole de Bibl., U. de M.)

2:173   **Besoushko, Wolodymyr**
Publications of Ukrainian Free Academy of Sciences, 1945-1955 [by]
W. Besoushko [and] J.B. Rudnyckyj. Winnipeg, Ukrainian Free Aca-
demy of Sciences. 1955. 22 p. Ukrainian Free Academy of Sciences.
Series: UVAN chronicle, no. 13.

2:174   **Besterman, Theodore**
A world bibliography of bibliographies and of bibliographical catalogues, calendars, abstracts, digests, indexes, and the like. Third and
final edition, revised and greatly enlarged throughout. Genève, Socie-
tas Bibliographica [1955-56, c1955]. 4 v. (xxviii p., 5701 columns)
V.1, col. 674-693 refer to Canada.

2:175   **Betts, Rachel Mary (Weaver)**
... Bibliography of the geology of Newfoundland, 1818-1936. St.
John's Nfld., 1936. v, 35 p. (Newfoundland, Dept. of Natural Re-
sources, Geological Section, Bulletin no. 5)

2:176   **Beugnot, Bernard**
Jean-Louis Guez de Balzac; bibliographie générale. Montréal, Presses
de l'Université de Montréal, 1967.
173 p.
Supplément I. Montréal, Presses de l'Université de Montréal, 1969.
94 p.

2:177   **Bibaud, Maximilien**
Bibliothèque canadienne; ou, Annales bibliographiques. Montréal,
Cérat et Bourguignon [1858]. 52 p.
Fait suite à Faribault, *Catalogue d'ouvrages sur l'histoire de l'Amérique.*
L'auteur a compilé, en vue d'une deuxième édition, un supplément demeuré en
manuscrit et daté de 1873. Ce ms. se trouve à la bibliothèque du Parlement.

2:178 **[Bibaud, Maximilien]**
Mémorial des honneurs étrangers conférés à des Canadiens ou domiciliés de la Puissance du Canada. Montréal, Beauchemin & Valois, 1885. 100 p.
'Bibliographie canadienne en dehors du Canada'; p. 83-94.

2:179 **Bibliographie de Michelle Le Normand** [Mme Léo-Paul Desrosiers].
1940. 40 p. (Ms. Ecole de Bibl., U. de M.)

2:180 **... Bibliographie d'histoire coloniale** (1900-1930); Grande-Bretagne et dominions, par MM. A.P. Newton [et autres]. Paris, Société de l'histoire des colonies françaises, 1932. 1 f., [5] – 149 p.
Extrait de *Bibliographie d'histoire coloniale (1900-1930),* publiée par les soins de MM. Alfred Martineau [et autres].
Canada: p. 103-149.

2:181 **Bibliographie pour servir à l'étude de l'histoire du Canada français;**
bulletin no. 1; 1966. [Montréal, Digital Computer Center, Sir George Williams University, 1966]
1 v. (non paginé) deux fois par année.
Compilateurs du no. 1, 1966: C. et E. Nish.

2:182 **Bibliographie sur Calixa Lavallée et "O Canada"**
(In *Le Passe-Temps,* août 1933, p. 42.)

2:183 **A bibliography in Canadian economics ...** 1920-1934.
(In *Contributions to Canadian economics ...* Toronto, 1928-1934.
v. I-VII, 1928-1934)
Compilers: H.A. Innis, V.L. Bladen, and A. Ewart.

2:184 **A bibliography of books published in Canada,** books by Canadians, and books about Canada, with the imprint 1917-[1920] Toronto, 1938-39. 4 v. (Ms. Toronto Univ. Libr. School)
1917, compiled by Rietta McRostie. 1939. iv, 26 *l.*
1918, compiled by E. Wilson. 1938. ii, 25 *l.*
1919, compiled by Margaret Elizabeth Rose. 1938. iv, 23 *l.*
1920, compiled by Sheila M. Bell. 1938. ii, 24 *l.*

2:185 **Bibliography of Canadian biological publications, 1946-1948**
[Toronto, 1949-1951] 3 v. (Ontario, Dept. of Lands and Forests, Biological bulletin, no. 3)
Compilers: J.M. Speirs, J.M. Johnston, and Ruth Kingsmill.

2:186 **Bibliography of Canadian botany ...**
(In Royal Society of Canada, *Transactions,* 1901-1916, sec. IV)
Compiler: A.H. MacKay.
Title varies: Botanical bibliography of Canada.

2:187   **Bibliography of Canadian entomology** ...
(In Royal Society of Canada, *Transactions,* 1901-1916, sec. IV)
Compilers: C.J.S. Bethune, and C.G. Hewitt.

2:188   **Bibliography of Canadian geology** ...
(In Royal Society of Canada, *Transactions,* 1901-1916, sec. IV)
Compilers: Henri Marc Ami, Leopold Reinecke, and Wyatt Malcolm.

2:189   **Bibliography of Canadian plant geography** ... Toronto, University
Press, 1928-1947. 9 pts.
The first 8 parts have appeared in the *Transactions of the Royal Canadian Institute.*
Compilers: J. Adams, M.H. Norwell, H.A. Senn.

2:190   **Bibliography of Canadian zoology** ...
(In Royal Society of Canada, *Transactions,* 1901-1916, sec. IV)
Compilers: for 1900-1906, J.F. Whiteaves; 1907-1912, Lawrence M. Lambe;
1913-1915, E.M. Walker.
Exclusive of entomology.

2:191   **Bibliography of Thomas Douglas,** earl of Selkirk. [N.p.] 1932. 30 *l.*
Prepared by AE. Fauteux and G. Lomer for W.S. Wallace's article in *Canadian historical review, 1932.* q.v.

2:192   **A bibliography of writings** [of] J.B. Rudnyćkyj, 1933-1963.
Winnipeg, 1964. 96 p. port.
'Compiled and published by Students and Friends of the Author on occasion of
the 30th anniversary of his scholarly activities, 1933-1963.'–p. [4]

2:193   **Bibliothèque de Canadiana.** [Montréal, 1967–
v.
Catalogues des ouvrages contenus dans la collection de la Bibliothèque Canadiana du Pavillon canadien à l'Expo 67.

2:194   **Bilodeau, Françoise**
Théâtre canadien-français, 1900-55. [Québec, 1956] 94 p. (Ms. Ecole
de Bibl., U.L.)

2:195   **Bineau, Gratien**
Bio-bibliographie de Monsieur Sylva Clapin, 1853-1928. 1948. 37 p.
(Mf. Ecole de Bibl., U. de M.)

2:196   **Binkley, Mildred B.**
Bibliography. Canadian artists and modern art movements. (In
*Ontario library review,* Nov. 1929, v. 14, no. 2, p. 42-46)

2:197   **Birney, Earle**
Malcolm Lowry (1909-1957). A bibliography prepared by Earle

Birney, with the assistance of Margerie Lowry. [Part I] (In *Canadian literature* no. 8, Spring 1961. p. 81-88)

[Part II] (In *Canadian literature* no. 9, Summer 1961. p. 80-84)

2:198 **Biron, Luc-André**
Bio-bibliographie de Charles-Yvon Thériault, journaliste (1948-1956) Lettre-préf. de Raymond Douville. Trois-Rivières, 1961. xi, 105 p. fac-sim.

2:199 **Biron, Monique**
Essai bio-bibliographique sur Joseph Lenoir-Rolland. 1948. iv, 10 p. (Ms. Ecole de Bibl., U. de M.)

2:200 **Bishop, Olga Bernice**
Checklist of historical works on Western Ontario in the libraries of the University of Western Ontario. (In *Western Ontario historical notes,* v. XIV, no. 1, Dec. 1957, pp. 24-30; no. 2, March 1958, pp. 30-37; no. 3, June 1958, pp. 42-47; no. 4, Sept. 1958, pp. 31-39; no. 5, Dec. 1958, pp. 39-49.

2:201 **Bishop, Olga Bernice**
Publications of the government of the Province of Canada, 1841-1867. Ottawa [Queen's Printer] 1963 [i.e. 1964] x, 351 p.
Thesis—University of Michigan, 1962.
Issued by the National Library of Canada.

2:202 **Bishop, Olga Bernice**
Publications of the governments of Nova Scotia, Prince Edward Island, New Brunswick, 1758-1952. Ottawa [Queen's Printer, 1958]. 237 p.
Published by the National Library of Canada.

2:203 **Bishop, Olga Bernice**
Thomas Chandler Haliburton; a bibliography of the biographical writings about the 'Father of American Humour.' [Ann Arbor, Mich.] 1951. 33 *l.*

2:204 **Black, Dorothy Miller**
Guide to lists of master's theses. Chicago, American Library Association, 1965.
144 p.
Includes Canadian universities.

2:205 **Blair, Mary Helen**
Bliss Carman; a bibliography. [Toronto, 1945] [3], 5 *l.* (Ms. Toronto Univ. Libr. School)

2:206 **Blais, Jeanne-d'Arc**
Bio-bibliographie du R.P. Marie-Alcantara Dion, o.f.m. Les Trois-Rivières, 1946. 123 p. (Ms. Ecole de Bibl., U. de M.)

2:207 **Blais, Micheline**
Notes bio-bibliographiques sur M. le chanoine Lionel Groulx. 1947. [7] p. (Ms. Ecole de Bibl., U. de M.)

2:208 **Blanchard, Thérèse**
Bibliographie de Maurice Hébert. 1944. 20 p. (Mf. Ecole de Bibl., U. de M.)

2:209 **Blanchet, Gaston**
Bibliographie du R.P. Gonzale Poulin, o.f.m. 1946. 76 p. (Mf. Ecole de Bibl., U. de M.)

2:210 **Blogg, Minnie Wright**
Bibliography of the writings of Sir William Osler; rev. and enl. Baltimore, Blogg, 1921. 96 p.

2:211 **Blois, Benoît de**
Le R.P. Victor Cardin, c.s.v. Essai de bio-bibliographie. 1951. 20 p. (Ms. Ecole de Bibl., U. de M.)

2:212 **Blouin, Berthe**
Bio-bibliographie de Cécile Lagacé. Préface de Marie-Claire Daveluy. 1947. 33 p. (Ms. Ecole de Bibl., U. de M.)

2:213 **Blouin, Gervaise**
Bibliographie analytique de Louis-Alexandre Bélisle. Québec, 1953. 70 p. (Ms. Ecole de Bibl., U.L.)

2:214 **Blouin, Gisèle**
Bibliographie analytique de Joseph-Thomas Leblanc. Préf. de M. Luc Lacourcière. Québec, 1950. 82 p. (Ms. Ecole de Bibl., U.L.)

2:215 **Blouin, Irène**
Notes bio-bibliographiques sur Monsieur Jules Tremblay. 1952. 16 p. (Mf. Ecole de Bibl., U. de M.)

2:216 **Blouin, Jeanne**
Bio-bibliographie de Edouard Montpetit. 1947. 12 p. (Mf. Ecole de Bibl., U. de M.)

2:217 **Blouin, Micheline**
Bio-bibliographie de Monsieur Casimir Hébert. Préface de Mlle Cécile Lagacé. 1947. 32 p. (Mf. Ecole de Bibl., U. de M.)

2:218 **Bock, Germaine-G.**
Notes bio-bibliographiques sur Mgr Henri Jeannotte, p.s.s. 1949. 14 p.
(Ms. Ecole de Bibl., U. de M.)

2:219 **Boily, Germaine (Tremblay)**
Flambeau saguenéen, l'abbé Charles-Elzéar Tremblay; bio-bibliographie. Préface de Mgr Victor Tremblay. Chicoutimi, 1964.
314 p. (Ms. Ecole de Bibl., U.L.)

2:220 **Bois, Jacqueline**
Bibliographie analytique de l'œuvre de Mgr Arthur Maheux,
précédée d'une biographie (années 1961-1964). Préf. de M. l'abbé
Benoît Garneau. 1964, xiv, 31(1) p. (Ms. Ecole de Bibl., U.L.)

2:221 **Boisclair, Thérèse**
Bio-bibliographie du chanoine Lionel Groulx. 1947. 8 p. (Ms. Ecole
de Bibl., U. de M.)

2:222 **Boissonnault, Henri**
Bio-bibliographie de M. Jean Bruchési, M.S.R.C., sous-secrétaire et
sous-régistraire. Préf. de Mgr Ferdinand Vandry. Québec, 1948. 76 p.
(Ms. Ecole de Bibl., U.L.)

2:223 **Boisvert, Marie A.**
Essai de bio-bibliographie: Sœur Marie Catherine Lavallée. 1953. 41 p.
(Ms. Ecole de Bibl., U. de M.)

2:224 **Boivin, Jean**
Bio-bibliographie de l'abbé Maheux (1945-1952) Préf. de l'abbé
Louis-Albert Vachon. Québec, 1954. 136 p. (Ms. Ecole de Bibl., U.L.)

2:225 **Bolduc, Marcel, frère**
Bio-bibliographie des anciens élèves des Frères maristes (1886-1963).
Québec, 1963. 111 p. (Ms. Ecole de Bibl., U.L.)

2:226 **Bolduc, Yolande**
Bio-bibliographie du chanoine Georges Robitaille. Préf. de M. Damien
Jasmin. 1951. v, 20 p. (Ms. Ecole de Bibl., U. de M.)

2:227 **Bonenfant, Gisèle**
Notes bio-bibliographiques sur Jean Bruchési, sous-secrétaire de la
province de Québec et membre de la Société royale. 1947. 19 p.
(Mf. Ecole de Bibl., U. de M.)

2:228 **Bonin, Fernande**
Essai de bio-bibliographie du R.P. Norbert-Marie Bettez, o.f.m. 1953.
vii, 17 p. (Ms. Ecole de Bibl., U. de M.)

2:229 **Bonin, Marie**
Bio-bibliographie analytique de Marthe Bergeron-Hogue. Préf. de Monsieur Eugène L'heureux. 1964. xxii, 152 (3) p. (Ms. Ecole de Bibl., U.L.)

2:230 **Bonin, Roger**
Bibliographie de Monsieur Ernest Gagnon. Préface du R.P. Gérard Houle, s.j. 1945. 77 p. (Mf. Ecole de Bibl., U. de M.)

2:231 **Book Publishers' Association of Canada**
Books & music presented by the Book Publishers' Association of Canada & the Canadian Music Publishers' Association, Stratford Festival, Canada, 1963. [Catalogue. Toronto, 1963] 30 p.

2:232 **Borduas, Jean-Rodolphe**
Notes bibliographiques sur Jean-Rodolphe Borduas, généalogiste. 1952. 58 p. (Mf. Ecole de Bibl., U. de M.)

2:233 **Boronkay, Dennis D.**
Canadian law; an annotated bibliography of reference books. Montreal, 1947. 14 *l.* (Ms. McGill Univ. Libr. School)

2:234 **Borowyk, Mychailo**
The Ukrainian press in Eastern Canada. Ottawa, University of Ottawa, Library School, 1959. 11, 8 p. (Ms. U. of O. Libr. School)

2:235 **Bosa, Réal**
Livres et lecteurs. 1967-68. 52f. (Ms. Ecole de Bibl., U. de M.)

2:236 **Boucher, Louis**
Bibliographie: les quotidiens de langue française. [Québec, 1957] 66 p. (Ms. Ecole de Bibl., U.L.)

2:237 **Boucher, Marie-Marthe**
Essai de bio-bibliographie de Paul Loyonnet. Préf. de Monsieur Henri Bosco. Montréal, 1961. viii, 69 p. (Ms. Ecole de Bibl., U. de M.)

2:238 **Boucher, Thérèse**
Notes bio-bibliographiques sur Charles Gill. 1948. iv, 13 p. (Mf. Ecole de Bibl., U. de M.)

2:239 **Boudreau, Gerald**
Education: separate schools in Ontario, 1960-1964. 1965. viii, 8 l. (Ms. U. of O. Libr. School)

2:240 **Boudreau, May**
Audio-visuel et enseignement au Québec, 1960-1965. 1966. [v] 6 l. (Ms. U. of O. Libr. School)

2:241 **Boult, Reynald**
Bibliographie du droit canadien. Etablie pour le Comité international pour la documentation des sciences sociales sous le patronage de l'Association internationale des sciences juridiques, avec le concours de l'Association canadienne de droit comparé et du Centre canadien de droit comparé. Montréal, Wilson et Lafleur, 1966.
xii, 393 p.

2:242 **Boult, Reynald**
A bibliography of Canadian law. Prepared for the International Committee for Social Sciences Documentation under the auspices of the International Association of Legal Science, with the support of the Canadian Association of Comparative Law and the Canadian and Foreign Law Research Centre. Montreal, Wilson and Lafleur, 1966.
xii, 393 p.

2:243 **Bourassa, Lucette**
Le roman au Canada français, 1925-1949. Lauzon, 1949. 38 p. (Ms. Ecole de Bibl., U.L.)

2:244 **Bourbonnais, Gabrielle**
Bio-bibliographie de Jean Dufresne [i.e., Marcel Valois, pseud.]. 1948. 8 p. (Mf. Ecole de Bibl., U. de M.)

2:245 **Bourdages, soeur**
Bibliographie analytique des écrits du R.P. Pascal, o.f.m. cap., précédée d'une biographie. Préface de Mgr Edgar Godin. Québec, 1962. 153 p. (Ms. Ecole de Bibl., U.L.)

2:246 **Bourgeois, Madeleine**
Bio-bibliographie de Monsieur Marcel Dugas. 1944. 75 p. (Mf. Ecole de Bibl., U. de M.)

2:247 **Bourget, Magdeleine**
Bio-bibliographie analytique de M. Elphège-J. Daignault. Québec, 1952. 27 p. (Ms. Ecole de Bibl., U.L.)

2:248 **Bourgoing, André**
Bibliographie analytique de l'œuvre de M. Gérard Tremblay, sous-ministre du Travail; précédée d'une biographie. Québec, 1963. 45 p. (Ms. Ecole de Bibl., U.L.)

2:249 **Bourinot, A.S.**
Edward William Thomson (1849-1924); a bibliography with notes and some letters. Ottawa, The Author [1955]. 28 p.

2:250 [Bourinot, Sir John George]
Bibliographie de M.G. Baillairgé. Extraite du volume des 'Transactions' pour 1894, de la Société royale du Canada. Addenda jusqu'à
ce jour, Québec, mai 1899. [Québec, 1899] xv p.

2:251 **Bourinot, Sir John George**
Bibliography of Parliamentary government in Canada ...
In American Historical Association. *Annual report,* 1891, p. 390-407.

2:252 **Bourinot, Sir John George**
Bibliography of the members of the Royal Society of Canada.
Printed by order of the Society, May 25th, 1894. [N.p.] 1894. 79 p.

2:253 **Bourinot, Sir John George**
Catalogue of the library of the late Sir John George Bourinot.
[N.p., 190–] 105 p.
Mostly Canadian items.

2:254 **Bourinot, Sir John George**
The library of the late Sir John Bourinot ... containing rare books,
pamphlets and maps relating to the progress of geographical discovery
and the history of Canada, including many relating to the American
revolution and the history of America in colonial times. For sale by
auction ... by the Anderson Auction Company ... New York. [New
York, Taylor] 1906. [2] , 175, [1] p.
Mostly Canadian items.

2:255 **Bourinot, Sir John George**
Short review of Canadian literature. London [n.d.] . (British Empire
series)
Bibliography, p. 192-217.

2:256 **Bourque, Jean-Paul**
Bio-bibliographie de S.E. Mgr M.-Antoine Roy, o.f.m. Préf. par le
R.P. Sylvère-M. Leblanc, o.f.m. 1948. xv, 16 p. (Ms. Ecole de Bibl.,
U. de M.)

2:257 **Bourret, Guy**
Bio-bibliographie de madame veuve Charles Gill. Préface de
Enguerrand Castelmann. 1944. 22 p. (Mf. Ecole de Bibl., U. de M.)

2:258 **Boutet, Odina**
Bio-bibliographie critique d'Anne Hébert. Québec, 1950. 28 p.
(Ms. Ecole de Bibl., U.L.)

2:259  **Boutin, Rose-Anne**
Bibliographie analytique de l'œuvre de l'honorable Cyrille Vaillancourt. Préface de M. Ferdinand Ouellet. Québec, 1961. 195 p. (Ms. Ecole de Bibl., U.L.)

2:260  **Bower, William J.**
A rough check list of the first editions of John Buchan (Lord Tweedsmuir). Compiled by William J. Bower, with the assistance of Paul Lemperly, Louis C. Stoneman [and] C. Hopkinson. London, Eng., First Edition Bookshop [1939]. 12 *l.*

2:261  **Bowman, Fred**
A bibliography of Canadian numismatics, by Fred Bowman and R.C. Willey. (In *Canadian numismatic journal,* 1959, v. 4, nos. 6-10.)
Addenda ... (In v. 5, no. 1, Jan., 1960.)

2:262  **Boyer, Alfred**
Bibliographie de Léopold Houlé, précédée d'une biographie de l'auteur. Lettre-préface de Mlle Juliette Chabot. 1942. 17 p. (Ms. Ecole de Bibl., U. de M.)

2:263  **Boyer, Marjorie M.**
A bibliography of English journalism in Canada from the middle of the nineteenth century to the present day. Montreal, 1939. 15 *l.* (Ms. McGill Univ. Libr. School)

2:264  **Boyer, Micheline**
La composition musicale au Canada. 1966. iv, 7 1. (Ms. U. of O. Libr School)

2:265  **Boyer, Simone**
Notes bio-bibliographiques sur Philippe Aubert de Gaspé. 1948. iv, 13 p. (Mf. Ecole de Bibl., U. de M.)

2:266  **Boyko, Max**
The Co-operative movement in Canada. 1962. vii [1] 6 1. (Ms. U. of O. Libr. School)

2:267  **Bradberry (Carroll E.) and Associates,** Los Altos, Calif.
Annotated bibliography on hydrology and sedimentation, 1959-1962 (United States and Canada) Compiled and edited under the auspices of the Subcommittees on Hydrology and Sedimentation, Inter-Agency Committee on Water Resources, by Carroll E. Bradberry and Associates, Los Altos, Calif. [Washington, U.S. Govt. Print. Off. 1964]
xii, 323 p. ([U.S.] Inter-Agency Committee on Water Resources. Joint hydrology-sedimentation bulletin, no. 8)

'Supplement to [American Geophysical Union] Annotated bibliography on hydrology 1951-54 and sedimentation 1950-54, United States and Canada, Joint hydrology-sedimentation bulletin no. 7 and U.S. Geological Survey water supply paper no. 1546, annotated bibliography on hydrology and sedimentation. United States and Canada, 1955-58.'

2:268 **Bradley, Annette**
Ontario library on wheels: a growing service in a vast and dispersed populated country, 1955-1965. 1966. [2] ii, 7 1. (Ms. U. of O. Libr. School)

2:269 **Bradley, Judith Ellen**
William Berczy and his settlers in Markham Township; a bibliography. [Toronto] 1965. ix, 18 *l.* (Ms. Toronto Univ. Libr. School)

2:270 **Brault, Lucien**
Bibliographie d'Ottawa. [Ottawa] 1954. (In *Revue de l'université d'Ottawa*, v. 24, no. 3, p. [345]-375)

2:271 **Brault, Lucien**
Francis-J. Audet et son œuvre. Bio-bibliographie par Lucien Brault, avec préface de Victor Morin. Ottawa [Hull, Leclerc] 1940. 92 p., 2f.

2:272 **Braun, Peter K.**
Canadian foreign trade, 1960-1964. 1967. vi, 8 1 (Ms. U. of O. Libr. School)

2:273 **Brazeau, Denis**
La Bibliothèque nationale du Canada de 1954 à 1967. 1967. [2] 16 1. (Ms. U. of O. Libr. School)

2:274 **Brazer, Shirley**
Young Canada's Book Week. 1964. v, 10 1. (Ms. U. of O. Libr. School)

2:275 **Bresolles, Judith de, soeur**
Bibliographie analytique de l'œuvre de Mère Marie-Berthe Thibault, précédée d'une biographie. Préface de l'abbé Roch Dancause. Québec, 1962. 101 p. (Ms. Ecole de Bibl., U.L.)

2:276 **Brewer, Charles**
The Halifax explosion of December 6th, 1917; a bibliography. [Toronto] 1966. 11 *l.* (Ms. Toronto Univ. Libr School)

2:277 **Brien, Fortunate**
Bio-bibliographie de Roger Brien, de l'Académie canadienne-française. Préface du chanoine Lionel Groulx. 1945. 306 p. (Mf. Ecole de Bibl., U. de M.)

2:278 **Brière, Maurice**
Bio-bibliographie de Rex Desmarchais. 1942. 89 p. (Mf. Ecole de Bibl., U. de M.)

2:279 **Brisebois, Eugène**
Bibliographie d'Albert Ferland, 1872-1943. 1945. 30 p. (Mf. Ecole de Bibl., U. de M.)

2:280 **British Columbia. Department of Agriculture**
List of publications issued by the Department of Agriculture, 1914–. Ottawa, King's Printer, 1914–.

2:281 **British Columbia. Department of Education. Division of Curriculum.**
A bibliography on British Columbia for elementary and secondary schools. Victoria, B.C., 1956. [1], 8 *l.*

2:282 **British Columbia. Department of Industrial Development, Trade and Commerce.**
Publications issued by Department of Industrial Development, Trade and Commerce. 19–?– Victoria [Queen's Printer] 19–?– annual.
Not published for 1956 or 1958.
Title varies:        -1961, Current publications.

2:283 **British Columbia. Department of Mines and Petroleum Resources**
List of publications. [Victoria, Queen's Printer, 19–? ]
Prior to 1960, issued by the Department of Mines.

2:284 **British Columbia. Provincial Library**
Simon Fraser centenary, 1808-1908. Checklist of books and pamphlets from the Provincial Library shown at the Provincial Exhibition, New Westminster, Sept. 29-Oct. 3, 1908. Victoria, King's Printer, 1908. 18 p.

2:285 **British Columbia. Provincial Library and Archives**
Ethnic groups in British Columbia; a selected bibliography based on a checklist of material in the Provincial Library and Archives. Victoria, B.C., Centennial Committee, 1957. [2], 64 p.

2:286 **British Columbia. Provincial Museum of Natural History and Anthropology**
Selected list of publications on the Indians of British Columbia, compiled by Wilson Duff. Rev. ed. Victoria, 1963. 32 p. map.
Previous editions: 1956 and 1961.

2:287 **British Columbia. Provincial Museum of Natural History and Anthropology**
Selected literature concerning birds in British Columbia. Victoria [Queen's Printer] 1965. 9 p.

2:288  **British Columbia. Public Library Commission**
Catalogue of books on Canada, Newfoundland and Labrador.
Victoria, B.C., The Commission, 1942. 24 p.

2:289  **British Columbia. University**
Publications of the faculty and staff ... Vancouver, 1950–. (University of British Columbia publications, Bibliographical series, nos. 1–)

2:290  **British Columbia. University**. Dept. of Chemistry
Scientific papers published July 1, 1964 to June 30, 1965. [Vancouver, 1965]
[11] p.
earlier edition. September 1, 1961 to August 31, 1962. [Vancouver, 1962]
folder (8 p.)

2:291  **British Columbia. University**. Faculty of Forestry
Lists of publications, 1950-1961. [Vancouver, 1961] , 7 *l.*

2:292  **British Columbia. University**. Library
Critical studies of John Milton and his works. 1958-1963.
[Vancouver, 1964]
15 *l.*
Supplement to John Milton; a bibliographical supplement 1929-1957, by Calvin Huckabay. (Pittsburgh, Duquesne University Press, 1960)
Supplement. 1963-1966. [Vancouver] 1968.
15 *l.*

2:293  **British Columbia. University**. Library
Current accessions; a classified list of materials newly added to the Library collections. Dec. 1, 1965. [Vancouver, 1965]
56 *l.* monthly.

2:294  **British Columbia. University**. Library
French Canadian literature. La littérature canadienne-française. A preliminary list of the holdings of the University of British Columbia Library. Vancouver, 1957. 68 *l.*

2:295  **British Columbia. University**. Library
Uncatalogued material available for borrowing. List no. 1; Jan. 1966. [Vancouver] 1966.
228 p.
Kept up to date by monthly supplements in current accessions, beginning Feb. 1966. A revised list will be issued periodically.

2:296  **British Columbia. University**. Library
Uncatalogued material available for borrowing. List no. 2; July 1967. [Vancouver, 1967]

696 p.
Cumulated list of uncatalogued items as of May 1, 1967.

2:297 **British Columbia. University. Library.** Special Collections Division Reference guide to Canadian newspapers; a checklist of major holdings in the library of the University of British Columbia. Vancouver, University of British Columbia Library, 1968.

19 *l.* (Reference publication no. 23)

2:298 **British Columbia Government Publications**
Monthly checklist, compiled by J. Gordon Chope. Victoria, B.C. Provincial Library. v. 1. no. 1– January, 1970–

'Includes all B.C. government publications received by the Provincial Library. Its aim is to provide a current bibliographical guide to Provincial Government Publications rather than to be an order catalogue.'

2:299 **British Columbia Library Association.** Bibliography Committee [Bibliographies]

Mimeographed.
(a) Cariboo district. Compiled by Helen Fairley. [1], 8 p. 1935.
(b) Columbia River Basin. [2], 46, [3] p. 1935.
(c) Gold and gold mining in British Columbia. Compiled by the Science Industry Division, Vancouver Public Library. [2], 18 p. 1936-37.
(d) Hudson's Bay Company. [2], 13, 10, 2, 10, 10 p. 1935.
(e) Simon Fraser. 3 p. 1935.
(f) Captain James Cook. 7 p. 1935-36.
(g) Captain Vancouver. 3 p. 1935.
(h) Similkameen Tulameen Valleys. Compiled by John Goodfellow & completed by Mabel M. Lanning. [8] p. 1935.
(i) Prince George district. Compiled by Helen Fairley. [1], 4 p. 1935.
(j) The Oregon question. Part 1. The Oregon question. Compiled by Franklin K. Lewis. Part 2. The Oregon question [1], 8, 7 p. 1935.
(k) The Okanagan district. Compiled by Margaret Ormsby. [1], 21 p. 1935.
(l) Nanaimo district. (Compiled by Jean Stewart & J.O. Swan) [1], 13 p. 1935.
(m) The Cranbrook Herald, 1900-1908. Compiled by Frances Matheson [2], 22 p. 1935-36.
(n) Duncan-Cowichan district. Compiled by Gerald Prevost. [1], 5, 7, 4 p. 1935.

2:300 **British Columbia library quarterly**
A checklist of recently published British Columbiana catalogued in the Provincial Archives. 1969–

2:301 **British Columbia Medical Library Service**
Recent and recommended texts; a selective list for hospital medical libraries, compiled by C. William Fraser. [Vancouver] 1966.

9 *l.*

'To be used as a supplement to basic lists published ... in 1961 and May 1964.'

2:302 **British Columbia Research Council**
Publications of the British Columbia Research Council. Vancouver, British Columbia Research Council at the University of British Columbia, 1964. 26 *l.*

2:303 **British Museum. Dept. of Printed Books**
Catalogue of the American books in the library of the British Museum at Christmas MDCCCLVI. By Henry Stevens. London, 1866. Nendeln, Liechtenstein, Kraus Reprint, 1969.
xxxii, 628, 14, 62, 17 p.
First published London, Printed by C. Whittingham at the Chiswick Press, for H. Stevens, 1866.

2:304 **Britten, Pauline**
Notes bio-bibliographiques sur Monsieur Hervé Biron. Trois-Rivières, 1947. 29 p. (Mf. Ecole de Bibl., U. de M.)

2:305 **Brooke, W. Michael**
Canadian adult basic education, compiled by W. Michael Brooke. Toronto, Canadian Association for Adult Education [1968?]
49 *l.* (Trends)

2:306 **Brosseau, Marguerite**
Essai de bio-bibliographie sur la personne et l'oeuvre littéraire, scientifique et historique de M. Edouard Montpetit. 1938. 41 p. (Ms. Ecole de Bibl., U. de M.)

2:307 **Broughton, Frederick**
Catalogue of a valuable collection of books and pamphlets relating to Canada and America and the fine arts, being the second portion of the library of Frederick Broughton, late manager of the Great Western Railway, to be sold by public auction at the salerooms of J.M. Macfarlane & Co. ... 29th and 30th of October, 1885 ... Prepared by W.R. Haight. Toronto, Hunter, Rose, 1885. 8, 44 p.

2:308 **Brousseau, Vincent**
Bio-bibliographie analytique de M. Albert Gervais. Québec, 1963. 186 p. (Ms. Ecole de Bibl., U.L.)

2:309 **Brown, C.R.**
Bibliography of Quebec or Lower Canada laws (1540-1841) Toronto, Carswell [1927?] 22 p.
Reprinted from *Law library journal,* January, 1927.

2:310 **Brown, Gene-Louise**
A bibliography of Canadiana. Ottawa, University of Ottawa, Library School, 1950. [55 p.] (Ms. U. of O. Libr. School)

2:311  **Brown, Marion E.**
The log cabin in Canada. [Toronto, 1934] [1], 7 *l*. (Ms. Toronto Univ. Libr. School)

2:312  **Brulotte, Marie-Berthe**
Bibliographie analytique de Mme Paule Daveluy, membre de la Société des Ecrivains canadiens, précédée d'une biographie. Préface du R.P. Jean-Paul Labelle, s.j. Montréal, 1964. 141 p. (Ms. Ecole de Bibl., U.L.)

2:313  **Brunel, Claire**
Notes bio-bibliographiques sur le professeur Jules Brunel. 1953. 63 p. (Ms. Ecole de Bibl., U. de M.)

2:314  **Brunet, Germaine**
Bio-bibliographie de Léopold Richer. 1946. ix, 100 p. (Ms. Ecole de Bibl., U. de M.)

2:315  **Brunet, Jean**
Bio-bibliographie du révérend Père Léo Boismenu, s.s.s. Montréal, Editions Pilon, 1953. 64 p.

2:316  **Brunet, Lise**
Bio-bibliographie d'Octave Crémazie. 1945. 59 p. (Mf. Ecole de Bibl., U. de M.)

2:317  **Brunet, Marguerite**
Bio-bibliographie de Berthelot Brunet. Préface de M. Robert Charbonneau. 1945. xviii, 138 p. (Mf. Ecole de Bibl., U. de M.)

2:318  **Bull, William Perkins**
M'n N Canadiana; books by Canadians or about Canada; a national wedding present from Wm. Perkins Bull, to his son Michael Bull, and his bride Noreen Hennessy, on the occasion of their visit (while on their honeymoon) to the parental home, Lorne Hall, Rosedale, Toronto, Canada, where Michael was born. Brampton, Charters Pub. Co., for Wm. Perkins Bull, 1933. xxii, 166 p.

2:319  **Bulteau, Eglantine**
Bio-bibliographie du Dr Jean-Baptiste Meilleur. Préface de M. Léon Lortie. 1945. 110 p. (Ms. Ecole de Bibl., U. de M.)

2:320  **Burkholder, Edgar Leroy, Jr.**
A bibliography about William Lyon Mackenzie King. Montreal, 1954. 9 *l*. (Ms. McGill Univ. Libr. School)

2:321 **Burns, Norma**
Changes in the way of life of the Eskimos during the last twenty-five years. 1963. vii, 11 1. (Ms. U. of O. Libr. School)

2:322 **Burpee, Lawrence Johnstone**
A Canadian bibliography for the year 1901. [Montreal] 1902. 233-344 p.
'From the *Transactions of the Royal Society of Canada,* 2nd ser., 1902-03, v. 8, sec. 2, English history, literature, archaeology, etc.'
Includes papers in the *Transactions of the R.S.C.,* pamphlets, and magazine articles. Newspapers have been omitted. Canadian work in English and American magazines and the contents of Canadian college magazines have also been included.

2:323 **Burpee, Lawrence Johnstone**
Sandford Fleming, empire builder. London, New York [etc.], Oxford University Press, 1915. 288 p.
Bibliography: p. 279-284.

2:324 **Burtniak, John**
Butler's Rangers; a bibliography about their organizer, their campaigns, and their contribution to settlement. [Toronto] 1965. 10 *l.* (Ms. Toronto Univ. Libr. School)

2:325 **Butcher, William W.**
W.W. Butcher's Canadian newspaper directory. Issued by W.W. Butcher, proprietor 'Canada Newspaper Advertising Agency,' (established 1880) Toronto, Ontario, Canada. First edition, December, 1886. London, Speaker, 1886. 46, [1] p.

2:326 **Byrnes, Mary M.**
Bibliography of Canadian costume. [Toronto] 1931. [2], 7 *l.* (Ms. Toronto Univ. Libr. School)

2:327 **Cadieux, Bernadette**
Bio-bibliographie de S.E. Mgr Joseph-Médard Emard. 1948. 7 p. (Ms. Ecole de Bibl., U. de M.)

2:328 **Cadieux, Diane-M.**
Notes bio-bibliographiques sur Fadette (Mme Maurice Saint-Jacques). 1948. 10 p. (Ms. Ecole de Bibl., U. de M.)

2:329 **Cadieux, Madeleine**
Notes bio-bibliographiques sur Mgr Félix Antoine Savard. 1952. 9 p. (Mf. Ecole de Bibl., U. de M.)

2:330 **Cahiers de bibliographie.** Québec, 1965 –
v.
Sous la direction de John Hare.

1. Index de *Gants du ciel* (1943-1946), préparé par G.E. Gélinas, c.s.v. [et autres] 1965.

2:331  **Cahill, Brian**
Library legislation in Canada, 1946-1966. 1967. [3] 8 1. (Ms. U. of O. Libr. School)

2:332  **Cambridge history of the British Empire**; general editors: J. Holland Rose, A.P. Newton, E.A. Benians. New York, Macmillan; Cambridge, The University Press, 1929–   . v.
V. 6. Canada and Newfoundland. Bibliography, p. [813]-885.

2:333  **Cameron, Charlotte E.**
Travel in Canada, 1900-1914, as revealed by books in the University of Toronto Library and the Toronto Reference Library. [Entries from A-L]. [Toronto 1938] 12 *l.* (Ms. Toronto Univ. Libr. School)

2:334  **Cameron, William James**
Robert Addison's library; a short-title catalogue of the books brought to Upper Canada in 1792 by the first missionary sent out to the Niagara frontier by the Society for the Propagation of the Gospel, compiled by William J. Cameron and George McKnight with the assistance of Michaele-Sue Goldblatt. Hamilton, Ont., Printed at McMaster University for the Synod of the Diocese of Niagara, 1967.
xliv, 98 p. illus., facsims.

2:335  **Campbell, Henry Cummings**
How to find out about Canada. Oxford, Pergamon Press [1967]
xiv, 248 p. illus. (The Commonwealth and international library of science, technology, engineering and liberal studies. Libraries and technical information division)

2:336  **Campbell, Joan**
Bytown. 1962. [3] ii, 7 1. (Ms. U. of O. Libr. School)

2:337  **Campbell, O.L.**
The group of seven; a bibliography. Montreal, 1957. iv, 6 *l.* (Ms. McGill Univ. Libr. School)

2:338  **[Campbell, William Wilfred]**
Bibliography. War of 1812-14. [N.p.n.d.] 38 *l.*

2:339  **Canada. Archives publiques**
... Catalogue des brochures aux Archives publiques du Canada ... avec index; préparé par Magdalen Casey. Ottawa, Imprimeur du roi, 1932. 2 v. (Publications des Archives publiques du Canada, no. 13)
Sommaire: v. 1, 1493-1877; v. 2, 1878-1931.

2:340  **Canada. Archives publiques**
Catalogue des brochures, journaux et rapports déposés aux Archives canadiennes, 1611-1867, suivi d'un index. Publié avec l'autorisation du ministre de l'agriculture, sous la direction de l'archiviste, 1911. Ottawa, Imprimerie nationale, 1911. 230 p.
Préparé par M. MacArthur.

2:341  **Canada. Archives publiques**
... Catalogue des cartes, plans et cartes marines, conservés au Dépôt des cartes des Archives canadiennes; classifiés et indexés par H.R. Holmden. Publié par l'ordre du secrétaire d'Etat sous la direction de l'archiviste. Ottawa, Imprimerie nationale, 1912. xii, 685 p. (Publications des Archives canadiennes, no 8)

2:342  **Canada. Archives publiques**
Rapport de l'archiviste ... Ottawa, 1872—.
La version en français et la version en anglais paraissent séparément depuis 1881.
N'a pas paru en 1906-1907. Les rapports pour chacune des périodes suivantes ont été fusionnés: 1914-15, 1917-18, 1919-21, 1922-23, 1924-26, 1927-28. Certains rapports contiennent en appendice des listes de livres, de brochures, de cartes et de manuscrits.
Depuis 1950, les rapports ne contiennent pas d'appendices.
Plusieurs autres publications des Archives, bien que n'étant pas considérées comme bibliographies, contiennent des renseignements précieux sur les documents disponibles, v.g. la série des Inventaires provisoires.

2:343  **Canada. Archives publiques**
Supplément du Rapport du Dr Brymner sur les Archives canadiennes, par M. Edouard Richard. 1899. (Annexe du *Rapport du ministre de l'Agriculture*) Imprimé par ordre du Parlement. Ottawa, Dawson, 1901. 1 f., 533 p. (Canada, Documents de la session, no 8c.)
Liste de documents canadiens du Ministère des colonies, Paris.

2:344  **Canada. Archives publiques. Division des Cartes géographiques**
Cartes géographiques du seizième siècle se rapportant au Canada. Liste préliminaire et bibliographie. Ottawa, 1958. 305 p. fac-sim.

2:345  **Canada. Bibliothèque nationale**
Bibliographie canadienne, 1867-1900. Compilée par R. Tanghe.
(*En cours de publication*)

2:346  **Canada. Bibliothèque nationale**
Inventaire des périodiques de sciences sociales et d'humanités que possèdent les bibliothèques canadiennes. Ottawa, 1968. 2 v.

2:347  **Canada. Bibliothèque nationale**
Liste collective des journaux non-canadiens dans les bibliothèques du
Canada par Stephen Rush. Ottawa, 1968. 69 p.

2:348  **Canada. Bibliothèque nationale**
... Thèses des gradués canadiens dans les humanités et les sciences
sociales [1921-1946]. [Ottawa, King's Printer, 1951] 194 p.
Compilé et publié sous les auspices du Conseil canadien de Recherches sur les
Humanités, et du Conseil de Recherche en Sciences sociales du Canada.

2:349  **Canada. Bureau de la statistique.** Division de l'*Annuaire du Canada,*
du *Canada* et de la bibliothèque.
Ouvrages sur le Canada. [Extrait] de l'*Annuaire du Canada 1965* ...
[Ottawa, Imprimeur de la Reine, 1965] 16 p.
'Signale les plus récentes éditions de livres parus durant la dernière décennie
et comprend des ouvrages publiés en anglais, en français ou dans les deux
langues.' –cf. p. 3.
Etabli par la Bibliothèque nationale.
Une revision annuelle est prévue.

2:350  **Canada. Bureau de la statistique.** Division de l'éducation
... Guide bibliographique de l'enseignement au Canada ... Document
de référence ... Ottawa, Imprimeur de la reine, 1958. 55 p. (Catalogue
no 81-506. Occasionnel. Irrégulier)

2:351  **Canada. Bureau de la statistique.** Division de l'éducation
... Guide bibliographique de l'enseignement au Canada. [2e éd.]
Ottawa, Imprimeur de la Reine, 1964. 55 p.
Première édition 1958.

2:352  **Canada. Bureau de la statistique.** Division de l'éducation
Relevé de l'enseignement au Canada ... Ottawa, Imprimeur du roi,
1933–
Le titre varie. 1933-1936. Aperçu annuel sur l'éducation au Canada. 1936/38–
Aperçu biennal sur l'éducation au Canada.
Publié en trois parties. Les deux premières parties, 'Relevé de l'enseignement
élémentaire et de l'enseignement secondaire' et 'Relevé de l'enseignement
supérieur' contiennent des bibliographies sur l'enseignement au Canada.

2:353  **Canada. Bureau de la statistique.** Section de presse et de publicité
... Publications du recensement du Canada de 1961 ... Ottawa,
Imprimeur de la Reine [1962–    ] formule.
La liste no 3, juin 1963, remplace les listes nos 1, mars 1962, et 2, oct. 1962.

2:354  **Canada. Bureau of Statistics**
Current publications ... Publications courantes. Ottawa, 1934–    .
Title varies: 1934-    ?, List of publications including reports, bulletins, press
releases, etc.; 19?    -1949, Publications including reports, bulletins, press
releases, etc.; 1950-    , Current publications.

2:355 **Canada. Bureau of Statistics.** *Canada year book, handbook* and Library Division.
Books about Canada. Reprinted from the *Canada year book 1965* ... [Ottawa, Queen's Printer, 1965] 16 p.

'Emphasizes the latest editions of books published within the past ten years, and includes titles issued in either or both English and French.' cf. p. 3.
Compiled in the National Library.
Revised edition to appear annually.

2:356 **Canada. Bureau of Statistics.** Education Division
A bibliographical guide to Canadian education ... Reference paper ... Ottawa, Queen's Printer, 1958. 55 p. (Catalogue no. 81-506. Occasional. Irregular)

2:357 **Canada. Bureau of Statistics.** Education Division
A bibliographical guide to Canadian education ... [2d ed.] Ottawa, Queen's Printer, 1964. 55 p.

First edition 1958

2:358 **Canada. Bureau of Statistics.** Education Division
Bibliography of Canadian studies in education, 1929-33. Ottawa, 1933. 17 p.

Continued in the *Survey of education in Canada.* 1933–

2:359 **Canada. Bureau of Statistics.** Education Division
Survey of education in Canada ... Ottawa, King's Printer, 1933–

Title varies. 1933-1936. Annual survey of education in Canada. 1936/38–
Biennial survey of education in Canada.
Issued in three parts. Pt. 1, Elementary and secondary education in Canada, and pt. 2, Higher education in Canada, contain bibliographies on Canadian education.

2:360 **Canada. Bureau of Statistics.** Library
Bibliographical list of references to Canadian railways, 1829-1938. Ottawa, The Department, 1938. 99 p.

2:361 **Canada. Bureau of Statistics.** Press and Publicity Section
... Publications of the 1961 census of Canada ... Ottawa, Queen's Printer [1962– ] form.

List no. 3, June 1963, replaces Lists 1, March 1962, and 2, Oct. 1962.

2:362 **Canada. Commission of Conservation**
Catalogue of publications, revised to 1913. [n.d.] 36 p.

2:363 **Canada. Defence Research Board**
Bibliography of Canadian reports in aviation medicine, 1939-1945, by W.K. Kerr. [Ottawa] 1962. 225, 95-187 columns. (DB 153)

'Abstracts of Reports Submitted to the Associate Committee on Aviation Medical Research, National Research Council, Canada.'

2:364  **Canada. Département des impressions et papeterie publiques**
... Liste des périodiques du gouvernement canadien. Ottawa,
Imprimeur de la Reine [1965] 15 p.

2:365  **Canada. Département des impressions et papeterie publiques**
... [Publications] Bureau fédéral de la statistique. [3e éd.] Ottawa,
Imprimeur de la Reine [1964] xxvii, 288 p. (Ses Publications du
gouvernement canadien, bibliographie no 14)
Deuxième édition 1960, Supplément 1962.

2:366  **Canada. Département des impressions et papeterie publiques**
... Publications du gouvernement canadien. Catalogue. Ottawa.
Le titre a subi plusieurs modifications depuis l'origine de la publication.

2:367  **Canada. Département des impressions et papeterie publiques**
Bibliothèque des documents.
... Publications du gouvernement canadien. Mines et relevés tech-
niques, Division des mines ... Ottawa, Imprimeur de la Reine [1957]
243 p. (Bibliographie no 12)
Deuxième édition: [1962] 301 p. 22 cm.

2:368  **Canada. Département des impressions et papeterie publiques**
... Publications du gouvernement canadien sur les sujets relatifs au
travail. [2e éd. bilingue] Ottawa, Imprimeur de la Reine [1963]
337 p. (Sa Bibliographie no 10)
Préparé sous la direction de Marie-Louise Myrand.
earlier edition. Ottawa, Imprimeur de la Reine [1958] 125 p.
(Bibliographie no 10)

2:369  **Canada. Département des impressions et papeterie publiques**
... [Publications] Ministère des Forêts ... Ottawa, Imprimeur de la
Reine, 1963. 137 p. ill., diagr. (Ses Publications du gouvernement
canadien, bibliographie no 13)

2:370  **Canada. Département des impressions et papeterie publiques.**
Bibliothèque des documents
... Publications. Nord canadien et Ressources naturelles ... Ottawa,
Imprimeur de la reine [1956] 182 p. (Bibliographie no 11)
Deuxième édition: 1963. 182 p.

2:371  **Canada. Department of Agriculture.** Agricultural Economics Division
A list of published material by members of the Economics Division,
1930-1956. Ottawa, Queen's Printer, 1957. 64 p.
1957 supplement. Ottawa, Queen's Printer, 1958. 5 p.
1957-1962 supplement. Ottawa [Queen's Printer] 40 p.

2:372  **Canada. Department of Agriculture.** Information Division
List of publications ... [Ottawa, Queen's Printer, 1878–   ] annual.
Not published for 1961.
Title varies: Previous to list for 1959, List of available publications.

2:373  **Canada. Department of Agriculture.** Information Division
Publications of the Canada Department of Agriculture, 1867-1959,
compiled by Ella S.G. Minter. Ottawa, Queen's Printer, 1963. 387 p.
'It does not include papers published in scientific journals or farm papers, re-
prints or items issued locally by units of the Department outside Ottawa.'–Cf.
Introd., p. 7.

2:374  **Canada. Department of Citizenship and Immigration**
Canadian immigration and emigration, 1946-1957; a bibliography.
Ottawa, 1958. 38 p.

2:375  **Canada. Department of Citizenship and Immigration.** Canadian
Citizenship Branch
Research on immigrant adjustment and ethnic groups; a bibliography
of published material, 1920-1953 ... Ottawa, 1956. [3], ii, 131 p.

2:376  **Canada. Department of Citizenship and Immigration.** Canadian
Citizenship Branch
Research on immigrant adjustment and ethnic groups; a bibliography
of unpublished theses, 1920-1953 ... Ottawa, 1955. [3], 31 p.

2:377  **Canada. Department of Citizenship and Immigration.** Canadian
Citizenship Branch
Research on immigrant adjustment and ethnic groups; an annual
bibliography ... Ottawa, 1954–   .

2:378  **Canada. Department of Citizenship and Immigration.** Economic and
Social Research Branch
Citizenship, immigration and ethnic groups in Canada; a bibliography
of research, published and unpublished sources. 1920-1958. Ottawa
[Queen's Printer] 1960 [i.e. 1961] [8], 190, [25] p. forms.
Citizenship ... 1959-1961. Ottawa [Queen's Printer] 1962. [6], iv, ivf, 55 p.
Citizenship ... 1962-1964. Ottawa [Queen's Printer] 1964. iii, iv, 127 p.

2:379  **Canada. Department of Forestry.** Forest Products Research Branch
List of publications of the Forest Products Research Branch, Ottawa
Laboratory and Vancouver Laboratory. Rev. Jan. 1962. [Ottawa,
Queen's Printer, 1962] v, 21 p.
Revised August 1963: v, 22, iii, 3 p.
Previous to Jan. 1962, issued by the Forest Products Laboratories Division,
Dept. of Northern Affairs and National Resources, under title: List of publica-
tions of the Forest Products Laboratories of Canada, Ottawa and Vancouver.

2:380 **Canada. Department of Forestry.** Information and Technical Services
Catalogue of Canadian forestry and other resources films ... Ottawa
[Queen's Printer, 1965] vii, 32 p.

2:381 **Canada. Department of Labour.** Economics and Research Branch
Canadian labour papers available on microfilm from the Department
of Labour Library ... Ottawa, 1958. 11 *l.*
Previous edition 1955.

2:382 **Canada. Department of Labour.** Economics and Research Branch
List of publications. May 1965. Ottawa [1965] 7 p.

2:383 **Canada. Department of Marine and Fisheries**
Catalogue of Canadian government publications of use to Canadian
mariners. Ottawa, King's Printer, 1915.
Other editions: 1922, 1924, 1928, 1932-33.

2:384 **Canada. Department of Mines.** Mines Branch
Catalogue of publications of the Mines Branch (1907-1911) containing tables of contents of the various technical reports, monographs,
bulletins, etc., together with a list of magnetometric survey maps,
working plans, etc., including also a digest of technical memoirs and
the annual summary reports of the superintendent of mines, issued
by the Department of the Interior, 1902-1906. Ottawa, Government
Printing Bureau, 1912. 134 p., 1 *l.* ([Publication] no. 104)
2nd to 16th editions appeared, up to 1939, with shortened title: 'Catalogue
of publications.'
A 17th edition was issued by the Bureau of Mines in 1946.

2:385 **Canada. Department of Mines and Resources.** Surveys and Engineering
Branch
Catalogue of maps, plans and publications issued by Legal Surveys
and Map Service. 7th ed. Ottawa, Patenaude, Printer to the King,
1939. 55 p.
Supplement to 1939 catalogue of maps ... corrected to December 2nd, 1942.
Ottawa, 1942. 30 p.

2:386 **Canada. Department of Mines and Technical Surveys**
Catalogue of Canadian hydrographic service nautical charts and sailing
directions for inland waters of Canada ... Ottawa, 1954. vi, 15 [i.e.,
26] p.

2:387 **Canada. Department of Mines and Technical Surveys**
Catalogue of Canadian hydrographic service nautical charts, tidal and
current publications, sailing directions, and other government publications of interest to mariners ... Ottawa, 1951. 40 p.
Another edition: 1955. v. 44, [i.e., 82] p.

2:388 **Canada. Department of Mines and Technical Surveys.** Geographical Branch
Bibliography of periodical literature on Canadian geography, 1930 to 1955 ... Ottawa, [Queen's Printer], 1959. 6 pts. (Its Bibliographical series, no. 22)
Contents: Pt. 1, Canada—General; 2, Atlantic Provinces; 3, Quebec and Ontario; 4, Prairie Provinces; 5, British Columbia; 6, Northern Canada.

2:389 **Canada. Department of Mines and Technical Surveys.** Geographical Branch
Canadian maps, 1949 to 1954. Ottawa, 1956. 82 p. (Its Bibliographical series, no. 16)
Canadian maps, 1955-1956. Ottawa, 1958. 40 p. (Its Bibliographical series, no. 21)

2:390 **Canada. Department of Mines and Technical Surveys.** Geographical Branch
Canadian urban geography. Ottawa, 1954. [3], 80 p. (Its Bibliographical series, no. 13)
Revised edition: 1957. 100 p.

2:391 **Canada. Department of Mines and Technical Surveys.** Geographical Branch
Colonization and settlement in the Americas; a selected bibliography ... Ottawa [Queen's Printer] 1960. 4 p. *l.,* 68 p. (Its Bibliographical series, no. 25)
Compiled by Dr S.C. Wiley.

2:392 **Canada. Department of Mines and Technical Surveys.** Geographical Branch
Cumulative list of theses and dissertations on Canadian geography ... Ottawa [Queen's Printer] 1964. 3 p. *l.,* 40 p. (Its Bibliographical series, 31)

2:393 **Canada. Department of Mines and Technical Surveys.** Geographical Branch
A list of periodical literature on topics related to Canadian geography for the period 1940-1950. 2d ed. Ottawa, 1954. vi, 131 p. (Its Bibliographical series, no. 9)
Arranged by area and subject.
First edition, 1952.

2:394 **Canada. Department of Mines and Technical Surveys.** Geographical Branch
List of publications ... Ottawa [195—?— ] irregular.

2:395  **Canada. Department of Mines and Technical Surveys.** Geographical
Branch
Pedogeography of Canada. Revised edition. Ottawa, 1956. 24 p.
(Its Bibliographical series, no. 12)

2:396  **Canada. Department of Mines and Technical Surveys.** Geographical
Branch
Selected bibliography of Canadian geography with imprint 1949–
Ottawa, 1950– . (Its Bibliographical series, nos. 2, 4-8, 10, 14-15,
17, 19, 23)
Some issues are cumulations: no. 5 includes no. 2; no. 7 includes nos. 4 and 6.
The 1959 issue includes maps published during the year.

2:397  **Canada. Department of Mines and Technical Surveys.** Geographical
Branch
Selected bibliography on Canadian permafrost. Annotations and
abstracts. By Frank A. Cook. Ottawa, 1958. 23 p. (Its Bibliographical
series, no. 20)

2:398  **Canada. Department of Mines and Technical Surveys.** Geographical
Branch
Selected bibliography on Canadian toponymy ... Ottawa [Queen's
Printer] 1964. 2 p. *l.,* 27 p. (Its Bibliographical series, no. 30)

2:399  **Canada. Department of Mines and Technical Surveys.** Geographical
Branch
Selected bibliography on colonization and land settlement in Canada.
Ottawa, 1950. 5 p. (Its Bibliographical series, no. 1)
Compiled by J. Matheson.

2:400  **Canada. Department of Mines and Technical Surveys.** Geographical
Branch
Selected bibliography on periglacial phenomena in Canada; annotations and abstracts, by Frank A. Cook. Ottawa [Queen's Printer]
1960. 1 p. *l.,* 22 p., 1 *l.* (Its Bibliographical series, no. 24)

2:401  **Canada. Department of Mines and Technical Surveys.** Geographical
Branch
Selected bibliography on sea ice distribution in the coastal waters of
Canada. Ottawa, 1957. 50 p. (Its Bibliographical series, no. 18)

2:402  **Canada. Department of Mines and Technical Surveys.** Geographical
Branch
A selected list of periodical literature on topics related to Canadian
geography for the period 1930-1939. Ottawa, 1954. [i] , iv. *l.,* 97 p.
(Its Bibliographical series, no. 11)

2:403   **Canada. Department of Mines and Technical Surveys.** Geographical Branch
University dissertations, theses and essays on Canadian geography. Cumulative edition, 1953. Ottawa, 1954. 19 p. (Its Bibliographical series, no. 3)
New titles are listed as addenda to the annual Bibliography of Canadian geography.

2:404   **Canada. Department of Mines and Technical Surveys.** Mines Branch
Bibliography of high temperature condensed states research in Canada and elsewhere ... Ottawa [Queen's Printer] 1960– quarterly.
First issue, March 1960.

2:405   **Canada. Department of Public Printing and Stationery**
Canadian Government publications ... Catalogue. Ottawa.
Title varies:   -1927, Price list of Government publications; 1928-39, Catalogue of official publications of the Parliament and Government of Canada; 1943-48, Government publications; annual catalogue.
Catalogue for 1953 and 1954 each issued in 2 v., listing separately publications in English and publications in French.
Beginning in 1953, issued daily with monthly and annual cumulations.

2:406   **Canada. Department of Public Printing and Stationery**
Canadian government publications relating to labour ... [3d ed.] Ottawa, Queen's Printer [1963] 337 p. (Its Sectional catalogue no. 10)
earliest edition. Ottawa, Queen's Printer [1958] 125 p. (Its sectional catalogue no. 10)

2:407   **Canada. Department of Public Printing and Stationery**
... Department of Forestry [publications] ... Ottawa, Queen's Printer, 1963. 137 p. illus., diagr. (Its Canadian government publications, Sectional catalogue no. 13)

2:408   **Canada. Department of Public Printing and Stationery**
... Dominion Bureau of Statistics [publications] ... [3d ed.] Ottawa, Queen's Printer [1964] xxvii, 288 p. (Its Canadian government publications, Sectional catalogue no. 14)
Second edition 1960, Supplement 1962.

2:409   **Canada. Department of Public Printing and Stationery**
List of Canadian government periodicals ... Ottawa, Queen's Printer [1965] 15 p.

2:410   **Canada. Department of Public Printing and Stationery.** Documents Library
Canadian Government publications ... Mines Branch, Mines and

Technical Surveys ... Ottawa, Queen's Printer [1957] 243 p. (Its
Sectional catalogue no. 12)

Second edition: [1962] 301 p.
18th and 19th editions as Catalogue and index of Mines Branch publications.

2:411  **Canada. Department of Public Printing and Stationery.** Documents
Library
Northern Affairs and National Resources publications ... Ottawa,
Queen's Printer [1956] 182 p. (Its Sectional catalogue no. 11)

Second edition: 1963. 182 p.

4:412  **Canada. Department of the Interior**
... Geographical publications of the Department of the Interior.
Ottawa, Government Printing Bureau, 1916. 10 p.

7th edition: 1939. 55 p.
Supplements: 1940, 12 p.; 1942, ii, 30 p.

2:413  **Canada. Department of the Interior.** Natural Resources Intelligence
Branch
Catalogue of publications of the Natural Resources Intelligence
Service ... Ottawa, [19—  .

2:414  **Canada. Department of the Interior.** Surveys Branch
... Catalogue of maps, plans, and publications of the Topographical
Survey. 4th ed. Ottawa, Acland, 1927. 19 p.

5th edition: 1930. 23 p.

2:415  **Canada. Department of the Interior.** Surveys Branch
... List of maps and publications issued by the Topographical Surveys
Branch and available for distribution. Ottawa, Taché, 1917. 11 p.

2:416  **Canada. Department of the Interior.** Surveys Branch
List of maps, plans, and publications issued by the Topographical
Survey of Canada. Ottawa, King's Printer, 1923.

2:417  **Canada. Fisheries Research Board**
Bibliography of parasites and diseases of fishes in Canada. Compiled
by L. Margolis. [N.p.] Fisheries Research Board of Canada, 1957.
14 p. (Manuscript reports of the Biological Stations no. 631)

2:418  **Canada. Fisheries Research Board**
Index and list of titles, publications of the Fisheries Research Board
of Canada, 1901-1954. Prepared by Yvonne Bishop [and others].
Ottawa, Queen's Printer, 1957. 209 p. (Its Bulletin no. 110)

2:419  **Canada. Geographic Board**
Catalogue of the maps in the collection of the Geographic Board.

List of the maps cor. to 1st January 1922. Ottawa, Acland, Printer to the King, 1922. 100 p. Maps and portfolio of 10 fold. maps.

Catalogue of maps of Canada pub. between January 1, 1922, and December 31, 1924. Supplement to Catalogue of the maps ... Ottawa, Acland, 1925. 19, [1] p.

earlier edition. Ottawa, 1918. 50 p.

2:420 **Canada. Geological Survey**
Annotated catalogue of and guide to the publications of the Geological Survey, Canada, 1847-1917 by W.F. Ferrier, assisted by Dorothy J. Ferrier. Ottawa, King's Printer, 1920. 544 p.

2:421 **Canada. Geological Survey**
Catalogue of publications of the Geological Survey of Canada ... Ottawa, Government Printing Bureau, 1906. 129 p.

Another edition: Revised to January 1, 1909. Ottawa, Parmelee, 1909. 181 p. Earlier editions under title: List of publications of the Geological Survey of Canada.

2:422 **Canada. Geological Survey**
... General index to reports, 1885-1906. Comp. by F.J. Nicolas. Ottawa, Government Printing Bureau, 1908. x p., 1 *l.*, 1014 p.

2:423 **Canada. Geological Survey**
Index of publications of the Geological Survey of Canada (1845-1958) By A.G. Johnston. [Ottawa, Queen's Printer, 1961] x, [1], 378 p. fold. map (in pocket)

... (Supplement for 1959, 1960) [By] H.M.A. Rice. [Ottawa, Queen's Printer, 1961] [3], iii, 83 p.

... Supplement for 1961, 1962, by H.M.A. Rice, [Ottawa, Queen's Printer, 1963] vii, 71 p.

... Author index. [Ottawa, Queen's Printer, 1963] 25 p.

2:424 **Canada. Geological Survey**
Index to Annual reports 1927-50, Economic geology series 1927-50, Geological bulletins 1927-50, Geological papers 1935-50, Maps without reports 1927-50, Museum bulletins 1927-50, Summary reports 1927-33, compiled by W.E. Cockfield, E. Hall and J.F. Wright. [Ottawa, Queen's Printer, 1962] viii, 723 p.

2:425 **Canada. Geological Survey**
... Index to Memoirs, 1910-1926; Bulletins, 1913-1926; Summary reports, 1917-1926; Sessional papers (administrative) 1921-1926. Compiled by Frank Nicolas. Ottawa, Acland, Printer to the King, 1932. vii, 666 p.

2:426 **Canada. Geological Survey**
... Index to paleontology (Geological publications). Compiled by
Frank Nicolas. Ottawa, Acland, 1925-30. 2v. (Miscellaneous series
no. 1-2)

2:427 **Canada. Geological Survey**
Index to reports of Geological Survey of Canada from 1951-59,
compiled by J.F. Wright. [Ottawa, Queen's Printer, 1965] xii, 379 p.

2:428 **Canada. Geological Survey**
List of publications of the Geological Survey of Canada ... Ottawa,
Government Printing Bureau, 1900. 58 p.
Earlier lists were printed in the *Report of progress* 1863, and separately in
1873, 1879, 1884, 1886, 1889, 1895 and 1898.
Title and imprint varies.

2:429 **Canada. Geological Survey**
Publications of the Geological Survey and National Museum (1909-
1947 inclusive). Ottawa, 1948. ciii p.
Cumulation of previous lists.

2:430 **Canada. Geological Survey**
Publications of the Geological Survey of Canada (1917-1952) compiled by Lorne B. Leafloor. Ottawa, 1952. v, 82 p.
Supplementary to the *Annotated catalogue of and guide to the publications of
the Geological Survey of Canada, 1845-1917,* by W.F. Ferrier.
Supplement to Aug. 1956. Ottawa, 1957. 11 p. Supersedes Supplement
[1952-1954] issued 1954.

2:431 **Canada. Geological Survey**
... Published maps (1917-1930 inclusive). List compiled by P.J. Moran.
Ottawa, Acland, 1931. 1 p. *l.,* 16 p.

2:432 **Canada. Interdepartmental Advisory Committee on Canadian
Participation in the Universal and International Exhibition in Brussels,
1958.** Library Advisory Committee
Books sent to the Library, Canadian Pavilion, Brussels Universal and
International Exhibition, 1958, selected by the Library Advisory
Committee. [Ottawa, 1958] [27] *l.*

2:433 **Canada. Ministère de l'Agriculture.** Division de l'économie
... Supplément aux Travaux publiés ... 1957-1962. Ottawa, 1964.
40 p. ([Publication] 64/3F, mars 1964)
Compilatrice: Helen I. Marquis.

2:434  **Canada. Ministère de l'Agriculture.** Division de l'Economie rurale
Travaux publiés par les membres de la Division de l'Economie,
1930-1956. Ottawa, Imprimeur de la reine, 1957. 64 p.
1957 supplément. Ottawa, Imprimeur de la reine, 1958. 5 p.

2:435  **Canada. Ministère de l'agriculture.** Division de l'information
Liste des publications. [Ottawa, Imprimeur de la Reine, 1923—   ]
annuel.
N'a pas paru en 1961.

2:436  **Canada. Ministère de l'Agriculture.** Service de l'information
Liste des publications disponibles ... Ottawa, 1923—. Annuel.

2:437  **Canada. Ministère de la Citoyenneté et de l'Immigration.** Direction
des recherches économiques et sociales
Citoyenneté, immigration et groupes ethniques au Canada; une
bibliographie des recherches, sources publiées et non publiées, 1920-
1958. Ottawa [Imprimeur de la Reine] 1960 [i.e. 1961] [8] , 190,
[25] p. form.
Citoyenneté ... 1959-1961. Ottawa [Imprimeur de la Reine] 1962. [6] , iv, ivf,
55 p.
Citoyenneté ... 1962-1964. Ottawa [Imprimeur de la Reine] 1962. iii, iv, 127 p.

2:438  **Canada. Ministère de la Citoyenneté et de l'Immigration.** Division
de la citoyenneté canadienne
... Recherches sur l'adaptation des immigrants et les groupes
ethniques; une bibliographie annuelle ... Ottawa, 1955—   .

2:439  **Canada. Ministère de la Citoyenneté et de l'Immigration.** Division
de la citoyenneté canadienne
... Recherches sur l'adaptation des immigrants et les groupes
ethniques; une bibliographie de thèses non publiées, 1920-1953.
Ottawa, 1955. [3] , 31 p.

2:440  **Canada. Ministère de la Citoyenneté et de l'Immigration.** Division
de la citoyenneté canadienne
... Recherches sur l'adaptation des immigrants et les groupes
ethniques; une bibliographie d'ouvrages publiés, 1920-1953. Ottawa,
1956. [3] , ii, 131 p.

2:441  **Canada. Ministère des Forêts.** Direction des recherches sur les produits
forestiers
Liste de publications de la Direction des recherches sur les produits
forestiers, laboratoires d'Ottawa et de Vancouver. Mise à jour août
1963. [Ottawa, Imprimeur de la Reine, 1963] iii, 3, 22, v p.

2:442 **Canada. Ministère des Forêts.** Service de l'information et des renseignements techniques
... Films canadiens sur les forêts et autres ressources renouvelables. Ottawa [Imprimeur de la Reine, 1965] vii, 32 p.

2:443 **Canada. Ministère des Mines et des Relevés techniques.** Direction de la géographie
... Bibliographie choisie d'ouvrages sur la géographie du Canada ...
1958– Ottawa [Imprimeur de la Reine] 1960– (Sa Série bibliographique nos 26-29, 32)

2:444 **Canada. Ministère des Mines et des Relevés techniques.** Direction de la géographie
... Bibliographie choisie d'ouvrages sur la toponymie au Canada ...
Ottawa [Imprimeur de la Reine] 1964. 2 f., 27 p. (Sa Série bibliographique, no 30)

2:445 **Canada. Ministère des Mines et Relevés techniques.** Direction de la géographie
Colonisation et peuplement dans les Amériques; bibliographie choisie ...
Ottawa [Imprimeur de la Reine] 1960. 4 f., 68 p. (Série bibliographique, no 25)
Compilé par Dr S.C. Wiley.

2:446 **Canada. Ministère des Mines et des Relevés techniques.** Direction de la géographie
... Liste de thèses et dissertations sur la géographie du Canada.
Ottawa [Imprimeur de la Reine] 1964. 3 f., 40 p. (Sa Série bibliographique, 31)

2:447 **Canada. Ministère des Mines et des Relevés techniques.** Direction de la géographie
... Liste des publications ... Ottawa [195–? ] irrégulier.

2:448 **Canada. National Library**
Canadian graduate theses in the humanites and social sciences, 1921-1946 ... [Ottawa, King's Printer, 1951] 194 p.
Compiled and published under the auspices of: Humanities Research Council of Canada, and Canadian Social Science Research Council.

2:449 **Canada. National Library**
Canadiana 1867-1900. Compiled by R. Tanghe. (*In progress*)

2:450 **Canada. National Library**
Periodicals in the social sciences and humanities currently received by Canadian libraries. Ottawa, 1968. 2 v.

2:451 **Canada. National Library**
Union list of non-Canadian newspapers held by Canadian libraries
[by] Stephan Rush. Ottawa, 1968. 69 p.

2:452 **Canada. National Museum**
Bibliography of Canadian anthropology for ... (In its *Annual report*
1954-55– )
Compiler: 1954/55– , T.F. McIlwraith.

2:453 **Canada. National Museum**
... Publications of the National Museum of Canada (1913-1951).
Issued under authority of the minister of Resources and Develop-
ment. Ottawa, 1952. 1 p. *l.*, vi, 127 p.
Supplements available to 1960.

2:454 **Canada. Parliament.** Library
Alphabetical catalogue of the library of Parliament: being an index
to the classified catalogues printed in 1857 and 1858, and to the
books since added to the library, up to 1st March, 1862. Printed by
authority. Quebec, Hunter, Rose & co., 1862.
313 p.

2:455 **Canada. Parliament.** Library
Alphabetical catalogue of the library of Parliament: being an index
to classified catalogues printed in 1857, 1858 and 1864, and to the
books and pamphlets since added to the library, up to 1st October,
1867. Printed by authority. Ottawa, Printed by G.E. Desbarats,
1867.
496 p.

2:456 **Canada. Parliament.** Library
Bibliography of Canadiana; a list of Canadian books and references
for public libraries, universities, the film industry, and others. Prepared
in co-operation with the Canadian Dept. of Trade and Commerce and
the Motion Picture Association of America, Inc. [Ottawa] 1949. 28 *l.*

2:457 **Canada. Parliament.** Library
Catalogue of books in the library of Parliament ... Quebec, J.
Lovell's Steam Printing Establishment, 1852.
vi p., 2 1., [11]-130 p.
Printed by order of the Legislative assembly.

2:458 **Canada. Parliament.** Library
... Catalogue of the library of Parliament ... Printed by order of the
Legislature. Toronto, J. Lovell, 1857-58.
2 v.

2:459  **Canada. Parliament.** Library
Catalogue of the Library of Parliament. Part I. Law; legislation;
political and social science; commerce and statistics. With index.
Published by authority. Ottawa, Printed by Maclean, Roger & Co.,
1880.
2v in 1.

2:460  **Canada. Parliament.** Library
Index to the catalogue of the library of Parliament: Part II. General
library 1879. Published by authority. Ottawa, Printed by the Citizen
Printing and Publishing Co., 1879.
x, [1], 683 p.
'This index will be found to comprise all the books in the Library of Parliament ...
with the exception of works on jurisprudence, political and social science and
political economy, forming the first part of the catalogue ...'

2:461  **Canada. Parliament.** Library
List of British and American official documents relating to the
history of the fisheries controversy. [Ottawa, 1888] 21 *l.*
Manuscript.

2:462  **Canada. Parliament.** Library
Reference list on the subject of reciprocity in trade between Canada
and the United States of America. Library of Parliament, Ottawa,
November, 1910. Ottawa, Government Printing Bureau, 1910. 68 p.

2:463  **Canada. Parliament.** Library
Report of the joint librarians, 1871-1900. (Sessional papers,
1871-1900)
A series of annual lists of copyright material bearing Canadian imprint, added
to the Library of Parliament.

2:464  **Canada. Public Archives**
Bibliography of materials at the Public archives of Canada relating to
the rebellion of 1837-38. [Ottawa, Patenaude, Printer to the King,
1940] [63]-138 p. [Its Report 1939, Appendix III]

2:465  **Canada. Public Archives**
... Catalogue of maps, plans and charts in the Map Room of the
Dominion Archives. Classified and indexed by H.R. Holmden. Pub-
lished by authority of the Secretary of State under the direction of
the Archivist. Ottawa, Government Printing Bureau, 1912. xii, 685 p.
(Publications of the Canadian Archives, no. 8)

2:466  **Canada. Public Archives**
Catalogue of pamphlets in the Public Archives of Canada ... with

index; prepared by Magdalen Casey. Ottawa, King's Printer, 1931-32.
2 v. (Publications of the Public Archives of Canada, no. 13)
Contents: v. 1, 1493-1877; v. 2, 1878-1931.

2:467 **Canada. Public Archives**
Catalogue of pamphlets, journals and reports in the Dominion
Archives, 1611-1867, with index. Published by authority of the
Minister of Agriculture under the direction of the Archivist. Ottawa,
Government Printing Bureau, 1911. 230 p.
'Prepared by Mr McArthur of the Archives Branch.'

2:468 **Canada. Public Archives**
Catalogue of pamphlets, journals and reports in the Public Archives
of Canada, 1611-1867, with index. 2d ed., prepared by Norman Fee.
Pub. by authority of the Secretary of State under the direction of
the Archivist. Ottawa, Taché, 1916. 2 p. *l.,* [3]-471 p. facsims.
Also issued in the same year as Appendix D to the *Report of the Archives
Dept. for 1914 and 1915.*

2:469 **Canada. Public Archives**
Catalogue of pictures including paintings, drawings and prints in the
Public Archives of Canada, with an introduction and notes by James
F. Kenney ... Published by authority of the secretary of state under
the direction of the keeper of the records. Ottawa [The Mortimer
Company, limited, 1925.

2:470 **Canada. Public Archives**
... A guide to the documents in the manuscript room at the Public
Archives of Canada ... Prepared by David W. Parker ... Ottawa,
Government Printing Bureau, 1914-
(Publications of the Archives of Canada, no. 10)

2:471 **Canada. Public Archives**
Reports of the Archivist ... Ottawa, 1872-.
Issued separately since 1881, in English and in French.
Not published in 1906-1907. Combined issues: 1914-15, 1917-18, 1919-21,
1922-23, 1924-26, 1927-28.
Some Reports contain lists of books, pamphlets, maps and charts, calendars.
Reports for 1950 and after have no appendices.

2:472 **Canada. Public Archives**
Supplemented to Dr Brymner's Report on Canadian Archives by Mr
Edouard Richard, 1899. (Being an appendix to *Report of the Minister
of Agriculture.*) Printed by order of Parliament. Ottawa, Dawson,
1901. 1 p. *l.,* 548 p. (Sessional papers, no. 8c)
A calendar of Canadian papers in the Ministère des colonies, Paris.

2:473 **Canada. Public Archives.** Manuscript Division
Checklist of census returns, New Brunswick, 1851-1871, Nova Scotia, 1871. [Ottawa, Queen's Printer] 1963 [i.e. 1964] i, 12 p.

2:474 **Canada. Public Archives.** Map Division
Sixteenth-century maps relating to Canada; a checklist and bibliography. Ottawa, 1956 [i.e., 1957]. 283 p. facsims.

2:475 **Canada. Wartime Information Board**
List of Dominion government publications. Ottawa, Wartime Information Board, The Library, 1944-45. 6 nos.
Jan.-June 1944, 36 p.; July-Sept. 1944, 20 p.; Oct.-Dec. 1944, 20 p.; Jan.-March 1945, 18 p.; April-June 1945, 16 p.; July-Sept. 1945, 16 p.

2:476 **Canada. Wildlife Service**
List of publications. Rev. June 1962. [Ottawa, Queen's Printer, 1962] 22 p.

2:477 **Canadian advertising, Canadian media authority** ... Toronto, Maclean-Hunter, 1928– . (v. –29, no. 2:) Bi-monthly.
Quarterly, 1928-52; 5 nos. a year, 1953.

2:478 **Canadian Association for Adult Education**
... Discussion materials on Canadian unity. [Montreal, Institut canadien d'éducation des adultes; Toronto, Canadian Association for Adult Education; Ottawa, Canadian Citizenship Council, 1964] [9] *l.*

2:479 **Canadian Association for Adult Education**
Non-degree research in adult education in Canada; an inventory. La recherche en éducation des adultes au Canada; un inventaire. 1968. Toronto, Canadian Association for Adult Education; Dept. of Adult Education, Ontario Institute for Studies in Education; Montréal, Institut canadien d'éducation des adultes, 1969.
103 p. annual.
First ed. 1968.

2:480 **Canadian Association for Adult Education**
A selective bibliography of Canadian plays. [Toronto] 1957. 15 *l.*

2:481 **Canadian Association of Law Libraries**
Periodicals in Canadian law libraries; a union list. Toronto, Published at York University Law Library for the Canadian Association of Law Libraries, 1968.
iii *l.,* 64 p.

2:482  **Canadian Association of Slavists**
A bibliography of publications of Canadian Slavists. Daniel Dorotich, editor. Vancouver, University of British Columbia, 1967.
51 *l.*

2:483  **Canadian author and bookman.** Montreal, Canadian Author's Association, 1923—.
Title varies. 1923-Apr. 1925, The Society's bulletin; May 1925-Sept. 1933, Authors' bulletin; Oct. 1933-Dec. 1939, Canadian author.

2:484  **The Canadian book at the Frankfurt Book Fair in West Germany,** 1965; an exhibition of books published during recent years sponsored by the Canada Council and the Department of Cultural Affairs of the province of Quebec and organized by a joint committee of the Book Publishers' Association of Canada and l'Association des éditeurs canadiens, with the collaboration of the Queen's Printer for Canada. List of titles and publishers. Ottawa, Queen's Printer, 1965. 3 p. *l.,* 54 p.

2:485  **Canadian booklist.** Mar.-Apr. 1961—Jan.-Feb. 1964. [Toronto] Published by *Quill & Quire* in co-operation with the National Library, 1961-64. 18 no. bimonthly.
Ceased publication with Jan.-Feb. issue, 1964.
List included in bimonthly issues of *Quill & quire,* v. 25, no. 6-v. 26, no. 4, Dec. 1959-Jan. 1960—Aug.-Sept. 1960.
Entries also appeared in list of new books included in *Canadiana,* Mar. 1960-Apr. 1962.
Compiled by the National Library from deposit copies of Canadian imprint books.

2:486  **The Canadian bookman.** V. 1-21; Jan. 1919/Nov. 1939. Toronto [etc., 1919-1939]. 21v.
Quarterly, 1919-Sept. 1921 (no numbers issued for Jan. and Apr. 1921); monthly (irregular) Dec. 1921-37; bimonthly, 1938-39.
V.1-4 called 'new series.'
Editors: 1919-22, B.K. Sandwell; 1923-37, F.I. Weaver; 1938-39, Howe Martyn.
Issues for Apr. 1923-Mar. 1937 have subtitle: A monthly devoted to literature and the creative arts (varies slightly).
Merged with *Canadian author* (later the *Canadian author and bookman*).

2:487  **Canadian book-prices current.** Toronto, McClelland and Stewart 1957-1959
Compiled by R.M. Hamilton.
2 v.
v. 1; 1950-55; v. 2; 1956-58

2:488 **Canadian books in print. Catalogue des livres canadiens en librairie**
[Toronto] Comité du catalogue des livres canadiens en librairie;
[distribué par Le Conseil supérieur du livre, and by University of
Toronto Press] 1967—
v. annual.

2:489 **Canadian bookseller and stationers' journal.** v. 1-20
Toronto, 1888-1907.
Subtitle varies.

2:490 **Canadian Broadcasting Corporation**
Catalogue of Canadian composers. [Compiled by J.J. Gagnier, and
others]. [Toronto? 1947] [136 *l*]
'A catalogue of about 250 living composers, presenting biographical information and a list of their compositions. The index by type of composition is a
valuable appendix.' cf. May, L. Music and composers of Canada.
Catalogue of Canadian composers. Edited by Helmut Kallmann. Revised and
enlarged edition. [Toronto, 1952] 254 p.
Includes living as well as dead.

2:491 **Canadian business and technical index.** v. 1-4; 1959-62. [Toronto]
Toronto Public Libraries, Reference Division, 1959-63. 4 v.
bimonthly.
Subject index to Canadian business and technical periodicals.
Published bimonthly with semi-annual and annual cumulations.
Ceased publication with v. 4, 1962.

2:492 **The Canadian catalogue of books published in Canada,** about
Canada, as well as those written by Canadians. [Toronto, Ontario
Dept. of Education, Public Libraries Branch] 1923-1950. Annual.
Compiled by the Toronto Public Libraries. Published 1945-1950 as a
supplement to the *Ontario library review.*

2:493 **The Canadian catalogue of books published in Canada,** about
Canada, as well as those written by Canadians, with imprint 1921-
1949; with cumulated author index. [2d] consolidated English
language reprint ed. [Toronto] Toronto Public Libraries, 1967.
1 v. (various pagings)
Reprint ed. of the English sections of the *Canadian catalogue,* published
annually 1921/22 to 1949.
First ed. 1959, in 2 v.

2:494 **Canadian Citizenship Council**
Educational aids available from the representatives of overseas
governments in Canada. [3d ed.] Ottawa [Canadian Committee for]
International Co-operation Year [1966]
25 *l.* (I.C.Y. series, 4)
First ed. 1945; 2d ed. 1950.

2:495 **Canadian Corrections Association**
Correctional and criminological literature published in Canada within the last five years and available to other countries ... [Ottawa, 1964–  ] semi-annual.

2:496 **Canadian Council for International Co-operation**
Bibliography of international development. Ottawa, 1969.
28 *l.*

2:497 **Canadian Council of Resource Ministers**
References. v. 1-   Dec. 1968-      Montreal.
v. monthly.
Supersedes Extracts.

2:498 **Canadian Council on Urban and Regional Research**
Urban & regional references urbaines & régionales, 1945-1962. Ottawa [1964]
1 v. (looseleaf) forms.
To be kept up to date by annual supplements.
Supplement. 1967. Ottawa [1968] [11], [29], 145 p.

2:499 **Canadian Cultural Information Centre**
Canadian cultural publications ... [Ottawa] Canadian Cultural Information Centre, 195–?]
Editions 1-9 list English language publications only.
Publisher varies:      -Rev. Mar. 1961, issued jointly by the Canada Foundation and the Canadian Citizenship Council.

2:500 **Canadian defence quarterly** (Indexes)
Author, review and subject indexes, *Canadian defence quarterly*, v. 1-16, 1923-1939, compiled by C.E. Dornbusch. Cornwallville, N.Y., 1956. [80 *l*]

2:501 **Canadian Education Association**
Graduate theses in education 1913-1952; partial list. Toronto, 1952.
33 p.

2:502 **Canadian Education Association.** Research and Information Division
Registry of Canadian theses in education. Series I: to 1955. Toronto [1959]-61. 15 nos.
The first 5 nos. issued as insets in the Association's *News letter,* Nov. 1959- Apr. 1960. The remaining nos. issued separately.
... 1955-1962. Toronto, 1963. iii, 24 p. (Its Bulletin no. A/1962-63. June 1963)

2:503 **Canadian education index**; a quarterly index to books, reports, pamphlets and periodical articles on education published in Canada ...

January to March 1965– Ottawa, Canadian Council for Research in Education, 1965– Quarterly.

Editor: Mavis R. Jones

2:504 **Canadian Federation of Mayors and Municipalities**
Municipal reference library catalogue. Bibliothèque de documentation municipale. [11th rev. Montreal, 1965]
1 v.

2:505 **Canadian Federation of Music Teachers Associations**
A list of Canadian music. Toronto, Published for the Canadian Federation of Music Teachers Associations, by the Oxford University Press [c1946]. 23 p.

2:506 **Canadian geographical journal** (Indexes)
A regional index of articles in the *Canadian geographical journal,* 1930 to 1959, compiled by J. Lewis Robinson. Ottawa, Royal Canadian Geographical Society [1960] 19 p.

2:507 **Canadian geophysical bulletin.** Ottawa, National Research Council of Canada, Associate Committee on Geodesy and Geophysics, 1947– . Quarterly.

2:508 **Canadian Health Education Specialists Society.** School Health Committee
Annotated guide to health instruction materials in Canada. 1st ed.; 1964-66. Ottawa, 1964.

iii, 87 p.

Supplement. 1964. Ottawa, 1964.
[18] p.

Supplement. 1965. Ottawa, 1966.
18 p. 22 cm.

2d ed. Ottawa, 1967. 105 p. 24 cm.

2:509 **Canadian historical review** (Indexes)
Index, v. I-IX, 1920-1929, by Julia Jarvis and Alison Ewart. [Toronto] University of Toronto Press, 1930. 3 p. *l.,* 284 p. *(University of Toronto studies.)*

Index, v. XI-XX, 1930-1939, compiled by the Editorial Department of the University of Toronto Press under the direction of Alison Hewitt. Toronto, University of Toronto Press, 1944. vi, 432 p. *(University of Toronto studies.)*

Index, v. XXI-XXX, 1940-1949 ... [1959] 3 p. *l.,* 404 p.

2:510 **Canadian index to periodicals and documentary films** 1948–.
Ottawa, Canadian Library Association and National Library of Canada. Monthly.

Continues: *Canadian periodical index.* Windsor, Ont., Public Library, 1928-32; Toronto, University Library, 1938-47.
Cumulated yearly.

2:511 **Canadian Institute of International Affairs.** Toronto. Men's Branch. Defence Study Group
Problems of national defence; a study guide and bibliography.
1961/62. Toronto, Canadian Institute of International Affairs, 1962.
[1], 12, 14 *l.*

2:512 **Canadian Institute of Mining and Metallurgy**
Transactions of the Canadian Mining Institute. Indices to names of authors and subjects of the papers presented to the Canadian Mining Institute, the Federated Canadian Mining Institute, and the antecedent provincial mining societies, 1891-1903 ... Ottawa, Published by authority of the Council of the Institute, 1904. 31 p.
Issued also in the *Journal of the Canadian institute of mining and metallurgy,* v. 6, p. 489-520.

2:513 **Canadian Institute of Mining and Metallurgy.** Transactions. (Indexes)
General index of the Journal of the Canadian Mining Institute, volumes XI to XIV (1908-1911), the Transactions of the Canadian Mining Institute, volumes XV to XXIII (1912-1920) and the Transactions of the Canadian Institute of Mining and Metallurgy and of the Mining Society of Nova Scotia, volumes XXIV to XXXVIII (1921-1935)
Montreal, Canadian Institute of Mining and Metallurgy, 1937. 229 p.

2:514 **Canadian Jewish Congress.** Archives Committee
Canadian Jewish archives; list of documents and material. Montreal, The Congress, 1939. 20 *l.*

2:515 **The Canadian law times** (Index)
Index of leading articles and editorials, etc., contained in volumes 1 to 42 (inclusive) with names of authors. Compiled by Lex. Toronto, Carswell, 1923. 72 p.

2:516 **Canadian League of Composers**
Catalogue of orchestral music (including works for small orchestra and band, concertos, vocal-orchestral and choral-orchestral works) composed by members of the Canadian League of Composers. Toronto, 1957. 58 p.

2:517 **Canadian Library Association**
... Checklist of Canadian periodicals in the field of education, by Lois J. Carrier. Ottawa, 1964. iii, 17 p. (Its Occasional papers, no. 44)

2:518  **Canadian Library Association**
[Exhibition of Canadian books. Catalogue. Ottawa, 1965] 1, 37 p.
Exhibition of books chosen by the National Library of Canada, the Ministry
of Cultural Affairs of Quebec (list published separately) and the C.L.A., held
at Cobo Hall, Detroit, during the American Library Association Conference,
July 1965.

2:519  **Canadian Library Association.** Microfilm Committee
Canadian newspapers on microfilm. Catalogue de journaux canadiens
sur microfilm. Ottawa, Canadian Library Association, 1959.
Contents: Pt. I, Cumulative microfilm catalogue of newspapers and periodicals
microfilmed by C.L.A.; II, Other Canadian newspapers on microfilm.

2:520  **Canadian Library Association.** Microfilm Committee
Catalogue of New Brunswick papers on microfilm, microfilmed by
the Microfilm Project of the Canadian Library Association. [Ottawa]
1961. iii, [15] *l.*
Information reprinted from *Canadian newspapers on microfilm,* part I, New
Brunswick section, 1959-1961.

2:521  **Canadian Library Association.** Microfilm Committee
Geographical list of CLA microfilms [and Alphabetical list of CLA
microfilms] July 1961. Ottawa [1961] 17 (i.e. 18) p.
... Supplement. Ottawa [1962–  ] annual.

2:522  **Canadian Library Association.** Microfilm Committee
Newspaper microfilming project. Microfilms de journaux. Catalogue ...
[Ottawa, 1948-1957] Irregular.

2:523  **Canadian Library Association.** Reference section
40 years of Kirkconnell; titles and selected articles. [Ottawa, 1962]
iii, 13 *l.*
Reprinted from the *Acadia bulletin,* v. 47, no. 1, p. 19-23, Jan. 1961, and
v. 48, no. 1, p. 22-25, Jan. 1962. Cf. *l.* ii.

2:524  **Canadian Library Association.** Young People's Section
Canadian books; a selection of books for young people's libraries,
compiled by the Committee on Canadian Books ... Ottawa, 1960–.
annual.
Some of the previous lists were issued as Occasional papers (nos. 13, 16 and 21)

2:525  **Canadian library literature index;** a preliminary checklist, prepared by
the Reference Section of the Canadian Library Association—Association canadienne des bibliothèques, in co-operation with the library
associations in Canada and their bulletins. Oct. 1956. Ottawa,
Canadian Library Association, 1956. 79 p.

2:526 **Canadian Library Week Council**
Some notable books, 1963, chosen for Canadian Library Week by
Toronto Public Libraries. [Ottawa, 1964] folder (6 p.)
List of 45 Canadian books.

2:527 **Canadian literature** (Indexes)
Canadian literature. The first three years. Index to numbers 1 to 12.
(In *Canadian literature* no. 13, Summer, 1962. p. [89]-100)

2:528 **Canadian Masonic Research Association**
List of papers read before the Association, May 9, 1949-Dec. 31,
1962. [Halifax, 1963?] [7] p.

2:529 **Canadian Medical Association**
Sir William Osler memorial number. [Montreal], Canadian Medical
Association Journal, 1920. 123 p.
'Classified bibliography of Sir William Osler's Canadian period (1858-1885) by
Maude E. Abbott,' p. 103-123.

2:530 **Canadian Music Library Association**
A bio-bibliographical finding list of Canadian musicians and those who
have contributed to music in Canada, compiled by a committee of the
Canadian Music Library Association, 1960-61. Ottawa, Canadian
Library Association [1961] v, 53 p.

2:531 **Canadian Music Library Association**
Musical Canadiana; a subject index. A preliminary ed. in which will
be found listed some 800 vocal and instrumental pieces of music
published ... up to 1921 ... Compiled by a committee of the Canadian
Music Library Association. [Ottawa, Canadian Library Association]
1967.
v, 62 p.
Introd. signed Helmut Kallmann, Laura Murray, Grace Pincoe.

2:532 **Canadian Music Library Association**
Union list of music periodicals in Canadian libraries. Ottawa,
Canadian Library Association, 1964.
v, 32 p.
Supplement. Ottawa, Canadian Library Association, 1967.
v, 27 p.

2:533 **Canadian National Railways.** Library
A selected bibliography on Canadian railways. [Montreal] 1965. 5 p.
(Its Special series, no. 25, 4th ed.)

2:534 **Canadian Nurses' Association**
Selected references on establishment of shortened programs in schools of nursing. [Ottawa] 1966.
11 *l.*

2:535 **Canadian Nurses' Association**
Selected references on geriatrics. [Ottawa] 1966.
12 *l.*

2:536 **Canadian Nurses' Association.** Library
[Bibliographies] Ottawa.
no.
Contents.
(a) Bibliography on higher education. Aug. 1965. Prepared for the Committee on Higher Education.
(b) Criteria for evaluating diploma schools of nursing. Apr. 26, 1965.
(c) Hospitals and schools of nursing: planning and construction; selected references for nurses. Nov. 1965.
(d) Selected bibliography for associate degree programs in nursing in junior and community colleges. Apr. 27, 1965.
(e) Selected bibliography for studies on nursing needs and education in Canada. Aug. 16, 1965.
(f) Selected bibliography on accreditation. Aug. 1965. Prepared for the Committee on Accreditation.
(g) Selected bibliography on Canadian Nurses' Association. Apr. 23, 1965.
(h) Selected bibliography on history and activities of Canadian Nurses' Association. Feb. 9, 1965.
(i) Selected bibliography on nursing; career choices. Aug. 1965.
(j) Selected bibliography on nursing education, with particular reference to baccalaureate programs. May 28, 1965.
(k) Selected bibliography on school health and nursing. Aug. 1965.
(l) Selected periodical references Report of Royal Commission on Health Services (Hall Report) Aug. 1965.
(m) Selected references on economic and social welfare. Mar. 22, 1965. Accompanied by Addendum I, Mar. 28, 1965, and Addendum II, Nov. 9, 1965.
(n) Selected references on establishment of shortened programs in schools of nursing. Mar. 1966.
(o) Selected references on evaluation of students. May 1966.
(p) Selected references on history of nursing in Canada. Feb. 12, 1965.
(q) Selected references on libraries (with particular reference to schools of nursing) Apr. 1965.
(r) Selected references on nursing education, graduate. Oct. 27, 1965.
(s) Selected references on occupational health nursing. Sept. 1965.
(t) Selected references on practical nurses and nursing. Aug. 1965.
(u) Selected references on professional roles. June 1, 1965.
(v) Selected references on public relations from CNA Library material. Nov. 1965.
(w) Selected references suggested for study of hospital nursing service. Jan. 8, 1965.

2:537  **Canadian Nurses Association.** Library
Index [of] Canadian nursing studies. [Rev. ed. Ottawa] 1967.
59 p.

2:538  **Canadian Pacific Railway Company**
Catalogue of Canadian books provided for the tour of the Duke and
Duchess of Cornwall and York. [Montreal, 1901] 3 p.

2:539  **Canadian Society of Authors**
Bibliography and general report. March, 1902. [Toronto, 1902] 29 p.

2:540  **Canadian Standards Association**
List of publications. 1966. Ottawa [1966]
44 p. form. annual.
Kept up to date by supplements published in the quarterly CSA news bulletin.

2:541  **Canadian Tax Foundation**
Guide to publications; a guide by subject and author to the publications of the Canadian Tax Foundation to December 31st, 1958.
Compiled by Reginald A. Rawkins. [Toronto, Foundation 1959]
42 p.

2:542  **Canadian Tax Foundation**
Index of publications to Dec. 31, 1964. Toronto, c1965.
iv, 107 p.
'A supplement will be issued as part of the last issue of the [*Canadian Tax*]
*Journal* each year.'–Foreword.
Supplement. 1965-68. [Toronto, c1969]
iv, 46 p.

2:543  **Canadian Tax Foundation**
A subject catalogue of the Foundation's published material.
[Toronto, 1957] 30 *l.*
Prepared by Reginald A. Rawkins.

2:544  **Canadian Teachers' Federation**
Books about Canada ... [Ottawa, 1963] [16] p. illus.
'Compiled for teachers in other countries'–p. [3]

2:545  **Canadian Teachers' Federation**
... Livres concernant le Canada. [Ottawa, 1963] [16] p.
'Destinés aux enseignants d'autres pays'–p.[3]

2:546  **Canadian theses.** 1960/61– Ottawa [Queen's Printer] 1962– annual.
First list published in 1953 under title: *Canadian theses, a list of theses*
*accepted by Canadian universities in 1952.* (50 p.)
Compiled by the National Library of Canada.

2:547  **Canadian Universities Foundation.** Research and Information Service
Current publications of the Canadian Universities Foundation and
the National Conference of Canadian Universities and Colleges ...
[Ottawa, 1962] 7 p.

2:548  **Canadian Welfare Council**
Catalogue of publications. Catalogue des éditions ... Ottawa, 1960-
annual.
Earlier editions 1957, 1959. Title varies.

2:549  **Canadian Welfare Council**
Pamphlets and reprints on problems in social welfare. Ottawa, 1940.
1 p. *l.*, 28 p., 1 *l.*, v p. (Its Catalogue of publications, no. 2, 1940.)

2:550  **Canadian Welfare Council**
Poverty; an annotated bibliography and references [by] Freda L.
Paltiel. [Ottawa] 1966.
x, 136 p.
Supplement, by Agnes Woodward. 1; Mar. 1967. Ottawa, [1967]
viii, 244 p.
Supplement, by Agnes Woodward. 2; Oct. 1967. Ottawa [1967]
viii, 123 p.
Supplement, by Agnes Woodward. 3; Apr. 1968. Ottawa [1968]
viii, 123 p.

2:551  **Canadian Welfare Council.** Research Branch
The day care of children; an annotated bibliography. Rev. ed. Ottawa,
1969.
68 *l.*

2:552  **Canadiana** ... Publications of Canadian interest noted by the
National Library ... [Ottawa, Queen's Printer, 1951–] . Monthly.
Cumulated yearly.

2:553  **Canadiana** ... Publications se rapportant au Canada notées par la
Bibliothèque nationale. [Ottawa, Imprimeur de la reine, 1951–]
Mensuel.
Refonte annuelle.

2:554  **Canadiana library.** Bibliothèque de Canadiana
[Montreal, 1967–
v.
On cover: The library and man and his world.
Text bilingual, English and French.
Catalogues of the holdings of the Canadiana library, Canadian Pavilion,
Expo 67.

2:555 **Canadiana selections** ... [Ottawa, Queen's Printer, 1956-63] 9 no. Annual.
Ceased publication with 1963 issue.

2:556 **Cannon, Velma R.**
A bibliography of vocational education in Ontario since 1900. Toronto, 1935. [1] 19 *l*. (Ms. Toronto Univ. Libr. School)

2:557 **Cantin, Gabrielle**
Bio-bibliographie du R.P. Fernand Porter, o.f.m. 1952. 75 p. (Ms. Ecole de Bibl., U. de M.)

2:558 **Cantin, Louise**
Bibliographie analytique de l'œuvre de Marcelle Lepage-Thibaudeau, précédée d'une biographie. Préface de M. Zéphirin Rousseau, sous-ministre des Terres et Forêts. Lévis, 1964. 97 p. (Ms. Ecole de Bibl., U.L.)

2:559 **Cappon, James**
Charles G.D. Roberts. Toronto Ryerson [1925]. 148 p. (*Makers of Canadian literature* ...)
Bibliography: p. 125-144.

2:560 **Carbonneau, Léo-Paul**
Bio-bibliographie analytique de Albert Rioux. Préface de J.-Chs Bonenfant ... Québec, 1958. 99 p. (Ms. Ecole de Bibl., U.L.)

2:561 **Cardin, Clarisse**
Bibliography of books on music by Canadian authors and books on Canadian music by foreign authors, 1900 to date. 20 p.

2:562 **Cardin, Clarisse**
Bibliography of Canadian historical bibliographies. 20 p.

2:563 **Cardin, Clarisse**
Bio-bibliographie de M. Marius Barbeau. Préface de M. Louvigny de Montigny. 1942. 101 p. (Mf. Ecole de Bibl., U. de M.)

2:564 **Cardin, Clarisse**
Bio-bibliographie de Marius Barbeau, précédée d'un hommage à Marius Barbeau par Luc Lacourcière et Félix-Antoine Savard. [Ottawa] Fides, 1947. 96 p. (*Publications de l'Université Laval. Archives de folklore, II.*)
Edition revisée de la précédente.

2:565 **Cardinal, Jacques**
Evolution du roman canadien-français (1940-1955). Bibliographie

annotée. Ottawa, Université d'Ottawa, Ecole de Bibliothécaires, 1961. 7 p. (Ms. Ecole de Bibl., U. d'O.)

2:566  **Carleton University, Ottawa.** Library
Selected list of current materials on Canadian public administration, prepared for the School of Public Administration no. 18; Jan. 1964. Ottawa [1964] 92 *l.*

2:567  **Carleton University, Ottawa.** Library
Sources of information for research in Canadian political science and public administration; a selected and annotated bibliography prepared for the Department of Political Science and the School of Public Administration. Ottawa, 1964–
25 1.

2:568  **Carnet bibliographique des publications de M. l'abbé Auguste Gosselin**
Petit souvenir à l'occasion de ses noces d'or sacerdotales, 30 septembre, 1866-1916. Québec, Laflamme, 1916. 24 p.

2:569  **Carney, R.J.**
A selected and annotated bibliography on the sociology of Eskimo education, prepared by R.J. Carney and W.O. Ferguson. With a foreword by B.Y. Card. Edmonton, Published [by] the Boreal Institute with the Dept. of Educational Foundations, University of Alberta, c1965.
v, 59 *l.* (Alberta. University. Boreal Institute. Occasional publication, no. 2)
A bibliography on Eskimo education in Alaska, Canada, and Greenland.

2:570  **Caron, Alfred**
Bio-bibliographie du R.P. Fernand Porter, o.f.m. Québec, 1952. 75 p. (Ms. Ecole de Bibl., U.L.)

2:571  **Carpentier, Denyse**
Bibliographie analytique de l'œuvre de Louis Hémon, précédée d'une biographie. Préface de Paul Charpentier. Québec, 1963. 52 p. (Ms. Ecole de Bibl., U.L.)

2:572  **Carrier, Hervé**
Sociologie du christianisme; bibliographie internationale. Sociology of Christianity; international bibliography [by] Hervé Carrier, s.j. [and] Emile Pin, s.j. Rome, Gregorian University Press, 1964.
313 p. (Studia socialia; series published by the Institute of Social Sciences of the Gregorian University, 8)

2:573  **Carrier, Lois J.**
Reference guide to educational literature in the Library of the University of British Columbia and in the Curriculum Laboratory of

the Faculty of Education, by Lois Carrier [and] Joseph Katz. Rev. Vancouver, University of British Columbia, Library and Faculty of Education, 1967.
51 p. (British Columbia. University. Library. Reference publication, no. 8)

2:574 **Carrier, Louis**
Books of French Canada. An exhibit prepared for the annual meeting of the American Library Association, Toronto, June 1927. Montreal, Carrier, 1927. 47, [1] p.

2:575 **Carrier, Nicole**
Almanachs et annuaires de la ville de Québec de 1780 à 1900. (Bibliographie) Préf. de M. André Beaulieu. 1964, viii, 91, xiii p. (Ms. Ecole de Bibl., U.L.)

2:576 **Carrière, Gaston**
Apôtres de la plume. Contribution des professeurs des facultés ecclésiastiques de l'Université d'Ottawa (1912 [i.e. 1932]-1951) à la bibliographie des Oblats de M.I. (Extrait des 'Missions' O.M.I. vol. 78, 1951, N. 277) Rome, Maison générale O.M.I., 1951. 32 p.
L'auteur annonce que ce travail sera continué dans la *Revue de l'Université d'Ottawa.*

2:577 **Carrière, Gaston**
Bibliographie des Oblats de langue française au Canada. Pour compléter Bernad. (In *Etudes oblates, Ottawa.* 10, 1951, p. 140-152, 291-304)

2:578 **Carrière, Gaston**
... Bibliographie des professeurs oblats des facultés ecclésiastiques de l'Université d'Ottawa (1932-1961) Ottawa [1962] 54 p., ix f.

2:579 **Carrière, Gaston**
Contribution des Oblats de Marie Immaculée de langue française aux études de linguistique et d'ethnologie du nord canadien. Québec, *Culture* [1951]. 14 p.

2:580 **Carrière, Gaston**
Une riche collection de manuscrits en langues indiennes (Extrait de Culture (1957) XVIII, 105-112) Québec, Culture [1957?] [105]-112 p.

2:581 **Carswell Company, Limited,** Toronto
Catalogue of Canadian publications, including historical and general books, statutes, and other government imprints, pamphlets, magazines, and miscellaneous books. Toronto, Carswell, 1900. 71 p.

2:582 **Cartier, Georges-E.**
Bio-bibliographie de Saint-Denys Garneau. Préf. par Robert Elie.
1952. 84 p. (Mf. Ecole de Bibl., U. de M.)

2:583 **Cartwright, Moira C.**
Special libraries in Canada, 1954-1966; an annotated bibliography.
Toronto, 1967. v, 27 p. (Ms. Toronto Univ. Libr. School)

2:584 **Casgrain, Philippe Baby**
La vie de Joseph-François Perrault surnommé le père de l'éducation
du peuple canadien ... Québec, Darveau, 1898. 176 p.
'Liste des ouvrages écrits par Joseph-François Perrault': p. 162-164.

2:585 **Casselman, Paul Hubert**
Coopération; bibliographie des ouvrages et des articles publiés en
français au Canada jusqu'à la fin de 1947. Ottawa, Centre social,
Université d'Ottawa [1953]. 191 p.

2:586 **Cassidy, Linda Anne**
The totem poles of the North Pacific coast of America; a bibliography. [Toronto] 1964. i, 6 *l*. (Ms. Toronto Univ. Libr. School)

2:587 **Catalogue de l'édition au Canada français.** 1969-70.
[Montréal] Conseil supérieur du livre [1969]
503 p.
Première éd. 1958.
Le titre varie: 1958, 1962, Catalogue collectif de l'édition au Canada français.
1965— Catalogue de l'édition au Canada français.

2:588 **Catalogue de livres canadiens** (section française). Londres, Exposition
de l'Empire britannique, Parc Wembley, 1924. 32 p.

2:589 **Catalogue des manuscrits et des imprimés en langues sauvages ainsi
que des reliques indiennes,** exposés à Québec à l'occasion du xve
Congrès international des Américanistes, septembre, 1906. Québec,
Dussault & Proulx, 1906. 50 p.

2:590 **Catalogue of a valuable collection of Canadian books and rare
pamphlets.** Includes some items of remarkable value and great
scarcity & choice extra illustrated works, history, biography, travel,
politics, geology, topography, agriculture, the Indian tribes, etc. ...
Toronto, Williamson, 1898. 34 p. (New series: no. 2, 1898)
Reproduced in facsimile in the *Papers of the bibliographical society of Canada,*
no. III, 1964.

2:591   **Catalogue of ancient documents relating to Acadia or Nova Scotia**
1710-1867. Halifax, N.S., 1886.

2:592   **Catholic press directory**; official media reference guide to Catholic
newspapers and magazines of the United States and Canada. 1923–
New York, Catholic Press Association, 1923–   annual.
Imprint varies: 1923–   Chicago, J.H. Meier.

2:593   **Céline-de-la-Présentation, sœur**
Bibliographie analytique de l'œuvre de l'abbé André Jobin, précédée
d'une biographie. Préface de l'abbé J.C. Racine. Pont-Rouge, 1964.
94 p. (Ms. Ecole de Bibl., U.L.)

2:594   **Centre d'information culturelle canadienne**
Canadian cultural publications. Publications culturelles canadiennes.
13e éd., printemps 1965. [Ottawa, 1965]
[16] p. annuel.

2:595   **Cercle linguistique de Montréal**
Jean-Paul Vinay: bibliographie chronologique, 1936-1962.
[Montréal] 1963.
15 p.

2:596   **Chabot, Evelyne**
Essai de bio-bibliographie: R.P. Jules Paquin, s.j. 1953. 23 p. (Ms.
Ecole de Bibl., U. de M.)

2:597   **Chabot, Juliette**
Bio-bibliographie d'écrivains canadiens-français; une liste des bio-
bibliographies présentées par les élèves de l'Ecole de Bibliothécaires,
Université de Montréal, 1937-1947. Montréal, 1948. 1 f., 12 p.

2:598   **Chabot, Juliette**
The history of Montreal; bibliography. Montreal, 1938. 22 *l.* (Ms.
McGill Univ. Libr. School)

2:599   **Chagnon, Berthe**
Bio-bibliographie de Claude Mélançon. Préface de Georges Préfontaine.
1945. 35 p. (Ms. Ecole de Bibl., U. de M.)

2:600   **Chagnon, Louise**
Béatrice Clément. Essai de bio-bibliographie. 1953. 52 p. (Mf. Ecole
de Bibl., U. de M.)

2:601   **Chagnon, Thaïs**
Bio-bibliographie de Honoré Parent. Préface de M. Léo-Paul Desrosiers.
1945. xix, 153 p. (Ms. Ecole de Bibl., U. de M.)

2:602 **Chalifoux, Jean-Pierre**
Bibliographie sur des questions actuelles. [Montréal] Bibliothèque.
Centre d'études canadiennes-françaises, McGill University, 1968.
[34] f.

2:603 **Chalifoux, Jean-Pierre**
Liste préliminaire de sources bibliographiques relatives à la littérature
canadienne-française. Montréal, Bibliothèque, Centre d'études
canadiennes-françaises, McGill University, 1966.
7 f.

2:604 **Champagne, André**
Bio-bibliographie analytique du docteur F.F. Osborne, géologue.
Préf. de M.I.W. Jones. 51 p. (Ms. Ecole de Bibl., U.L.)

2:605 **Champagne, Claude**
Bio-bibliographie de M. le chanoine Michel Couture. 1951. 55 p.
(Ms. Ecole de Bibl., U. de M.)

2:606 **Chan, Nancy**
Post secondary school education in Canada. 1967. [3] 12 1. (Ms.
U. of O. Libr. School)

2:607 **Chan, Yim-Sang**
The Royal Canadian Navy's operation in the Second World War:
1939-1945. 1963. vi, 4 1. (Ms. U. of O. Libr. School)

2:608 **Chandonnet, Gemma**
Bio-bibliographie de Ls-Ph. Audet. Québec, 1954. 100 p. (Ms. Ecole
de Bibl., U.L.)

2:609 **Chang, Liliane**
A Canadian bibliography of Canadian university library services. 1966.
ii, 7 1. (Ms. U. of O. Libr. School)

2:610 **Chapdelaine, Cécile**
Bibliographie sur la délinquance juvénile. Québec, 1966. 110 p.
(Ms. Ecole de Bibl., U.L.)

2:611 **Chaput, Gilles**
Yves Thériault dans la critique canadienne-française, 1948-1963. 1964.
[5] ii, 4 1. (Ms. U. of O. Libr. School)

2:612 **Charbonneau, Hélène**
Notes bio-bibliographiques sur Robert Prévost. 1952. vii, 39 p. (Ms.
Ecole de Bibl., U. de M.)

2:613 **Charbonneau, Jean-Maurice**
Bio-bibliographie du R.P. Emile Legault, c.s.c. 1945. 47 p. (Mf.
Ecole de Bibl., U. de M.)

2:614 **Charbonneau, Jeannine**
Bibliographie de la peinture au Canada. Québec, 1952. 37 p. (Ms.
Ecole de Bibl., U.L.)

2:615 **Charbonneau, Madeleine**
Notes bio-bibliographiques sur Ernest Pallascio-Morin. 1947. [6] p.
(Ms. Ecole de Bibl., U. de M.)

2:616 **Charbonneau, Pierrette**
Bio-bibliographie de Mme Allex Leduc Pelletier. 1947. 69 p. (Ms.
Ecole de Bibl., U. de M.)

2:617 **Charest, Pauline**
Bio-bibliographie analytique de M. Gérard Godin, journaliste. Préface
de M. Hervé Biron. Trois-Rivières, 1964. 72 p. (Ms. Ecole de Bibl.,
U.L.)

2:618 **Charland, Thomas**
Un gaumiste canadien: l'abbé Alexis Pelletier. Extrait de la *Revue
d'histoire de l'Amérique française,* septembre et décembre 1947.
Montréal, 1947. 48 p.
'Bibliographie de l'abbé Alexis Pelletier': p. 43-48.

2:619 **Charlotin, Marie-Joseph**
Bibliographie analytique du Rév. Père Philippe Deschamps. Québec,
1950. 22 p. (Ms. Ecole de Bibl., U.L.)

2:620 **Charron, Marguerite**
Bio-bibliographie de M. René Guénette. Préface de M. Rex Desmarchais. 1942. xv, 56 p. (Mf. Ecole de Bibl., U. de M.)

2:621 **Chartier, Yolande**
Essai de bio-bibliographie: M. l'abbé Jean-Baptiste Proulx. Préf. de
Sœur Marie Ernestine, f.c.s.c.j. Sherbrooke, 1952. xvii, 57 p. (Mf.
Ecole de Bibl., U. de M.)

2:622 **Chartrand, Georges-Aimé**
Notes bio-bibliographiques sur le R.P. Léon Pouliot, s.j. 1948. xii, 9 p.
(Ms. Ecole de Bibl., U. de M.)

2:623 **Chartrand, Marguerite**
Bio-bibliographie de Madame Ruth Lafleur-Hétu. 1949. v, 17 p.
(Mf. Ecole de Bibl., U. de M.)

2:624 **Chassé, Gertrude**
Bio-bibliographie de Françoise (Mlle Robertine Barry). Préface de Mlle Colette Lesage. 1945. x, 67 p. (Mf. Ecole de Bibl., U. de M.)

2:625 **Chaurette, Andrée**
Bio-bibliographie de Philippe La Ferrière. Préface de Me Jean-Marie Nadeau. 1944. 52 p. (Ms. Ecole de Bibl., U. de M.)

2:626 **[Checklist of Canadian newspapers]** (In American newspapers, 1821-1936, a union list of files available in the United States and Canada. Edited by Winifred Gregory under the auspices of the Bibliographical Society of America. New York, Wilson, 1937, p. 758-786)
Reprint: N.Y., Kraus Reprint Corp., 1967.

2:627 **A checklist of serial publications in the Law Library, University of Manitoba,** including those of the Law Society library. [n.p.] 1968.
14 *l.*

2:628 **A checklist of the law reports in the Law Library, University of Manitoba,** including those of the Law Society of Manitoba library. [n.p.] 1968.
22 *l.*

2:629 **Chéné, Jeanne**
Bibliographie d'écrivains canadiens-français. Une liste des bio-bibliographies présentées par les élèves de l'Ecole de Bibliothécaires de l'Université de Montréal, 1947-1960. Par Jeanne Chéné et Denise Martin. Préf. par Mlle Juliette Chabot. Montréal, 1961. xv, 65 p. (Ms. Ecole de Bibl., U. de M.)

2:630 **Cheng, Sin Kim Kee**
Higher education in Canada since 1961. 1966. v, 13 1. (Ms. U. of O. Libr. School)

2:631 **Chénier, André**
Canadian publishers and librarians; an annotated bibliography. Ottawa, University of Ottawa, Library School, 1955. 11, 9 p. (Ms. U. of O. Libr. School)

2:632 **Chew, Anne Rose** (Cushman)
References on the Great Lakes-Saint Lawrence waterway project, by Anne C. Chew and Arthur C. Churchill. Washington, 1940. 189 p. (U.S. Dept. of Agriculture, Library, Bibliographical contributions, no. 30, Ed. 2)

2:633 **Chiasson, Gilles**
La Gaspésie: histoire et tourisme. 1966. [6] 8 1. (Ms. U. of O. Libr. School)

2:634 **Chien, Ming-Yuan**
Reading interest in Canadian children's libraries. 1966. [3] i, 9 1. (Ms. U. of O. Libr. School)

2:635 **Chittick, Victor Levitt Oakes**
Thomas Chandler Haliburton ('Sam Slick') a study in provincial Toryism. New York, Columbia University Press, 1924. xi, 695 p., 1 *l.* (Columbia University studies in English and comparative literature.)
Thesis (Ph.D.), Columbia University, 1924.
Bibliography: p. 655-686.

2:636 **Chopin, Lucile**
Bio-bibliographie de René Chopin. 1944. 54 p. (Mf. Ecole de Bibl., U. de M.)

2:637 **Christensen, Ernest Martin**
Annotated bibliography of the college union. Edited by Porter Butts. Ithaca, N.Y., Association of College Unions-International, 1967.
iv [i.e. vi], 268 p. (College unions at work, 7)

2:638 **Christensen, Joanna**
Canadian economic thought since the Gordon report. 1967. xi, 10 1. (Ms. U. of O. Libr. School)

2:639 **Christin, Lise**
Essai de bio-bibliographie: R.P. Paul-Henri Barabé, o.m.i. Préf. du R.P. Sylvio Ducharme, o.m.i. 1953. 32 p. (Ms. Ecole de Bibl., U. de M.)

2:640 **Christine-Marie, soeur**
Bibliographie analytique de l'oeuvre du docteur Pierre Jobin, précédée d'une biographie. Préface de l'abbé André Jobin. Ancienne-Lorette, 1964. 146 p. (Ms. Ecole de Bibl., U.L.)

2:641 **Chumak, Oleh**
Toronto Public Library; new developments and techniques. 1964. vii, 5 1. (Ms. U. of O. Libr. School)

2:642 **Church, Elihu Dwight**
Catalogue of books relating to the discovery & early history of North & South America, forming a part of the library of E.D. Church, com-

piled and annotated by George Watson Cole. New York, Dodd, Mead; [Cambridge University Press] , 1907. 5 v. facsims.
Reprint: New York, Smith, 1951.

2:643  **Cimon, Constance**
Bibliographie analytique des écrits canadiens sur Cornélius Krieghoff, précédée d'une biographie. Lettre-préface de Marius Barbeau. Québec, 1964. 45 p. (Ms. Ecole de Bibl., U.L.)

2:644  **Clare, Ida M.**
[A bibliography of printed and manuscript material, in Toronto, concerning the settlement of Upper Canada by the United Empire Loyalists.] [Toronto] 1934. [1] , 29 *l.* (Ms. Toronto Univ. Libr. School)

2:645  **Clarence, frère**
Bibliographie analytique des œuvres de Jean-Marie Laurence. Montréal, 1964. 140 p. (Ms. Ecole de Bibl., U.L.)

2:646  **Clark, A.H.**
Contributions to geographical knowledge of Canada since 1945. (In *Geographical review*, v. XL, no. 2, p. 285-308, April 1950)

2:647  **Clark, Edith**
Niagara Falls. A partial bibliography ... (In *Bulletin of bibliography*. Boston, 1903. v. 3, p. [85]-91)

2:648  **Clarke, Irwin & Company Limited, Toronto**
Twenty-five years of Canadian publishing: W.H. Clarke; a memorial exhibition, 1930-1955. Toronto [1955] . 28 p.
A brief biographical sketch of W.H. Clarke, together with lists of the publications of Clarke, Irwin, 1931-1955, and of Oxford University Press (Canadian Branch), 1937-1949.

2:649  **Cleary, Marguerite**
A list of some general biographies of Canadians. 1941. 10 p. (Ms. Ecole de Bibl., U. de M.)

2:650  **Clemens, W.A.**
Canadian Pacific biological publications, 1922-1929 (incl.) [N.p.n.d.] 1 p. *l.,* 13 p.

2:651  **Clint, Harold C.**
Bibliographie du Colonel Wood. Préf. par George Cartwright. Québec, 1951. 40 p. (Ms. Ecole de Bibl., U.L.)

2:652  **Cloutier, Jeanne-Marce**
Notes bio-bibliographiques de M. Yvon Charron, p.s.s. 1952. vi, 7 p. (Ms. Ecole de Bibl., U. de M.)

2:653 **Cloutier, Laurette**
Bio-bibliographie de Mme Raoul Dandurand. Préface de Monsieur
Casimir Hébert. 1942. 54 p. (Mf. Ecole de Bibl., U. de M.)

2:654 **Cloutier, Thérèse**
Bibliographie du R.P. Léandre Poirier, o.f.m. 1947. 19 p. (Ms. Ecole
de Bibl., U. de M.)

2:655 **Coan, Otis W.**
America in fiction; an annotated list of novels that interpret aspects
of life in the United States, Canada, and Mexico [by] Otis W. Coan
[and] Richard G. Lillard. 5th ed. Palo Alto, Calif., Pacific Books,
1967.
viii, 232 p.
First ed. 1941.

2:656 **Cockburn, Gladys Edythe**
[Bibliography of the collections of the speeches of Canadian public
men. By Gladys Edythe Cockburn and Elsie G. Sumner. Toronto,
1932]. 2 pts. ([1], 10; 11 *l.*) (Ms. Toronto Univ. Libr. School)

2:657 **Coffey, Agnes**
A bibliography of the Honorable Thomas D'Arcy McGee, LL.D.
(1825-1868), orator, poet, patriot, statesman: the prophet of
Canadian nationality. Montreal, 1933. 15 *l.* (Ms. McGill Univ. Libr.
School)

2:658 **Collette, Lucille**
Petit essai de bio-bibliographie sur la personne et l'œuvre littéraire,
historique et bibliographique de Mlle Marie-Claire Daveluy. 1938-39.
35 p. (Mf. Ecole de Bibl., U. de M.)

2:659 **Collins, Carol**
Dr Wilder Graves Penfield. 1967. vi, 11 1. (Ms. U. of O. Libr. School)

2:660 **Comeau, Mildred**
Bibliography of bibliographies of the Maritime provinces. 1966.
iv, 4 1. (Ms. U. of O. Libr. School)

2:661 **Complete catalogue of blue books relating to Canada and the Arctic
Regions** from the earliest times to 1892. [N.p., 18–?] [2], 58 *l.*
Includes list of laws and command papers relating to Newfoundland.

2:662 **Complete list of Canadian copyright musical compositions** (entered
from 1868 to January 19th, 1889). Compiled from the official
register at Ottawa. [Toronto? 1889?] [32] p.
About 1400 items with date and number of entry.

2:663   **Cone, Gertrude E.**
A selective bibliography of publications on the Champlain Valley.
[Plattsburgh, N.Y., 1959] viii, 144 p.

2:664   **Connaught Medical Research Laboratories**
Starch-gel electrophoresis; a bibliography of observations made using
the technique of starch-gel electrophoresis. 2d ed. Willowdale, Ont.,
1967.
58 p.
First ed. Toronto, 1964.

2:665   **Connolly, M.E.**
Nova Scotia: travel and description. A bibliography. Montreal, 1952.
ii, 5 *l.* (Ms. McGill Univ. Libr. School)

2:666   **Conseil canadien de recherches urbaines et régionales**
Références urbaines & régionales, 1945-1962. Ottawa [1964]
1 v. (feuilles détachées) form.
Supplément. 1967. Ottawa [1968] [11], [29], 145 p.

2:667   **Conseil canadien des ministres des ressources**
Références. v. 1-     déc. 1968-     Montréal.
v. mensuel.

2:668   **Conseil canadien du bien-être**
Catalogue of publications. Catalogue des éditions ... Ottawa, 1960—.
annuel.
Edition précédente 1957.

2:669   **Conseil canadien du bien-être**
Poverty/Pauvreté; supplément [par] Agnes Woodward. 1; mars 1967.
Ottawa [1967]
viii, 244 p.
Supplément [par] Agnes Woodward. 2; oct. 1967. Ottawa [1967]
viii, 123 p.
Supplément [par] Agnes Woodward. 3; avril 1968. Ottawa [1968]
viii, 123 p.

2:670   **Contant, André**
Guide méthodique et alphabétique des périodiques en cours reçus par
la bibliothèque en 1965-66. L'Assomption, 1966. 67 f. (Ms. Ecole de
Bibl., U. de M.)

2:671   **Cooke, Alan**
Bibliography of the Quebec-Labrador Peninsula, compiled by Alan
Cooke and Fabien Caron. Boston, G.K. Hall, 1968.
2 v. (viii, 430, 383 p.)

2:672 **Cormier, Omer**
Notes bibliographiques sur le R.P. Gérard Petit, c.s.c. 1947. 13 p.
(Ms. Ecole de Bibl., U. de M.)

2:673 **Corrivault, Blaise**
Bibliographie analytique de l'histoire de l'Acadie. Church Point, N.E.,
1950. 60 p. (Ms. Ecole de Bibl., U.L.)

2:674 **Cossette, Angèle**
Bibliographie de l'œuvre de Louis-Philippe Audet. Québec, 1948.
60 p. (Ms. Ecole de Bibl., U.L.)

2:675 **Côté, Antonia**
Bio-bibliographie: Ginevra [Georgiana Lefebvre] et son œuvre.
Québec, 1948. 120 p. (Ms. Ecole de Bibl., U.L.)

2:676 **Côté, Athanase, frère**
Bibliographie analytique des ouvrages de langue française sur
l'histoire de la ville de Québec au XIXe siècle. Préface du frère
Robert Sylvain, é.c. Québec, 1964. 175 p. (Ms. Ecole de Bibl., U.L.)

2:677 **Côté, Augustin**
Catalogue de livres, brochures, journaux, etc., sortis de l'Imprimerie
générale, Québec ... depuis sa fondation, le 1er décembre, 1842.
[Québec] 1896. 1 f., 23 p.
Reproduced in facsimile in the *Papers of the bibliographical society of Canada*,
no. I, 1962.

2:678 **Côté, Berthe**
Bio-bibliographie du notaire Henri Turgeon, Laval. Québec,
1956. 63 p. (Ms. Ecole de Bibl., U.L.)

2:679 **Côté, Marielle**
Bio-bibliographie de Mme Jeanne L'Archevêque-Duguay. 1947. 25 p.
(Mf. Ecole de Bibl., U. de M.)

2:680 **Côté, Monique**
Essai de bio-bibliographie. Monsieur le docteur Jacques Olivier.
[Montréal] 1955. 34 p. (Ms. Ecole de Bibl., U. de M.)

2:681 **Côté, Paul**
Bibliographie des livres sur les beaux-arts publiés au Canada de 1750-
1899 et déposés à l'Université Laval. Préface de M. Marcel Hudon.
Québec, 1958. 48 p. (Ms. Ecole de Bibl., U.L.)

2:682 **Côté, Wilfrid**
Essai de bio-bibliographie: M. l'abbé Maurice O'Bready, 1952. 35 p.
(Ms. Ecole de Bibl., U. de M.)

2:683 **Côté, Paule**
Bio-bibliographie de Séraphin Marion. [s.d.] 14 p. (Mf. Ecole de Bibl., U. de M.)

2:684 **Coughlin, V.L.**
The St Lawrence river; a bibliography. Montreal, 1938. 13 *l.* (Ms. McGill Univ. Libr. School)

2:685 **Couillard, Anne**
Bio-bibliographie de Monsieur Albert Laberge. Préface de Paul-A. Martin, c.s.c. 1945. (Ms. Ecole de Bibl., U. de M.)

2:686 **Couillard, Claire**
Essai bio-bibliographique sur Louis Dupire. 1952. 43 p. (Mf. Ecole de Bibl., U. de M.)

2:687 **Coulombe, Marguerite**
Bio-bibliographie du R.P. Francis Goyer, s.s.s. 1948. vi, 46 p. (Ms. Ecole de Bibl., U. de M.)

2:688 **Coulombe, Marie-Anne**
Bibliographie analytique de la Côte Nord. Préf. de Damase Potvin. Québec, 1950. 110 p. (Ms. Ecole de Bibl., U.L.)

2:689 **Courrier du livre** Canadiana. Canadian history, archaeology, bibliography, numismatics, philately and genealogy ... Pub. mensuellement en anglais et en français ... Histoire, archéologie, bibliographie, numismatique, philatélie et généalogie canadiennes. V. 1-5, mai 1896-juin 1900. Québec, Brousseau [etc.] 1897-1901. 5 v.

2:690 **Cousineau, Léo**
Bio-bibliographie de Monsieur l'abbé Henri Gauthier, p.s.s. 1950. 91 p. (Mf. Ecole de Bibl., U. de M.)

2:691 **Cousineau, Léo**
Bio-bibliographie du R.P. Marie-Eugène Prévost. 1940. 34 p. (Ms. Ecole de Bibl., U. de M.)

2:692 **Couture, Marguerite**
Bibliographie analytique de Luc Lacourcière. Québec, 1950. 68 p. (Ms. Ecole de Bibl., U.L.)

2:693 **Couture, Raymonde**
Notes bio-bibliographiques de Mme Morin-Labrecque. 1951. vi, 23 p. (Ms. Ecole de Bibl., U. de M.)

2:694 **Couture, Raymonde**
Notes bio-bibliographiques de Mme Albertine Morin-Labrecque.
Préf. de Mme Françoise Desgranges. Montréal, 1961. xv, 38 p. (Ms.
Ecole de Bibl., U. de M.)

2:695 **Craig, Sheila Elizabeth Douglas**
Mackenzie King as a War Minister; a bibliography of monographs and
periodical articles, dealing with the activities of William Lyon
Mackenzie King during World War II. [Toronto] 1965. iv, 16 *l*. (Ms.
Toronto Univ. Libr. School)

2:696 **Creighton, M. Jean**
Reindeer in Alaska and Northern Canada: a bibliography. Ottawa,
University of Ottawa, Library School, 1949. 13 p. (Ms. U. of O.
Libr. School)

2:697 **Crépeau, Eliane**
Eloi de Grandmont; essai de bio-bibliographie. 1949. iv, 10 p. (Mf.
Ecole de Bibl., U. de M.)

2:698 **Crête, Raymond, frère**
Bio-bibliographie de Mlle Adrienne Maillet. 1947. 94 p. (Mf. Ecole
de Bibl., U. de M.)

2:699 **Crevier, Adrienne**
Bio-bibliographie du major Pierre Daviault. Préface de Monsieur
Victor Barbeau. 1952. 59 p. (Mf. Ecole de Bibl., U. de M.)

2:700 **Crombie, Jean Breakell**
A list of Canadian historical novels. Montreal, McGill University
Library School, 1930. 10 p. (On cover: McGill University publications,
Series VII (Library) no. 21.)

2:701 **Cross, Lowell Merlin**
A bibliography of electronic music. [Toronto] University of
Toronto Press [c1967]
ix, 126 p.

2:702 **Croteau, Daniel**
Notes bio-bibliographiques sur M. l'abbé Maurice O'Bready. 1953.
58 p. (Ms. Ecole de Bibl., U. de M.)

2:703 **Cruger, Doris M.**
A list of doctoral dissertations on Australia, covering 1933/34
through 1964/65; Canada, covering 1933/34 through 1964/65; New

Zealand, covering 1933/34 through 1964/65, compiled by Doris M.
Cruger. Ann Arbor, Mich., Xerox, 1967.
20 p.

2:704  **Cuffling, Jean**
The North-West rebellion. Montreal, 1957. 9 *l.* (Ms. McGill Univ.
Libr. School)

2:705  **Culture;** revue trimestrielle, sciences religieuses et sciences profanes
au Canada. Québec, 1940.
Publié par l'Association de recherches sur les sciences religieuses et profanes
au Canada.
V. 1 aussi numéroté v. 5, étant la continuation de 'Nos cahiers.'

2:706  **Cyrille, frère**
Bio-bibliographie de S.L. Irving. Les Trois-Rivières, 1956 [i.e., 1946]
28 p. (Ms. Ecole de Bibl., U. de M.)

2:707  **Dagenais, Gabrielle**
Essai bio-bibliographique sur Mlle Marguerite-Marie Léveillé. Préf.
par Juliette Chabot. 1955. 75 p. (Ms. Ecole de Bibl., U. de M.)

2:708  **Daigle, Corinthe**
Notes bio-bibliographiques sur S.E. Mgr Marie-Antoine Roy, o.f.m.
1947. 9 p. (Ms. Ecole de Bibl., U. de M.)

2:709  **Daigle, Irenée**
Essai de bibliographie sur M. l'abbé Jean-Baptiste-Antoine Ferland.
Préface de Mgr Paul Bernier. 1943. 84 p. (Ms. Ecole Bibl., U. de M.)

2:710  **Daigle, Louise**
Bibliographie analytique de M. Emile Castonguay, précédée d'une
biographie. Préf. de Ch.-M. Boissonnault, 1964. xi, 167 p. (Ms. Ecole
de Bibl., U.L.)

2:711  **Daigneault, Claire**
Bio-bibliographie de Sir Adolphe-Basile Routhier. Préface de M.
Jacques Rousseau. 1951. 43 p. (Mf. Ecole de Bibl., U. de M.)

2:712  **Dalhousie University, Halifax.** Institute of Public Affairs
Industrial Relations Reference Library [catalogues] Halifax, 1958–
no.

2:713  **Dalhousie University, Halifax.** Library
Catalogue of the William Inglis Morse collection of books, pictures,
maps, manuscripts, etc. at Dalhousie University Library, Halifax, Nova
Scotia, comp. by Eugenie Archibald, with a foreword by Carleton

Stanley and a pref. by William Inglis Morse. London, Curwen, 1938. 119 p.

2:714  **Dalhousie University, Halifax.** Library
Rudyard Kipling: a bibliographical catalogue. Compiled by James McG. Stewart, edited by A.W. Yeats. [Toronto] Dalhousie University Press and University of Toronto Press, 1959. xviii, 673 p. facsims.

2:715  **Dallaire, Françoise**
Notes bio-bibliographiques sur Adjutor Rivard. 1948. 12 p. (Ms. Ecole de Bibl., U. de M.)

2:716  **Dandurand, Thérèse**
Bio-bibliographie du chanoine Victor Tremblay. Québec, 1956. 110 p. (Ms. Ecole de Bibl., U.L.)

2:717  **Daoust, Lucille**
Notes bio-bibliographiques sur le Dr Edmond Grignon. 1948. iv, 6 p. (Ms. Ecole de Bibl., U. de M.)

2:718  **Dartmouth College,** Hanover, N.H. Library. Stefansson Collection. Selected bibliography on Eskimo ethnology with special emphasis on acculturation, compiled [by J.J. Bond] at the Stefansson Collection, Baker Library, Dartmouth College, Hanover, N.H., June, 1956. [N.p., 1956?] 11 *l.*

2:719  **Daudelin, Denise**
Essai de bio-bibliographie du R.P. Benoît Lacroix, o.p. Préf. par Jean Ménard. Montréal, 1961. xxxvii, 122 p. (Ms. Ecole de Bibl., U. de M.)

2:720  **Daveluy, Marie-Claire**
La Société de Notre-Dame de Montréal, 1639-1663: son histoire— ses membres—son manifeste. Préf. du chanoine Lionel Groulx. Montréal, Fides [c1965] 326, 127 p. (Collection Fleur de lys)
Bio-bibliographies publiées antérieurement par tranches, dans la *Revue d'histoire de l'Amérique française.*

2:721  **David, Ruth**
A select bibliography of Canadian history reference sources for a junior college library. Montreal, 1947. v, 9 *l.* (Ms. McGill Univ. Libr. School)

2:722  **Davidson, John**
A Scottish emigrant's contribution to Canada; record of publications and public lectures, 1911-1961. [Vancouver, 1961] 1 v. (various pagings) tables.
Bibliography of the author's works, chiefly in botany and related fields.

2:723 **Davidson, Margaret M.B.**
[A bibliography of the history of the city of Galt]. [Toronto, 1933]
[2], 4 *l.* (Ms. Toronto Univ. Libr. School)

2:724 **Davidson, Wendy Georgina**
A selected bibliography of the Canadian Parliament Buildings.
[Toronto] 1961. 18 *l.* (Ms. Toronto Univ. Libr. School)

2:725 **Davies, Raymond Arthur**
Printed Jewish Canadiana, 1685-1900; tentative checklist of books,
pamphlets, pictures, magazine and newspaper articles and currency,
written by or relating to the Jews of Canada. [Montreal, Davies,
1955] 56 p. facsims.

2:726 **Dawson, Barbara**
History of Canadian place-names; bibliography, books, pamphlets
and articles. [Toronto, 1933] [2], ix *l.* (Ms. Toronto Univ. Libr.
School)

2:727 **Dawson, Irene Joan**
The Dawson route, 1857-1883; a selected bibliography with annota-
tions. Toronto, 1966. 17 *l.* (Ms. Toronto Univ. Libr. School)
Published in *Ontario history*, v. 59, March 1967, p. 47-55.

2:728 **Deacon, William Arthur**
Peter McArthur. Toronto, Ryerson [1924]. 180 p. (Makers of
Canadian literature ...)
Bibliography: p. 167-174.

2:729 **De Bellefeuille, Madeleine**
Marie-Claire Blais. 1966. ix, 9 1. (Ms. U. of O. Libr. School)

2:730 **Décarie, Jean-J.**
Notes de bio-bibliographie sur Henri Bourassa, écrivain, orateur et
journaliste. 1941. [7] p. (Ms. Ecole de Bibl., U. de M.)

2:731 **Décary, Suzanne**
Bibliographie du R.P. [Richard] Arès, s.j. 1948. 48 p. (Ms. Ecole de
Bibl., U. de M.)

2:732 **Dechief, Hélène A.**
Trial bibliography: books and pamphlets relating to Canadian railways
in libraries of Montreal. 1953. vii, 118 p. (Ms. Ecole de Bibl., U. de M.)

2:733 **Deciry, Françoise**
Essai de bio-bibliographie du Dr Gustave Prévost. 1957. vii, 43 p.
(Ms. Ecole de Bibl., U. de M.)

2:734  **Defoy, Louisette**
Bibliographie analytique de monsieur Yvon Thériault. Québec, 1960.
22 p. (Ms. Ecole de Bibl., U.L.)

2:735  **De Guire, Juliette**
Bibliographie analytique de l'œuvre de monsieur Charles-Marie
Boissonnault, précédée d'une biographie. Québec, 1950. 75 p. (Ms.
Ecole de Bibl., U.L.)

2:736  **Deland, Berthe**
Bio-bibliographie de M. Félix-Gabriel Marchand. Préface de Mlle
Hélène Grenier. 1946. ix, 43 p. (Mf. Ecole de Bibl., U. de M.)

2:737  **Deland, Louis-Georges**
Bio-bibliographie de M. Etienne-Michel Faillon, p.s.s. Préface de Mgr
Olivier Maurault. Les Trois-Rivières, 1946. xiii, 68 p. (Mf. Ecole de
Bibl., U. de M.)

2:738  **Demers, Alphonse**
Essai de bibliographie sur l'œuvre du R.P. Paul-Victor Charland, o.p.
1938. 6 p. (Ms. Ecole de Bibl., U. de M.)

2:739  **Demers, Béatrice, sœur**
Essai de bio-bibliographie de M. le curé Joseph Urgel Demers. 1953.
36 p. (Ms. Ecole de Bibl., U. de M.)

2:740  **Demers, Françoise**
Essai bio-bibliographique de l'œuvre de Jean Pellerin. Trois Rivières,
1951. v, 61 p. (Mf. Ecole de Bibl., U. de M.)

2:741  **Demers, Henri**
Bio-bibliographie de l'hon. Edouard-Fabre Surveyer. Préf. de M$^e$
Pierre Beullac. 1957. vii, 81 p. (Ms. Ecole de Bibl., U. de M.)

2:742  **Demeter, Rosalie**
Bio-bibliographie de Mlle Germaine Bernier. Préface de Roger Duhamel.
Montréal, Ecole de Bibliothécaires, 1955. 508 p. (Ms. Ecole de Bibl.,
U. de M.)

2:743  **Denis, Roland**
Bio-bibliographie de Jean-Marie Nadeau. Préface de M. Jean-Jacques
Lefebvre. 1943. 86 p. (Ms. Ecole de Bibl., U. de M.)

2:744  **Denoncourt, Louise**
Bibliographie de Yves Leclerc, 1953-1961. Québec, 1964. 36 p. (Ms.
Ecole de Bibl., U.L.)

2:745 **Depatie, Lise**
Essai de bio-bibliographie du R.P. Gaston Carrière, o.m.i. 1953. 47 p.
(Ms. Ecole de Bibl., U. de M.)

2:746 **Déry, Claire**
Bibliographie de l'oeuvre de Mme Marthe Lemaire-Duguay. Préface
de Mgr Alphonse Roux. Victoriaville, 1963. 110 p. (Ms. Ecole de
Bibl., U.L.)

2:747 **Desaulniers, Hélène-L.**
Notes bio-bibliographiques sur François Lesieur-Desaulniers. 1947.
(Ms. Ecole de Bibl., U. de M.)

2:748 **Desautels, Adrien**
Bibliographie de Robert Rumilly. Québec, 1947. 21 p. (Ms. Ecole
de Bibl., U.L.)

2:749 **Desbarats Advertising Agency**
The Desbarats 'all Canada' newspaper directory ... Montreal,
Desbarats Advertising Agency, 1904-1932? Biennial.
Title varies: Desbarats newspaper directory; Canadian newspaper directory.

2:750 **Descarries, Andrée**
Bio-bibliographie de Sir Adolphe-Basile Routhier. Préface du Major
Gustave Lanctot. 1943. 116 p. (Mf. Ecole de Bibl., U. de M.)

2:751 **Deschene, Jean-Claude**
Bibliographie de l'oeuvre du Rév. Père Hector L. Bertrand. Montréal,
1963. 96 p. (Ms. Ecole de Bibl., U.L.)

2:752 **De Serres, Clorinde**
Bio-bibliographie de Errol Bouchette. 1944. 39 p. (Mf. Ecole de Bibl.,
U. de M.)

2:753 **Desjardins, soeur**
Bibliographie analytique de l'oeuvre du notaire Léonidas Bachand,
précédée d'une biographie. Préface de Mgr O'Bready. Sherbrooke,
1962. 45 p. (Ms. Ecole de Bibl., U.L.)

2:754 **Desjardins, Claire**
Bio-bibliographie de M. Narcisse-Henri-Edouard Faucher de Saint-
Maurice. 1940. 29 p. (Mf. Ecole de Bibl., U. de M.)

2:755 **Desjardins, Jeannette**
Bibliographie analytique de l'oeuvre du docteur Jean-Baptiste Jobin,
président du Collège des Médecins; précédée d'une biographie. Préface
de M. Charles-Marie Boissonnault. Québec, 1963. 97 p. (Ms. Ecole de
Bibl., U.L.)

2:756 **Desjardins, Lucienne**
Notes bio-bibliographiques: M. Henri Gauthier, p.s.s. 1952. xi, 13 p.
(Ms. Ecole de Bibl., U. de M.)

2:757 **Desjardins, Simone**
Bio-bibliographie de William Chapman. Préface de Marguerite Brunet.
1946. xii, 186 p. (Ms. Ecole de Bibl., U. de M.)

2:758 **Desjardins, Suzanne**
Notes bio-bibliographiques sur Marcel Dugas. 1948. 11 p. (Mf. Ecole
de Bibl., U. de M.)

2:759 **Deslandes, Germain**
Climatologie, pédologie et écologie forestières au Canada (1937-
1956); bibliographie. Préface du doyen L.-Z. Rousseau. Québec,
1958. 96 p. (Ms. Ecole de Bibl., U.L.)

2:760 **DesLauriers, Françoise**
Bio-bibliographie analytique de M. Aimé Plamondon. Québec, 1948.
111 p. (Ms. Ecole de Bibl., U.L.)

2:761 **Desnoyers, Paul-Henri**
Le Patronage, œuvre de formation pour la jeunesse. Québec, 1964.
105 p. (Ms. Ecole de Bibl., U.L.)

2:762 **Desrochers, Edmond**
Référence et bibliographie en sciences sociales. [Montréal] Ecole de
bibliothéconomie, Université de Montréal, 1967.
4 v.

2:763 **Desrochers, Guy**
Bio-bibliographie analytique de Marcel Trudel. Québec, 1948. 39 p.
(Ms. Ecole de Bibl., U.L.)

2:764 **Desrochers, Marthe**
Bio-bibliographie de l'abbé Azaile-Etienne Couillard-Després. [s.d.]
34 p. (Mf. Ecole de Bibl., U. de M.)

2:765 **Desroches, Denyse**
Notes bio-bibliographiques sur Francis Des Roches. 1949. 9 p. (Mf.
Ecole de Bibl., U. de M.)

2:766 **Desrosiers, Elphège, père**
Bibliographie franciscaine. Nos périodiques, nos auteurs, 1931-1941.
1941. 21 p. (Ms. Ecole de Bibl., U. de M.)

2:767 **DesRosiers, Emile**
Ontario Department of Education. 1964. iii, 5 l. (Ms. U. of O. Libr.
School)

2:768  **Dessureau, Laure**
Essai de bio-bibliographie: Marjorie MacCubbin. 1953. 26 p. (Mf. Ecole de Bibl., U. de M.)

2:769  **Destroismaisons, Simone**
Notes bio-bibliographiques sur le R.P. Jacques Tremblay, s.j. Préf. de Mgr Albert Tessier. 1956. xxi, 59 p. (Ms. Ecole de Bibl., U. de M.)

2:770  **De Varennes, Kathleen (Mennie)**
Sources généalogiques tirées de *Canadiana* 1951-1960. Genealogical materials compiled from *Canadiana* 1951-1960. Eastview, Ont., 1961. [2] , 26 f.

2:771  **De Varennes, Rosario**
National Library of Canada; an annotated bibliography. Term paper, bibliographical and research methods, Library School, University of Ottawa. Ottawa, 1954. [4] , ii-iv, [1] , 41 *l*.

2:772  **Deverell, Alfred Frederick**
Canadian bibliography of reading and literature instruction (English) 1760 to 1959. Toronto, Copp Clark [c1963] viii, 241 p.

2:773  **Devine, Gloria**
Ice hockey in the United States and Canada. 1967. [5] 5 1. (Ms. U. of O. Libr. School)

2:774  **Devoe, D.**
Labor mobility in Canada. 1967. xi, 12 1. (Ms. U. of O. Libr. School)

2:775  **De-Vreeze, Béatrice-A.**
Bio-bibliographie de Francis Reginald Scott. 1958. [x] , 96 p. (Ms. Ecole de Bibl., U. de M.)

2:776  **Dickinson, Judith E.**
Bibliography; Canadian paper. [Toronto] 1933. [7] *l.* (Ms. Toronto Univ. Libr. School)

2:777  **Dill, Charlotte E.**
A bibliography on soil conservation in Canada. Toronto, 1945. [1] , 22 *l.* (Ms. Toronto Univ. Libr. School)

2:778  **Dionne, Narcisse Eutrope**
Hennepin; ses voyages et ses œuvres ... Québec, Renault, 1897. 40 p.

2:779  **Dionne, Narcisse Eutrope**
Inventaire chronologique ... Québec, 1905-9. 4 v.
Le titre varie.
Publié par la Société royale du Canada. Parut aussi dans les *Mémoires et comptes rendus* de la société, 2e série, v. 10-12, 14; 1904-6, 1908.

Sommaire. [t. 1] Inventaire chronologique des livres, brochures, journaux et revues publiés en langue française dans la province de Québec, depuis l'établissement de l'imprimerie au Canada jusqu'à nos jours, 1764-1905. t. 2. Québec et Nouvelle France, bibliographie: inventaire chronologique des ouvrages publiés à l'étranger en diverses langues ... 1534-1906. t. 3. Inventaire chronologique des livres, brochures, journaux et revues publiés en langue anglaise dans la province de Québec ... 1764-1906. t. 4. Inventaire chronologique des cartes, plans, atlas relatifs à la Nouvelle-France et à la province de Québec, 1508-1908.

Inventaire chronologique des livres, brochures, journaux et revues publiés en diverses langues dans et hors la province de Québec. Premier supplément ... 1904-1912. Québec, 1912. 76 p.
Tiré à part des *Mémoires et comptes rendus de la Société royale du Canada*, 3e série, v. 5, 1911.

2:780 **Dionne, Narcisse Eutrope**
La Nouvelle-France de Cartier à Champlain, 1540-1603. Québec, Darveau, 1891. 395 p. fac-sim.
'Cartographie de la Nouvelle-France au XVIe siècle': p. [213]-255.

2:781 **Dionne, Narcisse Eutrope**
Samuel Champlain, fondateur de Québec et père de la Nouvelle-France; histoire de sa vie et de ses voyages. Québec, Côté, 1891-1906. 2 v.
'Bibliographie': v. 2, p. 485-495.

2:782 **Dionne, Narcisse Eutrope**
Travaux historiques publiés depuis trente ans, 1879-1909. Québec, Laflamme, 1909. 27 p.

2:783 **Dolbec, Aurée**
Essai de bio-bibliographie: le R.P. Laurent Tremblay, o.m.i. 1952. viii, 18 p. (Ms. Ecole de Bibl., U. de M.)

2:784 **Dominion annual register and review,** 1878-1886, imprint varies, 1879-1887. 8 v. edited by Henry James Morgan.
Publications of the year are given in each volume under the heading: Literature.

2:785 **Donald, William John Alexander**
The Canadian iron and steel industry; a study in the economic history of a protected industry. Boston, Houghton, Mifflin, 1915. xv, 376 p., 1 *l.* (Hart, Schaffner and Marx prize essay, no. 19)
Bibliography: p. 359-366.

2:786 **Donalda-Marie, soeur**
Essai de bio-bibliographie de M. l'abbé Edouard Gilbert, p.m.é. Préf. de M. l'abbé Léon Verschelden. 1957. xxiii, 68 p. (Ms. Ecole de Bibl., U. de M.)

2:787   **Donatien, frère**
Bibliographie de M. l'abbé Victorin Germain. Préface de M. Alphonse
Désilets. 1945. 71 p. (Ms. Ecole de Bibl., U. de M.)

2:788   **Donnelly, Joseph P.**
Thwaites' Jesuit relations; errata and addenda. Chicago, Loyola
University Press, 1967.
v. 269 p.
'Bibliography, 1906-66': p. [211]-266.

2:789   **Dorais, Rollande**
Bio-bibliographie de Monsieur Pierre-Georges Roy. Préface de M.
Victor Morin. 1943. x, 43 p. (Mf. Ecole de Bibl., U. de M.)

2:790   **Doray, Claire**
Bibliographie de M. l'abbé Etienne Blanchard. [s.d.] 23 p. (Mf. Ecole
de Bibl., U. de M.)

2:791   **Dorion, Anne-Marie**
Bio-bibliographie de Alfred-Duclos DeCelles. 1942. 60 p. (Mf.
Ecole de Bibl., U. de M.)

2:792   **Dornbusch, C.E.**
The Canadian army, 1855-1958; regimental histories and a guide to
the regiments. Cornwallville, N.Y., Hope Farm Press, 1959. 216 p.
facsims.

2:793   **Dosmond, Jean**
Revue de l'Université Laval. Table générale des années 1946-63.
(Titres des articles sujets, noms d'auteurs, comptes rendus bibliogra-
phiques.) Québec, 1965. 264 p. (Ms. Ecole de Bibl., U.L.)

2:794   **Doucet, Yolande**
Bibliographie de l'œuvre de Pascal Poirier, précédée d'une étude
biographique. 1941. 39 p. (Ms. Ecole de Bibl., U. de M.)

2:795   **Doughty, Arthur George**
Bibliography of the siege of Quebec, by A. Doughty and J.E. Middle-
ton, with a list of plans of Quebec by R. [*sic*] Lee-Phillips of the
Library of Congress, Washington.
(In *The siege of Quebec* ... by A.G. Doughty in collaboration with G.W.
Parmalee Fitzpatrick, ed. Quebec, 1901. V. VI, p. [149]-313)

2:796   **Dourte, Michelle (Bachand)**
Bio-bibliographie de M. Rodolphe de Repentigny, critique d'art.
Montréal, 1961. xi, 53 p. (Ms. Ecole de Bibl., U. de M.)

2:797 **Dow, Charles Mason**
Anthology and bibliography of Niagara Falls. Albany, New York State Library, 1921. 2 v.

2:798 **Dow, Robena M.**
Bibliography of the County of Wellington. Toronto, 1933. [10] *l.* (Ms. Toronto Univ. Libr. School)

2:799 **Drake, Everett N.**
Historical atlases of Ontario; a condensed checklist. Toronto, 1953. [2] p.

2:800 **Drapeau, Cécile**
Notes bio-bibliographiques sur Stanislas Drapeau. 1948. 10 p. (Ms. Ecole de Bibl., U. de M.)

2:801 **Drapeau, Jean**
Notice biographique et bibliographie de James Huston. 1947. 57 p. (Mf. Ecole de Bibl., U. de M.)

2:802 **Drapeau, Julien**
Essai de bibliographie sur le régime municipal dans la province de Québec. Préf. de Me Jean-Louis Doucet. Quebec, 1955. 98 p. (Ms. Ecole de Bibl., U.L.)

2:803 **Drolet, Antonio**
Bibliographie du roman canadien-français, 1900-1950. Québec, Presses universitaires de Laval, 1955. 125 p.

2:804 **Drolet, Antonio**
Répertoire de la bibliographie canadienne (ouvrages imprimés) [Québec] 1962.
36 f.

2:805 **Drolet, Bernadette**
Bibliographie analytique sur la Fédération des Guides catholiques de la province de Québec. Préface de Mlle Simone Paré. Québec, 1963. 56 p. (Ms. Ecole de Bibl., U.L.)

2:806 **Dubeau, Jean**
Bio-bibliographie analytique de Reine Malouin, de la Société des Ecrivains canadiens (1958-1963) Préface du R.P. Thomas-Marie Landry. Québec, 1963. 83 p. (Ms. Ecole de Bibl., U.L.)

2:807 **Dubois, Paul**
National Library of Canada. 1963. vii, 11 1. (Ms. U. of O. Libr. School)

2:808 **Dubuc, J.-H.**
Bibliographie des monographies paroissiales du diocèse de Sherbrooke.
1939. 11 p. (Ms. Ecole de Bibl., U. de M.)

2:809 **Dubuc, Richard**
Essai de bio-bibliographie sur Louis Francoeur, journaliste. 1950.
17 p. (Mf. Ecole de Bibl., U. de M.)

2:810 **Duchesne, Claude**
Bio-bibliographie de M. Philéas Gagnon. Préface de M. Casimir Hébert.
1947. 49 p. (Mf. Ecole de Bibl., U. de M.)

2:811 **Dufort, Gisèle**
Notes bibliographiques sur Joseph-Delvida Poirier. 1948. 50 p.
(Mf. Ecole de Bibl., U. de M.)

2:812 **Dufour, Hélène**
Bibliographie analytique de Marie-Claire Blais, précédée d'une
biographie. Préface de M. Gaston Dulong. Québec, 1964. 35 p.
(Ms. Ecole de Bibl., U.L.)

2:813 **Dufresne, Lise**
L'Institut des sourds-muets de Montréal (1848-1948) bibliographie.
Préface du frère Viateur Gervais, c.s.v. Charlesbourg, 1964. 165 p.
(Ms. Ecole de Bibl., U.L.)

2:814 **Dufresne, Thérèse**
Bibliographie de L.-O. David. 1944. [11], 44 p. (Mf. Ecole de Bibl.,
U. de M.)

2:815 **Duguay, Martine (Hébert)**
Liste des volumes sur les poissons du Canada. Montréal, 1961. 20 p.
(Ms. Ecole de Bibl., U. de M.)

2:816 **Duguay, Thérèse**
[Bio-bibliographie de Mme Jeanne L'Archevêque Duguay]. Préface
de Monseigneur Albert Tessier. 1951. 26 p. (Mf. Ecole de Bibl., U. de
M.)

2:817 **Duke, Dorothy Mary**
Agricultural periodicals published in Canada 1836-1960. M.L.S. thesis,
McGill University, 1961. 168 p. (Ms. McGill Univ. Libr. School)
[Ottawa] Canada Dept. of Agriculture, Information Division, 1962. iv, 101 p.

2:818 **Dulude, Paule-Andrée**
Essai de bio-bibliographie: R.P. Marcel-Marie Desmarais, o.p. 1950.
ix, 22 p. (Ms. Ecole de Bibl., U. de M.)

2:819   **Dumaine, Florence**
Notes bio-bibliographiques sur Monsieur Claude-Bernard Trudeau.
1953. 28 p. (Mf. Ecole de Bibl., U. de M.)

2:820   **Dumaresq, Frances M.**
Bibliography of folk tales and legends of French Canada. Montreal,
1932. [16] *l*. (Ms. McGill Univ. Libr. School)

2:821   **Dumas, Gabriel, père**
Bio-bibliographie du R.P. Alexis de Barbézieux. Québec, 1956. 94 p.
(Ms. Ecole de Bibl., U.L.)

2:822   **Dumoulin, Luce**
Bio-bibliographie de Révérende Sœur Saint-Ladislas, a.s.v. 1946.
x, 49 p. (Ms. Ecole de Bibl., U. de M.)

2:823   **Duncan, Marian Jane**
The rise of the United Farmers of Ontario, 1914-1920; a bibliography
of the materials available in Toronto libraries. [Toronto] 1964. v, 8 *l*.
(Ms. Toronto Univ. Libr. School)

2:824   **Duplessis, T., sœur**
Bibliographie nécrologique des religieuses hospitalières de Saint-
Joseph, province de Notre-Dame de l'Assomption. Préface du R.P.
Albert Guyot. Vallée-Lourdes, N.-B., 1962. xv, 111 p. (Ms. Ecole
de Bibl., U.L.)

2:825   **Dupré, Janine**
Reine Malouin. Bibliographie de Reine Malouin. Préface par l'abbé
Louis-Philippe Garon. Sainte-Anne-de-la-Pocatière, 1947. 78 p. (Mf.
Ecole de Bibl., U. de M.)

2:826   **Dupuis, Monique**
Bibliographie analytique de la chanson de folklore, ouvrages parus
au Canada de 1950 à 1962. 1964, xii, 41(1) p. (Ms. Ecole de Bibl.,
U.L.)

2:827   **Durand, Lucille**
Notes bio-bibliographiques sur l'abbé Pierre-E. Théoret. 1953. vi, 15 p.
(Ms. Ecole de Bibl., U. de M.)

2:828   **Durand, Marielle**
Essai de bio-bibliographie: M. Donat Durand. 1953. 29 p. (Mf.
Ecole de Bibl., U. de M.)

2:829   **Durnin, Thérèse**
Le chanoine Emile Chartier; biographie et bibliographie. 1938. 30 p.
(Mf. Ecole de Bibl., U. de M.)

2:830 **Durocher, Georges Etienne, père**
Bibliographie analytique du R.P. Paul-Emile Breton, o.m.i. Edmonton, 1961. 170 p. (Ms. Ecole de Bibl., U.L.)

2:831 **Durrell, Jean E.**
Folk culture in French Canada. Ottawa, University of Ottawa, Library School, 1961. vii, 6 p. (Ms. U. of O. Libr. School)

2:832 **Dutilly, Arthème A.**
Bibliography of bibliographies on the Arctic. Washington [1945]. 47 p. maps. (Catholic University of America, Publication no. 1 B)
Another edition: 1946. 50 p.

2:833 **Dutilly, Arthème A.**
A bibliography of reindeer, caribou and musk-ox. Contract W 44-109-qm-1297. Washington, 1949. x, 462 p. ([U.S.] Quartermaster Corps, Military Planning Division, Report no. 129)
'Will supplement the more general *Arctic bibliography* which is compiled by the Arctic Institute of North America under sponsorship of the Office of Naval Research.'

2:834 **Dwyer, Melva Jean**
A selected list of music reference materials. Edmonton, Edmonton Public Library, 1967.
15 *l.*

2:835 **Dymond, John Richardson**
Alfred Brooker Klugh; a bibliography. [By] J.R. Dymond and G.C. Toner. Gananoque, Ont., [Printed at the Reporter office], 1936. 12 p.

2:836 **Eady, David**
The extent to which Lord Durham's recommendations were carried out before the arrival of Lord Elgin as Governor-general in 1847. 1966. i, 10 1. (Ms. U. of O. Libr. School)

2:837 **Eakins, William George**
Bibliography of Canadian statute law. (In *Index to legal periodicals and Law library journal,* v. 1, no. 3, Oct. 1908, p. 61-78)
Includes bibliographical information and a checklist of laws of Upper Canada, 1792-1818.

2:838 **Eakins, William George**
Bibliography of Canadian statute law, Upper Canada, 1792-1840; Province of Canada, 1841-66. Reprinted from *Law library journal,* 1909. 1910.

2:839 **Eamon, Gladys M.**
Bibliography of the works of Adolphus Egerton Ryerson, 1803-1882.
[Toronto, 1932] 13 *l.* (Ms. Toronto Univ. Libr. School)

2:840 **Ecole des hautes études commerciales.** Institut d'économie appliquée.
Centre de recherches arctiques
Catalogue des coupures de presse [de la] Collection Gardner.
Montréal [1967-
nos

2:841 **Edgar, Pelham**
Across my path; edited by Northrop Frye. Toronto, Ryerson Press
[1952]. xiv, 167 p.
'Pelham Edgar: a bibliography of his writings, by Margaret Ray': p. 163-167.

2:842 **Edmond, frère**
Notes bio-bibliographiques: R.F. Patrice, s.c. 1953. 25 p. (Ms.
Ecole de Bibl., U. de M.)

2:843 **Edmonton Regional Planning Commission**
Regional planning: publications and maps, 1950-1964. [Edmonton,
1964] 16 *l.*

2:844 **Edouard, frère**
La Vie religieuse de Montréal au XIX$^e$ siècle. 1964. [2] 8 1. (Ms.
U. of O. Libr. School)

2:845 **Edwards, Everett Eugene**
References on the Great Lakes-Saint Lawrence waterway project.
Washington, G.P.O., 1936. 185 p. (U.S. Dept. of Agriculture, Library,
Bibliographical contributions, no. 30, Oct. 1936)

2:846 **Elisabeth-de-la-Trinité, soeur**
Bibliographie analytique de l'oeuvre de Mgr Albert Tessier, p.d.
(1946-1962), précédée d'une biographie. Préface de M. Raymond
Douville. Québec, 1962. vii, 144 p. (Ms. Ecole de Bibl., U.L.)

2:847 **Elisha, S. Sampson**
German reference aids in the University of Toronto Library,
Humanities & Social Sciences Division, prepared by S. Sampson
Elisha. Toronto, Reference Dept., University of Toronto Library,
1968.
iii, 72 *l.* (Reference series, no. 12)

2:848 **Eloi, frère**
Essai de bio-bibliographie: R.F. Marc, s.c. 1953. ix, 32 p. (Ms. Ecole
de Bibl., U. de M.)

2:849 **Engineering Institute of Canada**
Index of Transactions. v. I-XXIV. Montreal, Printed for the Society, 1911. 25 p.

2:850 **England, Robert**
Bibliography [and Curriculum vitae] of Robert England. [N.p. 196–?] 7 p.

2:851 **Entomological Society of Ontario**
General index to the thirty Annual reports of the Entomological Society of Ontario, 1870-1899. Prepared by Rev. C.J.S. Bethune. (Published by Ontario Department of Agriculture) Toronto, Cameron, 1900. 76 p.
General index to the thirty-eighth Annual ... 1900-1937. Prepared by C.E. Petch. Toronto, Bowman, Printer to the King, 1939. 267 p.

2:852 **Epp, Ingrid Ilse**
Bibliography of writing about John Wesley Dafoe. [Toronto] 1963. 5 l. (Ms. Toronto Univ. Libr. School)

2:853 **Ethier, Mireille**
Bio-bibliographie de Madeleine [Anne-Marie (Gleason) Huguenin]. Préface de Marie-Claire Daveluy. 1945. xxvii, 136 p. (Ms. Ecole de Bibl., U. de M.)

2:854 **Exposition de documents d'histoire du Canada** (1840-1880) à l'occasion du deuxième centenaire du Collège de Montréal avec l'aide financière de la Commission du Centenaire. [Catalogue] Exposition of documents pertaining to Canadian history (1840-1880) on the occasion of the bicentennial of the College of Montreal with the financial aid of the Centennial Commission. [Catalogue. Montréal, 1967]
[24] p. ill.

2:855 **Fabien, Cécile**
Essai bio-bibliographique sur Jeanne Grisé Allard. Préface de Casimir Hébert. 1945. 81 p. (Ms. Ecole de Bibl., U. de M.)

2:856 **Falardeau, Edith**
Bibliographie: artisanat au Canada français, 1900-50. Québec, 1956. 80 p. (Ms. Ecole de Bibl., U.L.)

2:857 **Falconer, Margaret**
Italian reference aids in the University of Toronto Library, Humanities and Social Sciences Division. Toronto, Reference Dept., University of Toronto Library, 1967.
48 l. (Reference series, no. 11)

2:858  **Fang, Irene Kuang-ching**
The regional library co-operatives in Ontario. 1967. vi, 9 *l* (Ms.
U. of O. Libr. School)

2:859  **Faribault, Georges Barthélemi**
Catalogue d'ouvrages sur l'histoire de l'Amérique et en particulier
sur celle du Canada, de la Louisiane, de l'Acadie, et autres lieux, ci-
devant connus sous le nom de Nouvelle-France; avec des notes
bibliographiques, critiques et littéraires. En trois parties. Québec,
Cowan, 1837. 207 p.
réimpression. [N.Y.] Johnson Reprint Corp., 1966. 207 p.

2:860  **Farmer, Dorothea B.**
Bibliography of Canadian wild flowers; periodical articles. [Toronto,
1932] 3 *l*. (Ms. Toronto Univ. Libr. School)

2:861  **Farrell, David M.**
The contracting out of work; an annotated bibliography. Kingston,
Ont., Queen's University, Industrial Relations Centre, 1965. 2 p. *l.,*
iii-v, 61 p. (Bibliography series, no. 1)

2:862  **Faucher, Blanche**
Bio-bibliographie de Eugène Achard. 1940. 41 p. (Mf. Ecole de
Bibl., U. de M.)

2:863  **Faucher, Gertrude**
Bio-bibliographie de Jeannine Lavalée. Préface de Hélène Charbonneau.
1945. 26 p. (Mf. Ecole de Bibl., U. de M.)

2:864  **Faucher, Suzanne**
Essai de bio-bibliographie de Geneviève de La Tour Fondue. Préf.
de Guy Boulizon. 1957. xiii, 45 p. (Ms. Ecole de Bibl., U. de M.)

2:865  **Faustin, frère**
Bibliographie compilée par ordre alphabétique d'auteurs, de tous les
articles composés par les religieux de Sainte-Croix et parus dans le
*Bulletin des études,* revue pédagogique, organe des Frères étudiants
de la Congrégation de Sainte-Croix (1918-1938). 1938. 172 p. (Ms.
Ecole de Bibl., U. de M.)

2:866  **Fauteux, Ægidius**
Bibliographie de la question universitaire Laval-Montréal (1852-1921)
... Montréal, Arbour et Dupont, 1922. 62 p.
Extrait de *l'Annuaire de l'Université de Montréal* pour 1922-1923.

2:867  **Fauteux, Ægidius**
Bibliographie de l'histoire canadienne. Montréal, 1926. 21 p.
Synthèse des travaux de bibliographie sur l'histoire du Canada.

2:868  **Favreau, Hélène**
Notes bio-bibliographiques sur Monsieur Albert Ferland, poète et
artiste. 1948. 14 p. (Mf. Ecole de Bibl., U. de M.)

2:869  **Favreau, J.-Etienne**
Essai de bibliographie de Louis Riboulet. Préf. par F. Camille
L'Heureux. Montréal, 1961. x, 39 p. (Ms. Ecole de Bibl., U. de M.)

2:870  **Favreau, Janyne**
Bio-bibliographie de Geneviève de Francheville [Berthe Potvin].
1952. ix, 38 p. (Mf. Ecole de Bibl., U. de M.)

2:871  **Fédération canadienne des maires et des municipalitiés**
Municipal reference library catalogue. Bibliothèque de documentation municipale. [11e rev. Montréal, 1965]
1 v.

2:872  **Fédération des collèges classiques.** Centrale de catalogage
Choix de livres à l'intention des bibliothèques. Liste no 1, déc. 1964.
Montréal, 1964. 90 f.
La plupart des ouvrages répertoriés dans ce numéro sont des ouvrages
canadiens-français.

2:873  **Fédération libérale provinciale.** Institut de recherches politiques
Problèmes politiques du Québec. Répertoire bibliographique des
commissions royales d'enquête présentant un intérêt spécial pour la
politique de la province de Québec, 1940-1957. Montréal, Québec,
1957. xiii, 218 p.
Compilateur: Gérard Bergeron.

2:874  **Fenton, William Nelson**
American Indian and white relations to 1830, needs & opportunities
for study: an essay by William N. Fenton; a bibliography by L.H.
Butterfield, Wilcomb E. Washburn, and William N. Fenton, Chapel
Hill. Published for the Institute of Early American History and
Culture, Williamsburg, Va., by the University of North Carolina
Press, 1957. x, 138 p. (Needs and opportunities for study series)

2:875  **Filion, Marthe**
Notes bio-bibliographiques du R.P. Arcade-M. Monette, o.p. 1952.
23 p. (Ms. Ecole de Bibl., U. de M.)

2:876  **[Finley, Eric Gault]**
Sources à consulter en vue d'une compilation bibliographique sur
l'évolution de l'éducation au Canada français. [Compilée par E. Gault

Finley. Montréal, Centre d'études canadiennes-françaises, Université McGill, 1966]
60 f.

2:877 **Firth, Edith G.**
Early Toronto newspapers, 1793-1867; a catalogue of newspapers published in the town of York and the city of Toronto from the beginning to Confederation. With an introd. by Henry C. Campbell. Toronto, Published by the Baxter Pub. Co. in co-operation with the Toronto Public Library, 1961. 31 p. facsims.

2:878 **Fish, Donald G.**
Simcoe County; an annotated bibliography. [Toronto] 1967. ii, 20 *l.* (Ms. Toronto Univ. Libr. School)

2:879 **Flemington, Frank**
Lorne Pierce; a bibliography. Toronto, 1959. 76 *l.*

2:880 **Florence-de-Marie, soeur**
Essai de bio-bibliographie de Joseph-Donat Dufour. 1953. 28 p. (Ms. Ecole de Bibl., U. de M.)

2:881 **Florence-du-Sacré-Coeur, soeur**
Bibliographie analytique sur le Forum catholique de Montréal (Catholic Inquiry Forum) (1952-1962). Préface du R.P. Irénée Beaubien. Montréal, 1963. 133 p. (Ms. Ecole de Bibl., U.L.)

2:882 **Foisy, Pierrette**
Catalogue des ouvrages canadiens à la Bibliothèque municipale de la cité des Sept-Iles. Préf. par R.P. Marcel Lavallée. Montréal, 1961. xvii, 135 p. (Ms. Ecole de Bibl., U. de M.)

2:883 **Fondation des universités canadiennes.** Service de recherches et de renseignements
... Publications courantes de la Fondation des universités canadiennes et [de] la Conférence nationale des universités et des collèges canadiens. [Ottawa, 1962] 7 p.

2:884 **Forget, Guy**
Bibliographie de Denis-Benjamin Viger, 1774-1861, précédée d'une notice biographique. 1946. 19 p. (Mf. Ecole de Bibl., U. de M.)

2:885 **Forget, Guy**
Bibliography of Canadian documents on alcoholic beverages, 1921-1956. Compiled by Guy Forget for the Association of Canadian Distillers. Ottawa, 1957. 356 p.

2:886   **Forgues, Yvette**
Notes bio-bibliographiques sur Léo-Pol Morin. 1949. iv, 9 p. (Ms.
Ecole de Bibl., U. de M.)

2:887   **Fortier, André**
Bio-bibliographie du Prof. L.-E. Fortier. Préf. du Dr Albert Lesage.
1952. xi, 39 p. (Ms. Ecole de Bibl., U. de M.)

2:888   **Fortier, Henriette**
Bio-bibliographie de Jules Fournier. Préface de Madame Thérèse
Surveyer-Fournier. 1942. 138 p. (Mf. Ecole de Bibl., U. de M.)

2:889   **Fortier, Suzanne**
Bibliographie de la poésie canadienne-française (1935-1958) Québec,
1961. 46 p. (Ms. Ecole de Bibl., U.L.)

2:890   **Fortin, Isabelle**
Bio-bibliographie analytique de Paul-Edouard Gagnon, du Conseil
national des Recherches. Préface de J.-B. Parent. Québec, 1958. 30 p.
(Ms. Ecole de Bibl., U.L.)

2:891   **Fortin, Rosario**
Bibliographie des monographies paroissiales. 1938. iii, 40 p. (Ms.
Ecole de Bibl., U. de M.)

2:892   **Fortunat, frère**
Bibliographie de Guy Laviolette [pseud.] (Michel-Henri Gingras) en
religion Frère Denis-Antoine des F.I.C. 1946. 40 p. (Ms. Ecole de
Bibl., U. de M.)

2:893   **Forty years of Kirkconnell titles.** (In *Acadia bulletin,* Jan. 1961,
vol. 47, no. 1, p. 19-23)
Bibliography of President Watson Kirkconnell of Acadia University.

2:894   **Fournier, Gisèle**
Notes bio-bibliographiques sur Albert Lozeau. 1947. [8] p. (Ms.
Ecole de Bibl., U. de M.)

2:895   **Fowler, Genevieve A.**
Canadian authors of books for children. [By Genevieve A. Fowler
and Mary K. Barton]. [Toronto] 1932. 2 pts. ([1], 7; [1], 8 *l.*)
(Ms. Toronto Univ. Libr. School)

2:896   **Francis, Laura E.**
Mapping in Canada. 1963. xiii, 9 1. (Ms. U. of O. Libr. School)

2:897   **Fraser, Bessie Fairbairn**
Bibliography of the geology of Gaspé. Montreal, 1932. [10] *l.* (Ms.
McGill Univ. Libr. School)

2:898 **Fraser, Ian Forbes**
Bibliography of French-Canadian poetry. Part 1: From the beginnings of the literature through the Ecole littéraire de Montréal ... New York, Institute of French Studies, Inc., Columbia University [c1935]. vi, 105 p.

2:899 **Fréchette, Edmée**
Essai de bio-bibliographie, Monsieur Pierre Baillargeon. 1949. 23 p. (Mf. Ecole de Bibl., U. de M.)

2:900 **Fréchette, Léandre-M.**
Bio-bibliographie du R.F. André [Alfred Bessette] c.s.c., fondateur de l'Oratoire Saint-Joseph du Mont-Royal. 1943. 195 p. (Ms. Ecole de Bibl., U. de M.)

2:901 **Fuller, Edna M.**
Bibliography of Canadian literary periodicals since 1900. [Toronto, 1931] 5 *l.* (Ms. Toronto Univ. Libr. School)

2:902 **Fulton, Jessie Eldred**
A first survey of material on Indian folk-tales and legends of Ontario, arranged according to subject and locality. By Jessie Eldred Fulton and Sadie I. Marston. Toronto, 1938. [1], v, 56 *l.* (Ms. Toronto Univ. Libr. School)

2:903 **Gaboriault, Victor, père**
Bio-bibliographie de Charles-Eusèbe Dionne. 1947. 237 p. fac-sim. (Ms. Ecole de Bibl., U. de M.)

2:904 **Gaboriault, Wilfrid**
Bio-bibliographie de M. Donatien Frémont. 1946. 138 p. (Mf. Ecole de Bibl., U. de M.)

2:905 **Gagné, Armand**
Catalogue des thèses de l'Ecole des Gradués de l'Université Laval, 1940-1960. Québec, 1960. vi p., [1] f., 76 p. (*Etudes et recherches bibliographiques*, no 1)

2:906 **Gagné, Armand**
Répertoire des thèses des facultés ecclésiastiques de l'Université Laval, 1935-1960. Québec, 1960. iii, [2], 19 f. (*Etudes et recherches bibliographiques*, no 2)

2:907 **Gagnon, Carmen**
Bio-bibliographie de Madame Françoise Gaudet-Smet. Préf. de Mlle Germaine Bernier. 42 p. (Mf. Ecole de Bibl., U. de M.)

2:908 **Gagnon, Françoise**
Bibliographie analytique de Simone Bussières. préc. d'une
biographie. Québec, 1963. 23 p. (Ms. Ecole de Bibl., U.L.)

2:909 **Gagnon, Huguette**
Bibliographie analytique de Alain Grandbois, précédée d'une
biographie. Préf. de Ch.-M. Boissonnault. 1964, xi (2), 120 p. (Ms.
Ecole de Bibl., U.L.)

2:910 **Gagnon, Jean**
Bio-bibliographie de M. Hermas Bastien. Montréal, 1961. xiii, 47 p.
(Ms. Ecole de Bibl., U. de M.)

2:911 **Gagnon, Marcelle**
Essai de bibliographie de Mme Hélène B. Beauséjour (1928-1964)
préc. d'une biographie. Préf. de Marguerite A. Hébert. 1964. xiv-87(2)
p. (Ms. Ecole de Bibl., U.L.)

2:912 **Gagnon, Philéas**
Essai de bibliographie canadienne: inventaire d'une bibliothèque
comprenant imprimés, manuscrits, estampes, etc., relatifs à l'histoire
du Canada et des pays adjacents ... Québec, L'Auteur, 1895-1913. 2 v.
'Avec des notes bibliographiques.'
Titre du v. 2: Essai ... ajoutés à la Collection Gagnon, depuis 1895 à 1909
inclusivement, d'après les notes bibliographiques et le catalogue de l'auteur.
Préface de l'échevin Victor Morin. Publié par la cité de Montréal, sous la
direction de Frédéric Villeneuve. Montréal, 1913.
Réimpression. Dubuque, Iowa, W.C. Brown Reprint Library [1962] 2 v. ill.,
fac-sim.

2:913 **Galarneau, Pierrette**
Essai bio-bibliographique sur Roland Goyette. 1952. 36 p. (Ms. Ecole
de Bibl., U. de M.)

2:914 **Gallup, Jennifer**
Reference guide to book reviews; a checklist of sources in the humanities, social sciences, and fine arts. Vancouver, University of British
Columbia Library, 1968.
19 *l.* (Reference publication no. 24)

2:915 **Gamelin, Lucienne**
Bio-bibliographie de M. Jean-Baptiste Lagacé. Préface de Me Victor
Morin. 1947. xiv, 73 p. (Mf. Ecole de Bibl., U. de M.)

2:916 **Garant, J.-Honorat**
Bio-bibliographie de M. Elphège Bois, D.Sc., directeur du Département
de biochimie. Préf. de M. Louis Cloutier. Québec, 1949. 53 p. (Ms.
Ecole de Bibl., U.L.)

2:917 **Garant, Maurice**
Bio-bibliographie du R.F. Magloire-Robert, f.é.c. [s.d.] 29 p. (Ms. Ecole de Bibl., U. de M.)

2:918 **Gardiner, Margaret**
Eskimo folklore; a bibliography. Montreal, 1957. v, 7 *l.* (Ms. McGill Univ. Libr. School)

2:919 **Garen, Robert John**
A bibliography of the poetry of Alden A. Nowlan. [Toronto] 1964. ii, 7 *l.* (Ms. Toronto Univ. Libr. School)

2:920 **Garigue, Philippe**
A bibliographical introduction to the study of French Canada. [Montreal] Department of Sociology and Anthropology, McGill University, 1956. 133 p.

2:921 **Garigue, Philippe**
Bibliographie du Québec (1955-1965) par Philippe Garigue avec la collaboration de Raymonde Savard. Montréal, Presses de l'Université de Montréal, 1967.
227 p.

2:922 **Garneau, Marthe**
Bibliographie de l'œuvre de M. Gérard Morissette, 1950-1962. Québec, 1964. 70 p. (Ms. Ecole de Bibl., U.L.)

2:923 **Garneau, Marthe**
Bibliographie analytique de Gérard Morrisset, de la Société royale du Canada (1950-1962) précédée d'une biographie. Préface de M. Paul E. Plamondon. Québec, 1964. 72 p. (Ms. Ecole de Bibl., U.L.)

2:924 **Garneau, Robert**
Bio-bibliographie de M. Rolland Dumais, 1938 à 1956. Courville, 1964. 164 p. (Ms. Ecole de Bibl., U.L.)

2:925 **Garratt, Hazel Jean**
A bibliography of the cartoons drawn by Mr John Wilson Bengough for the Toronto *Daily Globe,* for the year 1896, and also his verses, magazine articles, etc. [Toronto] 1932. [12] *l.* (Ms. Toronto Univ. Libr. School)

2:926 **[Garvin, Amelia Beers]**
Isabella Valancy Crawford, by Katherine Hale (Mrs John Garvin). Toronto, Ryerson [c1923]. 125 p. (*Makers of Canadian literature*)
Bibliography: p. 111-122.

2:927 **Gascon, Huguette**
Bio-bibliographie de Simone Routier. Préface de Michelle Le Normand.
1945. 47 p. (Mf. Ecole de Bibl., U. de M.)

2:928 **Gattinger, F. Eugene**
A bibliography of Canadian historical novels in English, 1930-1951.
Montreal, 1952. 8 *l.* (Ms. McGill Univ. Libr. School)

2:929 **Gaubert, Helen Anna**
Notes bio-bibliographiques sur Félix-Gabriel Marchand, dramaturge.
1949. v, 21 p. (Mf. Ecole de Bibl., U. de M.)

2:930 **Gaudet, Frederick Joseph**
The literature on labor turnover; a classified bibliography. [New
York] Industrial Relations News [c1960]
26 p.

2:931 **Gaudrault, Denise**
Bio-bibliographie de M. Rodolphe Laplante. 1952. xxvii, 68 p.
(Ms. Ecole de Bibl., U. de M.)

2:932 **Gaudreault, Delphis**
Le Canada et ses Ecoles de bibliothécaires. 1964. vii, 9 1. (Ms.
U. of O. Libr. School)

2:933 **Gauthier, Georges**
Bibliographie de Gabrielle Roy. Préf. de Mme Thérèse M. Miller.
Québec, 1960. 94 p. (Ms. Ecole de Bibl., U.L.)

2:934 **Gauthier, Jeanne, soeur**
Notes bio-bibliographiques sur M. Edouard Gagnon, p.s.s. Préface de
Mlle Juliette Chabot. 1953. 55 p. (Ms. Ecole de Bibl., U. de M.)

2:935 **Gauthier, Marcelle**
Notice bio-bibliographique: R.P. Dom Raoul Hamel, o.s.b. 1953. 20 p.
(Ms. Ecole de Bibl., U. de M.)

2:936 **Gauthier, Marguerite**
Bibliographie d'Edmond Lareau. 1943. xv, 36 p. (Mf. Ecole de Bibl.,
U. de M.)

2:937 **Gauthier, Monique**
Bio-bibliographie de Mme Thérèse Gouin-Décarie, psychologue.
Préface de Pierre Cléroux, ptre. Montréal, 1957. 24 p. (Ms. Ecole de
Bibl., U. de M.)

2:938 **Geddes, James**
Bibliographical outline of French-Canadian literature. [Chicago,
1940] 7-52 p.

'Reprinted from Bibliographical Society of America, *Papers,* v. VIII, nos. 1-2, 1914. First edition, 1904 ... Third revised edition, 1940.'

2:939 **Geddes, James**
Bibliographie linguistique du Canada français [par] James Geddes et Adjutor Rivard, continuée [par] Gaston Dulong. Québec, Presses de l'Université Laval; Paris, Librairie C. Klincksieck, 1966.
xxxii, 166 p. (Bibliothèque française et romane. Série E: langue et littérature françaises au Canada, 1)
Reproduit et continue Bibliographie du parler français au Canada; catalogue analytique des ouvrages traitant de la langue française au Canada, dressé par James Geddes, ... et Adjutor Rivard. (Paris, H. Champion; Québec, E. Marcotte, 1906)

2:940 **[Geddes, James]**
Bibliography of Geddes publications. 2nd ed. ... [N.p.] 1934. 15 p.
'Augmented from the 1912 first printing.'

2:941 **Geddes, James**
Canadian French. The language and literature of the past decade, 1890-1900, with a retrospect of the causes that have produced them. Erlangen, Junge; [etc., etc.] 1902. 66 p.
Reprinted from *Kritischer Jahresbericht über die Fortschritte der Romanischen Philologie,* v. 5. Continued in v. 6-13, 1901-1912.

2:942 **Gelly, Estelle**
Edouard Montpetit; essai bio-bibliographique. 1947. 16 p. (Ms. Ecole de Bibl., U. de M.)

2:943 **Gendreau, Jean-Yves**
Bio-bibliographie de Jovette-Alice Bernier. 1950. vii, 18 p. (Mf. Ecole de Bibl., U. de M.)

2:944 **Geneviève-de-Paris, mère**
Mémoire bibliographique [des écrivains de la Mauricie au cours des 45 dernières années]. 1938. 25 p. (Ms. Ecole de Bibl., U. de M.)

2:945 **Geoffrion, Renée**
Notes bio-bibliographiques sur l'honorable Fernand Rinfret. 1952. iv, 10 p. (Mf. Ecole de Bibl., U. de M.)

2:946 **Georges-André, soeur**
Bibliographie analytique de l'oeuvre de l'Abbé Pierre Gravel, curé de Boischâtel. 2e partie (1941-1957) Préface de M. Robert Rumilly. Sherbrooke, 1961. 100 p. (Ms. Ecole de Bibl., U.L.)

2:947 **Georges-Etienne, soeur**
Bio-bibliographie de Monsieur J.-D. Dufour, professeur à l'Ecole normale Marguerite Bourgeois. Sherbrooke, 1946. 64 p. (Mf. Ecole de Bibl., U. de M.)

2:948  **Georges-Maurice, frère**
Essai d'inventaire des livres, brochures, périodiques et autres
imprimés, publiés par la Congrégation des Frères Maristes. 1938.
34 p. (Ms. Ecole de Bibl., U. de M.)

2:949  **Germain, Pierre**
La musique d'orgue au Canada. 1964. vi, 12 1. (Ms. U. of O. Libr.
School)

2:950  **Germaine-Marie, sœur**
Psychologie rationnelle au Canada français. Bibliographie (1945-1963)
Préface de mère Marie-Lucienne, s.c.s.l. Pont-Rouge, 1964. 60 p.
(Ms. Ecole de Bibl., U.L.)

2:951  **Gervais, André**
Essai de bio-bibliographie de Armand Renaud-Lavergne. 1952. 48 p.
(Ms. Ecole de Bibl., U. de M.)

2:952  **Gervais, Claire**
Bio-bibliographie de Maréchal Nantel. Préface de M. Jean-Jacques
Lefebvre. 1945. viii, 59 p. (Ms. Ecole de Bibl., U. de M.)

2:953  **Gervais, Emile**
Pour mieux connaître nos fondateurs. Bibliographie pratique.
Montréal, Le Messager canadien [1942]. 32 p.

2:954  **Gervais, Germaine**
Bio-bibliographie de Louis Fréchette, poète. 1948. iv, 17 p. (Mf.
Ecole de Bibl., U. de M.)

2:955  **Gerwing, Howard**
A checklist of the Herbert Read Archive in the McPherson Library
of the University of Victoria. University of Victoria, 1969. 71 p.
(first published in *The Malahat review,* January, 1969).
Lists a substantial collection of Papers and MSS purchased by the University
of Victoria, and a definitive list of published works of Sir Herbert Read.
(see also 2:1050)

2:956  **Gibault, Janick**
Bio-bibliographie de Marie Thérèse Archambault. Préf. par Docteur
Madeleine Longtin. Montréal, 1961. xiii, 66 p. (Ms. Ecole de Bibl.,
U. de M.)

2:957  **Gignac, Françoise**
Bio-bibliographie analytique de Simone Paré, prof. à l'Université
Laval. Préface du R.P. Gilles-M. Bélanger, o.p. Québec, 1958. 80 p.
(Ms. Ecole de Bibl., U.L.)

2:958 **Gilbert, Rodolphe**
Esquisse bio-bibliographique du chanoine Arthur Sideleau. Lettre-préface de Mgr Emile Chartier, p.d. 1951. 26 p. (Ms. Ecole de Bibl., U. de M.)

2:959 **Gill, Theodore Nicholas**
... Material for a bibliography of North American mammals, prepared by Theodore Gill and Elliott Coues. Extracted from the eleventh volume of the final reports of the Survey, being Appendix B of the monographs of North American Rodentia. By Elliott Coues and Joel Asaph Allen. Washington, G.P.O., 1877. 1 p. *l.*, 951-1081 p.

2:960 **Gince, Liliane**
Bio-bibliographie de Robert Rumilly. Préface d'Eugène Achard. 1945. 119 p. (Mf. Ecole de Bibl., U. de M.)

2:961 **Gingras, Jean-Jules**
Bibliographie du Chanoine Paul-Emile Crépeault, 1944-1964. Québec, 1965. 71 p. (Ms. Ecole de Bibl., U.L.)

2:962 **Gingras, Marcel**
Bio-bibliographie du R.P. Louis Le Jeune, o.m.i. 1946. iv, 22 p. (Mf. Ecole de Bibl., U. de M.)

2:963 **Girard, Jeannine**
Bio-bibliographie de Yves Thériault. Préf. de M. Jean Bruchési. 1950. vii, 46 p. (Mf. Ecole de Bibl., U. de M.)

2:964 **Girard, Roland**
Essai de bio-bibliographie du R.P. Louis Chaussegros de Léry, s.j. Préface du R.P. Georges Van Belleghem. Montréal, 1957. xix, 98 p. (Ms. Ecole de Bibl., U. de M.)

2:965 **Giroux, Alice**
Bio-bibliographie de Georges Bugnet. Préface par l'abbé Arthur Maheux. 1946. 27 p. (Mf. Ecole de Bibl., U. de M.)

2:966 **Giroux, Pauline**
Bibliographie analytique du docteur Louis-George Godin (1897-1932) précédée d'une biographie. Préface de Mgr Albert Tessier, p.d. Trois-Rivières, 1964. 82 p. (Ms. Ecole de Bibl., U.L.)

2:967 **Giroux, Rollande**
Bibliographie de Léonie Valois. 1947. 21 p. (Mf. Ecole de Bibl., U. de M.)

2:968  **Giroux, Yvette**
Bibliographie analytique de André Giroux. Québec, 1948. 33 p.
(Ms. Ecole de Bibl., U.L.)

2:969  **Goard, Dean S.**
Rural British Columbia; a bibliography of social and economic research, compiled by Dean S. Goard. Vancouver, Dept. of Adult
Education, Faculty of Education, University of British Columbia,
1967.
26 p.

2:970  **Godbout, Claire**
Notre bibliothèque enfantine; essai de bibliographie canadienne-
française. Préface de M.-Claire Daveluy. Les Trois-Rivières, 1941.
x, 66 p. (Ms. Ecole de Bibl., U. de M.)

2:971  **Goggio, Emilio**
A bibliography of Canadian cultural periodicals (English and French
from colonial times to 1950) in Canadian libraries, compiled by
Emilio Goggio, Beatrice Corrigan [and] Jack H. Parker. [Toronto]
Department of Italian, Spanish and Portuguese, University of
Toronto, 1955. 45 p.

2:972  **Graham, Edith Margaret**
Bibliography of Canadian political biography. [Toronto, 1933] [21] *l.*
(Ms. Toronto Univ. Libr. School)

2:973  **Granger Frères**, Montréal
Bibliographie canadienne. France-Canada. Montréal, Granger, 1900.
83 p.
Préparée pour l'Exposition universelle de Paris.

2:974  **Granger Frères**, Montréal
Littérature nationale, bibliographie canadienne. Catalogue annoté
d'ouvrages canadiens-français. Montréal [1906]. 295, [1] p.
Nouvelle édition, augmentée et mise à jour.

2:975  **Grant, Donald H.**
Surveys of Canadian scientific achievements, 1867-1967. 1967. vii,
7 l. (Ms. U. of O. Libr. School)

2:976  **Grant, Mary Elspeth**
Women in the Canadian House of Commons. [Toronto] 1966. 25 *l.*
(Ms. Toronto Univ. Libr. School)

2:977 **Great Britain. Parliament. House of Commons.** Library
A bibliography relating to constitutional and economic developments
since the royal commission and the Newfoundland Act of 1933.
[London, 1949] 10 p. (House of Commons. Bibliographies, No. 59)
Addenda, 1949. Single leaf (2).

2:978 **Greenly, Albert Henry**
Lahontan: an essay and bibliography. [New York, Bibliographical
society of America, 1954] 59 p.

2:979 **Greenly, Albert Henry**
A selective bibliography of important books, pamphlets and broad-
sides relating to Michigan history; bibliography and notes by Albert
Henry Greenly. Lunenburg, Vt., Stinehour Press, 1958. xvii, 165 p.
facsims.
Includes publications relating to Canada.

2:980 **Greenway, Adele Joan**
Ontario folklore; a bibliography. [Toronto] 1964. 13 *l.* (Ms. Toronto
Univ. Libr. School)

2:981 **Greer, William Leonard Craig**
Bush flying in Canada; a bibliography. [Toronto, 1962. 6 *l.*] (Ms.
Toronto Univ. Libr. School)

2:982 **Grégoire, frère**
Essai de bio-bibliographie de M. Rolland Ricard, professeur. Préf. de
Conrad Lemieux. Montréal, 1960. x, 72 p. (Ms. Ecole de Bibl.,
U. de M.)

2:983 **Grégoire, Françoise (De Serres)**
Essai de bio-bibliographie: R.P. Alphonse de Grandpré, c.s.v. Préf.
de Mgr Joseph-Arthur Papineau. 1953. 40 p. (Mf. Ecole de Bibl.,
U. de M.)

2:984 **Grenon, Mireille**
Essai de bio-bibliographie: le R.P. Georges Lemoine, o.m.i. Préface
par R.P. Gaston Carrière. 1953. 32 p. (Ms. Ecole de Bibl., U. de M.)

2:985 **Griffin, Appleton Prentiss Clark**
... Bibliography of American historical societies. (The United States
and the Dominion of Canada.) (From the *Annual report of the
American historical association* for 1895, p. 677-1236.) (Reprinted,
with additions and revisions, from the Annual reports for 1890 and
1892.) Washington, G.P.O., 1896. 677-1236 p.

A list of the publications of 313 societies, classified by states, followed by an author index.
Second ed., rev. and enl.: [1907] 1374 p. 25 cm. (*American Historical Association, Annual reports*, 1905, v. 2.) Reprinted [Detroit, Gale Research Co., 1966] 1374 p.

2:986 **Griffin, Appleton Prentiss Clark**
The discovery of the Mississippi; a bibliographical account, with a fac-simile of the map of Louis Joliet, 1674. To which is appended a note on the Joliet map, by B.F. De Costa, with a sketch of Joutel's maps ... New York, Barnes, 1883. 20 p.
'Reprinted from the *Magazine of American history*, March and April, 1883.'

2:987 **Griffin, Grace Gardner**
Writings on American history, 1906-1918. A bibliography of books and articles on United States and Canadian history, published during the year[s] 1906-1918, with some memoranda on other portions of America. New Haven, Conn., Yale University Press, 1908-1921. 13 v.
Imprint varies.
1918-1921, issued as supplementary volumes to the *Annual report of the American historical association* for the corresponding years.

2:988 **Griffith, J.W.**
... A bibliography on the occurrence of uranium in Canada and related subjects. Ottawa, 1956. iii *l.*, 34 p. (Canada Department of Mines and Technical Survey. Geological survey. Paper 56-5)

2:989 **Grignon, Marcel**
Essai de bio-bibliographie: le R.P. Laurent Tremblay, o.m.i. 1950. viii, 18 p. (Mf. Ecole de Bibl., U. de M.)

2:990 **Groleau, Conrad**
Essai de bio-bibliographie: Monsieur le chanoine Dolor Biron. Sherbrooke, Préfecture des Etudes, Séminaire Saint-Charles-Borromée, 1951. vii, 18 p. (Mf. Ecole de Bibl., U. de M.)

2:991 **Grondin, Claire**
Bio-bibliographie de Alfred Desrochers. 1944. 35 p. (Mf. Ecole de Bibl., U. de M.)

2:992 **Grondin, François-Xavier**
Bio-bibliographie de Jacques Viger. 1947. 2 v. (Ms. Ecole de Bibl., U. de M.)

2:993 **Grondin, Madeleine**
Essai de bio-bibliographie: l'abbé J.-G. Gélinas. 1950. 12 p. (Ms. Ecole de Bibl., U. de M.)

2:994 **Grondin, Marguerite**
Notes bio-bibliographiques sur Monsieur Napoléon Bourassa. 1948.
8 p. (Mf. Ecole de Bibl., U. de M.)

2:995 **Grossman, Barbara Ann**
British Columbia through fiction; a reading list. Montreal, 1957. 7 *l.*
(Ms. McGill Univ. Libr. School)

2:996 **Growoll, Adolf**
Henry Harrisse; biographical and bibliographical sketch ... New York,
Dibdin club, 1899. 13 p. (Dibdin club, New York, Leaflets, no. 3)

2:997 **Guénin, Eugène**
La Nouvelle-France. Paris, Fourneau, 1896-1898. 2 v. (Histoire de la
colonisation française, 1-2)
Bibliographies: v. 1, p. 379-392; v. 2, p. 457-474.
Autre édition: Paris, Hachette, 1900. 414 p.

2:998 **Guérin, Gabrielle**
Bibliographie de M. l'abbé Hospice-Anthelme-Jean-Baptiste Verreau.
1939. 29 p. (Ms. Ecole de Bibl., U. de M.)

2:999 **Guérin, Germaine**
Bio-bibliographie de Mme Germaine Guèvremont. Lettre-préface de
Mlle Cécile Chabot. 1945. vi, 26 p. (Ms. Ecole de Bibl., U. de M.)

2:1000 **Guérin, Jeannette**
Bio-bibliographie de Jeanne Daigle. Préface de Mme Jeanne Grisé-
Allard. 1947. ix, 26 p. (Ms. Ecole de Bibl., U. de M.)

2:1001 **Guérin, Marc-Aimé**
Le lieutenant-colonel et arpenteur général du Bas-Canada, Joseph
Bouchette, père. 1951. xiii, 111 p. (Mf. Ecole de Bibl., U. de M.)

2:1002 **Guibault, Renée**
Bibliographie analytique de l'oeuvre de Bertrand Vac [pseud. d'Aimé
Pelletier.] précédée d'une biographie. Préface de M. Jean-Chs Bonen-
fant. Québec, 1963. 31 p. (Ms. Ecole de Bibl., U.L.)

2:1003 **Guilbault, Germaine**
Bibliographie analytique de l'oeuvre de Son Excellence Mgr N.A.
Labrie, c.j.m., évêque du Golfe St-Laurent, précédée d'une biographie.
Préface de M. Jean-Paul Pelletier. Québec, 1964. 170 p. (Ms. Ecole
de Bibl., U.L.)

2:1004 **Guilbert, Honoré**
Bibliographie du Tiers-Ordre séculier au Canada (province de Québec).
1940. 47 p. (Ms. Ecole de Bibl., U. de M.)
Supplément, pour les années 1931 à 1940, à l'oeuvre du R.P. Hugolin.

2:1005 **Guillemette, Marguerite**
Bio-bibliographie de Nérée Beauchemin, poète. [s.d.] 52 p. (Mf.
Ecole de Bibl., U. de M.)

2:1006 **Guitard, A. et Sansfaçon, J.**
L'accès documentaire aux sciences religieuses ou liste d'ouvrages de
consultation. 1968. 30 f. (Ms. Ecole de Bibl., U. de M.)

2:1007 **Guitard, André**
Bibliographie choisie d'études récentes sur le prêtre. Montréal, Office
national du clergé, 1969.
70 p.

2:1008 **Gutzwiller, Alois**
Guide du choix des livres en philosophie pour bibliothèques de
collèges. Préf. de E. Simard. Montréal, Fédération des collèges
classiques, 1966.
xii, 372 p. (Collection Livres et bibliothèques–L.B. 801)
Thèse (M.A.)–Catholic University of America, 1966.

2:1009 **Haché, Patricia**
Bio-bibliographie de Me Marie-Louis Beaulieu, prof. à Laval. Québec,
1957. 40 p. (Ms. Ecole de Bibl., U.L.)

2:1010 **Haight, Willet Ricketson**
Canadian catalogue of books, part 1. Toronto, Haight, 1896. 130 p.
Annual Canadian catalogue of books. First-[second] supplement to the
*Canadian catalogue of books,* 1791-1895. Toronto, Haight, 1898-1904. 2 v.
'An edition of 500 copies printed.'
Another edition by Canadian Book Co., same date.
Complete one-volume facsimile edition. London, Podres, 1959. '1,000 copies.'

2:1011 **Halasz de Beky, Ivan Leslie**
Bibliography of Hungarian dictionaries, 1410-1963. [Toronto]
University of Toronto Press [c1966]
xiv, 148 p.

2:1012 **Hale, Margaret A.**
The League for Social Reconstruction; a bibliography. [Toronto]
1967. iv, 20 *l.* (Ms. Toronto Univ. Libr. School)

2:1013 **Halifax. Memorial Library**
Around our lovely province. Halifax, 1964.
22 p.
An annotated bibliography.

2:1014 **Hallé, Blanche**
Essai de bibliographie des ouvrages écrits au Canada par des Canadiens

sur les sciences sociales, économiques et politiques. [s.d.] 26 p.
(Ms. Ecole de Bibl., U. de M.)

2:1015 **Hallé, Thérèse**
Bio-bibliographie d'Emile Nelligan. 1943. 14 p. (Mf. Ecole de Bibl.,
U. de M.)

2:1016 **Hallé, Thérèse**
Compilation bibliographique des travaux des médecins de l'Université
de Montréal, années académiques 1958-59, 1959-60. Préf. de Victor
Lacourcière. Montréal, 1961. xv, 33 p. (Ms. Ecole de Bibl., U. de M.)

2:1017 **Halley, Madeleine**
Essai de bibliographie des écrits des Récollets ou sur les Récollets,
depuis 1615. 1938. 28 p. (Ms. Ecole de Bibl., U. de M.)

2:1018 **Hamel, André**
Bibliographie sur le scoutisme catholique dans la province de Québec.
Québec, 1948. 45 p. (Ms. Ecole de Bibl., U.L.)

2:1019 **Hamel, Louis Bertrand, frère**
Relevé des thèses présentées par les Frères de l'Instruction chrétienne
du Canada en vue de l'obtention d'un diplôme universitaire.
[Montréal] 1960. xx, 48 p. (Ms. Ecole de Bibl., U. de M.)

2:1020 **Hamel, Réginald**
Cahiers bibliographiques des lettres québécoises (du 1er janv. au
15 mars 1966), par Réginald Hamel avec la collaboration de Madeleine
Corbeil et Nicole Vigeant. v. 1, no 1. [Montréal] Centre de documentation des lettres canadiennes-françaises, Université de Montréal 1966–
v. irregulier.

2:1021 **Hamelin, Jean**
Guide de l'étudiant en histoire du Canada [par] Jean Hamelin [et]
André Beaulieu. [Québec, Presses de l'Université Laval, 1965] iv,
274 f.

2:1022 **Hamelin, Louis Edmond**
Quelques matériaux de sociologie religieuse canadienne [par] Louis-
Edmond Hamelin [et] Colette L. Hamelin. Préf. du T.R.P. Georges-
Henri Lévesque, o.p. Montréal, Editions du Lévrier, 1956. 156 p.
(*Collection Sociologie et pastorale,* 1)

2:1023 **Hamelin, Louis-Edmond**
Recueil de travaux sur l'histoire de la géographie dans le Québec.
Québec, 1961. [4] f., 5 brochures, [1] f. graph., tabl.

Contient une 'Bibliographie annotée concernant la pénétration de la géographie dans le Québec': I. Manuels (Extrait des *Cahiers de géographie de Québec*, no 8, 1960, p. 345-359); II. Notes et documents ([1], 60 *l.*), formant les deux premières brochures du volume.

2:1024  **Hamilton, Kathleen E.**

Bibliography of Canadian printing. [Toronto, 1933] [7] *l.* (Ms. Toronto Univ. Libr. School)

2:1025  **Hanessian, John**

A select bibliography of the polar regions. New York, American Universities Field Staff [c1962]

30 p. (Polar area services, v. 2, no. 1)

2:1026  **Hanley, Annie Harvey (Ross) Foster**

British Columbia authors' index. Compiled by Mrs W. Garland Foster. White Rock, Semiahmoo Bay, B.C., [1941]. [127 *l*].

Addenda to 1949.

2:1027  **Hanna, Archibald**

John Buchan, 1875-1940; a bibliography. Hamden, Conn., Shoe String Press, 1953. 135 p.

A bibliography of writings by and about Lord Tweedsmuir, Governor General of Canada, 1935-1940.

2:1028  **Hare, John E.**

Bibliographie du roman canadien-français, 1837-1962 [par] John E. Hare. Préf. de Paul Wyczynski. Montréal, Fides [1965]

82 p.

Réimpression du: Roman canadien-français; évolution, témoignages, bibliographie. Montréal, Fides [c.1964] p. 375-456.

A paru dans *Archives des lettres canadiennes*, t. III, p. [275]-456.

2:1029  **Hare, John E.**

Les imprimés dans le Bas-Canada, 1801-1840; bibliographie analytique, par John Hare [et] Jean-Pierre Wallot. Préf. [de] Lionel Groulx. Montréal, Presses de l'Université de Montréal, 1967–

v.

'Publication no 1 du Groupe de recherche sur les idéologies de la société canadienne-française'.–[v.] 1, p. [vii]

L'ouvrage entier doit comprendre 4 v.

Sommaire.–[v.] 1. 1801-1810.

2:1030  **Harper, J. Russell**

Historical directory of New Brunswick newspapers and periodicals by J. Russell Harper. Foreword by Desmond Pacey. Fredericton, N.B., University of New Brunswick [c1961] xxii, 121 p. fold. facsim.

2:1031   **Harris, Frank E.**
French-Canadian claims in Canada. 1964. iv, 13 1. (Ms. U. of O.
Libr. School)

2:1032   **Harris, Robin Sutton**
An annotated list of the legislative acts concerning higher education
in Ontario. Compiled by Robin S. Harris, with the assistance of
Constance Allen and Mary Lewis. [Toronto] Innis College, University
of Toronto, 1966.
vi, 79 p.

2:1033   **Harris, Robin Sutton**
... Bibliographie de l'enseignement supérieur au Canada [par] Robin
S. Harris [et] Arthur Tremblay. [Toronto] University of Toronto
Press; [Québec] Presses Universitaires Laval [1960] xxv, 158 p.
*(Etudes dans l'enseignement supérieur au Canada, no 1)*
... Supplément 1965 de Bibliographie de l'enseignement supérieur au
Canada. [Toronto] University of Toronto Press; [Québec] Presses de
l'Université Laval [c1965] xxxi, 170 p. *(Etudes dans l'enseignement
supérieur au Canada, no 3)*

2:1034   **Harris, Robin Sutton**
A bibliography of higher education in Canada. Bibliographie de
l'enseignement supérieur au Canada [by] Robin S. Harris [and]
Arthur Tremblay. [Toronto] University of Toronto Press; [Quebec]
Presses Universitaires Laval [1960]
xxv, 158 p. *(Studies in higher education in Canada, no. 1)*
Supplement 1965 [by] Robin S. Harris. [Toronto] University of Toronto
Press; [Quebec] Presses de l'Université Laval [c1965]
xxxi, 170 p. *(Studies in higher education in Canada, no. 3)*

2:1035   **Harris, Robin Sutton**
A list of reports to the Legislature of Ontario bearing on higher education in the province. Compiled by Robin S. Harris, with the assistance of Constance Allen and Mary Lewis. [Toronto] Innis College,
University of Toronto, 1966.
v, 17 p.

2:1036   **Harris (Frederick) Music Co. Limited**
A complete catalogue of the published works of Boris Berlin.
Oakville, Ont. [1965] 8 p. port.

2:1037   **[Harrisse, Henry]**
Notes pour servir à l'histoire, à la bibliographie et à la cartographie

de la Nouvelle-France et des pays adjacents, 1545-1700. Par l'auteur de la *Bibliotheca americana vetustissima* ... Paris, Tross, 1872. 367 p.

Un supplément à cet ouvrage fut publié par Gabriel Marcel, en 1885. (*q.v.*)

Réimpression. Dubuque, Iowa, W.C. Brown. Reprint Library [1962] xxxiii, 367 p.

2:1038   **Harvard University.** Library

The Canadian collection at Harvard University, ed. by William Inglis Morse ... Cambridge, Mass., Harvard University printing office, 1944-1948/49. 6 v. map, facsim.

Bulletins 1-6.

2:1039   **Harvard University.** Library

Canadian history and literature; classification schedule, classified listing by call number, alphabetical listing by author or title, chronological listing. Cambridge, Mass., Published by the Harvard University Library; distributed by the Harvard University Press, 1968.

411 p. (*Its* Widener Library shelflist, 20)

2:1040   **Harvey, Léonise**

Bibliographie analytique des Iles-de-la-Madeleine. Préf. de M. Ovidge Hubert. 1964. xiii, 193 (2) p. (Ms. Ecole de Bibl., U.L.)

2:1041   **Hayne, David M.**

Bibliographie critique du roman canadien-français, 1837-1900 [par] David M. Hayne [et] Marcel Tirol. [Toronto] University of Toronto Press [c1968]

viii, 141 p.

ed. française. [Québec] Presses de l'Université Laval [1969].

2:1042   **Haywood, Charles**

A bibliography of North American folklore and folksong. 2d rev. ed. New York, Dover Publications [1961] 2 v. (xxx, [1], 1031 p.) maps (on lining papers)

First ed.: New York, Greenberg [1951].

2:1043   **Hébert, Raymonde**

Notes bio-bibliographiques sur Eva Circé-Côté. 1952. vii, 12 p. (Mf. Ecole de Bibl., U. de M.)

2:1044   **Hébert, Thérèse-Louise**

Bio-bibliographie de Pierre-Joseph-Olivier Chauveau. Préface de Casimir Hébert. 1944. 95 p. (Mf. Ecole de Bibl., U. de M.)

2:1045   **Hélène-de-la Présentation, sœur**

Bibliographie de la Croisade eucharistique (1949-1964) mouvement d' 'action catholique des enfants' (Pie XII) Préface du R.P. Blondin Dubé, s.j. Shawinigan-Sud, 1964. 109 p. (Ms. Ecole de Bibl., U.L.)

2:1046 **Hélène-de-Rome, soeur**
Bibliographie analytique de l'oeuvre du R.P. Jean Bousquet, o.p., précédée d'une biographie. Préface du R.P. Antonin Lamarche, o.p. Québec, 1964. 61 p. (Ms. Ecole de Bibl., U.L.)
Il en existe une édition limitée: Québec, 1964. 56, [2] f.

2:1047 **Hélène-Marguerite, soeur**
Bio-bibliographie: Mère Marie-Antoinette, soeur de Charité de la Providence. 1951. 26 p. (Ms. Ecole de Bibl., U. de M.)

2:1048 **Helwig, Margaret Jane**
J.M.S. Careless, historian; bibliography. [Toronto, 1964] vi, 11 *l.* (Ms. Toronto Univ. Libr. School)

2:1049 **Henderson, George Fletcher**
Federal royal commissions in Canada, 1867-1966; a checklist. [Toronto] University of Toronto Press [c1967] xvi, 212 p.

2:1050 **Herbert Read Archive**
A checklist of the Herbert Read Archive in the McPherson Library of the University of Victoria. [By] Howard Gerwing, with the assistance of Michael W. Pidgeon. [Victoria, B.C.] University of Victoria, 1969.
71 p. illus.
First published in *The Malahat review,* no. 9, Jan. 1969.
(see also 2:955)

2:1051 **Héroux, Jean**
Bibliographie analytique de l'oeuvre de Monsieur Omer Héroux, à l'exclusion des journaux, précédée d'une biographie. Québec, 1946. 77 p. (Ms. Ecole de Bibl., U. de M.)

2:1052 **Héroux, Lucie**
Essai de bio-bibliographie sur l'abbé Pierre Gravel, curé. 1954. v, 15 p. (Ms. Ecole de Bibl., U. de M.)

2:1053 **Héroux, Roch**
Bio-bibliographie de Mgr Charles-Philippe Choquette, p.d. Préface de M. Damien Jasmin. 1949. xx, 40 p. (Ms. Ecole de Bibl., U. de M.)

2:1054 **Herskowitz, Herbert**
A guide to reading in American history: the unit approach [by]

Herbert Herskowitz and Bernard Marlin. [Toronto] New American Library of Canada [1966]

2:1055 **Heung, Myra M.W.**
The economic relations between Canada and United States. 1964. vii, 6 1. (Ms. U. of O. Libr. School)

2:1056 **Higgins, Marion Villiers**
Canadian government publications; a manual for librarians ... With an introduction by Gerhard R. Lomer. Chicago, American Library Association, 1935. 4 p. *l.,* ix, 582 (i.e., 588) p.

2:1057 **Higgins, Ray Thomas**
Fox-farming on Prince Edward Island; an annotated bibliography. Toronto, 1962. 6 *l.* (Ms. Toronto Univ. Libr. School)

2:1058 **Hills, Theodore Lewis**
Caribbean topics; theses in Canadian university libraries, compiled by Theo L. Hills. [Montreal, Centre for Developing-Area Studies, McGill University] 1967.
11 *l.*

2:1059 **Hodge, Frederick Webb**
... Handbook of Indians of Canada. Published as an appendix to the *Tenth report of the Geographic Board of Canada* ... Ottawa, Parmalee, 1913. x, 632 p.
Reprinted by permission of Mr F.W. Hodge, ethnologist-in-charge, from *Handbook of American Indians north of Mexico,* published as Bulletin 30, Bureau of American ethnology.

2:1060 **Holmes, Marjorie C.**
Publications of the Government of British Columbia, 1871-1947. Being a complete revision and enlargement of Publications of the Government of British Columbia, 1871-1937, by Sydney Weston. [Victoria, B.C., King's Printer, 1950] 254 p.

2:1061 **Holmes, Marjorie C.**
Royal commissions and commissions of inquiry under the 'Public inquiries act' in British Columbia, 1872-1942; a checklist. [Victoria, B.C., King's Printer, 1945] 68 p.

2:1062 **Holmes, Maurice**
An introduction to the bibliography of Captain James Cook. London, Edwards, 1936. 59 p., 1 *l.*

2:1063 **Honey, Metta Edith**
Bibliography of periodical material on the writers of belles-lettres included in *A book of Canadian prose and verse* [by Edmund Kemper

Broadus and Eleanor Hammond Broadus] ... [Toronto] 1939. [8], 64 *l.* (Ms. Toronto Univ. Libr. School)

2:1064 **Horban, Petro**
Pottery and ceramics in Canada. 1962. [6] 8 1. (Ms. U. of O. Libr. School)

2:1065 **Horn, Betty Ann**
Bibliography of reference books on Canadian history, suitable for public libraries. Montreal, 1951. 6 *l.* (Ms. McGill Univ. Libr. School)

2:1066 **Horning, Lewis Emerson**
A bibliography of Canadian fiction (English) by Lewis Emerson Horning and Lawrence J. Burpee. Toronto, Printed for the Library, by William Briggs, 1904. 82 p. (Victoria University Library, Publication no. 2)

2:1067 **Horvath, Maria**
A Doukhobor bibliography, based on material available in the University of British Columbia Library. Vancouver, University of British Columbia, 1968
v. (University of British Columbia. Library. Reference publication no. 22)
To be completed in 2 pts.

2:1068 **Houde, Marguerite-A.**
Bio-bibliographie de Avila Bédard, sous-ministre des Terres et Forêts de Québec. Préface de J.-A. Breton. Québec, 1958. 205 p. (Ms. Ecole de Bibl., U.L.)

2:1069 **Houle, Alphonse**
Bibliographie de cinquante ouvrages traitant de l'adolescence. Québec, 1964. 217 p. (Ms. Ecole de Bibl., U.L.)

2:1070 **Houle, Blanche**
Bibliographie de Moïsette Olier. Préface d'Adrienne Choquette. 1946. 22 p. (Ms. Ecole de Bibl., U. de M.)

2:1071 **Houle, Gérard**
Inventaire chronologique des livres, brochures, journaux et revues imprimés au Canada pendant les années 1764 à 1820 et conservés aux archives du Collège Sainte-Marie. 1942. 47 p. (Ms. Ecole de Bibl., U. de M.)

2:1072 **Houle, Marcel**
Commission royale d'enquête (Commission Parent) 1966. v, 16 1. (Ms. U. of O. Libr. School)

2:1073 **Houle, Rosaire**
Bio-bibliographie du Cardinal Villeneuve. Québec, 1948. 72 p.
(Ms. Ecole de Bibl., U.L.)

2:1074 **Hruby, Georges-J.**
Bio-bibliographie de Dr Hans Selye, endocrinologue. Préface du Dr
Gaétan Jasmin. Montréal, 1956. x, 124 p. (Ms. Ecole de Bibl., U. de M.)

2:1075 **Huang, Ting-Young**
Canadian federal government publications 1935-1954. (An annotated
bibliography) Ottawa, University of Ottawa, Library School, 1955.
v, 8 p. (Ms. U. of O. Libr. School)

2:1076 **Huberdeau, Roger**
François-Joseph Cugnet, jurisconsulte canadien. Essai historique.
Saint-Rémi-de-Napierville, 1947. 115 p. (Mf. Ecole de Bibl., U. de M.)

2:1077 **Hubert-Marie, frère**
Notice bio-bibliographique sur le très cher Frère Célestin-Auguste
(Joseph Cavaleau). Préface du Frère Albert-Marie. 1954. xv, 109 p.
(Ms. Ecole de Bibl., U. de M.)

2:1078 **Hudson's Bay Company**
List of books relating to the Hudson's Bay Company. [Winnipeg?]
1935. 13 p.
A reprint of two articles which appeared originally in the *Beaver*.

2:1079 **Huet, François**
Le séparatisme au Québec, ses partisans et ses adversaires. 1967.
vi, 12 1. (Ms. U. of O. Libr. School)

2:1080 **Hughes, Margaret E.**
Books, pamphlets and documents relating to the history of the
County of Lambton, Ontario. [Toronto, 1934] [2], 11 *l*. (Ms.
Toronto Univ. Libr. School)

2:1081 **Hugolin, père**
Bibliographie antonienne; ou, Nomenclature des ouvrages, livres,
revues, brochures, feuilles, etc., sur la dévotion à S. Antoine de
Padoue, publiés dans la province de Québec de 1777 à 1909. Québec,
L'Evénement, 1910. 76 p.
Supplément jusqu'à l'année 1931. Montréal, 1932. 35 p.

2:1082 **Hugolin, père**
Bibliographie des ouvrages concernant la tempérance; livres, brochures,
journaux, revues, feuilles, cartes, etc., imprimés à Québec et à Lévis

depuis l'établissement de l'imprimerie (1764) jusqu'à 1910. Québec,
L'Evénement, 1910. 2 f., 7-165 p.

2:1083 **Hugolin, père**
Bibliographie du R.P. Hugolin. Montréal [Imprimerie des franciscains],
1932. 3 *l.*, [9]-50 p., 1 *l.*

2:1084 **Hugolin, père**
Bibliographie du R.P. Joachim-Joseph Monfette, o.f.m. Québec,
Imprimerie franciscaine missionnaire, 1931. 3 *l.*, [9]-42 p.

2:1085 **Hugolin, père**
Bibliographie du Tiers-Ordre séculier de Saint-François au Canada
(province de Québec). Montréal, Ménard, 1921. 149 p.
Supplément pour les années 1921 à 1931. Montréal Impr. franciscaine
missionnaire. 1932. 46 p.
Supplément pour les années 1931 à 1940, *voir* Guilbert, Honoré, o.f.m.

2:1086 **Hugolin, père**
Bibliographie et inconographie du serviteur de Dieu, le R.P. Frédéric
Jansoone [de Ghyvelde] o.f.m. (1838-1916). Québec, Imprimerie
franciscaine missionnaire, 1932. 62 p.

2:1087 **Hugolin, père**
... Bibliographie franciscaine; inventaire des revues, livres brochures
et autres écrits publiés par les franciscains du Canada de 1890 à 1915.
Québec, Imprimerie franciscaine missionnaire, 1916. 3 f., [9]-141 p.,
1 f.
Supplément jusqu'à l'année 1931. Québec, Imprimerie franciscaine missionnaire,
1932. 214 p.

2:1088 **Hugolin, père**
Bio-bibliographie du R.P. Ephrem Longpré, o.f.m. Québec, Imprimerie
franciscaine missionnaire, 1931. 40 p.

2:1089 **Hugolin, père**
Les Franciscains et la croisade antialcoolique dans la province de
Québec (Canada). Aperçu sommaire de leurs travaux. Montréal, 1915.
29 p.

2:1090 **Hugolin, père**
Inventaire des travaux, brochures et autres récits concernant la
tempérance, publiés par les Pères franciscains du Canada de 1906
à 1914. Montréal, 1915. 50 p.

2:1091 **Hugolin, père**
Notes bibliographiques pour servir à l'histoire des Récollects du
Canada ... Montréal [Imp. des Franciscains] 1932-36. 6 v.

2:1092  **Hunt, Norah F.**
Bibliography of Toronto newspapers. [Toronto, 1933] [13] *l.* (Ms.
Toronto Univ. Libr. School)

2:1093  **Hutchinson, Joan R.**
Bibliography of John Strachan, bp. of Toronto, 1778-1867.
[Toronto, 1933] [14] *l.* (Ms. Toronto Univ. Libr. School)

2:1094  **Imelda-des-Anges, soeur**
Notes autobio-bibliographiques: Noëlla Dionne (Soeur Imelda-des-
Anges, f.c.s.c.j.). 1953. 55 p. (Ms. Ecole de Bibl., U. de M.)

2:1095  **Index to Canadian legal periodical literature** 1963/65—
[Montreal] Canadian Association of Law Libraries
v. semi-annual.
Biennial 1963/65; annual 1966.
Final volume of each year cumulates and supersedes the first volume.
Editor: Marianne F. Scott.

2:1096  **Index to Canadian legal periodical literature.** 1963-65
[Montreal] Canadian Association of Law Libraries [c1966]
xxviii, 316 p.
Editor: Marianne Scott.

2:1097  **Informations bibliographiques et documentaires en science politique**
no 1; mai 1963. Montréal, Centre de documentation et de recherches
politiques, Collège Jean-de-Brébeuf, 1963.
14 f. irrégulier.

2:1098  **Inkel, Marcel**
Dominion-provincial relations in Canada; an annotated bibliography.
Ottawa, University of Ottawa, Library School, 1956. 18 p. (Ms.
U. of O. Libr. School)

2:1099  **Inkster, Jane-Claire**
Humor in Canada; bibliography of books published 1947-1963
(English) [Toronto] 1966. 23 *l.* (Ms. Toronto Univ. Libr. School)

2:1100  **Institut canadien d'éducation des adultes**
Documentation concernant l'unité canadienne ... [Montréal, Institut
canadien d'éducation des adultes; Toronto, Canadian Association for
Adult Education; Ottawa, Conseil canadien du civisme, 1964] [9] f.

2:1101  **Institut canadien d'éducation des adultes**
La recherche en éducation des adultes au Canada; un inventaire bibliographique. Non-degree-research in adult education in Canada, 1967-
1968; an annotated bibliography. Montréal, Institut canadien

d'éducation des adultes; Toronto, Canadian Association for Adult Education, Dept. of Adult Education, Ontario Institute for Studies in Education, 1968.

76 *l.*

2:1102 **Institut canadien d'outre-mer**
... Bibliographie sur l'aide canadienne aux pays en voie d'expansion. Ottawa, 1964. 8 p.

2:1103 **Institut Vanier de la famille**
An inventory of family research and studies in Canada (1963-1967). Un inventaire des recherches et des études sur la famille au Canada. Ottawa, 1967.

xiv, 161 p.

2:1104 **International congresses and conferences, 1840-1937**; a union list of their publications available in libraries of the United States and Canada. Edited by Winifred Gregory under the auspices of the Bibliographical Society of America. New York, 1938. [New York] Kraus Reprint Corp., 1967.

229 p.
First published New York, H.W. Wilson, 1938.

2:1105 **International Geographical Union.** Commission on Humid Tropics
A select annotated bibliography of the humid tropics. Une bibliographie choisie et annotée des régions tropicales humides. Compiled by Theo L. Hills. Montreal, Geography Dept., McGill University, 1960.

xiii, 238 p.

2:1106 **Iphigenia, soeur**
Bio-bibliographie de l'auteur de 'La foi en l'amour de Dieu.' 1947. 19 p. (Ms. Ecole de Bibl., U. de M.)

2:1107 **Isaak, David**
The Mennonites in Manitoba; an annotated bibliography based on books and periodicals found in the University of Toronto and Toronto Public Libraries. Toronto, 1963. [ii], 8 *l.* (Ms. Toronto Univ. Libr. School)

2:1108 **Isabelle, Lucile**
Essai de bio-bibliographie sur André Langevin. 1952. 57 p. (Mf. Ecole de Bibl., U. de M.)

2:1109 **Isbester, A.F.**
Industrial and labour relations in Canada; a selected bibliography, by A.F. Isbester, D. Coates [and C.B. Williams. Kingston, Ont., Queen's

University, Industrial Relations Centre, 1965. 5 p. *l.*, 100 p.
(Bibliography series, no. 2)

2:1110   **Isidore-Jean, frère**
L'œuvre pédagogique des Frères de l'Instruction chrétienne dans la
province de Québec, 1886-1953. Essai de bibliographie. Préface de
M.J.P. Labarre. 1955. xxii, 203 p. (Ms. Ecole de Bibl., U. de M.)

2:1111   **Jack, David Russell**
Acadian magazines. Ottawa, Hope, 1903. 173-203 p.
Reprinted from *Transactions of the Royal Society of Canada,* 2d series, 1903-
1904, v. IX, sec. II.

2:1112   **Jackson, Grace**
Bibliography of the tradition and folk-lore of the North American
Eskimo. Montreal, 1932. [11] *l.* (Ms. McGill Univ. Libr. School)

2:1113   **Jacques, Colette**
Bio-bibliographie de Jean-Charles Bonenfant. Québec, 1954. 159 p.
28 cm. (Ms. Ecole de Bibl., U.L.)

2:1114   **Jacques, Marthe**
Bibliographie analytique de l'œuvre de Antoine Goulet, de la Société
des poètes. Préface de M. Roger Brien. Québec, 1961. 37 p. (Ms.
Ecole de Bibl., U.L.)

2:1115   **Jacques, Mme Paul**
Bio-bibliographie de Olivette Lamontagne. Québec, 1957. 53 p.
(Ms. Ecole de Bibl., U.L.)

2:1116   **Jain, Sushil Kumar**
A classified guide to Canadian biographical sources. Windsor, Ont.,
1967.
[17] *l.*

2:1117   **Jain, Sushil Kumar**
French-Canadian literature in English translation; a short list compiled
from the library catalogues of the Regina Campus Library. Regina,
Regina Campus Library, Univ. of Saskatchewan, 1965. 9, [1] *l.*

2:1118   **Jain, Sushil Kumar**
Indian literature in English; a bibliography, being a checklist of works
of poetry, drama, fiction, autobiography and letters written by
Indians in English or translated from modern Indian languages into
English. Regina, Regina Campus Library, Univ. of Saskatchewan,
1965-67.
v.

2:1119  **Jain, Sushil Kumar**
Louis 'David' Riel & the North-West Rebellion; a list of references.
Regina, Regina Campus Library, Univ. of Saskatchewan, 1965. 19 *l.*

2:1120  **Jain, Sushil Kumar**
Poetry in Saskatchewan; a bibliography. Regina, Regina Campus
Library, University of Saskatchewan, 1965. 10 *l.*

2:1121  **James, Charles Canniff**
Bibliography of Canadian poetry (English). Toronto, Printed for the
Library by William Briggs, 1899. 71 p. (Victoria University Library,
Publication no. 1)

2:1122  **Jamieson, Edna Mary**
Camborne history; bibliography of materials, 1865-1965. [Toronto]
1965. 15 *l.* (Ms. Toronto Univ. Libr. School)

2:1123  **Jaraith, Juanita S.**
Canadian Flag. 1965. iv, 8 1. (Ms. U. of O. Libr. School)

2:1124  **Jarkiewicz, Bozena**
History and development of professional library training in Canada.
1966. vi, 9 1. (Ms. U. of O. Libr. School)

2:1125  **Jarry, Georgette**
Notes bio-bibliographiques sur Monsieur Jules-Paul Tardivel. 1951.
84 p. (Mf. Ecole de Bibl., U. de M.)

2:1126  **Jarvi, Edith T.**
Guide to basic reference books rev. ed. Canadian libraries, edited by
Edith T. Jarvi. [Toronto] University of Toronto, School of Library
Science, 1968.
viii, 235 p.
First ed.: Toronto, 1967.
3rd ed. 1970.

2:1127  **Jasmin, Denise**
Notes bio-bibliographiques sur Madame Michèle [!] Le Normand.
1947. 10 p. (Ms. Ecole de Bibl., U. de M.)

2:1128  **Jasmin, Laurette**
Notes bio-bibliographiques du Rév. Père Bernardin Verville, o.f.m.
1952. 28 p. (Ms. Ecole de Bibl., U. de M.)

2:1129  **Jeanne de l'Assomption, sœur**
Notice de bio-bibliographie [Joffre Proulx] [Montréal] 1953. 50 p.
(Ms. Ecole de Bibl., U. de M.)

2:1130   **Jeanne-Mance-Mercier, soeur**
Bibliographie analytique de l'œuvre de Béatrice Clément. Préface
de M. Jean-Charles Bonenfant. Québec, 1961. 172 p. (Ms. Ecole de
Bibl., U.L.)

2:1131   **Jobin, Françoise**
Essai de bio-bibliographie de Michel Brûlé. Montréal, 1961. xv, 22 p.
(Ms. Ecole de Bibl., U. de M.)

2:1132   **Johnsen, Julia E.**
... St Lawrence River ship canal. Briefs, references and reprints of
selected articles on both sides of the question. New York, Wilson
[1922]. 74 p. (The Reference shelf ... v. 1, no. 3)
'Bibliography': p. [8]-17.

2:1133   **Johnson, Marguerite**
Bio-bibliographie de Monsieur Clément Marchand. Préface de Raymond
Douville. Trois-Rivières, 1946. 93 p. (Mf. Ecole de Bibl., U. de M.)

2:1134   **Johnston, Isabel M.**
Bibliography of books and papers published by Adam Shortt.
[Toronto, 1933] [2], 8 *l*. (Ms. Toronto Univ. Libr. School)

2:1135   **Johnston, Joan Lillian**
The distribution of prehistoric Indian mounds and earthworks in
southern Ontario, and the excavation of the southwold earthworks
and the serpent mounds. [Toronto] 1962. 10 *l*. (Ms. Toronto Univ.
Libr. School)

2:1136   **Johnston, Marian B.**
Canada in Lord Durham's time; a bibliography. Toronto, 1930. [2],
26 *l*. (Ms. Toronto Univ. Libr. School)

2:1137   **Johnston, Viola M.**
Bibliography of one-act plays by Canadian authors. Montreal, 1932.
12 *l*. (Ms. McGill Univ. Libr. School)

2:1138   **Joliceur, Louis-Philippe**
Essai de bibliographie des Rédemptoristes de la province canadienne
de Sainte-Anne-de-Beaupré. 1878-1951. vii, 96 p. (Ms. Ecole de Bibl.,
U. de M.)

2:1139   **Joly, Monique**
Bio-bibliographie analytique de l'œuvre de Marcel Clément. Préf. de
M. Maurice Lebel. Québec, 1950. 74 p. (Ms. Ecole de Bibl., U.L.)

2:1140  **Jones, Marian Laybourne**
David Thompson in Canada. Toronto, 1966. 22 *l.* (Ms. Toronto Univ. Libr. School)

2:1141  **Joseph-Marie, sœur**
Bibliographie analytique de l'œuvre de l'abbé Anselme Longpré (1927-1947), précédée d'une biographie. St-Hyacinthe, 1963. 91 p. (Ms. Ecole de Bibl., U.L.)

2:1142  **Juchereau-Duchesnay, Marguerite**
Bio-bibliographie de monsieur Jean Vallerand, B.A., licencié ès lettres, diplômé de l'Université de Montréal. Québec, 1953.

2:1143  **Judd, William Wallace**
A bibliography of the natural history of Hamilton to the year 1950. [Hamilton, Ont.] Hamilton Naturalists' Club, 1960. 27 p.
Supplement to the *Wood duck,* v. 13, no. 5, Jan. 1960.

2:1144  **Judd, William Wallace**
Catalogues of columns on natural history, by W.E. Saunders and J.K. Reynolds, in London (Ontario) newspapers, 1929-1963 [compiled] by William W. Judd. [London, Ont., Lawson Memorial Library, University of Western Ontario, 1969]
69 p. (*Western Ontario history nuggets, no. 35*)
Columns appeared in the *London free press* and its earlier title the *London advertiser.*

2:1145  **Julien, Marie-Antoinette**
Bio-bibliographie du R.P. Alexandre Dugrés, s.j. 1942. 47 p. (Ms. Ecole de Bibl., U. de M.)

2:1146  **Julienne-de-l'Eucharistie, sœur**
Bio-bibliographie du R.P. Henri-Marie Guindon, s.m.m. [1958] [xxv], 126 p. (Ms. Ecole de Bibl., U. de M.)

2:1147  **Kain, Samuel K.**
Bibliography of scientific publications relating to the province of New Brunswick other than those contained in the bulletins of the Society, 1890-1895. (In *Bulletin of the natural history society of New Brunswick,* no. XIII, 1896 [i.e., 1895] p. 96-100)

2:1148  **Kaller, Elizabeth Genevieve**
T.C. Douglas; a bibliography of his speeches and writings accessible in Central Toronto. [Toronto] 1966. 20 *l.* (Ms. Toronto Univ. Libr. School)

2:1149  **Kallmann, Helmut**
A checklist of Canadian periodicals in the field of music. (In
*Canadian music journal,* winter 1957, p. 30-36.)

2:1150  **Karch, Gertrude**
Monseigneur Olivier Maurault, p.s.s.; essai bibliographique. 1937-38.
[95] p. (Mf. Ecole de Bibl., U. de M.)

2:1151  **Katz, Joseph**
A selected list of readings on international understanding for curriculum workers. Prepared for the Phi Delta Kappa Commission on International Relations in Education by Joseph Katz with the assistance
of William B. Johnson and the Summer Session, Comparative Education Class. Bloomington, Ind., Phi Delta Kappa International [1964]
49 p.

2:1152  **Kenney, James Francis**
The sources for the early history of Ireland: ecclesiastical; an introduction and guide, by James F. Kenney. New York, Octagon Books,
1966.
xviii, 815 p. fold. map. (Records of civilization; sources and studies, no. 11)

2:1153  **Kent, Doris M.**
Bibliography of books relating to the history of Kingston. Toronto,
1933. [3] , 18 *l.* (Ms. Toronto Univ. Libr. School)

2:1154  **Kerr, Lillian B.**
Bibliography of geology, coal, oil, natural gas and industrial minerals
in the post-Cambrian region of southern Manitoba to 1945. Winnipeg,
King's Printer, 1949. 25 p.

2:1155  **Kerr, W.B.**
Historical literature on Canada's participation in the Great War.
Reprinted from the *Canadian historical review,* Dec. 1933. [N.p.,
1933] 412-436 p. 26 cm.
Supplementary list of historical literature relating to Canada's part in the Great
War. Reprinted from the *Canadian historical review,* June 1934. [N.p., 1934]
[181]-190 p.
Canada's part in the Great War. Reprinted from the *Canadian historical review,*
Sept. 1935. [N.p., 1935] 364-366 p.

2:1156  **Keyes, Charles Rollin**
... A bibliography of North American paleontology, 1888-1892.
Washington, G.P.O., 1894. 251 p. (U.S. Geological Survey. Bulletin
no. 121)

2:1157  **Kingsford, William**
The early bibliography of the province of Ontario, Dominion of
Canada, with other information. A supplemental chapter of Canadian
archaeology. Toronto, Rowsell & Hutchison, 1892. 140 p.
Arranged chronologically. A bibliography of pamphlets, books, etc., from
1783-1840, fully annotated.

2:1158  **Kingston. Queen's University.** Douglas Library
Canadiana 1698-1900 in the possession of the Douglas Library,
Queen's University, Kingston, Ontario ... Kingston, 1932. ii, 86 p.
Compiled by Janet S. Porteous.

2:1159  **Kingston. Queen's University.** Douglas Library
A catalogue of Canadian manuscripts collected by Lorne Pierce, and
presented to Queen's University. Toronto, Ryerson, 1946. xii, 164 p.
'Compiled by D. Harlowe, and edited and introduced by E.C. Kyte.'

2:1160  **Kingston. Queen's University.** Douglas Library. Buchan Collection
A checklist of works by and about John Buchan in the John Buchan
Collection, Queen's University. [Compiled by B.C. Wilmot] Kingston,
1958. iii, 31 *l.*
Revised, augmented and indexed edition: Boston, Hall, 1961. 38, 24 p.

2:1161  **Klein, Suzanne**
Essai de bio-bibliographie de Gérard Pelletier, journaliste. Préface par
Pierre Juneau. [Montréal] 1959. xii, 79 p. (Ms. Ecole de Bibl., U. de M.)

2:1162  **Klinck, Carl F.**
Canadian literature: theses in preparation (ed.), The University of
Western Ontario, London, Vols. 1-11. (1959-1967), 1960-1970.

2:1163  **Klinck, Carl F.**
Canadian literature in English: a select reading list. In *The association
for commonwealth literature and language studies.* Bulletin No. 4,
1967 (Leeds, University of Leeds, 1968) 32 p.

2:1164  **Klinck, Carl F.**
Wilfred Campbell, a bibliography. 1943. 32 p.

2:1165  **Klinck, George Alfred**
Bibliographie, Louis Fréchette, prosateur. [S.l.n.d.] [132]-146 p.
Extrait de la *Revue d'histoire de l'Amérique française,* juin 1953.

2:1166  **Knill, William Douglas**
A classification of theses in education completed at the University of

Alberta, 1929-1966 [compiled by] Wm. D. Knill [and others] 3d rev.
ed. [Edmonton, 1967]

iv, 67 p.
First ed. 1964; rev. ed. 1965.

2:1167 **Knox, John**
An historical journal of the campaigns in North America for the
years 1757, 1758, 1759, and 1760 ... edited ... by Arthur G. Doughty
... Toronto, The Champlain Society, 1916. 3 v.
Bibliography, in Appendix, v. 3, p. 423-456.

2:1168 **Knox, Vera Huntingdon**
Public finance: information sources. Pref. by C. Lowell Harriss.
Detroit, Gale Research Co. [c1964]
142 p. (Management information guide, no. 3)

2:1169 **Koester, Charles B.**
A bibliography of selected theses in the library of the University of
Alberta (Edmonton) relating to western Canada, 1915-1965, com-
piled for Western Canada Research Project by C.B. Koester.
Edmonton, 1965.
21 *l.*

2:1170 **Kohli, Dev**
Library education in Canada for the period 1955-1966. 1967.
[iv] 6 1. (Ms. U. of O. Libr. School)

2:1171 **Kolesnyk, Petro**
Library schools in Canada, 1938-1961. 1962. iv, 6 1. (Ms. U. of O.
Libr. School)

2:1172 **Kuehl, Warren Frederick**
Dissertations in history; an index to dissertations completed in history
departments of United States and Canadian universities, 1873-1960.
[Lexington] University of Kentucky Press, 1965.
xi, 249 p.

2:1173 **Kula, Sam**
Bibliography of film librarianship. [London] Library Association
[1967]
68 p. (Library Association. Bibliographies, no. 8)

2:1174 **Kupsch, Walter Oscar**
Annotated bibliography of Saskatchewan geology 1823-1951 (incl.).
Regina [Queen's Printer] , 1952. 106 p. (Geological Survey, Report
no. 9)

2:1175 **Kwan, Bernard**
Growth of population in Canada since her discovery. 1963. v, 6 1.
(Ms. U. of O. Libr. School)

2:1176 **Labbé, Edith**
Bibliographie analytique de l'œuvre de l'abbé Honorius Provost,
archiviste à l'Université Laval, précédée d'une biographie. Préface de
Mgr P.-E. Gosselin. Québec, 1962. 49 p. (Ms. Ecole de Bibl., U.L.)

2:1177 **Labelle, Jean-Paul**
Bio-bibliographie de Henri d'Arles [abbé Henri Beaudé]. [s.d.] 23 p.
(Mf. Ecole de Bibl., U. de M.)

2:1178 **Labelle, Juliette**
Essai de bio-bibliographie de l'abbé Paul Lachapelle. 1949. vi, 13 p.
(Ms. Ecole de Bibl., U. de M.)

2:1179 **Labelle, Pierre**
Notes bio-bibliographiques sur le frère Marie-Victorin (Conrad
Kirouac). 1952. 96 p. (Mf. Ecole de Bibl., U. de M.)

2:1180 **Laberge, Raymond-Marie**
Bibliographie analytique de M. C.-J. Magnan (1865-1942). Préf. de
M. J.-Chs Magnan. Québec, 1953. 73 p. (Ms. Ecole de Bibl., U.L.)

2:1181 **Labrecque, Hélène**
Essai de bio-bibliographie sur la personne et l'œuvre de Robert
Choquette. 1939. xvii p. (Mf. Ecole de Bibl., U. de M.)

2:1182 **Labrie, Hilda**
Bio-bibliographie de Mgr Elias Roy. Québec, 1954. 37 p. (Ms. Ecole
de Bibl., U.L.)

2:1183 **Labrie, Jean-Marc**
Bibliographie analytique des écrits de Jean Hubert, journaliste,
précédée d'une biographie. Préface de Alfred Rouleau. Lévis, 1964.
327 p. (Ms. Ecole de Bibl., U.L.)

2:1184 **Labrie, R.**
Notes bio-bibliographiques sur Mgr Louis-Adolphe Paquet. 1947. 7 p.
(Ms. Ecole de Bibl., U. de M.)

2:1185 **Lachance, Andrée**
Essai de bio-bibliographie sujet: Les Oblats Missionnaires de Marie
Immaculée. Montréal, 1961. xiii, 42 p. (Ms. Ecole de Bibl., U. de M.)

2:1186  **Lachs, John**
Marxist philosophy; a bibliographical guide. Chapel Hill, University
of North Carolina Press [c1967]
xiv, 166 p.

2:1187  **Lacourcière, Luc**
Bibliographie raisonnée des traditions populaires françaises
d'Amérique. (*En cours de publication.* Comprendra 2 vol.)
Déjà paru: *Bibliographie raisonnée de l'anthroponymie canadienne.*

2:1188  **Lacoursière, Mme M.-A.**
Bio-bibliographie de M. l'abbé Joseph-Fidèle Raîche. Préface de Mgr
Patrick J. Nicholson et de l'hon. J.-A. Brillant. 1946. xv, 28 p. (Mf.
Ecole de Bibl., U. de M.)

2:1189  **Lacroix, Céline**
Bio-bibliographie analytique de Joseph Risi, professeur à Laval.
Préface de Lucien Montreuil. Québec, 1959. 41 p. (Ms. Ecole de
Bibl., U.L.)

2:1190  **Lacroix, Denise**
Les activités et les publications du Centre canadien des Cercles
Lacordaire et Sainte-Jeanne-d'Arc depuis sa fondation en décembre
1939. Québec, 1953. 45 p. (Ms. Ecole de Bibl., U.L.)

2:1191  **Lacroix, Francine**
Bio-bibliographie de Jean Charbonneau. Préface de M. Jean-Marie
Nadeau. 1943. viii, 72 p. (Mf. Ecole de Bibl., U. de M.)

2:1192  **Lacroix, Jacqueline**
Bio-bibliographie de Benoît Brouillette. Lettre-préface de M. Paul
Riou. 1943. viii, 61 p. (Ms. Ecole de Bibl., U. de M.)

2:1193  **Laflamme, Claire**
Bibliographie analytique de la littérature musicale canadienne-française.
Préf. de M. Henri Gagnon. Québec, 1950. 75 p. (Ms. Ecole de Bibl.,
U.L.)

2:1194  **Laforest, Marthe**
Bibliographie analytique de l'œuvre de Marcel Dubé, précédée d'une
autobiographie. Préface de Louis-Georges Carrier. Montréal, 1964.
135 p. (Ms. Ecole de Bibl., U.L.)

2:1195  **Laforte, Conrad**
Le catalogue de la chanson folklorique française. Préf. de Luc
Lacourcière. Québec, Presses universitaires Laval, 1958. [1], xxix,
397 p. (*Publications des archives de folklore, Université Laval*)

2:1196   **Laforte, Conrad**
Essai de bio-bibliographie de Mgr Joseph-Victor-Alphonse Huard, p.d.
1949. vii, 295 p. (Ms. Ecole de Bibl., U. de M.)

2:1197   **Lafortune, François**
Bio-bibliographie de M. Napoléon Lafortune, journaliste. Préface de
M. Léo-Paul Desrosiers. 1944. 66 p. (Mf. Ecole de Bibl., U. de M.)

2:1198   **Lafrance, Lucie**
Bio-bibliographie de M. Honoré Beaugrand, 1849-1906. Préface de
Me Victor Morin. 1948. 67 p. (Mf. Ecole de Bibl., U. de M.)

2:1199   **Lafresnière, Cécile-G.**
Essai bibliographique de l'auteur canadien-français Harry Bernard.
1938. 10 p. (Mf. Ecole de Bibl., U. de M.)

2:1200   **Laird, Edith M.**
Conservation and wildlife: bibliography, edited by Edith M. Laird.
Coconut Grove, Fla., Field Research Projects, 1967–
v. (Man and nature series)
Vols. 1 and 2 issued as *Natural area studies*, no. 3-4.

2:1201   **Lakhanpal, Sarv Krishna**
Indian women: a bibliography. Saskatoon, University of Saskatchewan,
1967.
ii, 14 *l.* (Bibliography publication no. 2)

2:1202   **Laki, Georgette**
Bibliographie analytique de l'œuvre de Bruno Lafleur, préc. d'une
notice biographique. Préf. de J.-Ch. Bonenfant. 1964. xv, 70(1) p.
(Ms. Ecole de Bibl., U.L.)

2:1203   **Lalande, Louise**
Le Séparatisme au Québec. 1967. [ii] 7 1. (Ms. U. of O. Libr. School)

2:1204   **Laliberté, Francine**
L'Office national du film. 1967. 17 1. (Ms. U. of O. Libr. School)

2:1205   **Lalime, Hélène**
Notes bio-bibliographiques de l'abbé Elie-Joseph Auclair. 1946. 13 p.
(Ms. Ecole de Bibl., U. de M.)

2:1206   **Lalonde, Emile**
Bio-bibliographie analytique de monseigneur Antoine D'Eschambault,
p.d., diocèse de Saint-Boniface, Manitoba. Préface par le R.P. Lucien
Hardy, s.j. Saint-Boniface, Collège de Saint-Boniface, 1962. xi, 104 f.
portr.

2:1207 **Lalonde, Monique**
Bio-bibliographie de Monsieur Casimir Hébert. 1948. iii, 11 p. (Mf.
Ecole de Bibl., U. de M.)

2:1208 **Lamarche, Hermance**
Notes bio-bibliographiques sur le Dr Auguste Panneton. 1947.
[10] p. (Ms. Ecole de Bibl., U. de M.)

2:1209 **Lamarre, Françoise**
Monsieur Wilfrid Lemoine; essai de bio-bibliographie. 1953. 15 p.
(Mf. Ecole de Bibl., U. de M.)

2:1210 **Lamb, Barbara Elizabeth**
Selkirk's Red River Colony as a cause of the collapse of the North-
West Company; a bibliography. [Toronto] 1964. 12 *l.* (Ms. Toronto
Univ. Libr. School)

2:1211 **Lamonde, Francine (Neilson)**
Répertoire bibliographique des documents du Bureau d'aménagement
de l'est du Québec. Québec, Conseil d'orientation économique,
Bureau d'étude en aménagement régional, 1968.
ii, 118 p. (Planification du développement régional. Série 1: Inventaire et
méthodologie. Cahier 1/5)

2:1212 **Lamontagne, Léopold**
Arthur Buies, homme de lettres. Québec, Presses universitaires Laval,
1957. 258 p. fac-sim.
Bibliographie: p. [251]-254.

2:1213 **Lamontagne, Onésime**
Bibliographies spéciales du Monastère franciscain de Québec. 1941.
[39] p. (Ms. Ecole de Bibl., U. de M.)

2:1214 **Lamothe, Elisabeth**
Bibliographie de l'œuvre de Sir Thomas Chapais précédée de notes
biographiques. 1940. 45 p. (Ms. Ecole de Bibl., U. de M.)

2:1215 **Lamy, Françoise**
Essai de bio-bibliographie de Blandine Neault. [Montréal] 1960.
xii, 97 p. (Ms. Ecole de Bibl., U. de M.)

2:1216 **Lamy, Gabrielle**
Essai de bio-bibliographie sur Juliette Chabot. 1949. v, 12 p. (Ms.
Ecole de Bibl., U. de M.)

2:1217 **Lanctot, Gustave**
François Xavier Garneau. Toronto, Ryerson [1926?]. 197 p.
(Makers of Canadian literature ...)
Bibliographie: p. 177-185.

2:1218 **Lanctot, Gustave**
L'œuvre de la France en Amérique du Nord; bibliographie sélective et critique. Montréal, Fides, 1951. 185 p.

2:1219 **Land, R. Brian**
City and trade directories published in Canada. [N.p., 1958] 5 p.
Reprinted from *Canadian business*, v. 31, April 1958, p. 32.

2:1220 **Land, R. Brian**
Directory of publications issued by Canadian financial and investment houses. [N.p., 1958] 8 p.
Reprinted from *Canadian business*, v. 31, Sept. 1958, p. 102.

2:1221 **Land, R. Brian**
Directory of publications issued periodically by chambers of commerce and boards of trade in Canada. (In *Canadian business*, v. 31, Nov. 1958, p. 82.)

2:1222 **Land, R. Brian**
Labor publications distributed in Canada. (In *Canadian business*, v. 31, June 1958, p. 40.)

2:1223 **Landormy, Lucette**
Essai de bio-bibliographie de M. Réginald Boisvert. Montréal, 1957. 35 p. (Ms. Ecole de Bibl., U. de M.)

2:1224 **Langevin, Herménégilde**
Bio-bibliographie du R.P. Valentin-M. Breton, o.f.m. [s.d.] 28 p. (Mf. Ecole de Bibl., U. de M.)

2:1225 **Langlais, Jacques**
Bio-bibliographie analytique de Régis Roy. Préface de Marie-Claire Daveluy. 1947. iv, 106 p. (Mf. Ecole de Bibl., U. de M.)

2:1226 **Langlois, Laurette**
Bio-bibliographie du R.F. Antoine Bernard, c.s.v., professeur à l'Université de Montréal. Préface du R.P. Alphonse de Grandpré, c.s.v. 1945. 172 p. (Mf. Ecole de Bibl., U. de M.)

2:1227 **Lanoue, Yvonne**
Les Bibliothèques régionales au Canada. 1967. v, 9 l. (Ms. U. of O. Libr. School)

2:1228 **Lanthier, Réal**
Essai de bio-bibliographie: M. Jean Delorme. 1952. 22 p. (Ms. Ecole de Bibl., U. de M.)

2:1229 **Laperrière, Lucienne**
Bio-bibliographie de Joseph Quesnel. Préface de M. Eugène Lapierre.
1943. 43 p. (Mf. Ecole de Bibl., U. de M.)

2:1230 **Lapierre, Juliette**
Notes bio-bibliographiques sur Jules Fournier, journaliste. 1948. 8 p.
(Mf. Ecole de Bibl., U. de M.)

2:1231 **Lapointe, Irène**
Bio-bibliographie de Gédéon Boucher, ex-professeur au Collège de
l'Assomption. 1948. 13 p. (Mf. Ecole de Bibl., U. de M.)

2:1232 **Lapointe, Madeleine**
Bio-bibliographie analytique de l'œuvre de Charles-Marie Boissonnault
(1950-1959). Préface de Francis Desroches. Québec, 1959. 45 p.
(Ms. Ecole de Bibl., U.L.)

2:1233 **Laporte, Suzanne**
Notes bio-bibliographiques sur Monsieur Adolphe Nantel. Préf. de
M. Pierre Laporte. 1952. 18 p. (Mf. Ecole de Bibl., U. de M.)

2:1234 **Laquerre, Françoise**
Essai de bio-bibliographie du Dr J.-Henri Charbonneau. Montréal,
1960. iv, 241 p. (Ms. Ecole de Bibl., U. de M.)

2:1235 **Lardy, Moïsette**
Essai de bio-bibliographie de Guy Boulizon, 1946-1960. Montréal,
1961. vii, 131 p. (Ms. Ecole de Bibl., U. de M.)

2:1236 **Larned, Josephus Nelson**
The literature of American history; a bibliographical guide. Boston,
Houghton, 1902. 588 p. (American Library Association Annotated
list.)
Pt. 5, Canada, p. 395-440.

2:1237 **Laroche, Médard**
Notes bio-bibliographiques sur le R.P. Lorenzo Gauthier, c.s.v. 1947.
13 p. (Ms. Ecole de Bibl., U. de M.)

2:1238 **Laroche, Thérèse**
Bibliographie de M. Claude Aubry, conservateur adjoint à la
Bibliothèque publique d'Ottawa. 1949. v, 10 p. (Mf. Ecole de Bibl.,
U. de M.)

2:1239 **Laroque, Lédéanne**
Notes bio-bibliographiques sur Hélène Grenier. 1953. vi, 73 p.
(Ms. Ecole de Bibl., U. de M.)

2:1240 **Larose, Lucille**
Notes bio-bibliographiques sur Monsieur Georges Bouchard, député fédéral, professeur d'agriculture. 1949. 10 p. (Mf. Ecole de Bibl., U. de M.)

2:1241 **Larrivée, Micheline**
Bibliographie de M. Richard Joly (début à 1954) précédée d'une biographie. Préface de M. Eddy Slater. Québec, 1964. 46 p. (Ms. Ecole de Bibl., U.L.)

2:1242 **Larrivée, Pierrette**
Bibliographie de M. Richard Joly (1955-1963) précédée d'une biographie. Préface de M. l'abbé Roch Duval. Québec, 1964. 59 p. (Ms. Ecole de Bibl., U.L.)

2:1243 **Larue, Roger**
Robert Charbonneau; bio-bibliographie. 1945. 35 p. (Mf. Ecole de Bibl., U. de M.)

2:1244 **Lasnier, Rina**
Bio-bibliographie de Victor Barbeau. 1940. 94 p. (Ms. Ecole de Bibl., U. de M.)

2:1245 **Latourelle, René**
Etude sur les écrits de saint Jean de Brébeuf. Préf. de Guy Frégault. Montréal, Editions de l'Immaculée-Conception, 1952-53. 2 v. (*Studia Collegii maximi Immaculatæ Conceptionis, 9-10*)
Bibliographie: v. 1., p. [v]-xv.

2:1246 **Latulippe, Louise**
Bibliographie analytique de l'œuvre du révérend Frère Clément Lockquell, é.c. Québec, 1952. 110 p. (Ms. Ecole de Bibl., U.L.)

2:1247 **Laure-de-l'Euchariste, sœur**
Bio-bibliographie de M. l'abbé Georges-Emile Gervais. Lettre-préface de Sœur Marie Amédée, f.c.s.c.j. 1953. 46 p. (Ms. Ecole de Bibl., U. de M.)

2:1248 **Laurendeau, Adrien**
Notes bio-bibliographiques sur Mgr Cyprien Tanguay. 1949. 23 p. (Mf. Ecole de Bibl., U. de M.)

2:1249 **Laurendeau, Marielle**
Essai de bio-bibliographie: M. Joseph-Eugène Lapierre. 1950. 23 p. (Ms. Ecole de Bibl., U. de M.)

2:1250 **Lauriston, Victor**
Arthur Stringer, son of the North; biography and anthology, by
Victor Lauriston. Toronto, Ryerson [1941]. 178 p. (Makers of
Canadian literature ...)
Bibliography: p. 169-173.

2:1251 **Lauvrière, Emile**
M. Emile Lauvrière (autobiographie). Introd. et bibliographie par
René Baudry, c.s.c. [Memramcook, N.-B.] Université Saint-Joseph,
1952. 40 p. (*Cahiers acadiens*, no 1)
Bibliographie: p. [33]-40.

2:1252 **Lauzon, Madeleine**
Compilation bio-bibliographique du R.P. Henri Béchard, s.j.
Montréal, 1961. xv, 58 p. (Ms. Ecole de Bibl., U. de M.)

2:1253 **Lavigueur, Lucile**
Bio-bibliographie de Octave Crémazie. 1948. iii, 6 p. (Mf. Ecole de
Bibl., U. de M.)

2:1254 **Lavoie, Amédée**
Bibliographie relative à l'histoire de la Nouvelle-France, 1516-1700.
Préf. de M. Rodolphe Laplante. Giffard, 1949. 82 p. (Ms. Ecole de
Bibl., U.L.)

2:1255 **Lavoie, Cécile**
Essai de bio-bibliographie: M. l'abbé Charles-Honoré Laverdière.
1948. viii, 22 p. (Ms. Ecole de Bibl., U. de M.)

2:1256 **Lavoie, Delores Joan**
The development of ballet in Canada; a bibliography. [Toronto]
1966. 5, [2] *l*. (Ms. Toronto Univ. Libr. School)

2:1257 **Lavoie, Marie-Thérèse**
Notes bio-bibliographiques sur Nérée Beauchemin. 1948. 17 p.
(Mf. Ecole de Bibl., U. de M.)

2:1258 **Law, Jean Thorum**
Winnipeg women authors; a selected bibliography. [Toronto] 1966.
16 *l*. (Ms. Toronto Univ. Libr. School)

2:1259 **Lawrence, Bertha**
A survey of the materials to be found in the Provincial Legislative
Library, Alberta, for the study of Canadian history, and more partic-
ularly that of Western Canada. 1936. 419 *l*.

2:1260  **Lawrence, Robert Gilford**
A descriptive bibliography of the manuscript material in the Rufus
Hathaway collection of Canadian literature, University of New
Brunswick. 1947. 3 p. *l.*, 200 p.
Thesis (M.A.), University of New Brunswick.

2:1261  **Lawrence Lande Foundation for Canadian Historical Research**
Confederation pamphlets; a checklist–liste abrégée. Montreal,
McGill University, 1967.
67 p. illus. (1 fold. laid in), facsims. (*Its* [Publications] no. 3)

2:1262  **Laycock, Anna L.**
List of publications of the Department of External Affairs, and
publications related to the work of the Department, 1910-55.
[Toronto] 1956. [2], iv, 21 *l.* (Ms. Toronto Univ. Libr. School)

2:1263  **Lazure, Rachel**
Bibliographie d'Oscar Massé. Préface de Louis-Philippe Robidoux.
1946. 30 p. (Mf. Ecole de Bibl., U. de M.)

2:1264  **Lea, Elizabeth M.**
Bibliography on John Strachan, first bishop of Toronto, 1778-1867.
[Toronto, 1933] [1], 8 *l.* (Ms. Toronto Univ. Libr. School)

2:1265  **Lebel, Diane**
Eskimo art. 1967. [viii] 11 1. (Ms. U. of O. Libr. School)

2:1266  **Le Bel, Madeleine**
Adolphe Poisson; essai de bio-bibliographie. Préface par Alphonse
Désilets. 1951. 80 p. (Mf. Ecole de Bibl., U. de M.)

2:1267  **Le Bel, Marcelle-T.**
Bibliographie de l'honorable Juge Gonzalve Desaulniers. 1945. 25 p.
(Mf. Ecole de Bibl., U. de M.)

2:1268  **Lebel, Maurice**
Le voyage de Grèce: bibliographie des voyageurs français en Grèce au
XXe siècle (1900-1968) Sherbrooke, Editions Paulines, 1969.
61 p.

2:1269  **Leblanc, Jeanne**
Bio-bibliographie de Marie-Rose Turcot. Préface de Mlle Marie-Claire
Daveluy. 1943. 26 p. (Ms. Ecole de Bibl., U. de M.)

2:1270  **Le Breton, Pierre**
Notes bio-bibliographiques sur le P. Maurice-H. Beaulieu, s.j. 1948.
vii, 6 p. (Ms. Ecole de Bibl., U. de M.)

2:1271  **Leclerc, Marcel**
Bibliographie de l'île d'Orléans. Québec, 1950. 40 p. (Ms. Ecole de
Bibl., U.L.)

2:1272  **Leclerc, Thérèse**
Bio-bibliographie de M. Marcel Raymond. Préface de Jacques
Rousseau. 1945. xviii, 19 p. (Mf. Ecole de Bibl., U. de M.)

2:1273  **Lecompte, Georges-Ernest**
Essai de bibliographie de M. l'abbé J.-E.-C. Laferrière (1874-1936).
Préface de M. le Chan. Lucien Beauregard. 1949. 52 p. (Ms. Ecole
de Bibl., U. de M.)

2:1274  **Lecomte, Julienne**
Essai de bibliographie de Mme Emmanuel-Persillier. Benoît. Préface
de M. l'abbé N.-Paul Desrochers. 1949. 29 p. (Mf. Ecole de Bibl.,
U. de M.)

2:1275  **LeCours, Claire**
Vanier. 1967. viii, 8 l. (Ms. U. of O. Libr. School)

2:1276  **Lectures**; revue mensuelle de bibliographie critique ... Montréal,
1946-1954.
Publiée par le Service de bibliographie et de documentation de Fides.
Nouvelle série tirée à part de la section littéraire de *Notre temps*. 1954-1955.
Nouvelle série. Deux fois par mois. 1955 –.

2:1277  **Leduc, Joseph**
Bio-bibliographie du sénateur Léon-Mercier Gouin, K.C. 1942. 37 p.
(Mf. Ecole de Bibl., U. de M.)

2:1278  **Leduc, Lucienne**
Bio-bibliographie de M. l'abbé Albert Tessier. Préface du R.P. Paul-A.
Martin, c.s.c. 1946. xxviii, 146 p. (Ms. Ecole de Bibl., U. de M.)

2:1279  **Leduc, Lucienne (Desrochers)**
Bibliographie analytique de la reliure au Canada français. Québec,
1953. 30 p. (Ms. Ecole de Bibl., U.L.)

2:1280  **Leechman, John Douglas**
Bibliography of Harlan I. Smith, 1889-1936. (In Canada, National
Museum, Bulletin, no. 112, p . 9-14)

2:1281  **Leechman, John Douglas**
Bibliography of W.J. Wintemberg, 1899-1947. (In Canada, National
Museum, Bulletin, no. 112, p. 39-41)

2:1282 **Lefaivre, Louise**
Bibliographie analytique de l'œuvre de l'abbé Jean Holmes, un des fondateurs de l'Université Laval, précédée d'une biographie. Préface de Don. Guay. Québec, 1964. 68 p. (Ms. Ecole de Bibl., U.L.)

2:1283 **Lefebvre, Esther, sœur**
Bio-bibliographie du R.P. Marcel-Marie Desmarais, o.p. Préface de la Très R.M. Rivard, r.h. 1949. 130 p. (Ms. Ecole de Bibl., U. de M.)

2:1284 **Lefebvre, Françoise**
Bio-bibliographie du R.P. Thomas-Marie Charland, o.p. Préface du R.P. A. Papillon, o.p. 1944. xxi, 27 p. (Ms. Ecole de Bibl., U. de M.)

2:1285 **Lefebvre, Gérard, frère**
Bibliographie analytique du Rév. Frère M. Cyrille Côté. Québec, 1965. (Ms. Ecole de Bibl., U.L.)

2:1286 **Lefebvre, Marguerite**
Bio-bibliographie analytique du chanoine Lionel Groulx. Québec, 1947. 24 p. (Ms. Ecole de Bibl., U.L.)

2:1287 **A legal bibliography of the British Commonwealth of Nations ...**
London, Sweet & Maxwell, 19—. v.
V. 3, Canadian and British-American colonial law from earliest times to December, 1956.
Compiled by C.R. Brown, L.F. Maxwell, P.A. Maxwell.

2:1288 **Légaré, Claire**
Bibliographie analytique de M. Jean-Charles Falardeau. Préf. du R.P. Gonzalve Poulin o.f.m. Québec, 1953. 68 p. (Ms. Ecole de Bibl., U.L.)

2:1289 **Légaré, Denise**
Bibliographie de M. Stanislas Vachon. Québec, 1955. 41 p. (Ms. Ecole de Bibl., U.L.)

2:1290 **Légaré, Hélène**
Bibliographie de l'œuvre de M. Jean-Baptiste Caouette, précédée d'une biographie. Préface de M. Mario Bussanca. Québec, 1964. 70 p. (Ms. Ecole de Bibl., U.L.)

2:1291 **Legault, Agathe**
Bio-bibliographie de la R.S. Paul-Emile, s.g.c. Préf. par M. Séraphin Marion. [Montréal] 1959. xvii, 106 p. (Ms. Ecole de Bibl., U. de M.)

2:1292 **Legendre, Georges**
Répertoire des travaux de l'Association Canadienne des Bibliothèques de Langue Française. 1964. iv, 15 1. illus., diagr. (Ms. U. of O. Libr. School)

2:1293 **Léger, Jacqueline**
Bio-bibliographie du R.P. Paul-Aimé Martin, c.s.c. Préface de Cécile
Martin. 1947. 35 p. (Ms. Ecole de Bibl., U. de M.)

2:1294 **LeGresley, J.-E.**
Bibliographie analytique de monsieur Alphonse Désilets. Québec,
1950. 81 p. (Ms. Ecole de Bibl., U.L.)

2:1295 **Legris, Denyse**
Notes bio-bibliographiques sur Monsieur Hervé Biron. Louiseville,
1950. 31 p. (Mf. Ecole de Bibl., U. de M.)

2:1296 **Leigh, Dawson M.**
Huronia in print. [New ed.] Midland, Ont., Huronia Historic Sites
and Tourist Association [1963?] [12] p.
First edition: 1952.

2:1297 **Leitch, Isabel**
A bibliography of reference books in Canadian literature. Montreal,
1949. iii, 16 *l*. (Ms. McGill Univ. Libr. School)

2:1298 **Lemaire, Gyslaine**
Bio-bibliographie analytique de M. Hervé Biron. Québec, 1963. 123 p.
(Ms. Ecole de Bibl., U.L.)

2:1299 **Lemay, Clotilde**
Bibliographie analytique de Maxine [Mme Taschereau-Fortier].
Québec, 1950. 46 p. (Ms. Ecole de Bibl., U.L.)

2:1300 **Lemay, Gisèle**
Bio-bibliographie de Albert Lévesque. Préface de M. Léo-Paul
Desrosiers. 1945. 26 p. (Ms. Ecole de Bibl., U. de M.)

2:1301 **Lemay, Léona**
Bibliographie analytique de la généalogie dans les comtés de Saint-
Maurice, Maskinongé, Champlain. Saint-Barnabé-Nord, 1964. 141 p.
(Ms. Ecole de Bibl., U.L.)

2:1302 **Lemay, Philippe**
L'Acte de Québec, 1774—son sens et ses conséquences vue en 1774
et aujourd'hui. 1966. viii, 7 1. (Ms. U. of O. Libr. School)

2:1303 **Lemieux, Sir François Xavier**
Collection de premiers numéros de journaux, 1764-1915. Index
alphabétique reproduit du catalogue de M.F.X. Lemieux d'Ottawa.
Partie canadienne. Ottawa, L'auteur [s.d.] 12 p.

2:1304 **Lemieux, Marthe**
Bio-bibliographie de Monsieur l'abbé Georges Dugas. 1948. 8 p.
(Mf. Ecole de Bibl., U. de M.)

2:1305 **Lemieux, Marthe**
Essai d'une bibliographie sur la ville de Chicoutimi. 1953. viii, 96 p.
(Ms. Ecole de Bibl., U. de M.)

2:1306 **Lennox, Hattie Jean**
A bibliography of the poetical works of E.J. Pratt. [Toronto] 1945.
10 *l.* (Ms. Toronto Univ. Libr. School)

2:1307 **Lennoxville, Que. Bishop's University.** Library
Catalogue of the Eastern Townships historical collection in the John
Bassett Memorial Library. Lennoxville, 1965. 38 p.

2:1308 **[Lenox, James]**
... The Jesuit relations, etc. New York, Printed for the Trustees,
1879. 19 p. (Contributions to a Catalogue of the Lenox library, no. 2)
Ed. by G.H. Moore.

2:1309 **[Lenox, James]**
... The voyages of Thévenot. New York, The Trustees, 1879. 20 p.
(Contributions to a Catalogue of the Lenox library, no. 3)
Ed. by G.H. Moore.

2:1310 **Léon-Pierre, frère**
Notes bio-bibliographiques sur Rex Desmarchais. 1947. 18 p. (Mf.
Ecole de Bibl., U. de M.)

2:1311 **LeSage, Aline**
Bio-bibliographie de Cécile Chalifoux. Préface du R.P. Léonard-Marie
Puech. 1946. xi, 203 p. (Mf. Ecole de Bibl., U. de M.)

2:1312 **Lescarbot, Marc**
The history of New France, with an English translation, notes and
appendices by W.L. Grant, and an introduction by H.P. Biggar.
Toronto, Champlain Society, 1914. 3v. (Added t.-p.: The publica-
tions of the Champlain Society [I, VII, XI])
List of Lescarbot's works, v. 3, p. 515-535.

2:1313 **Le Sieur, P.B.**
Bibliographie; études podologiques des sols de la province de Québec.
Québec, 1956. 160 p. (Ms. Ecole de Bibl., U.L.)

2:1314  **Lespérance, Odette**
Bibliographie de Raymond Tanghe, précédée de notes biographiques.
Préface de M. Raymond Tanghe. 1943. 79 p. (Ms. Ecole de Bibl.,
U. de M.)

2:1315  **Letourneau, Solange**
Notes bio-bibliographiques sur M. Jean Charbonneau. 1948. iv, 18 p.
(Mf. Ecole de Bibl., U. de M.)

2:1316  **Lett, E.M.**
Shipbuilding in Canada; bibliography. Ottawa, University of Ottawa,
Library School, 1948. 9 p. (Ms. U. of O. Libr. School)

2:1317  **Letters in Canada.** 1935– . Toronto. Annual.
Reprinted from *University of Toronto quarterly.*

2:1318  **Leury, Berthe**
Bibliographie du roman historique canadien. 1940. 34 p. (Ms. Ecole
de Bibl., U. de M.)

2:1319  **Levasseur, Carmelle**
Bibliographie analytique de Reine Malouin. Préf. de M. Gérard Martin.
Québec, 1950. 67 p. (Ms. Ecole de Bibl., U.L.)

2:1320  **Levasseur, Georgette**
Bio-bibliographie canadienne des oeuvres de Mgr Emile Chartier,
1938-1962. Sherbrooke, 1963. 138 p. (Ms. Ecole de Bibl., U.L.)

2:1321  **Léveillé, Jean-Bernard**
Bio-bibliographie de M. l'abbé Léon Provancher. Préf. du R.P. Emile
Deguire, c.s.c. 1949. 156 p. (Ms. Ecole de Bibl., U. de M.)

2:1322  **Lévêque, Isabella**
Bio-bibliographie de Monsieur Gérard Filion (1935-1949) Chicoutimi,
1964. 134 p. (Ms. Ecole de Bibl., U.L.)

2:1323  **Levesque, Ginette**
Bibliographie de l'oeuvre de Louis Bérubé, i.p., précédée d'une
biographie. Préface de l'abbé Raymond Boucher. La Pocatière, 1962.
57 p. (Ms. Ecole de Bibl., U.L.)

2:1324  **Liboiron, Albert A.**
Federalism and intergovernmental relations in Australia, Canada, the
United States and other countries; a bibliography, compiled by Albert
A. Liboiron. Kingston, Ont., Institute of Intergovernmental Relations,
Queen's University, 1967.
vi, 231 *l.*

2:1325  **Lippens-Giguère, Magdeleine**
Bio-bibliographie du Frère Robert, é.c., professeur au Mont-Saint-Louis. Québec, 1947. 44 p. (Ms. Ecole de Bibl., U.L.)

2:1326  **Literary and Historical Society of Quebec**
Index to the archival publications of the Literary and Historical Society of Quebec, 1824-1924. Quebec, L'Evenement, 1923. 215 p.

2:1327  **The Literary Garland** (Indexes)
An index to the *Literary garland* (Montreal 1838-1851). Toronto, Bibliographical Society of Canada, Société bibliographique du Canada, 1962. x, 61 p.
Compiler: Mary Markham Brown.

2:1328  **Litster, Joyce M.**
A bibliography of works by and about Robert W. Service. [Toronto, 1967] v, 13 *l.* (Ms. Toronto Univ. Libr. School)

2:1329  **Le livre canadien à la Foire du livre de Francfort en Allemagne de l'Ouest, 1965**; une exposition d'ouvrages publiés durant les dernières années, organisée sous le patronage du Conseil des arts du Canada et du ministère des Affaires culturelles de la province de Québec, par un comité conjoint de l'Association des Editeurs canadiens et de la Book Publishers' Association of Canada, avec la collaboration de l'Imprimeur de la Reine du Canada. Liste des titres et des éditeurs. Ottawa, Imprimeur de la Reine, 1965. 3 f., 54 p.

2:1330  **Livres et auteurs canadiens** 1961—  Panorama de la production littéraire de l'année. [Montréal, 1962—  ] annuel.

2:1331  **Lizotte, Jean**
Notes bio-bibliographiques sur le R.P. Henri Mousseau, o.m.i. 1949. 30 p. (Ms. Ecole de Bibl., U. de M.)

2:1332  **Lizotte, Jean**
Répertoire bibliographique des revues canadiennes-françaises, 1900-1957. Préface par Hélène Grenier. Montréal, 1957. xvi, 64 p. (Ms. Ecole de Bibl., U. de M.)

2:1333  **Lochhead, Douglas**
A bibliography of reference sources in Canadian literature. Montreal, 1951. v, 11 *l.* (Ms. McGill Univ. Libr. School)

2:1334  **Lockwell, Huguette**
Bibliographie de madame Emma Boivin-Vaillancourt. Québec, 1954. 32 p. (Ms. Ecole de Bibl., U.L.)

2:1335 **Logan, John Daniel**
Thomas Chandler Haliburton. Toronto, Ryerson [1923?]. 176 p.
(Makers of Canadian literature ...)
Bibliography: p. 155-173.

2:1336 **Lomer, Doris A.**
Books printed in Canada before 1837 that are in McGill University
Library. Montreal, McGill University, Library, 1929. 32 p.
A chronological list.

2:1337 **Lomer, Gerhard Richard**
A catalogue of scientific periodicals in Canadian libraries, prepared
by Gerhard R. Lomer and Margaret S. Mackay. Montreal, McGill
University, 1924. xx, 255 p.

2:1338 **Lomer, Gerhard Richard**
List of publications. (May 1, 1958.) [Montreal] 1958. 6 *l.*
rev. ed. [Ottawa, 1960] 5 *l.*

2:1339 **Lomer, Gerhard Richard**
Stephen Leacock; a checklist and index of his writings. Ottawa,
National Library of Canada, 1954. 153 p.

2:1340 **Lomme, Léo**
Biographies de missionnaires venus au Canada sous la domination
française. 1940. 13 p. (Ms. Ecole de Bibl., U. de M.)

2:1341 **London, Ont. Public Library and Art Museum**
Films, 16 mm. sound; recent additions, 1963-1965. [London, Ont.,
1965]
5 p.

2:1342 **London, Ont. Public Library and Art Museum**
London through the century; London centennial, 1855-1955.
[London, Ont., 1955] [8] p.
List of books and articles pertaining to London and its citizens, chosen from
the Library collection.
Compiled by Elizabeth Spicer.

2:1343 **London, Ont. University of Western Ontario**
... Bibliography of publications by members of the faculties to
December 31, 1928. London, Ont., 1929. 35 numb. *l.*

2:1344 **Long, Robert James**
Nova Scotia authors and their work; a bibliography of the province.
East Orange, N.J., The Author, 1918. 4, 7-312, [4] p.

2:1345 **Longtin, Marcel**
Essai de bio-bibliographie de Gérard Pelletier, journaliste. Préface
par Jean-Paul Lefebvre. [Montréal] 1960. xv, 40 p. (Ms. Ecole de
Bibl., U. de M.)

2:1346 **Loranger, Fernande**
Bio-bibliographie de Monsieur Jean Bruchési, sous-secrétaire de la
province de Québec. 1940. 55 p. (Mf. Ecole de Bibl., U. de M.)

2:1347 **Loranger, Marguerite**
Bio-bibliographie de Monseigneur Napoléon Caron. Lettre-préface
de M. l'abbé Albert Tessier. 1943. 63 p. (Mf. Ecole de Bibl., U. de M.)

2:1348 **Loranger, Ursule**
Bio-bibliographie de l'honorable Juge Thomas-Jean-Jacques Loranger.
Préface de M. Léo-Paul Desrosiers. 1943. 53 p. (Ms. Ecole de Bibl.,
U. de M.)

2:1349 **Lord, Fernande**
Bio-bibliographie de Marie-Louise d'Auteuil. Préface de M. Arthur
Saint-Pierre. 1946. 39 p. (Ms. Ecole de Bibl., U. de M.)

2:1350 **Lord, Marcel-A.**
Bibliographie du 'Rocher de Grand'Mère' (monument sis en la cité
du même nom) Grand'Mère, 1964. 25 p. (Ms. Ecole de Bibl., U.L.)

2:1351 **Lord, Marie-Paule**
Bibliographie analytique de l'œuvre de Charles E. Harpe, poète et
écrivain. Préface de M. Roger Brien. Lettre préface de l'Abbé Moïse
Roy. Québec, 1961. 171 p. (Ms. Ecole de Bibl., U.L.)

2:1352 **Lortie, Lucien**
Bibliographie analytique de l'œuvre de l'abbé Arthur Maheux,
précédée d'une biographie. Préface de Mgr Camille Roy. Québec,
1942. 159 p.

2:1353 **Lotz, James Robert**
... Yukon bibliography. Preliminary edition. Ottawa, Northern
Co-ordination and Research Centre, Department of Northern Affairs
and National Resources, 1964. vii, 155 p. (Yukon Research Project
series, no. 1)

2:1354 **Louis-Armand, frère**
Essai d'inventaire des livres, brochures, périodiques et autres imprimés
publiés par la congrégation des Frères Maristes au Canada. Préf. du
Frère Pierre Marien, mariste. Montréal, 1961. xxiv, 129 p. front.
(fac-sim.) (Ms. Ecole de Bibl., U. de M.)

2:1355  **Louis-Bernard**
Bibliographie de l'œuvre du Rév. Père Gaston Carrière, o.m.i.
Shawinigan, 1963. 113 p. (Ms. Ecole de Bibl., U.L.)

2:1356  **Louis-Ernest, sœur**
Bibliographie analytique de l'œuvre d'un grand chroniqueur, Louis-
Philippe Audet, 1953-1962. Québec, 1963. 246 p. (Ms. Ecole de
Bibl., U.L.)

2:1357  **Louisville, Ky. Free Public Library**
... Books and magazine articles on Oliver Hazard Perry and the battle
of Lake Erie. [Louisville] 1913. 7, [1] p.

2:1358  **Lowther, Barbara J.**
A bibliography of British Columbia; laying the foundations, 1849-
1899, by Barbara J. Lowther with the assistance of Muriel Laing.
[Victoria, B.C., University of Victoria, 1968]
xii, 328 p.

2:1359  **Luce, Barbara Gene**
Niagara's history; a bibliography of the first publications of the
Niagara Historical Society. Montreal, 1957. 11 *l.* (Ms. McGill Univ.
Libr. School)

2:1360  **Luchkiw, Vasyl**
Library science periodicals in Canadian library schools. 1962. vi, 20 1.
(Ms. U. of O. Libr. School)

2:1361  **Lucier, Juliette**
Bio-bibliographie de M. Guy Frégault, historien (1918–  ). Préface
de M. le chanoine Lionel Groulx. 1945. 40 p. (Mf. Ecole de Bibl.,
U. de M.)

2:1362  **Ludovic, frère**
Bio-bibliographie de Mgr Camille Roy, recteur de l'Université Laval.
Préface de M. Ægidius Fauteux. Québec [Imprimé pour la Procure des
F.E.C.] , 1941. 180 p.
Autre édition sur microfilm. 1939-40. 105 p. (Ecole de Bibl., U. de M.)

2:1363  **Luke, Lorna**
The life of Etienne Brulé. Toronto, 1965. iv, 10 *l.* (Ms. Toronto
Univ. Libr. School)

2:1364  **Lunn, Jean**
Bibliography of the history of the Canadian press. (Reprinted from
the *Canadian historical review,* Dec. 1941) 416-433 p.
Thesis, McGill Univ., Library School.

2:1365 **Lunn, Jean**
Canadian newspapers before 1821, a preliminary list. [Toronto, 1944]
417-420 p.
Reprinted from the *Canadian historical review,* Dec. 1944.

2:1366 **Lusignan, Lucien**
Essai bibliographique sur les écrits des saints martyrs Jean de Brébeuf
et Isaac Jogues. 1938. 10 p. (Ms. Ecole de Bibl., U. de M.)
revu et augmenté. Extrait du *Bulletin des recherches historiques,* juin 1944.
[s.l.n.d.] 23 p.

2:1367 **Lussier, Louise**
Bio-bibliographie du Dr Joseph-Edmond Dubé. Préface de M. Albert
Lesage. 1942. xv, 116 p. (Ms. Ecole de Bibl., U. de M.)

2:1368 **Lyonnais, Mariette**
Notes bio-bibliographiques sur Monsieur le docteur Auguste Panneton.
1949. xvi, 8 p. (Mf. Ecole de Bibl., U. de M.)

2:1369 **McAllister, Donald Evan**
Bibliography of the marine fishes of Arctic Canada, by D.E. McAllister.
Vancouver, Institute of Fisheries, University of British Columbia,
1966.
16 p. (British Columbia. University. Institute of Fisheries. Museum contribution,
no. 8)

2:1370 **McArthur, Peter**
Stephen Leacock. Toronto, Ryerson [c1923] . 176 p. (Makers of
Canadian literature ...)
Bibliography: p. 167-173.

2:1371 **McAtee, Waldo Lee**
Ornithological publications of Percy Algernon Taverner, 1895-1945.
(In Canada, National Museum, Bulletin, no. 112, p. 103-113)
'Known to be incomplete with respect to newspaper contributions. Mimeo-
graphed items have been omitted.'

2:1372 **McCalib, Patricia**
Guide to reference materials in anthropology in the Library of the
University of British Columbia. Vancouver, University of British
Columbia Library, 1968.
v, 64 p. (Reference publication, no. 25)

2:1373 **McConnell, Ruth E.**
Teaching English as an additional language; annotated bibliography,

by R. McConnell and P. Wakefield. Vancouver, Extension Dept.,
University of British Columbia [1969]
74 *l.*

2:1374 **McCormick, Mary**
Canadian Pacific Railway. Bibliography. Books and pamphlets
relating to the Canadian Pacific Railway in the Library of the Department of Transport, Ottawa, Ontario. Library School, University of
Ottawa, 1960. [3], 19, iv p. (Ms. U. of O. Libr. School)

2:1375 **MacCougan, David V.**
Music education in Canada and the United States of America. 1964.
iv, 8 l. (Ms. U. of O. Libr. School)

2:1376 **McCoy, James Comly**
Canadiana and French Americana in the library of J.C. McCoy; a
hand-list of printed books. Grasse, 1931. 87, [1] p.

2:1377 **McCoy, James Comly**
Jesuit Relations of Canada, 1632-1673; a bibliography by James C.
McCoy, with an introduction by Lawrence C. Wroth. Paris, Rau, 1937.
2 p. *l.,* xv, [3], 3-310, [36] p.

2:1378 **McCready, Warren Thomas**
Bibliografía temática de estudios sobre el teatro español antiguo.
[Toronto] University Toronto Press [c1966]
xix, 445 p.
Bibliography of studies published 1850-1960 covering period from the Middle
Ages to the 18th century.

2:1379 **MacDermot, Hugh Ernest**
A bibliography of Canadian medical periodicals, with annotations.
Montreal, Printed for McGill University by Renouf, 1934. 21 p.

2:1380 **Macdonald, John Ford**
William Henry Drummond. Toronto, Ryerson [1923?]. 132 p.
(Makers of Canadian literature ...)
Bibliography: p. 121-129.

2:1381 **MacDonald, Mary Christine**
Historical directory of Saskatchewan newspapers, 1878-1950.
Saskatoon, Office of the Saskatchewan Archives, University of
Saskatchewan, 1951. 114 p.
Lists 493 papers.

2:1382 **Macdonald, Mary Christine**
Publications of the Governments of the North-West Territories, 1876-

1905, and of the province of Saskatchewan, 1905-1952. Regina, Legislative Library, 1952. 109, [1] p.
Preliminary checklist: 1948. 84 *l.*

2:1383 **McDormand, Ruth M.**
Canadian history; a selective bibliography of reference books for advanced students. Montreal, 1956. iii, 9 *l.* (Ms. McGill Univ. Libr. School)

2:1384 **McDormand, Ruth M.**
Cape Breton in history and romance; a reading list ... Montreal, 1956. iv, 7 *l.* (Ms. McGill Univ. Libr. School)

2:1385 **McFarlane, William Goodsoe**
New Brunswick bibliography. The books and writers of the province. St John, N.B., Sun, 1895. 98 p.

2:1386 **McGill University, Montreal.** French Canada Studies Programme
Bibliography: Canadian political parties, 1791-1867, 1867- (including books, review articles, graduate theses and pamphlets). [Montreal, 1966]
70 *l.*

2:1387 **McGill University, Montreal.** Institute of Islamic Studies
Publications 1952-59. [Montreal, 1959] 9 *l.*

2:1388 **McGill University, Montreal.** Library
... List of McGill University publications to December 31, 1926. Montreal, McGill University Library, 1927. 17 p.
Supplement, Jan.-Dec. 1927. (... Publications ... no. 11.)
Supplement, Jan.-Dec. 1928. (... Publications ... no. 16.)

2:1389 **McGill University, Montreal.** Library
List of University publications in print to Aug. 1, 1930. Montreal, McGill University, 1930. 27 p.

2:1390 **McGill University, Montreal.** Library
McGill University bibliography: publications and lectures. Montreal, 1930-31.

2:1391 **McGill University, Montreal.** Library. Blacker-Wood Library of Zoology and Ornithology
A dictionary catalogue of the Blacker-Wood Library of Zoology and Ornithology. Boston, G.K. Hall, 1966.
9 v.
'C.A. Wood Collection of Oriental Manuscripts': v. 9, p. 681-684.

2:1392 **McGill University, Montreal.** Library. Lawrence Lande Collection
of Canadiana
The Lawrence Lande Collection of Canadiana in the Redpath Library
of McGill University; a bibliography, collected, arranged and annotated by Lawrence Lande, with an introduction by Edgar Andrew
Collard. Montreal, Lawrence Lande Foundation for Canadian
Historical Research, 1965.
xxxv, 301 p. illus., maps.

2:1393 **McGill University, Montreal.** Library School
A bibliography of Canadian bibliographies compiled by the 1929
and 1930 classes in bibliography of the McGill University Library
School under the direction of Marion V. Higgins. Montreal, 1930.
iv, 45 p.

2:1394 **McGill University, Montreal.** Library School
A bibliography of scientific articles by Henry Mousley. Emma
Shearer Wood Library of Ornithology, McGill University. Prepared
by the class in reference work and bibliography, 1929-1930. Montreal,
McGill University Library School, 1930. 10 *l.*

2:1395 **McGill University, Montreal.** Library School
A bibliography of Stephen Butler Leacock, compiled by the class of
1935, McGill University Library School, under the direction of
Marion Villiers Higgins. Montreal, 1935. 31, [5] p. facsims.

2:1396 **McGill University, Montreal.** Library School
Quebec in books; comp. by the class of 1934, McGill University
Library School, for the fifty-sixth annual convention of the American
Library Association, Montreal, June 25-30, 1934. Montreal, McGill
University Library, 1934. 56 p.

2:1397 **MacGown, Magdalene Coul**
A bibliography of the wine industry in Canada. [Toronto, 1963] iii,
6 *l.* (Ms. Toronto Univ. Libr. School)

2:1398 **McGrigor, G.D.**
Bibliography of Newfoundland, with some reference to Labrador.
[N.p.] 1923.

2:1399 **McIntosh, Jean A.**
Lawrence Johnstone Burpee, 1873-1946; a bibliography of his
separately published works which are included in the holdings of
seven Toronto libraries. Toronto, 1947. 6 *l.* (Ms. Toronto Univ. Libr.
School)

2:1400 **McIntyre, Ruth Anne**
The Hutterites in North America; a bibliography of the resources available in the Toronto Public Library and the Library of the University of Toronto. Toronto, 1966. iii, 9, [1] *l.* (Ms. Toronto Univ. Libr. School)

2:1401 **MacKay, Edith Christine**
Lord Elgin in Canada, 1847-1854. [Toronto] 1956. ii, 10 *l.* (Ms. Toronto Univ. Libr. School)

2:1402 **McKenzie, Ruth I.**
A survey of the proletarian movement in Canadian literature ... [Toronto] 1938. [3], 42 *l.* (Ms. Toronto Univ. Libr. School)

2:1403 **MacKerracher, Christina J.**
Bibliography of imprints in London, Ontario. [Toronto] 1939. [1], 28 *l.* (Ms. Toronto Univ. Libr. School)

2:1404 **MacKerracher, Christina J.**
Bibliography of the history of London, Ontario. Toronto, 1936. [1], 20 *l.* (Ms. Toronto Univ. Libr. School)

2:1405 **McKim's directory of Canadian publications**
Montreal, McKim, 1892-1942.
Title and frequency vary.
Newspapers and periodicals published in the Dominion of Canada and Newfoundland.

2:1406 **McLaren, Margaret F.**
Bibliography; early history of Hudson Bay. [Toronto, 1931] 7 *l.* (Ms. Toronto Univ. Libr. School)

2:1407 **Maclean, John**
Canadian savage folk; the native tribes of Canada. Toronto, Briggs; [etc., etc.] 1896. 641 p.

2:1408 **MacLean, Joyce Merlyn**
A bibliography of the creative works of A. Earle Birney published from 1950 to the present. [Toronto, 1962. ii], 8, [2] *l.* (Ms. Toronto Univ. Libr. School)

2:1409 **Maclean's magazine** (Indexes)
An index to Maclean's magazine, 1914-1937. Compiled by Peter Mitchell. Ottawa, Canadian Library Association, Association canadienne des bibliothèques, 1965. 1 p. *l.*, 140 p. (CLA-ACB, Occasional papers, no. 47)

2:1410 **McLetchie, Margaret**
French-Canadian folk literature; a bibliography. Montreal, 1957.
ii, 10 *l*. (Ms. McGill Univ. Libr. School)

2:1411 **MacMechan, Archibald McKellar**
Halifax in books. [St John? N.B., 1906] 103-122, 201-217 p.
Reprinted from *Acadiensis*, v. 6, April and July.

2:1412 **MacMillan, Jean Ross**
Music in Canada, a short bibliography. (In *Ontario library review*,
v. XXIV, no. 4, Nov. 1940, p. 386-396.)
Music and composers of Canada. [Lucille May, comp.] (In *Ontario library
review*, v. 33, no. 3, Aug. 1949, p. 264-270.)
Canadian music and composers since 1949. [Nancy J. Williamson, comp.]
(In *Ontario library review*, v. 38, no. 2, May 1954, p. 118-122.)

2:1413 **McNeil, Eva Mary Ogreta**
Music in nineteenth century Toronto; a bibliography. [Toronto]
1953. 13 *l*. (Ms. Toronto Univ. Libr. School)

2:1414 **MacTaggart, Hazel Isabel**
Publications of the government of Ontario, 1901-1955; a checklist
compiled for the Ontario Library Association. Toronto, Printed and
distributed by the University of Toronto Press for the Queen's
Printer, 1964. xiv, 303 p.

2:1415 **Madeleine-de-Galilée**
Bio-bibliographie analytique de son Exc. Mgr Jean-Marie Fortier.
Québec, 1965. 194 p. (Ms. Ecole de Bibl., U.L.)

2:1416 **Madeleine-de-la-Croix, soeur**
Bibliographie analytique de l'œuvre de Mgr Louis-Joseph Aubin, p.d.
Préface de l'abbé Jacques Tremblay. Chicoutimi, 1961. 116 p. (Ms.
Ecole de Bibl., U.L.)

2:1417 **Magee, William Henry**
A checklist of English-Canadian fiction, 1901-1950. 1952. 65 p.

2:1418 **Magloire, frère**
Bio-bibliographie du colonel C.E. Marquis. Québec, 1947. 53 p.
(Ms. Ecole de Bibl., U.L.)

2:1419 **Magnan, Françoise**
Bio-bibliographie du docteur Philippe Panneton. Préface de M.
Philippe Beaudoin. 1942. xvi, 81 p. (Mf. Ecole de Bibl., U. de M.)

2:1420  **Magnan, Monique**
Mademoiselle Marguerite Gauvreau; notes bio-bibliographiques. 1953.
29 p. (Mf. Ecole de Bibl., U. de M.)

2:1421  **Maheux, Arthur**
Les trois Gosselin (Bibliographie). (In *Société canadienne d'histoire de
l'Eglise catholique, Rapport,* 1944-45, p. 27-35)
Trois historiographes du XIXe siècle qui ont porté le nom de Gosselin: David,
Auguste et Amédée.

2:1422  **Mainguy, Louise**
Bio-bibliographie analytique de Jean Simard. Préface de Georges
Mainguy. Québec, 1959. 29 p. (Ms. Ecole de Bibl., U.L.)

2:1423  **Mair, Edweena**
Cessation of the publication of the *Canadian Dietetic Association
Journal.* An annotated bibliography. Ottawa, University of Ottawa,
Library School, 1961. 11 p. (Ms. U. of O. Libr. School)

2:1424  **Majeau, Thérèse**
Dr Eugène Robillard, titulaire de physiologie à l'Université de
Montréal. 1957. xiv, 29 p. (Ms. Ecole de Bibl., U. de M.)

2:1425  **Malchelosse, Gérard**
Cinquante-six ans de vie littéraire. Benjamin Sulte et son oeuvre.
Essai de bibliographie des travaux historiques et litté raires (1860-
1916) de ce polygraphe canadien ... Montréal, Le Pays laurentien,
1916. 78 p. (Collection laurentienne.)

2:1426  **[Malchelosse, Gérard]**
En hommage aux 'Dix,' à l'occasion du 25e anniversaire de la fonda-
tion des Dix célébré par un banquet au Cercle universitaire de
Montréal le 24 septembre 1960, la Librairie Ducharme limitée ...
présente ... l'éminent groupe des Dix et les *Cahiers des Dix* ...
Montréal [Librairie Ducharme] 1961. 16 p. ill., portr.
'Liste des articles parus dans les vingt-cinq premiers *Cahiers des Dix (1936-
1960)*': p. 6-13.

2:1427  **Mallen, Bruce E.**
A basic bibliography on marketing in Canada, compiled and edited by
Bruce E. Mallen [and] I.A. Litvak. [Chicago, American Marketing
Association, c1967]
x, 119 p. (*AMA bibliography series,* no. 13)

2:1428  **Maltais, L. Adhémar**
Livres ou articles de revues sur l'histoire du Canada publiés de 1955
à 1960 (inclusivement). 1962. iv, 14 1. (Ms. U. of O. Libr. School)

2:1429   **Management index**; the international monthly guide to business literature. v. 3, no. 1; Jan. 1965. Ottawa, Keith Business Library, 1965.

36 p. monthly.
Supersedes *Business methods literature* issued June 1959-Dec. 1960; *Business methods index* issued Jan. 1960-Dec. 1962.

2:1430   **Mandryka, Mykyta Ivan**
... Bio-bibliography of J.B. Rudnyc'kyj. Winnipeg, Published by the Academy, 1961. 72 p. (Ukrainian Free Academy of Sciences. Ser.: Ukrainian Scholars, No. 10)

2:1431   **Manitoba.** Department of Mines and Natural Resources. Mines Branch
... Bibliography of geology, palaeontology, industrial minerals, and fuels in the Post-Cambrian regions of Manitoba, 1950 to 1957. Compiled by B.A. Mills. Winnipeg, 1959. 32 p. (Publication no. 57-4)

2:1432   **Manitoba. Legislative Library**
Canadian imprints and books about Canada, 1949-1956. Compiled by the Provincial Library. Winnipeg [1957] [2], 71 *l.*

2:1433   **Manitoba. Public Archives**
Preliminary inventory. 1955. Winnipeg, 1955. 52, [7] p.

A preliminary description of the manuscript collection in the Legislative Library of Manitoba.

2:1434   **Manitoba. Public Archives**
Transactions and proceedings of the Historical Society of Manitoba. [Winnipeg, 1953] 9 *l.*

2:1435   **Manitoba. University.** Faculty of Medicine. Library.
A catalogue of books on the history of medicine in the Ross Mitchell Room. Winnipeg, 1966.

133 p. facsims.

2:1436   **Mantha, Madeleine**
Bio-bibliographie de M. Maurice Ollivier. Préface de l'honorable juge Robert Taschereau. 1953. vi, 46 p. (Ms. Ecole de Bibl., U. de M.)

2:1437   **Marburg. Universität.** Bibliothek
Katalog der Kanada-Bibliothek, Stand Frühjahr 1963. [Marburg, 1963] 75 p.

2:1438   **Marcel, Gabriel Alexandre**
Cartographie de la Nouvelle France. Supplément à l'ouvrage de M. Harrisse. Publié avec des documents inédits par Gabriel Marcel ... Paris, Maisonneuve et Leclerc, 1885. 41 p.

2:1439  **Marchand, Cécile**
Bio-bibliographie du Révérend Frère Gilles [Noël-Joseph-Achillas Gosselin] o.f.m. Préface de Monsieur Omer Héroux. 1945. 61 p. (Mf. Ecole de Bibl., U. de M.)

2:1440  **Marchand, Louise**
Bio-bibliographie de Robert Laroque de Roquebrune. Préface de Madame Jean-Louis Audet. 1941. x, 60 p. (Mf. Ecole de Bibl., U. de M.)

2:1441  **Marchildon, Camille**
Bio-bibliographie de Marguerite Bourgeois [Soeur Marguerite du Saint-Sacrement, carmélite]. Préface de Claire Godbout. Trois-Rivières, 1946. 27 p. (Ms. Ecole de Bibl., U. de M.)

2:1442  **Marcotte, Béatrice**
Bio-bibliographie du R.P. Marcel Dubois. Québec, 1957. 48 p. (Ms. Ecole de Bibl., U.L.)

2:1443  **Marcotte, Claire**
Bio-bibliographie de Léo-Pol Morin. 1942. 76 p. (Ms. Ecole de Bibl., U. de M.)

2:1444  **Marcoux, Lucile**
Bibliographie analytique de l'amiante au Canada. Québec, 1953. 40 p. 28 cm. (Ms. Ecole de Bibl., U.L.)

2:1445  **Margrett, Barbara H.**
A bibliography of Jack Miner. Toronto, 1945. [1], 7 *l.* (Ms. Toronto Univ. Libr. School)

2:1446  **Marguerite de Varennes, soeur**
Bibliographie analytique des écrits publiés par les Soeurs de la Charité de Québec (1942-1961) Lettre-préface de très révérende mère Marie-de-Grâces, s.c.q., supérieure générale. Québec, 1964. 167 p. (Ms. Ecole de Bibl., U.L.)

2:1447  **Maria Albert**
Bibliographie de Mère Isabelle Sormany dite Ladauversière. Québec, 1962. 161, LVII, p. (Ms. Ecole de Bibl., U.L.)

2:1448  **Maria-Bernadette, soeur**
Notes bio-bibliographiques sur Jeanne de Montigny. 1951. 39 p. (Ms. Ecole de Bibl., U. de M.)

2:1449  **Marie-Agénor, soeur**
Notice bio-bibliographique du R.F. Magloire-Robert, é.c. 1953. 33 p. (Ms. Ecole de Bibl., U. de M.)

2:1450 **Marie-Agnès-de-Jésus, soeur**
Biographie et bibliographie de Madame Maurice Saint-Jacques
[Henriette (Dessaules)]. 1939. 88 p. (Ms. Ecole de Bibl., U. de M.)

2:1451 **Marie-Aimée-des-Anges, soeur**
Bibliographie analytique de l'oeuvre de Jeanne d'Aigle. Préface de
Madame Reine Malouin. St-Hyacinthe, 1961. 76 p. (Ms. Ecole de
Bibl., U.L.)

2:1452 **Marie-Anita-de-Jésus, soeur**
Notes bio-bibliographiques sur Mgr Charles-Philippe Choquette.
1951. 25 p. (Mf. Ecole de Bibl., U. de M.)

2:1453 **Marie-Anne-Aline, soeur**
Bio-bibliographie de M. le chanoine Emile Dubois. Préface par Mlle
Marie-Claire Daveluy. 1947. 73 p. (Ms. Ecole de Bibl., U. de M.)

2:1454 **Marie-Anne-Victoire, soeur**
Bio-bibliographie de Mère Marie-Irène, s.s.a. Préface de Mlle Marie-
Claire Daveluy. 1947. 80 p. (Ms. Ecole de Bibl., U. de M.)

2:1455 **Marie-Antonin, soeur**
Bibliographie analytique de l'oeuvre de Sr Saint-Ignace de Loyola,
c.n.d. Lettre préface de Mère Ste-Madeleine du Sacré-Coeur, c.n.d.
Québec, 1962. 137 p. (Ms. Ecole de Bibl., U.L.)

2:1456 **Marie-Aurélienne, soeur**
Bibliographie de Mère Marie-Elise, s.s.a. Préface de M. l'abbé Emile
Lambert. 1947. 87 p. (Ms. Ecole de Bibl., U. de M.)

2:1457 **Marie-Bibiane, soeur**
Bio-bibliographie de la R.S. Marie-Rollande, s.s.a. Préface de M. le
chanoine Lionel Groulx. 1947. ix, 63 p. (Ms. Ecole de Bibl., U. de M.)

2:1458 **Marie-Carmen René, soeur**
Bio-bibliographie de Mgr Antonio Camirand. 1947. iv, 15 p. (Ms.
Ecole de Bibl., U. de M.)

2:1459 **Marie-Clément, frère**
Bio-bibliographie analytique du révérend Frère Marc, s.c. Lettre-
préface du révérend Frère Gaétan, s.c., ill. du révérend Frère Jean-
Vital, s.c. Causapscal, 1964. 84 p. (Ms. Ecole de Bibl., U.L.)

2:1460 **Marie-de-la-Charité, soeur**
Bibliographie analytique de l'oeuvre de Mlle Gertie Kathleen Hart,
précédée d'une biographie. Préface de Mlle Hart. Québec, 1962. 30 p.
(Ms. Ecole de Bibl., U.L.)

2:1461　**Marie-de-la-Croix, soeur**
Bibliographie analytique de l'oeuvre de M. l'Abbé J. Alfred Tremblay. Préface de l'abbé Raymond Desgagné. Chicoutimi, 1961. 32 p. (Ms. Ecole de Bibl., U.L.)

2:1462　**Marie de la Grâce, soeur**
Bibliographie de l'Hotel-Dieu St-Vallier de Chicoutimi, 1879-1889. Chicoutimi, 1962. 66 p. (Ms. Ecole de Bibl., U.L.)

2:1463　**Marie-de-l'Ange-Gardien, soeur**
Bibliographie analytique de M. Louis Gérard 'Gerry' Gosselin, précédée d'une biographie. Préface de Sr Sainte-Marie-de-la-Présentation, c.n.d. Québec, 1962. xxiii, 136 p. (Ms. Ecole de Bibl., U.L.)

2:1464　**Marie-de-la-Protection, soeur**
Bio-bibliographie des biographies des religieuses Augustines, Hospitalières de la Miséricorde de Jésus décédées au monastère de l'Hotel-Dieu de Lévis, 1892-1962. Lévis, 1962. 216 p. (Ms. Ecole de Bibl., U.L.)

2:1465　**Marie-de-la-Recouvrance, soeur**
Bibliographie analytique de Marie-Thérèse, 1944-1961. Rimouski, 1962. 106 p. (Ms. Ecole de Bibl., U.L.)

2:1466　**Marie-de-la-Réparation, soeur**
Bibliographie de Monsieur le commandeur Charles-Joseph Magnan, précédée d'une biographie. 1938. 46 p. (Ms. Ecole de Bibl., U. de M.)

2:1467　**Marie-de-la-Sainte-Enfance, soeur**
Bibliographie de M. l'abbé Emile Bégin, ouvrages et articles de revues (1933-1963). Préc. d'une notice biographique. Préf. de M. Pierre-Paul Turgeon. 1963. xi [176] p.

2:1468　**Marie-de-la-Salette, soeur**
Bibliographie analytique de Me Eugène L'Heureux, journaliste (1950-1960) précédée d'une biographie. Préface de M. Raymond Dubé, rédacteur au Soleil. Québec, 1964. 491 p. (Ms. Ecole de Bibl., U.L.)

2:1469　**Marie-de-Massabielle, soeur**
Bibliographie des congrégations de femmes à Montréal. 1941. 52 p. (Ms. Ecole de Bibl., U. de M.)
'Les oeuvres éditées à Montréal ont seules été consignées ici.'

2:1470　**Marie de Montciel, soeur**
Bibliographie analytique de l'oeuvre du Dr Jean-Charles Miller,

médecin-psychiatre à l'Ecole La Jemmerais, 1898-1952. Québec, 1963. 190 p. (Ms. Ecole de Bibl., U.L.)

2:1471  **Marie-de-Rouen, soeur**
Travaux scientifiques des médecins de l'Hôpital Saint-Michel Archange et de la clinique Roy-Rousseau. Québec, 1963. 186 p. (Ms. Ecole de Bibl., U.L.)

2:1472  **Marie de St Alphonse de Jésus, soeur**
Bibliographie analytique de l'oeuvre de M. le Chanoine Georges Panneton. Rimouski, 1963. 87 p. (Ms. Ecole de Bibl., U.L.)

2:1473  **Marie de Saint-Alphonse de Liguori, soeur**
Bibliographie analytique de l'oeuvre du Dr Louis-Edmond Hamelin. Québec, 1962. 100 p. (Ms. Ecole de Bibl., U.L.)

2:1474  **Marie-de-Saint-Camille-de-Jésus, soeur**
Bio-bibliographie analytique (1918-1961) de l'abbé Ernest Arsenault, missionnaire colonisateur. Préface de M. Guy Hamel. Québec, 1963. 148 p. (Ms. Ecole de Bibl., U.L.)

2:1475  **Marie-de-Saint-Denis l'Aréopagite**
Bibliographie analytique précédée d'une biographie de Mgr Alphonse-Marie Parent. Québec, 1964. 136 p. (Ms. Ecole de Bibl., U.L.)

2:1476  **Marie-de-St-Didier, soeur**
Bibliographie de monsieur l'abbé Henri Grenier, docteur en philosophie, théologie, droit canon. Québec, 1948. 32 p. (Ms. Ecole de Bibl., U.L.)

2:1477  **Marie de St Gilles, soeur**
Bibliographie de l'oeuvre de Madame Françoise Gaudet-Smet, 1929-1962. Shawinigan Sud, 1963. 193 p. (Ms. Ecole de Bibl., U.L.)

2:1478  **Marie-de-Saint-Jean, soeur**
Bio-bibliographie de monsieur le commandeur Georges Bellerive (1859-1935) Québec, 1950. 67 p. (Ms. Ecole de Bibl., U.L.)

2:1479  **Marie-de-Saint-Jean-d'Ars, soeur**
Bio-bibliographie de M. l'abbé Auguste-Honoré Gosselin. 1945. ix, 73 p. (Mf. Ecole de Bibl., U. de M.)

2:1480  **Marie-de-Saint-Jean-du-Calvaire, soeur**
Bio-bibliographie de S.E. Mgr Albert-François Cousineau, c.s.c., évêque de Cap Haïtien. Montréal, 1956. 112 p. (Ms. Ecole de Bibl., U. de M.)

2:1481   **Marie-de-S.-Jeanne-d'Orléans, soeur**
Bibliographie de Laure Conan, [Félicité Angers]. [s.d.] 16 p.
(Mf. Ecole de Bibl., U. de M.)

2:1482   **Marie-de-St-Joseph-du-Rédempteur, soeur**
Bibliographie analytique de Marie de St-Paul-de-la Croix, s.c.i.m.
(Georgianna Juneau) 1873-1940. Préface de Mgr Victorin Germain.
Québec, 1962. 100 p. (Ms. Ecole de Bibl., U.L.)

2:1483   **Marie-de-Saint-Joseph Jean, soeur**
Bibliographie analytique de la vallée de la Matapédia. Préface de M.
Dominique Laberge. Conclusion par l'honorable Bona Arsenault.
Rimouski, 1964. 107 p. (Ms. Ecole de Bibl., U.L.)

2:1484   **Marie-de-S.-Martin-du-Sacré-Coeur, soeur**
Essai de bio-bibliographie sur les ouvrages de la Congrégation des
soeurs de Ste-Croix et des Sept-Douleurs, 1847-1948. 1948. 85 p.
(Ms. Ecole de Bibl., U. de M.)

2:1485   **Marie-de-Ste-Berthe-Martyre, soeur**
Notes bio-bibliographiques sur M. le chan. Alphonse-Charles Dugas.
1948. 10, [5] p. (Ms. Ecole de Bibl., U. de M.)

2:1486   **Marie de Sainte-Jeanne-de-Domrémy**
Bibliographie analytique des écrits publiés au Canada français de
1930 à 1960 sur la peinture religieuse. Québec, 1964. 254 p. (Ms.
Ecole de Bibl., U.L.)

2:1487   **Marie-de-Sion, soeur**
Bibliographie analytique du Révérend Père Jean-Paul Dallaire, s.j.
Préf. du Rév. Père Florian Larivière, s.j. Québec, 1960. 106 p. (Ms.
Ecole de Bibl., U.L.)

2:1488   **Marie-de-Sion, soeur**
Bibliographie d'Albert Lozeau. 1938. 16 p. (Mf. Ecole de Bibl.,
U. de M.)

2:1489   **Marie-des-Anges, soeur**
Bibliographie de monsieur l'abbé Paul-Emile Gosselin, professeur de
philosophie au Séminaire de Québec. Québec, 1948. 43 p. (Ms.
Ecole de Bibl., U.L.)

2:1490   **Marie-des-Anges, soeur**
Bibliographie mariale. 1964. (Ms. Ecole de Bibl., U.L.)

2:1491 **Marie des Chérubins, soeur**
Bibliographie analytique de l'œuvre de M. l'abbé Jean-Baptiste
Gauvin. Québec, 1963. 157 p. (Ms. Ecole de Bibl., U.L.)

2:1492 **Marie-des-Lys, soeur**
Bibliographie analytique de l'œuvre d'Ernest Pallascio-Morin.
Préface de Roger Brien. Québec, 1961. 172 p. (Ms. Ecole de Bibl.,
U.L.)

2:1493 **Marie-des-Miracles, soeur**
Bibliographie analytique de M$^e$ Eugène L'Heureux, journaliste
(1929-1940) précédée d'une biographie. Préface de Mgr Arthur
Maheux. Québec, 1964. 426 p. (Ms. Ecole de Bibl., U.L.)

2:1494 **Marie-des-Neiges, soeur**
Bibliographie analytique de l'œuvre de révérende Mère Sainte-Louise
de Marillac, o.s.a., précédée d'une biographie. Préface du R.P.
A. Léveillé. Gaspé, 1962. 52 p. (Ms. Ecole de Bibl., U.L.)

2:1495 **Marie-des-Sept-Douleurs, soeur**
Bibliographie analytique de l'Hôtel-Dieu d'Alma (1950-1960)
Préface de Mgr Victor Tremblay. Alma, 1961. 67 p. (Ms. Ecole de
Bibl., U.L.)

2:1496 **Marie-des-Stigmates, soeur**
Essai de bio-bibliographie du R.P. Ferdinand Coiteux, o.f.m. 1949.
x, 38 p. (Ms. Ecole de Bibl., U. de M.)

2:1497 **Marie-du-Perpétuel-Secours, soeur**
Bibliographie analytique de la Rév. Sr Marie-de-St-Jean Martin.
Préf. de Mgr Ferdinand Vandry. Québec, 1955. 75 p. (Ms. Ecole de
Bibl., U.L.)

2:1498 **Marie-du-Perpétuel-Secours, soeur**
Bibliographie analytique de l'œuvre de Mgr Paul-Eugène Roy
(1859-1926) précédée d'une biographie. Préface de Mgr Arthur
Maheux. Québec, 1964. 199 p. (Ms. Ecole de Bibl., U.L.)

2:1499 **Marie-du-Thabor, soeur**
Bio-bibliographie de M. l'abbé Auguste Lapalme. Préface de l'abbé
J.-O. Maurice. 1947. xv, 63 p. (Ms. Ecole de Bibl., U. de M.)

2:1500 **Marie-Elie, frère**
Bibliographie du R.F. Robert, é.c., D.Sc., précédée d'une biographie.
Montréal, 1963. 60 p. (Ms. Ecole de Bibl., U.L.)

2:1501 **Marie-Elphège, soeur**
Notice bio-bibliographique de Soeur Marie-de-Saint-Paul-de-la-Croix, s.c.i.m. (1873-1940). 1953. 38 p. (Ms. Ecole de Bibl., U. de M.)

2:1502 **Marie-Gemma, soeur**
Bibliographie analytique de l'œuvre du Dr Marcel Langlois. Préface du Dr Roland Cauchon. Québec, 1961. 50 p. (Ms. Ecole de Bibl., U.L.)

2:1503 **Marie-Henriette-de-Jésus, soeur**
Bio-bibliographie de M. l'abbé Joseph-Marie Mélançon. Préface de Monsieur Casimir Hébert. 1946. xviii, 53 p. (Mf. Ecole de Bibl., U. de M.)

2:1504 **Marie-Irene, soeur**
Bio-bibliographie de Mgr Louis-Joseph-Arthur Mélanson. Québec, 1963. 237 p. (Ms. Ecole de Bibl., U.L.)

2:1505 **Marie-Jean-du-Cénacle, soeur**
Bio-bibliographie de Monsieur Gratien Gélinas. 1949. [52] p. (Mf. Ecole de Bibl., U. de M.)

2:1506 **Marie-Jean-Gabriel, soeur**
Bibliographie des ouvrages publiés par les membres de la Congrégation des Saints Noms de Jésus et de Marie. 1938. 5 p. (Ms. Ecole de Bibl., U. de M.)

2:1507 **Marie-Libératrice, soeur**
Bibliographie analytique de l'œuvre de Mgr Victorin Germain. Thetford-Mines, 1962. 221, 17 p. (Ms. Ecole de Bibl., U.L.)

2:1508 **Marie-Liberman, soeur**
Les Instituts familiaux de notre province (1937-1961) Bibliographie analytique. Préface de Mgr A. Tessier. Québec, 1961. 80 p. (Ms. Ecole de Bibl., U.L.)

2:1509 **Marie-Louis-André, soeur**
Bibliographie de S.E. le cardinal Jean-Marie-Rodrigue Villeneuve, o.m.i. 1939. 43 p. (Ms. Ecole de Bibl., U. de M.)

2:1510 **Marie-Louis-Ferdinand, soeur**
Bibliographie partielle de M. l'abbé Elie-J.-A. Auclair. 1939. 76 p. (Ms. Ecole de Bibl., U. de M.)

2:1511 **Marie-Madeleine-du-Bon-Pasteur, soeur**
Bibliographie de Monsieur Léo-Paul Desrosiers. Saint-Hyacinthe, 1939. 85 p. (Mf. Ecole de Bibl., U. de M.)

2:1512  **Marie-Magloire-des-Anges, soeur**
Bio-bibliographie de M. l'abbé Ovila Fournier, L.Sc., professeur à
l'Institut de biologie de l'Université de Montréal, 1935-1955. Préf.
de Louis-Philippe Audet. Montréal, Cercles des jeunes naturalistes,
1962 [c1960] xx, 89 p. portr.
éd. précédente [Montréal] 1960. xxv, 95 p. (Ms. Ecole de Bibl., U. de M.)

2:1513  **Marie-Maurice, soeur**
Bio-bibliographie de Mère Marie-Odilon, s.n.j.m. Préf. par Sr M.-Aimé
de Jésus, s.n.j.m. Montréal, 1961. xvii, 32 p. (Ms. Ecole de Bibl.,
U. de M.)

2:1514  **Marie-Monique d'Ostie, soeur**
Compilation bibliographique des thèses des Soeurs des Saints Noms
de Jésus et de Marie, 1920-1961. Préf. par Sr M.-Jeanne-Madeleine,
s.n.j.m. Montréal, 1961, xxi, 52 p. (Ms. Ecole de Bibl., U. de M.)

2:1515  **Marie-Patricia, soeur**
Bibliographie analytique sur l'hygiène mentale préventive (1925-
1955). Préface de Sr Marie-du-Cénacle. Pont-Rouge, 1963. 49 p.
(Ms. Ecole de Bibl., U.L.)

2:1516  **Marie-Paule, soeur**
Les Soeurs missionnaires de l'Immaculée-Conception, premier institut
d'origine canadienne. Bibliographie analytique (1902-1932) Préface
de Mgr Edgar Larochelle, p.a. Montréal, 1964. 368 p. (Ms. Ecole de
Bibl., U.L.)

2:1517  **[Marie-Raymond, soeur]**
Bio-bibliographie du R.P. Georges Simard, o.m.i., par une Religieuse
des Saints Noms de Jésus et de Marie. [Montréal] , Beauchemin
[1939] . 3 f., [9] -64 p., 2 f.

2:1518  **Marie-St-Edouard, soeur**
Notes bio-bibliographiques sur Soeur Marie-Aimée-de-Jésus, r.p.m.
1953. 27 p. (Ms. Ecole de Bibl., U. de M.)

2:1519  **Marie Saint-Jean-Eudes, soeur**
Bibliographie de l'oeuvre de la vénérable Anne-Marie Rivier.
Marieville, 1964. 45 p. (Ms. Ecole de Bibl., U.L.)

2:1520  **Marie St-Salvy, soeur**
Le Très Révérend Père Frédéric (1838-1916); biographie et bibliographie. Québec, 1963. 88 p. (Ms. Ecole de Bibl., U.L.)

2:1521 **Marie-Siméon, soeur**
Bibliographie analytique du docteur Jean-Paul Gélinas, précédée d'une biographie. Préface du Dr Raymond Lecours. Montréal, 1962. 43 p. (Ms. Ecole de Bibl., U.L.)

2:1522 **Marie-Stanislas, soeur**
Notes bio-bibliographiques sur Madeleine (Mme W.A. Huguenin) 1948. 17 p. (Mf. Ecole de Bibl., U. de M.)

2:1523 **Marie-Sylvia, soeur**
Essai bibliographique: Soeur Jean-Baptiste, f.c.s.p. 1951. 47 p. (Ms. Ecole de Bibl., U. de M.)

2:1524 **Marin, Armand**
L'honorable Pierre-Basile Mignault. Montréal, Fides, 1946. 132 p. (Bibliographies d'auteurs canadiens d'expression française.) éd. précédenté. 1941. xv, 56 p. (Ms. Ecole de Bibl., U. de M.)

2:1525 **Marin-Etienne**
Essai de bio-bibliographie: Frère Martin-Grégoire, f.é.c. 1953. 71 p. (Ms. Ecole de Bibl., U. de M.)

2:1526 **Marsh, Alan D.**
The case for the fluoridation of the public water supplies in Canada, 1959-1964. 1965. vi, 8 1. (Ms. U. of O. Libr. School)

2:1527 **Martel, Claire**
Bio-bibliographie de Mgr Arsène Goyette. 1947. 17 p. (Ms. Ecole de Bibl., U. de M.)

2:1528 **Martel, Louise**
Bibliographie de Joseph Costisella, précédée d'une biographie. Québec, 1964. 69 p. (Ms. Ecole de Bibl., U.L.)

2:1529 **Marten, Luella**
The social and economic implications of automation in Canada. 1967. v, 13 1. (Ms. U. of O. Libr. School)

2:1530 **Martigny, Marie de**
Bio-bibliographie de Jean-Marie Gauvreau. 1943. 102 p. (Ms. Ecole de Bibl., U. de M.)

2:1531 **Martin, Gérard**
Bibliographie sommaire du Canada français, 1854-1954. Québec, 1954. 104 p.

2:1532 **Martin, Gérard**
Bio-bibliographie de J.-Edmond Roy. Préface de Antoine Roy. 1945.
158 p. (Mf. Ecole de Bibl., U. de M.)

2:1533 **Martin, J.D.P.**
A bibliography of reference sources for Canadian literature.
Montreal, 1949. iv, 16 *l.* (Ms. McGill Univ. Libr. School)

2:1534 **Martin, Madeleine**
... Madame Marguerite Aubin-Tellier. Chicoutimi, 1951. 60 p.
(Mf. Ecole de Bibl., U. de M.)

2:1535 **Martin, Margaret Elizabeth Burns**
A bibliography of the published work of Thomas Head Raddall,
together with a short bibliography of biographies of the writer.
Toronto, 1953. 11 *l.* (Ms. Toronto Univ. Libr. School)

2:1536 **Martinus-Ephrem**
Essai de bio-bibliographie [du Frère Olympius-Georges (Henri
Tremblay) f.é.c.]. Montréal, 1953. 42 p. (Ms. Ecole de Bibl., U. de M.)

2:1537 **Mary Stella, sœur**
Bio-bibliographie de Guy Laviolette [pseud. de Michel-Henri Gingras,
en religion Frère Achille, f.i.c.]. Québec, 1954. 150 p. (Ms. Ecole de
Bibl., U.L.)

2:1538 **Mascaro, Beatrice**
Early Canadian furniture. 1962. v, 8 1. (Ms. U. of O. Libr. School)

2:1539 **Massé, Jogues**
Bio-bibliographie du R.P. Odoric-Marie Jouve, o.f.m. 1943. 68 p.
(Ms. Ecole de Bibl., U. de M.)
Publié dans la *Chronique franciscaine,* 5e livraison, 1945.

2:1540 **Massicotte, Louisia**
Bio-bibliographie de Emile Miller. 1944. 71 p. (Ms. Ecole de Bibl.,
U. de M.)

2:1541 **Massicotte-Boutin, Françoise**
Notes bio-bibliographiques sur Edouard-Zotique Massicotte. 1948.
14 p. (Ms. Ecole de Bibl., U. de M.)

2:1542 **Masson, Louis François Rodrigue**
Catalogue of the late Hon. L.R. Masson's magnificent private library,
to be sold at public auction on ... 9th, 11th, 12th April 1904 ... at the
residence, 286 Prince Arthur street, Montreal Canada. [Montreal]
La Patrie, 1904. 1 p. *l.,* 153 p.
Canadiana, p. 51-153.

2:1543 **Mathieu, Denise**
Essai de bio-bibliographie: R.P. Ludger Brien, s.j. 1953. vii, 34 p. (Ms. Ecole de Bibl., U. de M.)

2:1544 **Mathieu, Jacques**
Valdombre [Claude-Henri Grignon] et ses pamphlets. Compilation bibliographique. 1943. 33 p. (Mf. Ecole de Bibl., U. de M.)

2:1545 **Mathieu, Marie-Gisèle**
Notes bio-bibliographiques sur Mademoiselle Béatrice Clément. 1952. ix, 19 p. (Mf. Ecole de Bibl., U. de M.)

2:1546 **Matte, Pierre**
Bibliographie de M. le chan. Hervé Trudel. Préface par M. l'abbé François Trudel. 1949. xi, 183 p. (Ms. Ecole de Bibl., U. de M.)

2:1547 **Matthews, William**
Canadian diaries and autobiographies. Berkeley, University of California Press, 1950. 130 p.
A bibliography covering both British and French Canada and including published and unpublished material.

2:1548 **Maxwell, William Harold**
A complete list of British and colonial law reports and legal periodicals, arranged in alphabetical and in chronological order, with bibliographical notes. 3d ed., with a checklist of Canadian statutes, comp. by W. Harold Maxwell, for Sweet & Maxwell Limited, and C.R. Brown, for the Carswell Company Limited. Toronto, Carswell, 1937. viii, 141, [1] p., 2 l., 59 p.
Previous edition: 1913.
Supplement: 1946.

2:1549 **Mayer, Raymonde**
Bio-bibliographie du R.P. Marc-Antonio Lamarche, o.p. 1940. 117 p. (Ms. Ecole de Bibl., U. de M.)

2:1550 **Médéric-Rodrigue, frère**
Bio-bibliographie de Nérée Tremblay, éducateur. Préf. de Frère Jacques, f.c. [Montréal] 1959. x, 48 p. front. (fac-sim). (Ms. Ecole de Bibl., U. de M.)

2:1551 **Meikle, W.**
Canadian newspaper directory; or, Advertisers' guide, containing a complete list of all the newspapers in Canada, the circulation of each, and all information in reference thereto. Toronto, Blackburn, 1858. 60 p.

2:1552 **Meister, Marilyn**
'The little magazines of British Columbia: a narrative bibliography,'
*British Columbia library quarterly,* vol. 31, no. 2 (October, 1967),
3-19.

2:1553 **Ménard, Germaine, soeur**
Bio-bibliographie de Madame Albertine Ferland-Angers, conseillère
à la Société historique de Montréal. 1947. 19 p. (Mf. Ecole de Bibl.,
U. de M.)

2:1554 **Mercier, Marcel**
Bibliographie de Louis Dantin [Eugène Seers]. St-Jérôme, Labelle,
1939. 69 p.
Autre édition sur microfilm. 1938. 38 p. (Ecole de Bibl., U. de M.)

2:1555 **Mercier, Marguerite**
Bio-bibliographie de E.-Z. Massicotte. 1940. 85 p. (Mf. Ecole de Bibl.,
U. de M.)

2:1556 **Mercier, Yvette**
Bibliographie de biographies et mémoires sur les journalistes, les
hommes de lettres canadiens français, depuis 1764 à nos jours.
Préface de Mlle Marie-Claire Daveluy. 1943. 335 p. (Ms. Ecole de
Bibl., U. de M.)

2:1557 **Mercure, Henri**
Bio-bibliographie analytique de Gérard Morisset, N.P., de la Société
royale du Canada. Québec, 1947. 20 p. (Ms. Ecole de Bibl., U.L.)

2:1558 **Mews, Marjorie**
A selective bibliography on the ancient colony of Newfoundland.
Montreal, 1935. 5 *l.* (Ms. McGill Univ. Libr. School)

2:1559 **Michaelson, David**
State of instruction in the use of the library in Canada. 1966.
vi, 13 1 (Ms. U. of O. Libr. School)

2:1560 **Michaud, Irma**
Antoine Dessane. (In *Bulletin des recherches historiques,* v. XXXIV,
no 2, 1933, p. 73-76.)
Notice biographique suivie de la liste de ses œuvres.

2:1561 **Michaud, Marguerite**
La reconstruction française au Nouveau-Brunswick: Bouctouche,
paroisse-type. Frédéricton, N.-B., Presses universitaires [1955].
223 p.

2:1562 **Miedzinska, K.M.**
The St Lawrence, a short list of materials published in 1939-1940.
1962. [3] 5 1. (Ms. U. of O. Libr. School)

2:1563 **Miko, Eugénie**
Bio-bibliographie analytique de Roger Chartier, directeur du personnel à l'Hydro-Québec, précédée d'une biographie. Préface de M. Marcel Hudon. Québec, 1962. 38 p. (Ms. Ecole de Bibl., U.L.)

2:1564 **Milette, Denyse**
Bio-bibliographie de l'abbé Paul-Emile McCaughan. Préface de G. Chaput, p.s.s. 1951. xii, 32 p. (Ms. Ecole de Bibl., U. de M.)

2:1565 **Miller, Genevieve**
Bibliography of the history of medicine of the United States and Canada, 1939-1960. With a historical introd. by W.B. McDaniel. Baltimore, Johns Hopkins Press [c1964] xvi, 428 p.
Reissue in consolidated form of the *Bibliography of the history of medicine of the United States and Canada,* published annually in the *Bulletin of the history of medicine,* since 1940.

2:1566 **Miller, Genevieve**
A bibliography of the writings of Henry F. Sigerist. Montreal, McGill University Press, 1966.
vi, 112 p. port.

2:1567 **Millo, Valentino**
Bio-bibliographie de Jacques Rousseau. [Montréal] 1959-60.
vii, 166 p. (Ms. Ecole de Bibl., U. de M.)

2:1568 **Mills, Judith Eileen**
Sir Oliver Mowat; a bibliography of primary sources and biographical materials. Toronto, 1966. ii, 17 *l.* (Ms. Toronto Univ. Libr. School)

2:1569 **Mills, Judith Eileen**
University of Toronto doctoral theses, 1897-1967; a bibliography, compiled by Judy Mills and Irene Dombra. [Toronto] Published for University of Toronto Library by University of Toronto Press [c1968] xi, 186 p.

2:1570 **Milne, William Samuel**
Canadian full-length plays in English; a preliminary annotated catalogue. [Ottawa] Dominion Drama Festival [1964] viii, 47 p.
supplement. [Ottawa] Dominion Drama Festival, 1966. vii, 39 p.

2:1571 **Milot, Arthur-F.**
La politique extérieure du Canada. 1964. iv, 16 1. (Ms. U. of O. Libr. School)

2:1572 **Mitchell, James G.**
A bibliography of Canadian poetry, 1911-1915, in the Toronto Public Library, the University of Toronto Library, and Victoria College Library. [Toronto] 1947. [1], ii, 7 *l.* (Ms. Toronto Univ. Libr. School)

2:1573 **Moir, Elizabeth**
List of books on Canadian bibliography in the reference department of the Toronto Public Library. (In *Library world,* n.s., v. 13, 1907, p. 111-113)
Arranged alphabetically by author. Covers 1508-1909, but majority of list covers the early 19th century.

2:1574 **Moisan, Pierrette**
Bio-bibliographie de Madame Jeanne Grisé-Allard [s.d.] 36 p. (Mf. Ecole de Bibl., U. de M.)

2:1575 **Moissac, Elisabeth de, soeur**
Notes bio-bibliographiques sur Donatien Frémont. 1947. 15 p. (Mf. Ecole de Bibl., U. de M.)

2:1576 **Molinaro, Julius A.**
A bibliography of sixteenth-century Italian verse collections in the University of Toronto Library, compiled by Julius A. Molinaro. [Toronto] University of Toronto Press [c1969]
xxxiii, 124 p. illus.

2:1577 **Monfette, Brigitte**
Essai de bio-bibliographie: Rév. Sœur Sainte-Marie-Pia. 1953. 16 p. (Ms. Ecole de Bibl., U. de M.)

2:1578 **Monkhouse, Valerie**
The role of the ombudsman in Canada. 1967. iv, 8 1 (Ms. U. of O. Libr. School)

2:1579 **Montigny, Louvigny Testard de**
Antoine Gérin-Lajoie. Toronto, Ryerson [1925]. 130 p. (Makers of Canadian literature)
Bibliographie: p. 119-125.

2:1580 **Montréal. Ecole des Hautes Etudes commerciales**
... Contribution des professeurs de l'Ecole des Hautes Etudes commerciales de Montréal à la vie intellectuelle du Canada. Livres,

conférences, ouvrages en collaboration, brochures, mémoires ...
Catalogue des principaux écrits. [Montréal] 1960. iii, 132 f.

2:1581 **Montreuil, Denise**
Bibliographie du roman canadien-français des débuts à 1925.
Québec, 1949. 30 p. (Ms. Ecole de Bibl., U.L.)

2:1582 **Morgan, Henry James**
Bibliotheca Canadensis; or, A manual of Canadian literature.
Ottawa, Desbarats, 1867. xiv, 411 p.

2:1583 **Morgan, Jean E.**
A bibliography of descriptive and historical material relating to
Prince Edward Island. Montreal [1940]. 11, 14 *l*. (Ms. McGill Univ.
Libr. School)

2:1584 **Morgan, Judith**
A bibliography of printed materials concerning Mackenzie King's
external policy, 1939-1945. [Toronto] 1967. iv, 12 *l*. (Ms. Toronto
Univ. Libr. School)

2:1585 **Morin, Jacqueline**
Bio-bibliographie de Jean-Charles Harvey. 1943-44. 312 p. (Mf.
Ecole de Bibl., U. de M.)

2:1586 **Morin, Jacques**
Bio-bibliographie de M. Rolland Dumais, 1957 à 1960. Giffard,
1964. 86 p. (Ms. Ecole de Bibl., U.L.)

2:1587 **Morin, Maurice**
Bibliographie analytique de 'T.D. Bouchard' (discours et conférences)
précédée d'une biographie. Préface de M. Gustave Morin. Loretteville,
1964. 143 p. (Ms. Ecole de Bibl., U.L.)

2:1588 **Morin, Mme Romuald**
Bibliographie analytique de l'œuvre de l'abbé Louis O'Neill,
précédée d'une biographie. Préface du R.F. Gustave Tardif. Québec,
1962. 37 p. (Ms. Ecole de Bibl., U.L.)

2:1589 **Morisset, Anne-Marie**
Bio-bibliographie de Esdras Minville. Préface de M. Edouard
Montpetit et du R.P. Emile Bouvier, s.j. 1943. 80 p. (Ms. Ecole de
Bibl., U. de M.)

2:1590 **Morissette, Rachel**
Bibliographie analytique de Madame Yolande Chéné, précédée d'une
biographie. Préface de Guy Laviolette [pseud.] Québec, 1963. 28 p.
(Ms. Ecole de Bibl., U.L.)

2:1591  [Morley, E. Lillian]
A Perth county bibliography. [Milverton? Milverton Sun, 1949?]
[14] p.

2:1592  Morley, Marjorie
A bibliography of Manitoba, selected from holdings in the Legislative
Library of Manitoba. Winnipeg, Provincial Library, 1948. 17 *l.*
Revised edition: 1953. 45 *l.*

2:1593  Morley, Marjorie
Royal commissions and commissions of inquiry under 'The Evidence
Act' in Manitoba; a checklist. [Winnipeg, Legislative Library, 1952]
11, 10 *l.*

2:1594  Morley, William F.E.
The Atlantic provinces; Newfoundland, Nova Scotia, New Brunswick,
Prince Edward Island, by William F.E. Morley. [Toronto] University
of Toronto Press [c1967]
xx, 137 p. illus., maps (part fold.) (Canadian local histories to 1950: a
bibliography. v. 1)

2:1595  Morley, William F.E.
A bibliographical study of Charlevoix's *Histoire et description générale
de la Nouvelle-France.* (In *Bibliographical society of Canada. Papers,
no. 2, 1963, p. 21-45*)

2:1596  Morrison, Hugh M.
A guide to reading on Canada for high school teachers and students
of social studies. Compiled by Hugh M. Morrison, and Fred E.
Whitworth. Ottawa, Canadian Council of Education for Citizenship,
1945. 116 p.

2:1597  Morse, Hazel Gordon
Acadia authors; a bibliography. Wolfville, N.S., 1922. 44 p.
'From *Acadia bulletin* XI, no. 1, December 1922.'

2:1598  Moss, Harold Charles
A partial bibliography of Saskatchewan soil science, containing
papers, reports and theses from the Department of Soil Science and
the Saskatchewan Soil Survey for the period 1921 to 1957. [Saska-
toon, Sask.] Dept. of Soil Science, University of Saskatchewan, 1958.
25 p.

2:1599  Motiuk, Laurence
Canadian Forces college reading guide for the study of war, national
defence and strategy [by] L. Motiuk. [Ottawa, 1967]
vii, 345 p.

2:1600 **Moulton, Alice Marian**
Louisbourg, fortress of the Atlantic; a bibliography of its history
from 1713 to 1758. Toronto, 1965. iv, 11 *l.* (Ms. Toronto Univ.
Libr. School)

2:1601 **Muchin, John**
Ballet in Canada. 1963. v, 12 1. (Ms. U. of O. Libr. School)

2:1602 **Munger, Angèle**
La vie personnelle de l'infirmière d'après la documentation des
revues de langue française de la province de Québec. (Bibliographie
analytique) 1951-1961. Chicoutimi, 1962. 26 p. (Ms. Ecole de Bibl.,
U.L.)

2:1603 **Munns, Edward Norfolk**
... A select bibliography of North American forestry. Washington,
U.S., Government Printing Office, 1940. 2 v. (1142 p.) (U.S. Dept.
of Agriculture. Miscellaneous publications, no. 364)
'... Includes references to the more important literature on forestry published
in Canada, Mexico, and the United States prior to 1930.'–Cf. Introd. p. 3.

2:1604 **Murdock, George**
Ethnographic bibliography of North America. New Haven, Pub. for
the Dept. of Anthropology, Yale University, by the Yale University
Press; London, Milford, Oxford University Press, 1941. xvi, 168 p.
(*Yale anthropological studies,* v. 1)
Second ed.: New Haven, Human Relations Area Files, 1953. xvi, 239 p.
28 cm. (*Behavior science bibliographies*)
Third ed.: New Haven, Human Relations Area Files, 1960. xxiii, 393 p.
(*Behavior science bibliographies*)

2:1605 **Murphy, Henry Cruse**
Catalogue of the magnificent library of the late Hon. Henry C. Murphy
of Brooklyn, Long Island, consisting almost wholly of Americana or
books relating to America. New York, Leavitt, 1884. viii, 434 p.
'Le Canada occupe un espace considérable dans cette collection importante.'–
Cf. Gagnon I, 413.

2:1606 **Murray, Elsie McLeod**
A bibliography of the works of George MacKinnon Wrong. [Toronto]
1938. [10] *l.* (Ms. Toronto Univ. Libr. School)

2:1607 **Murray, Elsie McLeod**
A checklist of early newspaper files located in local newspaper offices
in western Ontario. London, Ont., Lawson Memorial Library, Univ.
of Western Ontario, 1947. 23 *l.* (*Western Ontario history nuggets, 12*)

2:1608  **Myers, R. Holtby and company**
... Complete catalogue of Canadian publications, containing carefully prepared lists of all the newspapers and periodicals published in the Dominion of Canada. Toronto, Myers, 1890. 30 p.

2:1609  **Myres, Miles Timothy**
An introduction to the literature of the effects of biocides on wildlife and fish; a select bibliography. Calgary, Dept. of Biology, University of Alberta at Calgary, 1964.
ii, 28 *l.*

2:1610  **Nadeau, Charles**
Saint Joseph dans l'édition canadienne; bibliographie. Montréal, Oratoire Saint-Joseph du Mont-Royal, 1967.
v, 81 p.

2:1611  **Nadeau, Marie-Marthe**
Bibliographie analytique de l'œuvre de l'abbé Arthur Maheux pour les années 1942–1943–1944. Québec, 1947. 58 p. (Ms. Ecole de Bibl., U.L.)

2:1612  **Narcisse, frère**
Notes bio-bibliographiques sur M. l'abbé Jules-Bernard Gingras. 1950. iv, 13 p. (Ms. Ecole de Bibl., U. de M.)

2:1613  **National Committee for Friendly Relations with Overseas Students**
A Canadian reading list. Toronto [1960] 12 p.
'Prepared with the cooperation of the University of Toronto Library.'

2:1614  **National Committee for Research on Co-operatives**
Bibliography of Canadian writings on co-operation, 1900 to 1959. Ottawa, Co-operative Union of Canada, 1960. 48 p. (Its Research paper no. 1)
Compiled by the Dept. of Co-operation and Co-operative Development of Saskatchewan. Cf. p. 4.

2:1615  **National Research Council, Canada.** Division of Building Research
A bibliography of Canadian papers of interest in building research to June 30, 1951, by R.J. Brodie, J. O'Flanagan, and M.K. Anderson, January 1952. [Ottawa, 1952] 43 p. (Its Bibliography no. 4)

2:1616  **National Research Council, Canada.** Division of Building Research
List of publications, 1947-1962 inclusive. Ottawa, 1962. 60, [1] p.
Previous editions under title: List of [and] index to publications ...
Supplement no. 1 ... April, 1963. Ottawa, 1963. 4, [1] *l.*
Supplement no. 2 ... September, 1963. Ottawa, 1963. [7] *l.*

2:1617 **National Research Council, Canada.** Division of Building
Research Bibliography. Ottawa, 1951.

2:1618 **National Research Council, Canada.** Division of Information Services
Publications of the National Research Council of Canada. 3d ed.,
1918-1952 (N.R.C. nos. 1-2900) Ottawa, 1953. 263 p.
Kept up to date by mimeographed, bimonthly lists.
First ed. 1939, issued by the Research Plans and Publications Branch. Second
ed. 1947, issued by the Public Relations Branch.
Supplement. 1953-58. [Ottawa, n.d.] 180 p.
Supplement. 1958-63. Ottawa, 1964. v, 438 p.

2:1619 **Naud, Denise**
Bibliographie analytique de l'œuvre du Dr Georges Maheux, ento-
mologiste. (1ère partie, 1915-1940) Préface de M. Jean-Charles
Magnan. Québec, 1963. 120 p. (Ms. Ecole de Bibl., U.L.)

2:1620 **Neill, Edward Duffield**
The writings of Louis Hennepin, Recollect missionary. Prepared for
the monthly meeting of the Department of American history,
Minnesota historical society, on September 6, 1880, at Minneapolis.
[Minneapolis? 1880] 10 p.

2:1621 **New Brunswick.** Department of Education. Audio-Visual Bureau
Catalog of motion pictures and filmstrips, 1963. Fredericton, 1963.
739 p.
Title page in English. Text bilingual.
Supplement, 1964. Fredericton, 1964. 743-786 p.
Supplement, 1965. Fredericton, 1965. 789-831 p.

2:1622 **New Brunswick.** Legislative Library
New Brunswick government documents. A checklist of New Brunswick
government documents received at the Legislative Library, Fredericton,
N.B., during the calendar year ... Fredericton, N.B., 1955–. Annual.

2:1623 **New Brunswick. University.** Library
A catalogue of the Rufus Hathaway collection of Canadian literature,
University of New Brunswick. Fredericton, 1935. vi, 53 p.

2:1624 **New Brunswick Museum.** Dept. of Canadian History. Archives Division
Inventory of manuscripts. [Saint John, N.B.] 1967.
154 p.

2:1625 **New Brunswick Research and Productivity Council**
... Bibliography of New Brunswick geology. D. Abbott, editor.
Fredericton, 1965. 79 p. (Its Record 2, pt. C)

2:1626  **New York.** Museum of French art, French institute in the United States
Publications contemporaines de langue française aux Etats-Unis et au Canada; exposition. New York, French institute, 1942. 4 f., 11-45 p., 1 f.

2:1627  **New York.** Public Library
Canada; an exhibition commemorating the four hundredth anniversary of the discovery of the Saint Lawrence by Jacques Cartier, 1534-1535; a catalogue with notes. New York, New York Public library, 1935. 59 p.
'Compiled by Stanley R. Pillsbury under the direction of Mr McCombs.'–p. 4.
'Reprinted from the *Bulletin of the New York public library* of July and August 1935.'

2:1628  **Newberry Library,** Chicago. Edward E. Ayer Collection
Narratives of captivity among the Indians of North America; a list of books and manuscripts on this subject in the Edward E. Ayer Collection of the Newberry Library. Chicago, Newberry Library [1912]. 120 p. (Publications of the Newberry Library, no. 3)
Supplement I. By Clara A. Smith. Chicago, Newberry Library, 1928.

2:1629  **Newcombe, Hanna**
Bibliography on war and peace. [Clarkson, Ont., Canadian Peace Research Institute, 1963]
19 *l.*

2:1630  **Newcombe, Hanna**
Short bibliography on war and peace. [Clarkson, Ont.] Canadian Peace Research Institute [1963?]
2 *l.*

2:1631  **Newfoundland.** Geological Survey
Bibliography of the geology of Newfoundland, 1936-1954; bibliography of the geology of Labrador, 1814-1954. By D.M. Baird, C.R. Gillespie and J.H. McKillip. St John's, Nfld., 1954. 47 p.

2:1632  **Nickle, Elizabeth Anne Margaret**
Harold Adams Innis; a bibliography of biographical, critical and bibliographical materials. [Toronto] 1965. iv, 9 *l.* (Ms. Toronto Univ. Libr. School)

2:1633  **Nish, James Cameron**
Bibliographie pour servir à l'étude de l'histoire du Canada français, compilée par Cameron et Elizabeth Nish. [Montréal, Digital Computer Center, Sir George Williams University, 1966]

1 v. (non paginé) deux fois par année
Bulletin no 1 publié par le Centre de recherche en histoire économique du
Canada français et le Centre d'étude du Québec.
Title varies.

Bulletins 3 & 4, Montréal, Centre d'étude du Québec, Sir George Williams
University, 1968.

2:1634 **Nish, James Cameron**
Inventaire sommaire des documents historiques de la Société historique de Montréal. [Montréal, 1968]

vi, 174 f.
Publié sous les auspices du Centre de recherche en histoire économique du
Canada français et du Centre d'étude du Québec de l'Université Sir George
Williams.

2:1635 **Nolin, Louisette**
Notes bibliographiques sur Marius Barbeau. 1947. 19 p. (Ms. Ecole
de Bibl., U. de M.)

2:1636 **Normand, Rita**
Bio-bibliographie analytique de Gérard Martin. Préf. de Charles-Marie
Boissonnault. Québec, 1953. 65 p. (Ms. Ecole de Bibl., U.L.)

2:1637 **Normandin, Georges**
Bio-bibliographie de Olivar Asselin. 1947. 9 p. (Mf. Ecole de Bibl.,
U. de M.)

2:1638 **North** (Indexes)
Subject and author index. [Vol. 6, no. 2-v. 9, no. 2; May-June 1959–
Mar.-Apr. 1964. Ottawa, Northern Administration Branch, Dept. of
Northern Affairs and National Resources, 1964] 31 *l.*

'Issues previous to Volume VI, Number 2, were not available to the public and
have not been indexed. The title was *Northern affairs bulletin* until Volume VII,
Number 3.'–Pref.

2:1639 **Nova Scotia.** Legislative Library
A finding-list of Royal Commissions appointed by the province of
Nova Scotia, 1908-1954. Halifax, 1956. 5 *l.*

2:1640 **Nova Scotia.** Public Archives
... A catalogue of maps, plans and charts in the Public Archives of
Nova Scotia. Comp. by Marion Gilroy, under the direction of D.C.
Harvey. Halifax, Public Archives, 1938. 95 p. (Bulletin, v. 1, no. 3)

2:1641 **Nova Scotia.** Public Archives
A catalogue of the Akins Collection of books and pamphlets. Comp.
by Sheila I. Stewart. Halifax, Imperial Publishing Co., 1933. 206 p.
(Publication no. 1)

2:1642 **O'Bready, Maurice**
Les journaux publiés dans les Cantons de l'Est depuis 150 ans. Texte de la conférence prononcée sur les ondes de CHLT, Sherbrooke, le 11 avril 1965, à l'occasion de la 7e semaine des bibliothèques canadiennes. [Sherbrooke, 1965] 9 f.
Composé en majeure partie de la liste de ces journaux.

2:1643 **O'Brien, Arthur Henry**
... Haliburton ('Sam Slick'): A sketch and bibliography ... Montreal, Gazette, 1910. 26 p.
Reprinted from Royal Society of Canada, *Transactions,* 3rd series, 1909-1910, v. III, sec. II.

2:1644 **O'Brien, Elmer L.**
Theology in transition; a bibliographical evaluation of the 'decisive decade,' 1954-1964. [Montreal] Palm Publishers; [New York] Herder and Herder [1965]
282 p. (*Contemporary theology,* v. 1)

2:1645 **O'Callaghan, Edmund Bailey**
Jesuit relations of discoveries and other occurrences in Canada and the northern and western states of the Union, 1632-1672. New York, 1847. 22 p. (New York Historical Society, *Proceedings,* Nov. 1847)

2:1646 **O'Callaghan, Edmund Bailey**
Relations des Jésuites sur les découvertes et les autres événements arrivés en Canada, et au nord et à l'ouest des Etats-Unis (1611-1672). Par le Dr E.B. O'Callaghan. Tr. de l'anglais avec quelques notes, corrections et additions [par Félix Martin]. Montréal, Bureau des Mélanges religieux, 1850. vi, [7]-70 p.

2:1647 **O'Dea, Agnes C.**
Bibliography of Newfoundland. (*In progress*)
Includes a checklist of periodical articles on Newfoundland and Labrador.

2:1648 **L'Œuvre du chanoine Lionel Groulx**; témoignages, bio-bibliographie. Montréal [Académie canadienne-française, 1964] 197 p. portr. (Les publications de l'Académie canadienne-française)
'Ce volume a été conçu et réalisé par Victor Barbeau. La bibliographie est l'œuvre de Juliette Rémillard et de Madeleine Dionne ...'–p. [4] Bibliographie: p. 19-189.

2:1649 **Okanagan Regional Library**, Kelowna, B.C.
British Columbia. [Kelowna, B.C., 1965]
23, ii p. map.
Bibliography of books about British Columbia, and books by British Columbia authors.

2:1650 **Okanagan Regional Library,** Kelowna, B.C.
A list of selected non-fiction catalogued during the year, from
August, 1966 to August, 1967. [Kelowna, 1967]
101, iv p.

21651 **Okanagan Regional Library,** Kelowna, B.C.
Recent additions. 1966. [Kelowna, B.C., 1966]
93, iv p.

2:1652 **Olivier, Gabrielle**
Bio-bibliographie de Mère Saint-Louis-du-Sacré-Cœur, c.n.d. Lettre-
préface du R.P. E.-A. Langlais, o.p. Préface de M. Henri Garrouteigt,
p.s.s. 1945. xi, 54 p. (Ms. Ecole de Bibl., U. de M.)

2:1653 **Ontario. Department of Education.** Public Libraries Branch
Dominion, British Columbia, Ontario and Quebec Government
publications, 1938; received by the Inspector of Public Libraries.
Toronto, King's Printer, 1938. 19 p.

2:1654 **Ontario. Department of Mines**
Bibliography of theses on the Precambrian geology of Ontario,
compiled by R.M. Ginn. [Toronto] 1961. ii, 49, [1] *l.* map. (Its
Miscellaneous paper MP-2)

2:1655 **Ontario. Department of Mines**
General index of the reports of the Bureau of Mines, Ontario, v. I to
XXV (1891-1916) compiled by F.J. Nicolas. Printed by order of the
Legislative Assembly of Ontario. Toronto, King's Printer, 1921. vi,
871 p.
General index to the reports ... v. XXVI to XXXV (1917-1927) ... Toronto,
King's Printer, 1928. vi, 668 p.

2:1656 **Ontario. Department of Mines**
... List of publications. [10th ed.] rev. to Oct. 1963. Compiled by
the Publications Office ... Toronto, Queen's Printer, 1963. ix, 96 p.
(fold. maps in pocket) (Its Bulletin no. 25)

2:1657 **Ontario. Department of Mines.** Report. (Indexes)
General index to the Reports of the Ontario Department of Mines ...
1891-[1950] Toronto, Queen's Printer, 1921-1954. 4 v.
Contents.–V. 1. 1891-1916. (1921);-2. 1917-27. (1928);-3. 1927-40.
(1949);-4. 1941-50. (1954)

2:1658 **Ontario. Education Department**
Catalogue of the books relating to Canada: historical and biographical,
in the library of the Education Department for Ontario, arranged

according to topics and in alphabetical order. Toronto, Warwick, 1890. 122 p.

Another edition: 1897. 268 p.

2:1659  **Ontario. Legislative library,** Toronto
Catalogue of books in the Legislative library of the province of Ontario on November 1, 1912. Printed by order of the Legislative assembly of Ontario. Toronto, Printed by L.K. Cameron, 1913.

1 p. 1., v-viii, 3-929 p.

2:1660  **Ontario. Legislative library,** Toronto
Catalogue of the library of the Parliament of Ontario. Toronto, Printed by Hunter, Rose & co., 1875.

viii, 308 p.

Supplementary catalogue ... 1876. Toronto, Printed by Hunter, Rose & company, 1876.
33 p.

2:1661  **Ontario. Legislative library,** Toronto
Catalogue of the library of the Parliament of Ontario: with alphabetical indexes of authors and of subjects. 1881. Comp. by John Watson. Toronto, Printed by C.B. Robinson, 1881.

xi, [3]-558 p.

2:1662  **Ontario. Office of King's Printer**
Catalogue of publications issued by the government of Ontario (Rev. to August 1st, 1916) Toronto, Wilgress, Printer to the King, 1916. 16 p.

2:1663  **Ontario Library Association**
Selected books [displayed at the] Ontario Library Association Conference. Catalogue by the Ryerson Press. 1966. [Toronto, 1966]

24 *l.* annual.
Title varies: 1955, O.L.A. booklist.–1956-61, Selected books, assembled and displayed by the Ryerson Press [at the] Ontario Library Assoc. Conference.

2:1664  **Ontario library review** ... Toronto, Public Libraries Branch, Ontario Department of Education [1916]. Quarterly.

Title varies: June 1916-May 1928, *Ontario library review and book selection guide*; Aug. 1928-Feb. 1938, *Ontario library review,* published quarterly ...; May 1938-Nov. 1947, *Ontario library review and periodical index.*
Suspended Feb.-May 1932, Aug. 1933.

2:1665  **Oregon Historical Society,** Portland
A bibliography of Pacific Northwest history. [Portland, 1958?]

[ii], 44 *l.* (Its *Oregon centennial publications.*)

2:1666 **Osekre, B.A.**
Canadian bilateral agreements. 1963. ii, 10 l. (Ms. U. of O. Libr.
School)

2:1667 **Osler, Sir William**
Bibliotheca osleriana: a catalogue of books illustrating the history
of medicine and science, collected, arranged and annotated by Sir
William Osler, and bequeathed to McGill University. Montreal,
McGill-Queen's University Press, 1969.
xli, 792 p.
First ed. Oxford, Clarendon Press, 1929.

2:1668 **Ostiguy, Flore-Ella**
Bibliographie de madame Ella Charland-Ostiguy. Québec, 1950. 45 p.
(Ms. Ecole de Bibl., U.L.)

2:1669 **Ottawa. Public Library**
Canada, a reading list. Comp. by W.J. Sykes. Ottawa, Carnegie Public
Library, 1931. 23 p.

2:1670 **Ottawa. Public Library**
Canadian scene; a selected list of recent Canadian books in the
Ottawa Public Library. [Ottawa, 1959] 8 *l.*

2:1671 **Ottawa. Public Library**
Ottawa and district; a selected list of books. [Ottawa, 1954] 5 *l.*
Signed: Elizabeth L. Hunter.

2:1672 **Ottawa. Université.** Centre canadien de documentation—sport et
fitness
Periodicals received by the Canadian Documentation Centre.
Périodiques auxquels le Centre canadien de documentation est
abonné. [Ottawa, 1965]
24 p.

2:1673 **Ottawa. University.** Canadian Documentation Centre—Fitness and
Sport
Periodicals received by the Canadian Documentation Centre.
Périodiques auxquels le Centre canadien de documentation est
abonné. [Ottawa, 1965]
24 p.

2:1674 **Ouellet, Thérèse**
Bibliographie du théâtre canadien-français avant 1900. Thèse ...
Univ. Laval ... D. de Bibliothéconomie. Québec, 1949. 53 p.

2:1675 **Ouimet, Jacqueline**
Bio-bibliographie de Charles Gill. Préface de Mlle Marie-Claire Daveluy. 1945. 35 p. (Ms. Ecole de Bibl., U. de M.)

2:1676 **Ouimet, Lucile**
Bio-bibliographie du Dr Oscar Mercier. 1944. 27, 7 p. (Ms. Ecole de Bibl., U. de M.)

2:1677 **Ouimet, Yves**
L'Opinion contemporaine sur le gouvernement de monsieur Duplessis, en dehors du Québec. 1967. iv, 9 1. (Ms. U. of O. Libr. School)

2:1678 **Outremont, Qué.** Maison provinciale des Clercs de Saint-Viateur. Bibliothèque
Section Canadiana; [catalogue] Outremont, 1955. 59 p.

2:1679 **Overseas Institute of Canada**
Bibliography on Canadian aid to the developing countries ... Ottawa, 1964. 8 p.

2:1680 **Ower, Bernard A.**
Railways—Canada; a select bibliography. Montreal, 1935. [6] *l.* (Ms. McGill Univ. Libr. School)

2:1681 **Oyama, Midori**
The work of Marius Barbeau published in Canada since 1948. 1964. xiii, 16 1. (Ms. U. of O. Libr. School)

2:1682 **Packard, Alpheus Spring**
The Labrador coast. A journal of two summer cruises to that region. With notes on its early discovery, on the Eskimo, on its physical geography, geology and natural history. New York, Hodges; [etc., etc.] 1891. 6 p., 1 *l.,* 513 p.
'Bibliography of books and articles relating to the geography and civil and natural history of Labrador': p. 475-501.

2:1683 **Page, Céline V.**
Frère Robert Sylvain. Bibliographie analytique précédée d'une biographie. Préf. de Maurice Lebel. 1964. (Ms. Ecole de Bibl., U.L.)

2:1684 **Page, Jean-Pierre**
Bio-bibliographie de Henri de Saint-Denys Garneau. Préface de M. Stanislas Vachon. Québec, 1964. 48 p. (Ms. Ecole de Bibl., U.L.)

2:1685 **Pagé, May-Andrée**
Essai de bio-bibliographie: Mgr Joseph Chevalier, p.a. 1953. 37 p. (Ms. Ecole de Bibl., U. de M.)

2:1686 **Palfrey, Thomas Rossman**
Guide to bibliographies of theses, United States and Canada. Compiled by Thomas Rossman Palfrey and Henry E. Coleman. Chicago, American Library Association, 1936. 48 p.
Second edition: 1940. 54 p.

2:1687 **Paltsits, Victor Hugo**
Bibliography of the works of Father Louis Hennepin. Chicago, McClurg, 1903. 1 p. *l.*, [xlv]-lxiv p.
'Separate (twenty-five copies printed) from Hennepin's *A new discovery*, edited by Reuben Gold Thwaites.'

2:1688 **Paltsits, Victor Hugo**
A bibliography of the writings of Baron Lahontan. Chicago, McClurg, 1905. [ii]-xciii p.
'Separate (twenty-five copies) from the Reprint of Lahontan's *New voyages to North America* (London, 1703). Edited, with introduction, notes and index, by Reuben Gold Thwaites,' 1904.

2:1689 **Papillon, Lucien**
Maître Adjutor Rivard. 1949. vi, 77 p. (Mf. Ecole de Bibl., U. de M.)

2:1690 **Paquette, Irène**
Bio-bibliographie de M. l'abbé Elie-J. Auclair. 1948. 9 p. (Ms. Ecole de Bibl., U. de M.)

2:1691 **Paquette, Jacques**
Essai de bio-bibliographie. M. Robert Lionel Séguin. Montréal, 1961. 39 p. (Ms. Ecole de Bibl., U. de M.)

2:1692 **Paquette, Marcelle**
Bibliographie de Félix Leclerc. Préface de Lucien Thériault. 1945. xxii, 49 p. (Mf. Ecole de Bibl., U. de M.)

2:1693 **Paquette, Monique**
Essai de bio-bibliographie: R.P. Germain Lesage, o.m.i. Préface du R.P. Hector Matton, o.m.i. 1953. 25 p. (Ms. Ecole de Bibl., U. de M.)

2:1694 **Paquin, Denise**
Notes bio-bibliographiques sur Louis-Honoré Fréchette. 1947. 13 p. (Ms. Ecole de Bibl., U. de M.)

2:1695 **Paquin, Madeleine**
Bio-bibliographie du R.P. Bonaventure Péloquin, o.f.m., missionnaire apostolique. 1947. 10 p. (Ms. Ecole de Bibl., U. de M.)

2:1696 **Paquin, Marie-Antoinette, soeur**
Bibliographie de la Révérende Mère Gérin-Lajoie, n.d. du b.c. 1939. ii, 33 p. (Ms. Ecole de Bibl., U. de M.)

2:1697  **Paradis, André**
Bibliographie du Rév. Père Arcade-M.-Monette, o.p. Québec, 1964.
41 p. (Ms. Ecole de Bibl., U.L.)

2:1698  **Paradis, Gabrielle**
Bio-bibliographie du R.P. Antonio Dragon, s.j. Lettre-préface du
R.P. Léon Pouliot, s.j. 1944. 53 p. (Ms. Ecole de Bibl., U. de M.)

2:1699  **Paradis, Germaine**
Bio-bibliographie de Mademoiselle Adrienne Choquette. Préf. de
Monsieur Robert Choquette. 1947. 42 p. (Mf. Ecole de Bibl., U. de M.)

2:1700  **Paré, Rosario**
Bibliographie de l'œuvre de Maurice Lebel, précédée d'une biographie.
Québec, 1947. 25 p. (Ms. Ecole de Bibl., U.L.)

2:1701  **Parent, Amand**
Bibliographie de Georges-Emile Marquis. 1938. 28 p. (Ms. Ecole de
Bibl., U. de M.)

2:1702  **Parent, Jean-Baptiste**
Bio-bibliographie de Monseigneur Alexandre Vachon, archevêque
d'Ottawa. Préf. de M. Cyrias Ouellet. Québec, 1947. 25 p. (Ms.
Ecole de Bibl., U.L.)

2:1703  **Paris.** Exposition rétrospective des colonies françaises de l'Amérique
du Nord. 1929.
... Catalogue illustré. Analyse des documents, objets et peintures
exposés, par M.A.-Léo Leymarie. Paris, Société d'éditions géographiques, maritimes et coloniales [1929] lxv, 312 p.

2:1704  **Park, Maria**
Canadian folk-songs. 1963. vi, 7 1 (Ms. U. of O. Libr. School)

2:1705  **Parke-Bernet Galleries**
The celebrated collection of Americana formed by the late Thomas
Winthrop Streeter, Morristown, New Jersey, sold by order of the
trustees. v. 6 [compiled by Caroline F. Hover, Paul Jordan Smith
[and] David Lasswell] New York, 1969.
2284-2766, [11] p. facsims.
Contents.—The Pacific West.—Orgeon.—British Columbia.—Alaska 1751-1865.—
Alaska and the Klondike 1873-1925.—Canada.—Hawaii.—Maps.—Reference
books (p. [2767-2769])

2:1706  **Parker, David W.**
Guide to the materials for United States history in Canadian archives.

Washington, D.C. Carnegie Institution of Washington, 1913. New York, Kraus Reprint Corp., 1965.
x, 339 p. (Carnegie Institution of Washington. Publication no. 172)

2:1707   **Parker, Franklin**
Canadian education; bibliography of 131 doctoral dissertations. Austin, Tex. [n.d.] 9 *l.*

2:1708   **Parmenter, Ross**
Explorer, linguist and ethnologist; a descriptive bibliography of the published works of Alphonse Louis Pinart, with notes on his life. Introd. by Carl Schaefer Dentzel. Los Angeles, Southwest Museum, 1966.
xi, 57 p. illus., ports. (F.W. Hodge Anniversary Publication Fund. [Publications] 9)

2:1709   **Parry, Norah H.**
Bibliography of Rt. Hon. Sir Gilbert Parker, bart. [Toronto] 1933. [1], 15 *l.* (Ms. Toronto Univ. Libr. School)

2:1710   **Partridge, Florence G.**
Handicrafts in Canada; bibliography. [Toronto] 1932. [12] *l.* (Ms. Toronto Univ. Libr. School)

2:1711   **Paul de Rome**
Bibliographie analytique de l'œuvre du docteur de la Broquerie Fortier. Québec, 1962. 82 p. (Ms. Ecole de Bibl., U.L.)

2:1712   **Paul-du-Sauveur, soeur**
Essai de bio-bibliographie de la Révérende Mère Gamelin. 1958. [xxiii], 149 p. (Ms. Ecole de Bibl., U. de M.)

2:1713   **Paulhus, Euchariste**
Essai de bio-bibliographie du R.P. Noël Mailloux, o.p. 1952. vi, 14 p. (Ms. Ecole de Bibl., U. de M.)

2:1714   **Pauline-Marie, soeur**
Les Sœurs missionnaires de l'Immaculée-Conception. Montréal, 1964. 363 p. (Ms. Ecole de Bibl., U.L.)

2:1715   **Payette, Ange-Albert**
Bibliographie de l'œuvre de l'honorable Maurice Tellier. Préface de Lorenzo Pouliot. Québec, 1960. 25 p. (Ms. Ecole de Bibl., U.L.)

2:1716   **Peart, Helen**
Bibliography on the report compiled by the Royal Commission [Rowell-Sirois] on dominion-provincial relations. Montreal, 1941. 34 *l.* (Ms. McGill Univ. Libr. School)

2:1717   **Peel, Bruce Braden**
Alberta imprints before 1900. (In *Alberta historical review,* v. 3,
no. 3, Summer 1955, p. 41-46)

2:1718   **Peel, Bruce Braden**
A bibliography of the Prairie Provinces to 1953. [Toronto] Published
in co-operation with the Saskatchewan Golden Jubilee Committee
and the University of Saskatchewan by University of Toronto Press
[1956] . xix, 680 p.
Supplement. [Toronto] University of Toronto Press, 1963. x, 130 p.

2:1719   **Peel, Bruce Braden**
How the Bible came to the Cree. (In *Alberta historical review,* v. 6,
no. 2, Spring 1958, p. 15-19) facsim.
A bibliography of early religious writings in the language of the Cree Indians.

2:1720   **Peel, Bruce Braden**
Saskatchewan imprints before 1900. (In *Saskatchewan history,* v. 6,
no. 3, Autumn 1953, p. 91-94)
An enlargement of an article which appeared originally in the *Bulletin of the
Saskatchewan library association,* v. 4, no. 2, Spring 1951.

2:1721   **Pelletier, Carmen**
Bibliographie analytique de Pierre-Paul Turgeon, précédée d'une
biographie. 1964. xiv, 59(1) p. (Ms. Ecole de Bibl., U.L.)

2:1722   **Pelletier, Charles**
Le Tourisme au Québec (1949-1967). 1967. vii, 8 l. (Ms. U. of O.
Libr. School)

2:1723   **Pelletier, J.-Antoine**
Bio-bibliographique de l'abbé Joseph-William-Ivanhoe Caron, 1875-
1941. Québec, 1947. 42 p. (Ms. Ecole de Bibl., U.L.)

2:1724   **Pelletier, Jacqueline**
Bio-bibliographie de l'abbé Arthur Maheux (1953-54-55). Québec,
1956. 38 p. (Ms. Ecole de Bibl., U.L.)

2:1725   **Pelletier, Jacqueline (Desaulniers)**
Bio-bibliographie de l'abbé Jean-Charles Beaudin. Préface par Mlle
Jeanne-Marguerite Saint-Pierre. 1947. 55 p. (Ms. Ecole de Bibl.,
U. de M.)

2:1726   **Pelletier, Suzanne-D.**
Bio-bibliographie de Claude-Henri Grignon. 1946. 32 p. (Mf. Ecole
de Bibl., U. de M.)

2:1727 **Pelletier, Virginie**
Bio-bibliographie de Georges Pelletier. 1942. 165 p. (Ms. Ecole de Bibl., U. de M.)

2:1728 **Penhallow, David Pearce**
A review of Canadian botany from 1800-1895. Montreal, 1898. 56 p. (McGill University. Papers from the Department of Botany, no. 7)
(Reprinted from Royal Society of Canada, *Transactions*, sec. 4, 1897) Bibliography, p. 27-56.

2:1729 **Pennsylvania. University.** Library
Catalogue of manuscripts in the libraries of the University of Pennsylvania to 1800, compiled by Norman P. Zacour and Rudolf Hirsch. Assisted by John F. Benton and William E. Miller. Philadelphia, University of Pennsylvania Press [c1965]
viii, 279 p. illus.

2:1730 **Pépin, Isabelle**
Notes bio-bibliographiques sur M. Henry Laureys. 1948. iv, 19 p. (Ms. Ecole de Bibl., U. de M.)

2:1731 **Perrault, Arthur**
Bio-bibliographie de Maximilien Bibaud, avocat. 1942. 35 p. (Mf. Ecole de Bibl., U. de M.)

2:1732 **Perrault, Eustelle**
Notes bio-bibliographiques du R.P. Lorenzo Gauthier, c.s.v. 1948. 16 p. (Ms. Ecole de Bibl., U. de M.)

2:1733 **Perrault, Pauline**
Bio-bibliographie de Michel Bibaud, journaliste, poète, historien. Lettre-préface de Harry Bernard. 1951. 69 p. (Mf. Ecole de Bibl., U. de M.)

2:1734 **Perreault, Honoré**
Essai de bibliographie de Joseph-François Perrault. 1950. 77 p. (Mf. Ecole de Bibl., U. de M.)

2:1735 **Perreault, Jean**
Bio-bibliographie du R.P. Paul-Emile Farley, c.s.v. 1948. 26 p. (Ms. Ecole de Bibl., U. de M.)

2:1736 **Perreault, Jeannette**
Bibliographie de Jean-Marie Laurence, précédée de notes biographiques. 1946. 36 p. (Ms. Ecole de Bibl., U. de M.)

2:1737 **Perret, Robert**
La géographie de Terre-Neuve. Préface de Marcel Dubois. Paris, Guilmoto, 1913. 372 p.
'Bibliographie': p. [353]-370.

2:1738 **Perron, Marc-A.**
Un grand éducateur agricole, Edouard-A. Barnard, 1835-1898; étude historique sur l'agriculture de 1760 à 1900. Préf. de Jean-Charles Magnan. [S.l., c1955] xxxi, 355 p.
Bibliographie: p. [xvii]-xxxi.

2:1739 **Pérusse, Claire**
Bio-bibliographie de l'abbé Armand Dubé. Québec, 1957. 60 p. (Ms. Ecole de Bibl., U.L.)

2:1740 **Petit, Madeleine**
Bio-bibliographie de M. l'abbé Georges Robitaille. Préface de M. Léo-Paul Desrosiers. 1945. xi, 26 p. (Ms. Ecole de Bibl., U. de M.)

2:1741 **Pettigrew, Renée**
Bibliographie des journaux de Québec, 1899-1940. Préf. de M. Bruno Lafleur. Québec, 1952. 32 p. (Ms. Ecole de Bibl., U.L.)

2:1742 **Philion, Dorothy**
Bio-bibliographie de W.A. Baker, c.r. Préface de Andrée Chaurette. 1951. 45 p. (Mf. Ecole de Bibl., U. de M.)

2:1743 **Piersol, Elizabeth M.**
Bibliography of Charles George Douglas Roberts. [Toronto, 1933] [2], 28 *l.* (Ms. Toronto Univ. Libr. School)

2:1744 **Pilling, James Constantine**
... Bibliography of the Algonquian languages. Washington, G.P.O., 1891. 614 p. (Smithsonian Institution, Bureau of [American] ethnology [Bulletin, no. 13])

2:1745 **Pilling, James Constantine**
... Bibliography of the Athapascan languages. Washington, G.P.O., 1892. 125 p. [U.S. Bureau of American Ethnology, Bulletin no. 14]

2:1746 **Pilling, James Constantine**
... Bibliography of the Chinookan languages (including the Chinook jargon). Washington, G.P.O., 1893. 81 p. (Smithsonian Institution, Bureau of Ethnology [Bulletin, no. 15])

2:1747 **Pilling, James Constantine**
... Bibliography of the Eskimo language. Washington, G.P.O., 1887.

116 p. (Smithsonian Institution, Bureau of Ethnology [Bulletin, no. 1].)

2:1748  **Pilling, James Constantine**
... Bibliography of the Iroquoian languages. Washington, G.P.O., 1888. 208 p. [U.S. Bureau of American Ethnology, Bulletin, no. 6]

2:1749  **Pilling, James Constantine**
... Bibliography of the Muskhogean languages. Washington, G.P.O., 1889. 114 p. [U.S. Bureau of American Ethnology, Bulletin no. 9]

2:1750  **Pilling, James Constantine**
... Bibliography of the Salishan languages. Washington, G.P.O., 1893. 86 p. (Smithsonian Institution, Bureau of Ethnology ... [Bulletin, no. 16])

2:1751  **Pilling, James Constantine**
... Bibliography of the Siouan languages. Washington, G.P.O., 1887. 87 p. (Smithsonian Institution, Bureau of Ethnology ... [Bulletin, no. 5])

2:1752  **Pilling, James Constantine**
... Bibliography of the Wakashan languages. Washington, G.P.O., 1894. 70 p. (Smithsonian Institution, Bureau of Ethnology [Bulletin, no. 19])

2:1753  **Pilling, James Constantine**
Proofsheets of a bibliography of the languages of the North American Indians (distributed only to collaborators) Smithsonian institution, Bureau of Ethnology, J.W. Powell, director. Washington, G.P.O., 1885. xl, 1135 p. 29 facsims.

2:1754  **Pilon, André**
Notes bibliographiques sur le Frère Antoine Bernard, c.s.v. 1947. 6 p. (Ms. Ecole de Bibl., U. de M.)

2:1755  **Pilon, Huguette**
Essai de bio-bibliographie. Monsieur l'abbé Adrien Brault. 1952. iii, 8 p. (Mf. Ecole de Bibl., U. de M.)

2:1756  **Pintal, Angèle**
Essai bio-bibliographique du R.P. Roger Gauthier. 1951. 20 p. (Ms. Ecole de Bibl., U. de M.)

2:1757  **Plante, Thérèse**
Bio-bibliographie du major Louis-Alexandre Plante. Préf. de M. Alphonse Désilets. Québec, 1953. 64 p. (Ms. Ecole de Bibl., U.L.)

2:1758  **Platzmann, Julius**
Verzeichniss einer Auswahl Amerikanischer Grammatiken Wörter-
bücher, Katechismen, u.s.w. Gesammelt von Julius Platzmann.
Leipzig, Köhler, 1876. 3 p. *l.*, 38 p.

2:1759  **Plourde, Marthe**
Bio-bibliographie de M. l'abbé L.E. Otis, préface de M. l'abbé Pascal
Tremblay. 1964, 35(1) p. (Ms. Ecole de Bibl., U.L.)

2:1760  **Plympton, Charles William**
... Select bibliography on travel in North America. Submitted for
graduation, New York state library school, June 1891. Revised
1896 ... [Albany, University of the state of New York, 1897] 1 p. *l.*,
[37]-60 p. (*New York state library bulletin.* Bibliography [v. 1]
no. 3, May 1897)

2:1761  **Poisson, Lise**
Bio-bibliographie du R.P. Marcel de Grandpré, c.s.v. 1953. vii, 49 p.
(Ms. Ecole de Bibl., U. de M.)

2:1762  **Poisson, Louis-Philippe**
Bibliographie de Raymond Douville. Préface de Clément Marchand.
1946. 114 p. (Ms. Ecole de Bibl., U. de M.)

2:1763  **Polgar, Anna-R.**
Essai de bio-bibliographie de Louis-Philippe Audet. Préf. par Georges
Maheux. Montréal, 1956. xxiii, 67 p. (Ms. Ecole de Bibl., U. de M.)

2:1764  **Pollin, Burton Ralph**
Godwin criticism; a synoptic bibliography [by] Burton R. Pollin.
[Toronto] University of Toronto Press [c1967]
xlvi, 659 p.

2:1765  **Pop, Sever**
... Jaroslav Bohdan Rudnyćkyj: notice biographique et bibliographique,
et résumé de sa communication: Recherches dialectologiques en
Amérique du Nord et enquêtes linguistiques sur place envisagées en
1933. Louvain, Centre international de Dialectologie générale près
l'Université catholique de Louvain, 1958. 29, [4] p. (Centre international de Dialectologie générale près l'Université catholique de
Louvain. Biographies et conférences. 13)

2:1766  **Poroniuk, Mychajlo**
The Ukrainian Catholic Church in Canada. 1963. viii, 13 l. (Ms.
U. of O. Libr. School)

2:1767 **Porter, Peter Augustus**
Father Hennepin; an attempt to collect every edition of his works. A brief bibliography thereof. Niagara Falls [Adams], 1910. 17 p.

2:1768 **Porter, Peter Augustus**
The works of Father Hennepin; a catalogue of the collection brought together by Peter A. Porter of Niagara Falls, N.Y. New York, Dodd & Livingston, 1910. 13 p.

2:1769 **Potvin, Claude**
Bibliographie des écrits de Claude Aubry, 1949-1965. 1966. iii, 5 1. (Ms. U. of O. Libr. School)

2:1770 **Potvin, Micheline**
Bio-bibliographie du docteur Louis-Paul Dugal. Préf. du docteur Rosario Potvin. Québec, 1950. 20 p. (Ms. Ecole de Bibl., U.L.)

2:1771 **Poulin, Daniel**
Teilhard de Chardin; essai de bibliographie (1955-1966) Préf. de Fernand Dumont. Québec, Presses de l'Université Laval, 1966. xiii, 157 p.

2:1772 **Pouliot, Aline**
Bibliographie analytique de l'œuvre de l'abbé Roch Duval, licencié en orientation, précédée d'une biographie. Préface de l'abbé Gérard Dion. Québec, 1964. 65 p. (Ms. Ecole de Bibl., U.L.)

2:1773 **Pouliot, Ghislaine**
Bio-bibliographie de Francis Desroches. Québec, 1959. 25 p. (Ms. Ecole de Bibl., U.L.)

2:1774 **Pouliot, Marcelle**
Bio-bibliographie de monsieur Jean-Charles Bonenfant, attaché à la bibliothèque de la Législature provinciale. Québec, 1947. 49 p. (Ms. Ecole de Bibl., U.L.)

2:1775 **Pratt, Phebe Gross**
A bibliography of Canadian opinion on national defence since the statute of Westminster, 1931-1938. Montreal, 1939. 21 *l*. (Ms. McGill Univ. Libr. School)

2:1776 **Préfontaine, Jacques**
Le peintre de la forêt: Marie Le Franc. [1953] 5 p. (Mf. Ecole de Bibl., U. de M.)

2:1777 **Prime, Frederick**
A catalogue of official reports upon geological surveys of the United States and territories, and of British North America. Philadelphia,

Sherman, 1879. 71 p.

From vol. VII, *Transactions of the American institute of mining engineers.*
A 'proof copy' (1 p. *l.*, 51 p.) had been issued the same year.

... Supplement I ... [Easton, Pa., 1880] 13 p.
Reprinted from the *Transactions of the American institute of mining engineers,*
v. 8, p. 466-478.

... Supplement II ... [Easton, Pa., 1881] 12 p.
Reprinted from the *Transactions of the American institute of mining engineers,*
v. 9, p. 621-632.

2:1778  **Primeau, Marguerite**
Notes bio-bibliographiques sur le R.P. Henri Bernard, c.s.c. 1953.
22 p. (Ms. Ecole de Bibl., U. de M.)

2:1779  **Primeau, Monique**
Essai de bio-bibliographie de Mlle Gabrielle Carrière. 1953. viii, 22 p.
(Mf. Ecole de Bibl., U. de M.)

2:1780  **Prince, Madeleine**
Bio-bibliographie de Gérard Langlois. Québec, 1954. 112 p. (Ms.
Ecole de Bibl., U.L.)

2:1781  **Principe, Walter Henry**
Bibliographies and bulletins in theology. Toronto, 1967.
44 *l.*

2:1782  **Pringle, Doris E.**
... A bibliography of material relating to the subject of interior
decoration in Canada. Toronto, 1934. [3] 15 *l.* (Ms. Toronto Univ.
Libr. School)

2:1783  **Pross, Catherine A.**
Should public servants have the right to strike? a bibliography of the
Canadian debate, January 1957-February 1967. Toronto, 1967. iii,
12 *l.* (Ms. Toronto Univ. Libr. School)

2:1784  **Providence, R.I. Public Library**
*Monthly bulletin of Providence Public Library* ... Providence, R.I.,
Published by the Library, 1895.
The October, 1895, issue is a bibliography of Canada.

2:1785  **Prowse, Daniel Woodley**
A history of Newfoundland from the English, colonial, and foreign
records, by D.W. Prowse. With a prefatory note by Edmund Gosse.
London and New York, Macmillan, 1895. xxiii, 742 p.
Bibliography: p. 666-690.

2:1786 **Prud'homme, Luce**
Notes bio-bibliographiques sur Monsieur Edmond de Nevers [Edmond Boisvert] . 1949. 11 p. (Mf. Ecole de Bibl., U. de M.)

2:1787 **Prud'homme, Marie-Line**
Bibliographie de Monsieur Camille Bertrand, archiviste paléographe aux Archives nationales. 1946. 20 p. (Mf. Ecole de Bibl., U. de M.)

2:1788 **... Publications culturelles canadiennes ...** [Ottawa] Centre d'information culturelle, 195—?—
Les éditions 1-9 ne comprennent que les publications en anglais.

2:1789 **Publications de Louis-Edmond Hamelin,** professeur de géographie et directeur du Centre d'études nordiques. Québec, Université Laval, 1969.
1 v. (pag. div.)

2:1790 **Pulp and Paper Research Institute of Canada**
List of library books and periodicals. Montreal, 1964.
iii, 131 p.
Supplement no. 1, March 1965. Montreal, [1965]
iii, 15 p.
List of library books and periodicals, July 1967. Pointe Claire, Que. [1967]
v. 145 p.
Supplement no. 1. Sept. 1968. [Pointe Claire, Que.] 1968.
iii, 11 p.

2:1791 **Quebec (Province) Department of Mines**
... Annotated list of publications of the Department of Mines of the province of Quebec, 1883-1944. Quebec, Paradis, Printer to the King, 1944. 39 p.

2:1792 **Quebec (Province) Department of Mines**
List of geological maps published by the Quebec Department of Mines. Honorable Jonathan Robinson, minister. A.O. Dufresne, deputy minister. [Quebec, 1944?] 4;4 p.

2:1793 **Quebec (Province). Department of Trade and Commerce.** Geographical Service
... Bibliography of New Quebec. Quebec, 1955. 4 *l.,* [11]-321 p. (Its Publication no. 1)
Compiled by Jacques Cousineau.

2:1794 **Québec (Province) Législature.** Bibliothèque
Catalogue de la bibliothèque de la Législature de la province de Québec. Préparé sous la direction de l'honorable T.-D. Bouchard. Québec, Paradis, imprimeur du roi, 1932. xxxii, 293 p.
'Première partie contient tous les ouvrages canadiens, moins ceux ayant trait au droit.'—Avant-propos.

2:1795 **Québec (Province). Ministère de l'Industrie et du Commerce.**
Service de géographie
Bibliographie du Nouveau-Québec ... Québec, 1955. 4 f., [11]-321 p.
(Publication no 1)
Compilée par Jacques Cousineau.

2:1796 **Québec (Province). Ministère des Mines**
... Liste annotée des publications du ministère des Mines de la
province de Québec, 1883-1944. Québec, Paradis, imprimeur du roi,
1944. 39 p.

2:1797 **Québec (Province). Office d'information et de publicité**
Les publications gouvernementales du Québec. [Québec? 1965]
1 v. (non paginé)

2:1798 **Québec (Ville). Université Laval.** Ecole des gradués
Liste des thèses, 1940 à 1965. [Québec] 1965.
v. 82 p.

2:1799 **Quebec Literary and Historical Society**
Index to [their] archival publications, 1824-1924. Québec, L'Evénement, 1923. 215 p.

2:1800 **Queen's University,** Kingston, Ont. Library
Catalogue of Canadian newspapers in the Douglas Library, Queen's
University, [compiled by Lorraine C. Ellison, Peter E. Greig, and
William F.E. Morley] Kingston [Ont.] Douglas Library, Queen's
University, 1969.
xxi [i.e. xxxi], 195 p. (*Douglas Library occasional papers,* no. 1)

2:1801 **Racine, Henri-Dominique**
Bibliographie du Père Pierre-Théophile-Dominique-Ceslas Gonthier,
o.p. [s.d.] 26 p. (Mf. Ecole de Bibl., U. de M.)

2:1802 **Racine, Laurette**
Bibliographie sur le saumon de la province de Québec. 1937-38. 21 p.
(Ms. Ecole de Bibl., U. de M.)

2:1803 **Rainville, Clothilde**
Bio-bibliographie de M. Roger Brien. Préface de M. Léo-Paul
Desrosiers. 1943. 52 p. (Mf. Ecole de Bibl., U. de M.)

2:1804 **Rainville, Lucie**
Bibliographie analytique des recueils biographiques canadiens
français et anglais. Préf. de Mme Emilia B. Allaire. 1964, ix, 99(1) p.
(Ms. Ecole de Bibl., U.L.)

2:1805 **Rajan, Kamala**
Writings of Rev. Auguste-M. Morisset. 1965. ix, 9 1. (Ms. U. of O.
Libr. School)

2:1806 **Rankin, Reita A.**
Bibliography of materials in Fort William Public Library relating to
Fort William, Port Arthur, and northwestern Ontario. (In *Ontario
library review,* v. XLIII, no. 2, p. 140-146)

2:1807 **Ratté, Anna**
La coopération dans la province de Québec; bibliographie. 1944. 95 p.
(Ms. Ecole de Bibl., U. de M.)

2:1808 **Ray, Margaret Violet**
Raymond Knister; a bibliography of his works. [Toronto, 1950] 8 p.
Reprinted from the *Collected poems of Raymond Knister,* edited by Dorothy
Livesay (Toronto, Ryerson Press, 1949).

2:1809 **Raymond, Claire**
Bibliographie de Antonio Perrault, précédée de notes biographiques.
1942. 21 p. (Ms. Ecole de Bibl., U. de M.)

2:1810 **Raymond-Marie**
Bibliographie de l'œuvre du docteur Albert Jobin, 1867 à 1952.
Ancienne Lorette, 1964. 153 p. (Ms. Ecole de Bibl., U.L.)

2:1811 **Reading list on Canada and Montreal** (In *Library journal,* v. 25,
March, 1900, p. 120-141)

2:1812 **Redenstan, William**
History of paper-making in Canada. 1966. [8] 1. (Ms. U. of O.
Libr. School)

2:1813 **Reeves-Morache, Marcelle**
Notes bio-bibliographiques sur M. Arthur Laurendeau. 1953. 77 p.
(Ms. Ecole de Bibl., U. de M.)

2:1814 **Reid, Robie Lewis**
British Columbia; a bibliographical sketch. [Chicago, 1928] [19]-44 p.
Reprinted from the *Papers of the bibliographical society of America,* v. 22,
pt. 1, 1928.

2:1815 **Reiss, Nellie**
French Canadian culture today; a bibliography. Montreal, 1957. 7 *l.*
(Ms. McGill Univ. Libr. School)

2:1816 **[Une Religieuse des SS.NN. de J. et M.]**
Essai de bio-bibliographie: Mgr Ambroise Leblanc, o.f.m. Préf. par
M. le chanoine Omer Bonin. 1953. 28 p. (Ms. Ecole de Bibl., U. de M.)

2:1817 **Remington, Cyrus Kingsbury**
The ship-yard of the Griffon, a brigantine built by René Robert
Cavelier, sieur de La Salle, in the year 1679, above the falls of
Niagara ... Together with the most complete bibliography of Hen-
nepin that has ever been made in any one list ... Buffalo, N.Y.
[Clement] , 1891. 78 p., 1 *l.*
'Bibliography of Hennepin': p. [51]-74.
'Bibliography of La Salle': p. [75]-78.

2:1818 **Remington brothers' newspaper manual** ... a complete catalogue of
the newspapers of the United States, Canada, Porto Rico, Cuba, and
Hawaii ... New York, Remington brothers' newspaper advertising,
1892—
Title varies: 1892-96, 1898, Remington brothers' newspaper manual ... A
catalogue of the newspapers of United States and Canada. With supplementary
lists of the best agricultural, religious, scientific and trade papers, leading
magazines and principal daily and weekly papers ...

2:1819 **Renaud, Huguette**
Essai de bio-bibliographie: le R.P. Zacharie Lacasse, o.m.i. Préface
du R.P. Gaston Carrière, o.m.i. 1953. 41 p. (Ms. Ecole de Bibl.,
U. de M.)

2:1820 **Renault, Raoul**
Bibliographie de Sir James M. Lemoine. Québec, Brousseau, 1897.
11 p.
Réimprimé du *Courrier du livre,* jan./mars 1897, t. 1, nos 9/11, p. 141-146.

2:1821 **Renault, Raoul**
Faucher de Saint-Maurice; son œuvre. Québec, Brousseau, 1897.
16 p.

2:1822 **Renault, Raoul**
Mémoires et documents historiques. Notice bibliographique.
Québec, Brousseau, 1897. 14 p.

2:1823 ... **Répertoire canadien sur l'éducation;** index trimestriel des livres,
rapports, brochures et articles de revue traitant d'éducation et publiés
au Canada. Janvier à mars 1965— Ottawa, Conseil canadien pour la
recherche en éducation, 1965— trimestriel.
Rédactrice: Mavis R. Jones

2:1824 **Research Council of Alberta**
... Athabasca oil sands; bibliography (1789-1964) by M.A. Carrigy.
[Rev. ed.] Edmonton, Research Council of Alberta, 1965. ix, 91 p.
(Its Preliminary report, 65-3)
Previous edition 1962.

2:1825 **Review of historical publications** relating to Canada, 1896-1919.
Toronto, Briggs [etc.] 1897-1919. 22 v. (Half-title: *University of
Toronto studies*)

Edited by G.M. Wrong and others. Succeeded by *Canadian historical review.*

Index, v. I-X. By H.H. Langton. Toronto, Morang, 1907. 202 p.

Index, v. XI-XX. By Laura Mason. [Toronto] Univ. of Toronto, 1918. 218 p.

2:1826 **Revue canadienne**
Index par noms d'auteurs des matières contenues dans les seize
premiers volumes de la *Revue canadienne.* [Montréal, 1881?] xii p.

Table analytique des matières contenues dans les seize premiers volumes de la
*Revue canadienne.* [Montréal, 1881?] xvi p.

Tables générales des 53 premiers volumes de la *Revue canadienne,* 1864 à
1907. Montréal, La Revue canadienne [1907] 142 p.

2:1827 **Revue de L'Université Laval**; troisième série du Parler français ...
publication de l'Université Laval, organe de la Société du Parler
français au Canada. Québec, Université Laval [1946—

2:1828 **Rhodenizer, Vernon Blair**
At the sign of the Hand and Pen. Halifax, Canadian Authors'
Association, Nova Scotia Branch [n.d.] . 43 p.

2:1829 **Rhodenizer, Vernon Blair**
Canadian literature in English. [Montreal, Printed by Quality Press,
c1965]

1055 p. index published separately, cf. 2:2148.

2:1830 **Richard, Denise**
Bio-bibliographie analytique de M. Antonio Barbeau. Préface du Dr
J.-Roméo Pépin. 1942. x, 47 p. (Mf. Ecole de Bibl., U. de M.)

2:1831 **Richard, Marie-France**
Bio-bibliographie analytique du poète Adolphe Poisson. Québec, 1952.
60 p. (Ms. Ecole de Bibl., U.L.)

2:1832 **Richer, Yvon**
Le Nationalisme québécois. 1965. vii, 14 1. (Ms. U. of O. Libr.
School)

2:1833 **Richmond, Mary G.**
A bibliography of the Rideau river and canal system. Montreal,
1939. vii, 12 *l.* (Ms. McGill Univ. Libr. School)

2:1834 **Riddell, William Renwick**
John Richardson. Toronto, Ryerson, [1923] . 226 p. (Makers of
Canadian literature ...)

Bibliography: p. 211-222.

2:1835 **Riddell, William Renwick**
William Kirby. Toronto, Ryerson [1923] 176 p. (Makers of
Canadian literature ...)
Bibliography: p. 167-172.

2:1836 **Rideout, Eric Brock**
City school district reorganization: an annotated bibliography;
centralization and decentralization in the government of metropolitan
areas with special emphasis on the organization, administration, and
financing of large-city school systems [by] E. Brock Rideout and
Sandra Majat. [Toronto] Ontario Institute for Studies in Education
[c1967]
v, 93 p. (*Educational research series,* no. 1)

2:1837 **Rimouski, Qué. Séminaire.** Bibliothèque
Répertoire par ordre alphabétique d'auteurs des publications des
anciens élèves (cours classique) du Séminaire de Rimouski. Rimouski,
1964. 36 (i.e. 37) f. (Ses Publications, 1)

2:1838 **Rinfret, Carmen**
Bio-bibliographie de M. Gustave Lanctot. [s.d.] 35 p. (Mf. Ecole de
Bibl., U. de M.)

2:1839 **Ringuet, Gemma**
Notes bibliographiques sur Charles E. Harpe. 1952. 10 p. (Mf. Ecole
de Bibl., U. de M.)

2:1840 **Riopel, Marie-Ange**
Bibliographie de Georges Boucher de Boucherville, avocat. Précédée
d'une notice biographique. 1945. 30 p. (Mf. Ecole de Bibl., U. de M.)

2:1841 **Robb, Marion D.**
Sources of Nova Scotian history, 1840-1867. 296 p.

2:1842 **Robert, frère**
Essai bibliographique. La religion et le français. Manuels pour les
élèves de langue française, approuvés par le Comité catholique du
Conseil de l'Instruction publique de la province de Québec (1950-
1959) Préface de Me Charles Bilodeau. Jonquière, 1961. 112 p.
(Ms. Ecole de Bibl., U.L.)

2:1843 **Robert, Bernard**
Poetry of and by librarians in Canadian, American and British
library periodicals. 1963. v, 8 l. (Ms. U. of O. Libr. School)

2:1844  **Robert, Cécile**
Bio-bibliographie de Mgr Th.-G. Rouleau. Préface de M. Damien
Jasmin. Montréal, 1955. x, 40 p. (Ms. Ecole de Bibl., U. de M.)

2:1845  **Robert, Lionel, frère**
Bibliographie sur le Sacré-Cœur chez les Missionnaires du Sacré-
Cœur, français et canadiens. Québec, 1962. 59 p. (Ms. Ecole de
Bibl., U.L.)

2:1846  **Robert, Michèle**
Essai de bio-bibliographie de Richard Bergeron, directeur général des
écoles à la Commission des écoles catholiques de Sherbrooke. Préf.
par M. Jean-Claude Corbeil, [Montréal] 1960. xvi, 42 p. (Ms. Ecole
de Bibl., U. de M.)

2:1847  **Robertson, Marjorie Grace**
Ombudsmen in Canada? a selected bibliography. Toronto, 1967.
ii, 8, [1] *l.* (Ms. Toronto Univ. Libr. School)

2:1848  **Robertson, William Murdoch**
Selected bibliography of Canadian forest literature, 1917-1946.
Ottawa, 1949. 332 p. (Canada, Dept. of the Interior, Forestry
Branch, Miscellaneous silvicultural research note, no. 6)

2:1849  **Robidoux, G.-L.**
Notes bio-bibliographiques sur Laure Conan [Félicité Angers]. 1948.
iv, 9 p. (Mf. Ecole de Bibl., U. de M.)

2:1850  **Robinson, Betty Belle**
Bibliography of population and immigration, with special reference
to Canada, with foreword by Gilbert E. Jackson. Prepared under the
direction of Professor W. Burton Hurd, Head of the Department of
Political Economy, McMaster University. [Hamilton, Ont., McMaster
University] 1949. 20 *l.*

2:1851  **Robitaille, Alphéda**
Bio-bibliographie de Mgr Amédée Gosselin. Préface de Mgr Adjutor
Faucher. Trois-Rivières, 1946. 215, [3] p. (Mf. Ecole de Bibl.,
U. de M.)

2:1852  **Robitaille, Lucie**
Bio-bibliographie de M. le chan. Georges Robitaille. Préface de
Donatien Frémont. 1952. 93 p. (Ms. Ecole de Bibl., U. de M.)

2:1853  **Robitaille, Noémi**
Bibliographie d'auteur: Mgr Camille Roy, prélat romain, écrivain et
critique littéraire. Montréal, 1931. 5 *l.* (Ms. McGill Univ. Libr. School)

2:1854  **Roch, Madeleine**
Bio-bibliographie de M. l'abbé Arthur Lacasse. 1946. 141 p.
(Mf. Ecole de Bibl., U. de M.)

2:1855  **Roch, Thérèse**
Bio-bibliographie de M. le Dr Georges-A. Boucher. Préface de
M. J.-A. Brunet. Lettre manuscrite de G.-A. Boucher. 1946. 79 p.
(Mf. Ecole de Bibl., U. de M.)

2:1856  **Rocheleau, Jeannette**
Bibliographie de François-Xavier Garneau. [s.d.] 28 p. (Mf. Ecole de
Bibl., U. de M.)

2:1857  **Rodger, Elizabeth A.**
Tait McKenzie, 1867-1938; a centenary bibliography. [Toronto,
1967] xi, 16 *l.* (Ms. Toronto Univ. Libr. School)

2:1858  **Roenicke, J.E.**
The political career of C.D. Howe. 1967. [4] 4 1. (Ms. U. of O.
Libr. School)

2:1859  **Rogeau, Mme Charles**
Bio-bibliographie de l'abbé H.-R. Casgrain. 1940. 78 p. (Mf. Ecole
de Bibl., U. de M.)

2:1860  **Rogers, Amos Robert**
Books and pamphlets by New Brunswick writers, 1890-1950.
[Fredericton, N.B., 1953] 2 p. *l.*, ii-vi, 73 *l.*
'Bibliography submitted in part fulfilment of the requirement for University of
London Diploma in Librarianship ... May 1953.'
Includes only material in English.

2:1861  **Rogers, Gertrude**
Laurentia, a bibliography designed as a guide to knowledge of the
Laurentian mountains. Montreal, 1938. iii, 17 *l.* (Ms. McGill Univ.
Libr. School)

2:1862  **Rogers, William Ross**
... List of publications including Reports (vols. I-XXXV, 1891 to
1926) also maps and Bulletins. Accompanied by index map of the
province of Ontario (in pocket) showing areas covered by geological
maps, 1891 to 1926, scale 35 miles to the inch. Toronto, Printed and
published by the printers to the King's Most Excellent Majesty, 1927.
34 p., 1 *l.* (Ontario. Dept. of Mines. Bulletin no. 25. (Rev. ed.))
... (vols. I-XL, 1891-1931) maps and bulletins. (Revised to May, 1932)
Toronto, Ball, 1932. 47 p. (Ontario. Dept of Mines. Bulletin no. 25 (3d ed.))

2:1863 **Roland, Jacqueline**

Bibliographie analytique de monsieur Paul Legendre. Préf. de M. Charles de Koninck. Québec, 1953. 67 p. (Ms. Ecole de Bibl., U.L.)

2:1864 **Rolland, Paule**

Bio-bibliographie de Roger Duhamel. Préf. par Alain Grandbois. [Montréal, L'auteur, 1954] 208 p.

2:1865 **Rome, David**

Jews in Canadian literature; a bibliography. Rev. ed. Montreal, Canadian Jewish Congress and Jewish Public Library, 1964. 2 v. (2, xiv, 252 *l.*)

First ed. 1962.

2:1866 **Rome, David**

... A selected bibliography of Jewish Canadiana. Montreal, Canadian Jewish Congress and The Jewish Public Library, 1959. 1 v. (unpaged)

2:1867 **Romuald, frère**

Monsieur Arthur Charlebois; essai de bio-bibliographie. 1953. 22 p. (Mf. Ecole de Bibl., U. de M.)

2:1868 **Ross, Carolyn M.**

Books and pamphlets on Laura Ingersoll Secord, 1775-1868. [Toronto, 1933] [2], 2 *l.* (Ms. Toronto Univ. Libr. School)

2:1869 **Ross, Nancy**

A bibliography of Marshall McLuhan: his books and articles published in English in this decade. 1967. vii, 15 1. (Ms. U. of O. Libr. School)

2:1870 **Rouillard, Eugène**

Les premiers almanachs canadiens. Lévis, Roy, 1898. 80 p. (*Bibliothèque canadienne*)

2:1871 **Rouillard, Joseph, frère**

Bio-bibliographie d'Eugénie Rouillard. Préface de M. Jean-Chs Bonenfant. Vaudreuil, 1963. 137 p. (Ms. Ecole de Bibl., U.L.) (*en religion:* Colomban)

2:1872 **Rouleau, Ernest**

... Bibliographie des travaux concernant la flore canadienne, parus dans 'Rhodora' de 1899 à 1943 inclusivement, précédée d'un index alphabétique de tous les noms botaniques nouveaux proposés dans cette revue. Montréal, Université de Montréal, Institut botanique, 1944. 2 f., [7]-367 p. (*Contributions de l'Institut botanique de l'Université de Montréal,* no 54)

2:1873 **Rouse, Irving**
An anthropological bibliography of the eastern seabord, ed. by
Irving Rouse and John M. Goggin. New Haven, The Federation,
1947 [i.e. 1948]. 174 p. (*Eastern States Archeological Federation
Research publication* no. 1)

2:1874 **Rousseau, Jacques**
... Bibliographie des travaux botaniques contenus dans les 'Mémoires
et comptes rendus de la Société royale du Canada,' de 1882 à 1936
inclusivement, par Jacques Rousseau, Marcelle Gauvreau, et Claire
Morin ... New York, Fiedler; Montréal, Institut botanique de
l'Université de Montréal; [etc., etc.] 1939. 117 p. (*Contributions de
l'Institut botanique de l'Université de Montréal,* no 33)

2:1875 **Rousseau, Jacques**
La cartographie de la région du lac Mistassini. Extrait de la *Revue
d'histoire de l'Amérique française,* livraison de septembre 1949,
pp. 289-312. Montréal, 1949. 24 p.

2:1876 **Rousseau, Jacques**
Curriculum vitæ et bibliographie. [Montréal, 1955] 60 [i.e. 71] f.
Feuilles 43A-I, 46A, 52A insérées.

2:1877 **Rousseau, Jacques**
Le docteur J.-A. Crevier, médecin et naturaliste (1824-1889). Etude
biographique et bibliographique. Extrait des *Annales de l'Acfas,*
v. 6, 1940. [Montreal? 1940] 96 p. portr.

2:1878 **Rousseau, Jacques**
Essai de bibliographie botanique canadienne. (In *Naturaliste canadien,*
3e série, v. 60, no 4 à v. 61, no 5, 1933-1934)
Aussi tirage à part sans changement de pagination.

2:1879 **Rousseau, Jacques**
Essai bibliographique sur la région du lac Mistassini. Montréal, 1954.
155 f.

2:1880 **Roussy, William**
Compilation bibliographique, sur le livre et la lecture, des articles
parus dans dix revues canadiennes-françaises du ler janvier 1950 au
30 juin 1960, et précédée d'un essai sur la lecture 'ferment de vie ou
de mort.' Préf. de Armand Gauthier. Montréal, 1960. xv, 127 p.
(Ms. Ecole de Bibl., U. de M.)

2:1881 **Rouyn, Solange de**
Bibliographie analytique sur 'le Centre de Service social du diocèse

des Trois-Rivières.' Préface de M. Jules Perron. Québec, 1962. 109 p. (Ms. Ecole de Bibl., U.L.)

2:1882 **Rowe, Judith E.**

Bibliography on Canadian constitutional law [1946-1959] Library School, University of Ottawa, 1960. iv, 12 p. (Ms. U. of O. Libr. School)

2:1883 **Rowell's American newspaper directory,** containing a description of all the newspapers and periodicals pub. in the United States and territories, Dominion of Canada and Newfoundland, and of the towns and cities in which they are pub., together with a statement or estimate of the average number of copies printed by each publication catalogued. [1st]-40th year; 1869-1908. New York, Rowell [etc.] 1869-1908. 40 v. in 61.

Annual, 1869-77; quarterly, Jan. 1878-Oct. 1879; annual, 1880-96; quarterly, June 1897-Dec. 1901; semiannual, Apr.-Oct. 1902; annual 1903-08.
Title varies: 1869, Geo. P. Rowell & Co's American newspaper directory; 1870 (in 3 pt.) 1. The men who advertise; 2. American newspaper ratebook; 3. Geo. P. Rowell & Co's American newspaper directory; 1871-85, Geo. P. Rowell & Co's American newspaper directory (Jan.-Oct. 1878, American newspaper directory); 1886-1904, American newspaper directory; 1905-08, Rowell's American newspaper directory.
Published by the Printers' ink publishing company, 1905-08.
Merged into N.W. Ayer & son's American newspaper annual (q.v.).

2:1884 **Rowland, Mary K.N.**

Bibliography of the history of Prince Edward County, 1784-1900. [Toronto, 1934] [1], 13 *l.* (Ms. Toronto Univ. Libr. School)

2:1885 **Roy, André**

Notes bio-bibliographiques sur Adrien Leblond de Brumath. 1948. 16 p. (Ms. Ecole de Bibl., U. de M.)

2:1886 **Roy, Antoine**

L'œuvre historique de Pierre-Georges Roy. Bibliographie analytique ... Paris, Jouve, 1928. 268 p.

2:1887 **Roy, Carmen**

La littérature orale en Gaspésie. Ottawa [Imprimeur de la Reine] 1955 [i.e., 1956]. 389 p. (Musée national du Canada, Bulletin no 134, Série anthropologique, no 36)

2:1888 **Roy, George Ross**

Canadian poetry; a supplementary bibliography, compiled by G. Ross Roy and Michael Gnarowski. Quebec, Culture, 1964. 13 p.

Bibliography of items published before 1950, located in the George Ross Roy Collection of Canadiana in the Library of the University of Montreal and the

Library of Lakehead College of Arts, Sciences and Technology, Port Arthur, Ont.

2:1889 **Roy, Irène**
Bibliography of adult education through libraries in Canada from 1945 to 1961. Ottawa, University of Ottawa, Library School, 1961. xi, 14 p. (Ms. U. of O. Libr. School)

2:1890 **Roy, Jean**
Bibliographie analytique de l'oeuvre du Rév. Père Eugène Lefebvre, c.s.s.r., directeur de l'Œuvre des pèlerinages au Sanctuaire de Ste-Anne de Beaupré. Préface du Rév. Père Lucien Gagné, c.s.s.r. Québec, 1960. 36 p. (Ms. Ecole de Bibl., U.L.)

2:1891 **Roy, Jean-Luc, frère**
Bibliographie sur le cinéma (publications et écrits du Canada français (1940-1960). Québec, 1963. 121 p. (Ms. Ecole de Bibl., U.L.) (*en religion*: Prosper.)

2:1892 **Roy, Marguerite-Marie**
Bio-bibliographie de M. l'abbé Victor Tremblay. 1945. 25 p. (Ms. Ecole de Bibl., U. de M.)

2:1893 **Roy, Pierre Georges**
Bibliographie de la poésie franco-canadienne ... Lévis, 1900. 14 p.

2:1894 **Roy, Pierre Georges**
Bibliographie lévisienne. Lévis, 1932. 24 p.

2:1895 **Roy, Reina L.**
Bibliographie analytique de l'oeuvre de Léopold Lamontagne, doyen de la Faculté des lettres de Laval, précédée d'une biographie. Préface de M. Luc Lacourcière. Québec, 1964. 146 p. (Ms. Ecole de Bibl., U.L.)

2:1896 **Roy, Rhéal-A.**
Ernest Pallascio-Morin; essai de bio-bibliographie. Préface de Jean Dufresne. 1945. x, 91 p. (Mf. Ecole de Bibl., U. de M.)

2:1897 **Roy, Rita**
Bio-bibliographie de M. le chan. Henri Vallée. Lettre-préface de M. l'abbé Albert Tessier. 1949. 68 p. (Ms. Ecole de Bibl., U. de M.)

2:1898 **Roy, Ulysse**
Participation des bibliothèques canadiennes à l'éducation des adultes. 1965. vi, 6 l. (Ms. U. of O. Libr. School)

2:1899 **Royal Astronomical Society of Canada**

... General index to the publications of the Astronomical and physical society of Toronto 1890-1899, Toronto astronomical society 1900-1901, Royal astronomical society of Canada 1902-1931, being the *Transactions* 1890-1905, *Journal* 1907-1931, volumes 1 to 25 inclusive. Compiled by W.E. Harper. Toronto, Royal astronomical society [1932] 122 p.

2:1900 **Royal Canadian Institute, Toronto**

... General index to publications, 1852-1912. Comp. and ed. by John Patterson ... Toronto, University Press, 1914. 516 p.

2:1901 **Royal Colonial Institute, London.** Library

Catalogue of the library of the Royal Colonial Institute to October 1881. [Chilworth and London, Unwin, 1881] 29 p.

Catalogue of the library of the Royal Colonial Institute, 1886. London, Spottiswoode, 1886. 3 p. *l.,* [v]-1, 179 p.

Catalogue of the library of the Royal Colonial Institute. (Founded 1868. Incorporated by royal charter, 1882) London, The Institute, 1895. clv, 543 p. By James R. Boosé, librarian.

First supplementary catalogue of the library of the Royal Colonial Institute. Compiled by James R. Boosé. London, The Institute, 1901. cclxxviii, 793 p.

2:1902 **Royal Empire Society, London.** Library

Subject catalogue of the library of the Royal Empire Society, formerly Royal Colonial Institute, by Evans Lewin. v. 3. The Dominion of Canada and its provinces, the Dominion of Newfoundland, the West Indies and colonial America. [London, The Society] 1932. xvii, 822 p.

Formerly Royal Colonial Institute, now Royal Commonwealth Society.

2:1903 **Royal Society of Canada**

General index, proceedings and transactions of the Royal Society of Canada; first and second series. 1882-1906. Toronto, Copp, Clark, 1908. 133 p.

A subject index ... third series, v. I-XXXI, 1907-1937, comp. by May Alice Martin. Ottawa, Canadian Library Association, 1947. 2 p. *l.,* 143 p. (*Canadian Library Association, Reference publication,* no. 1)

Author index, transactions of the Royal Society of Canada, sections I-V, third series: v. I-XXXV, 1907-1941 ... [Toronto, University of Toronto Press, 1942?] 90 p.

2:1904 **Rozon, René**

Yousuf Karsh. 1963. v, 5 1. (Ms. U. of O. Libr. School)

2:1905 **Rumsey, Fay**

Economics of forestry; a bibliography for the United States and

Canada, 1955-1959. [Syracuse, N.Y.] State University College of
Forestry at Syracuse University [1964?]

136 p. (State University College of Forestry at Syracuse University. Bulletin
45)

1960-1962. Washington, U.S. Dept. of Agriculture, Forest Service, 1965.
iv, 45 p. (U.S. Dept. of Agriculture. Forest Service. Miscellaneous
Publication 1003)

2:1906 **Rupsys, Emilija**
Expo 67. 1965. vi, 4 1. (Ms. U. of O. Libr. School)

2:1907 **Rush, Stephan**
Canadian petroleum after the Second World War. 1962. vii, 8 1.
(Ms. U. of O. Libr. School)

2:1908 **Russell, Bertrand, 3d Earl Russell**
A detailed catalogue of the archives of Bertrand Russell. [Edited by]
Barry Feinberg. London, Produced and designed by Continuum 1
Ltd.; [Hamilton, Ont.] Mills Memorial Library, McMaster University
[c1967]

343 p. facsims., port.

2:1909 **Ryder, Dorothy E.**
Bibliography of reference material on Canadian history. Montreal,
1951. iii, 10 *l.* (Ms. McGill Univ. Libr. School)

2:1910 **Ryerson, Margaret E.**
Canadian railways to 1867; a list of sources in the libraries of
Toronto ... [Toronto] 1935. [1] , ii, 31 *l.* (Ms. Toronto Univ. Libr.
School)

2:1911 **S.-C., soeur**
Notice bio-bibliographique de M. Paul Coderre. 1951. 31 p. (Ms.
Ecole de Bibl., U. de M.)

2:1912 **Sabin, Joseph**
Bibliotheca americana. A dictionary of books relating to America,
from its discovery to the present time. Begun by Joseph Sabin, continued by Wilberforce Eames and completed by R.W.G. Vail, for the
Bibliographical Society of America. New York, 1868-1936. 29 v.

Imprint varies.
Issued in 172 parts.

2:1913 **Sabin, Joseph**
A list of the editions of the works of Louis Hennepin and Alonso
[i.e., Antonio] de Herrera; extracted from *Dictionary of books
relating to America.* New York, Sabin, 1876. 16 p.

2:1914 **Saint-Achillas, soeur**

Bibliographie analytique sur 'l'artisanat canadien (1945-1962).' Préface de Mgr Albert Tessier, P.D. Québec, 1962. 137 p. (Ms. Ecole de Bibl., U.L.)

2:1915 **Saint-Antoine-de-Padoue, soeur**

Bibliographie analytique de l'œuvre du R.P. Henri-Marie Guindon, s.m.m., précédée d'une biographie. Préface de M. l'abbé Hervé Gagné. Lévis, 1962. 145 p. (Ms. Ecole de Bibl., U.L.)

2:1916 **Saint-Augustin**

Bio-bibliographie de Alcide Fleury. Arthabasca, 1963. 75, XXXIV p. (Ms. Ecole de Bibl., U.L.)

2:1917 **St-Claude-Marie, soeur**

L'enseignement ménager au Canada français. Bibliographie analytique (1955-1963) Préface de Sr Ste-Isabelle, s.s.c.m. Québec, 1964. 70 p. (Ms. Ecole de Bibl., U.L.)

2:1918 **Saint-Clément, soeur**

Les fêtes du Troisième centenaire de l'Hôtel-Dieu de Québec (1639-1939) bibliographie analytique avec appendices et illustrations. Préface de madame Edguarda Leczinska. Québec, 1964. 544 p. (Ms. Ecole de Bibl., U.L.)

2:1919 **Saint-Damase-Marie, soeur**

Bibliographie analytique de l'œuvre du R.P. J. Herman Poisson, o.f.m., précédée d'une biographie. Lettre-préface de Son Excellence Mgr Damase Laberge. Sorel, 1962. 74 p. (Ms. Ecole de Bibl., U.L.)

2:1920 **Saint-Denis, soeur**

Gaspésiana. Avant-propos de l'abbé Claude Allard. Préface du docteur Guy Fortier. Montréal et Paris, Fides [c1965] xix, 180 p. ill., cartes. Bibliographie de l'histoire de la Gaspésie du 16e au 20e siècle inclusivement, rédigée pour l'obtention d'un diplôme en bibliothéconomie à l'Université Laval, Québec.

2:1921 **Saint-Donat-Joseph, soeur**

Bibliographie analytique du Rév. Père Francis Goyer, s.s.s., 1948-1962. Plessisville, 1963. 39 p. (Ms. Ecole de Bibl., U.L.)

2:1922 **Saint Emile, soeur**

Bibliographie analytique des travaux de M. Jean Charles Bonenfant, 1954-1964. Québec, 1965. (Ms. Ecole de Bibl., U.L.)

2:1923 **Saint-Evariste, soeur**

Essai de bio-bibliographie de Soeur Sainte-Théophanie, c.n.d. Préface

de Sœur Ste-Marguerite-du-Rosaire, c.n.d. Montréal, 1957. xxi, 48 p.
(Ms. Ecole de Bibl., U. de M.)

2:1924 **Saint-Fidèle, soeur**
Bibliographie analytique de l'œuvre de M. Louis-Philippe Robidoux,
journaliste, précédée d'une biographie. Préface de M. l'abbé Conrad
Groleau, du Séminaire St-Charles-Borromée. Sherbrooke, 1964.
359 p. (Ms. Ecole de Bibl., U.L.)

2:1925 **Saint-François-Georges, soeur**
Bibliographie du R.P. Louis Lalande, s.j. 1938. 10 p. (Ms. Ecole de
Bibl., U. de M.)

2:1926 **Saint-Gérard, soeur**
Bio-bibliographie de l'abbé Pascal Potvin, principal de l'Ecole normale
de Lévis. Préface de Mgr Arthur Maheux. Lévis, 1962. 180 p. (Ms.
Ecole de Bibl., U.L.)

2:1927 **Saint-Gérard-de-l'Eucharistie**
Notes bio-bibliographiques sur M. l'abbé Gérard Blais. 1953. 47 p.
(Ms. Ecole de Bibl., U. de M.)

2:1928 **Saint-Gérard-du-Sauveur, soeur**
Notes bio-bibliographiques sur M. l'abbé Ernest Arsenault.
1953. 24 p. (Mf. Ecole de Bibl., U. de M.)

2:1929 **Saint-Germain, Estelle**
Bio-bibliographie de Rina Lasnier de l'Académie canadienne-française.
1950. xiii, 33 p. (Mf. Ecole de Bibl., U. de M.)

2:1930 **St-Gilbert-de-la-Croix, soeur**
Bio-bibliographie de 'Tante Chantal' (Mme Cécile Lachaîne-Brosseau).
Préface de Sr Ste-Julienne Falconieri, c.n.d. Danville, 1963. 85 p.
(Ms. Ecole de Bibl., U.L.)

2:1931 **Saint-Hilaire, Alphonse**
Nos grands prix de la province (1944-1954); biographie et bibliogra-
phie des artistes vainqueurs des concours. Québec, 1955. 123 p.
(Ms. Ecole de Bibl., U.L.)

2:1932 **St-Hilaire, Marie-Thérèse**
Essai de bio-bibliographie du R.P. Richer-Marie Beaubien, o.f.m.
Préface du T.R.P. Hervé Blais, o.f.m. 1951. xv, 45 p. (Ms. Ecole de
Bibl., U. de M.)

2:1933 **St-Hilaire, Simone**
Notes bibliographiques sur Ambroise Lafortune, ptre. 1952. [16] p.
(Ms. Ecole de Bibl., U. de M.)

2:1934 **Saint-Hyacinthe, soeur**
Bienheureuse Marguerite d'Youville. Bibliographie canadienne, 1938-1949. Sherbrooke, 1963. 98 p. (Ms. Ecole de Bibl., U.L.)

2:1935 **Saint-Ignace-de-Loyola, soeur**
Notice bio-bibliographique de Monsieur Louis-C. O'Neil. Sherbrooke, 1953. 41 p. (Mf. Ecole de Bibl., U. de M.)

2:1936 **Saint-Jacques, Lise**
Bio-bibliographie de François-Albert Angers. Préf. de M. Jean Bruchési. 1947. x, 67 p. (Ms. Ecole de Bibl., U. de M.)

2:1937 **St James, Man. Public Library**
A bibliography of Canadiana. Centennial ed. [St James, Man.] 1967.
1 v. (various pagings)
First ed. 1961; suppl., 1963.

2:1938 **St-Jean, Jean-Guy**
Les bibliobus au Canada. 1967. [4] 9 1. (Ms. U. of O. Libr. School)

2:1939 **St-Jean-Brébeuf, soeur**
Bio-bibliographie du R.P. Edm. Gaudron, o.f.m. Québec, 1956. 62 p. (Ms. Ecole de Bibl., U.L.)

2:1940 **Saint-Jean-Marie, soeur**
Bibliographie analytique de Françoise L. Roy, précédée d'une biographie. 1964, xiii, 139 (2) p. Préface de Mgr Paul E. Gosselin (Ms. Ecole de Bibl., U.L.)

2:1941 **Saint-Jorre, Cécile**
Essai de bio-bibliographie sur Pamphile Lemay. 1939. 19 p. (Ms. Ecole de Bibl., U. de M.)

2:1942 **Saint-Joseph-de-la-Charité, soeur**
Bibliographie analytique de monseigneur Joseph Ferland, curé de St-Roch de Québec. Préf. de Sr St-François de l'Alverne, c.n.d. Québec, 1960. 107 p. (Ms. Ecole de Bibl., U.L.)

2:1943 **St Lawrence Seaway Development Corporation.** Office of Information
Seaway bibliography. [Rev. ed.] Washington, 1957. 21 *l.*
'Publications and articles relating to Great Lakes and St Lawrence River navigation and St Lawrence Seaway and power development.'
A cumulation of the 1st ed., dated Aug. 1, 1955, and its supplements 1-6.
Supplement[s]. [7th-14th] Washington, 1957-60.
28-G-28-O *l.*

2:1944 **Saint-Léonce, soeur**
Bibliographie analytique de l'oeuvre du docteur Marcel Lapointe

(pseud. Marcel Portal), précédée d'une biographie. Préface du R. Père Conrad E. Brunet. Chicoutimi, Hôtel-Dieu, 1962. 191 p. (Ms. Ecole de Bibl., U.L.)

2:1945  **Saint-Louis, Rose-Adeline**
François Hertel [M. l'abbé Rodolphe Dubé] et son œuvre; bio-bibliographie. Préface de M. l'abbé E. Hamelin. 1943. 33 p. (Ms. Ecole de Bibl., U. de M.)

2:1946  **Saint-Louis-Daniel, sœur**
Bibliographie analytique de Me Eugène L'Heureux, journaliste (1940-1949) précédée d'une biographie. Préface de M. Lorenzo Paré, rédacteur en chef à *l'Action.* Beauce, 1964. 559 p. (Ms. Ecole de Bibl., U.L.)

2:1947  **Saint-Majella, sœur**
Bibliographie analytique de l'œuvre du docteur Louis-Philippe Roy, M.D., journaliste (1920-1948) précédée d'une biographie. Préface de Me Wheeler Dupont. Québec, 1964. 524 p. (Ms. Ecole de Bibl., U.L.)

2:1948  **Saint-Marc Bédard, mère**
Bibliographie analytique de l'œuvre du R.P. Philias F. Bourgeois, c.s.c., précédée d'une biographie. St-Léonard, N.-B., 1964. 110 p. (Ms. Ecole de Bibl., U.L.)

2:1949  **Saint-Michel, sœur**
Essai de bibliographie, par ordre chronologique, des écrits publiés sur Jeanne Mance. 1938. iii, 47 p. (Ms. Ecole de Bibl., U. de M.)

2:1950  **Saint-Philippe-André**
Les actes de Sa Sainteté le Pape Jean XXIII. Québec, 1963. 238 p. (Ms. Ecole de Bibl., U.L.)

2:1951  **Saint-Pierre, Jacqueline**
Bibliographie collective des auteurs de la région du Saguenay (1838-1964) Préf. de Mgr Victor Tremblay. 1964, 113(1) p. (Ms. Ecole de Bibl., U.L.)

2:1952  **St-Pierre, Jeanne**
Bibliographie canadienne sur les archives médicales d'un hôpital (2e partie, 1951-1956) Préface de M. René Bureau. Québec, 1961. 80 p. (Ms. Ecole de Bibl., U.L.)

2:1953  **Saint-Pierre, Jeanne-Marguerite**
Bibliographie de Arthur Saint-Pierre, précédée de notes biographiques. 1940. 27 p. (Ms. Ecole de Bibl., U. de M.)

2:1954 **Saint-Raymond-du-Sauveur, soeur**
Bibliographie analytique de l'oeuvre de M. Pierre H. Ruel, doyen de la Faculté des Sciences de l'éducation de l'Université de Sherbrooke, précédée d'une biographie. Préface de Mgr Maurice O'Brady. p.d., vice-recteur de l'Université de Sherbrooke. Sherbrooke, 1964. 126 p. (Ms. Ecole de Bibl., U.L.)

2:1955 **St-Roger, soeur**
Bibliographie sur 'quelques monuments historiques de Québec (1854-1901).' Québec, 1963. 80 p. (Ms. Ecole de Bibl., U.L.)

2:1956 **Saint-Roger, soeur**
Essai bio-bibliographique de Monsieur Henri-Myriel Gendreau. 1953. 29 p. (Mf. Ecole de Bibl., U. de M.)

2:1957 **Sainte-Agilberte**
Bibliographie analytique du Rév. Père Florian Larivière, S.J. Saint-Joseph de Beauce, 1963. 54 p. (Ms. Ecole de Bibl., U.L.)

2:1958 **Sainte-Agnès, soeur**
Notes bio-bibliographiques du R.F. Benjamin, s.c. Préface de M. le chan. Léon Marcotte. 1951. 50 p. (Ms. Ecole de Bibl., U. de M.)

2:1959 **Sainte-Angèle, soeur**
Bibliographie de l'oeuvre de l'abbé Anselme Longpré (1947-1964) 2e ptie, précédée d'une biographie. Saint-Hyacinthe, 1964. 84 p. (Ms. Ecole de Bibl., U.L.)

2:1960 **Sainte-Anne-de-Marie, soeur**
Bibliographie analytique de l'oeuvre de Odilon Arteau, journaliste (1920-1960) précédée d'une biographie. Préface du Dr Louis-Philippe Roy. Thetford Mines, 1964. 560 p. (Ms. Ecole de Bibl., U.L.)

2:1961 **Sainte-Antonie, soeur**
Bibliographie canadienne sur les archives médicales d'un hôpital (1ère partie, 1944-1950) Préface du docteur Mathieu Samson. Québec, 1961. 62 p. (Ms. Ecole de Bibl., U.L.)

2:1962 **Sainte-Apollonie**
Bibliographie analytique de l'oeuvre de Rév. Sr Sainte-Claire-de-Rimini, s.c.q. Québec, 1962. 75 p. (Ms. Ecole de Bibl., U.L.)

2:1963 **Sainte-Bibiane, soeur**
Essai de bio-bibliographie: R.F. Marie-Maximin, f.e.c. 1953. 40 p. (Ms. Ecole de Bibl., U. de M.)

2:1964 **Sainte-Blandine-de-France, soeur**
Vénérée Mère Saint-Victor; essai de bio-bibliographie. [s.d.] 9 p.
(Ms. Ecole de Bibl., U. de M.)

2:1965 **Ste-Candide, soeur**
Bio-bibliographie de l'abbé Roland Dufour. Préface de Mgr Gérard
Desgagné. Chicoutimi, 1962. 100 p. (Ms. Ecole de Bibl., U.L.)

2:1966 **Sainte-Catherine de Saint-Augustin, soeur**
Bibliographie des biographies des religieuses décédées à l'Hôtel-Dieu
du Sacré-Cœur de Jésus de Québec (1925-1960) Préface de la R. Sr
Saint-Zéphirin, o.s.a., supérieure. Québec, 1961. 91 p. (Ms. Ecole
de Bibl., U.L.)

2:1967 **Sainte-Catherine-de-Sienne Massicotte, mère**
Bio-bibliographie de Mère Marguerite-Marie Lasalle, o.s.u. Shawinigan,
1964. 29 p. (Ms. Ecole de Bibl., U.L.)

2:1968 **Ste-Cécile, soeur**
Bio-bibliographie du révérend Père Ovila Melançon, c.s.c. St-Jean-sur-
Richelieu, 1962. 169 p. (Ms. Ecole de Bibl., U.L.)

2:1969 **Sainte-Claire-de-la-Trinité, soeur**
Bibliographie analytique de la Rév. Sr Sainte-Blanche. Préf. de la
T. Rév. Mère Sainte-Marie-Ange. Québec, 1955. 108 p. (Ms. Ecole
de Bibl., U.L.)

2:1970 **Sainte Daniella**
Bibliographie analytique de l'œuvre de M. Eugène l'Heureux.
(1918-1929) Québec, 1962. 140 p. (Ms. Ecole de Bibl., U.L.)

2:1971 **Sainte-Elisabeth-d'Hebron, soeur**
Bio-bibliographie de M. l'abbé Jean-Baptiste Desrosiers, p.s.s. 1947.
54 p. (Ms. Ecole de Bibl., U. de M.)

2:1972 **Sainte-Fernande, soeur**
Bibliographie 1950-1958, de la Bienheureuse Marguerite d'Youville.
Québec, 1963. 63 p. (Ms. Ecole de Bibl., U.L.)

2:1973 **Sainte-Gilberte, soeur**
Essai bio-bibliographique de Monsieur Louis Bouhier, p.s.s., ancien
curé de Notre-Dame de Montréal. Rock-Island, 1951. 54 p. (Mf.
Ecole de Bibl., U. de M.)

2:1974 **Sainte-Héliène-de-Marie**
Bibliographie des notices biographiques et des écrits des soeurs de la
Charité de Québec décédées, 1851-1917. Québec, 1963. 157 p. (Ms.
Ecole de Bibl., U.L.)

2:1975 **Ste-Hildegarde, soeur**
Bibliographie analytique de l'oeuvre de 'Béraud de St-Maurice'
(Mère Clothilde [sic] -Angèle-de-Jésus, o.s.u.) Précédée d'une
biographie. Préface de M. Hervé Biron. Trois-Rivières, 1963. 43 p.
(Ms. Ecole de Bibl., U.L.)

2:1976 **Sainte-Janvière, soeur**
Bibliographie analytique de l'honorable juge Sir Adolphe Routhier.
Préf. de M. l'abbé Paul-Emile Gosselin. Québec, 1952. 71 p. (Ms.
Ecole de Bibl., U.L.)

2:1977 **Sainte-Janvière, soeur**
Essai de bio-bibliographie du T.R.P. Lucien Pagé, c.s.v., supérieur
général. Préface de Mgr Irénée Lussier. Montréal, 1957. xxxix, 91 p.
(Ms. Ecole de Bibl., U. de M.)

2:1978 **Sainte-Jeanne d'Annecy, soeur**
Bibliographie analytique de l'oeuvre de Sr St-François de l'Alverne,
c.n.d., précédée d'une biographie. Préface de Sr Saint-Jean, c.n.d.
Sherbrooke, 1963. 113 p. (Ms. Ecole de Bibl., U.L.)

2:1979 **Sainte-Jeanne-de-Jésus, soeur**
Bibliographie analytique de Soeur-Madeleine-des-Anges, c.n.d.
Québec, 1952. 50 p. (Ms. Ecole de Bibl., U.L.)

2:1980 **Sainte-Julienne-Falconièri**
Notes bio-biographiques sur 'tante Chantal,' Mme Cécile Lachaîne-
Brosseau. 1963. 83 p. (Ms. Ecole de Bibl., U.L.)

2:1981 **Sainte-Léonie, soeur**
L'Hôtel-Dieu de Québec (1639-1900). Notices historiques et
dépouillement des registres. (2e partie, 1759-1900). Préface du
docteur Jean-Baptiste Jobin. Québec, 1964. 438 p. (Ms. Ecole de
Bibl., U.L.)

2:1982 **Sainte-Louise, soeur**
Essai bio-bibliographique de Monsieur Alexis-Edouard Hains. 1953.
25 p. (Mf. Ecole de Bibl., U. de M.)

2:1983 **Sainte-Lydie, soeur**
Bibliographie analytique de l'oeuvre de M. René Pomerleau, de la
Société royale du Canada, précédée d'une biographie. Préface de M.
Georges Maheux, i.f.D.Sc. Québec, 1964. 110 p. (Ms. Ecole de Bibl.,
U.L.)

2:1984 **Sainte-Madeleine, soeur**
Bibliographie analytique de la Rév. Sr Marie-Emmanuel, o.s.u.
Québec, 1955. 32 p. (Ms. Ecole de Bibl., U.L.)

2:1985   **Sainte-Madeleine-du-Calvaire, soeur**
Bibliographie analytique de l'œuvre de Jean-Paul Légaré, journaliste
(1945-1961) précédée d'une biographie. Préface de Adrien Bégin.
Québec, 1964. 323 p. (Ms. Ecole de Bibl., U.L.)

2:1986   **Ste-Marguerite, soeur**
Bibliographie: l'Hôpital St-Michel-Archange. Québec, 1957. 90 p.
(Ms. Ecole de Bibl., U.L.)

2:1987   **Sainte-Marie, Lise**
Essai de bio-bibliographie du R.P. Raymond-Marie Voyer. Préface de
Pierre Morin, o.p. Montréal, 1958. xi, 48 p. (Ms. Ecole de Bibl.,
U. de M.)

2:1988   **Sainte-Marie-Camille, soeur**
Bio-bibliographie de Mgr Arsène Goyette, p.d. 1949. vi, 36 p. (Ms.
Ecole de Bibl., U. de M.)

2:1989   **Sainte-Marie-Christine, soeur**
Bio-bibliographie de M. Jean Flahault. 1945. viii, 38 p. (Ms. Ecole de
Bibl., U. de M.)

2:1990   **Sainte-Marie-Cléophas, soeur**
Bibliographie analytique de l'œuvre du docteur Louis-Philippe Roy,
M.D., journaliste (1949-1960) précédée d'une biographie. Préface de
M. Omer-Jules Desaulniers, surintendant de l'Instruction publique de
Québec. Québec, 1964. 924 p. (Ms. Ecole de Bibl., U.L.)

2:1991   **Sainte-Marie-de-Pontmain, soeur**
Bio-bibliographie analytique de l'œuvre des Sœurs de la Congrégation
de Notre-Dame de Montréal. Québec, 1952. 175 p. (Ms. Ecole de Bibl.,
U.L.)

2:1992   **Sainte-Marie-Emma, soeur**
Bio-bibliographie de Sœur Sainte-Marie-Vitaline, c.n.d. 1947. viii, 38 p.
(Ms. Ecole de Bibl., U. de M.)

2:1993   **Sainte-Marie-Gédéon, soeur**
Bio-bibliographie analytique de Sr Saint-Damase-de-Rome, c.n.d.
Québec, 1963. 153 p. (Ms. Ecole de Bibl., U.L.)

2:1994   **Sainte-Marie-Madeleine, soeur**
Bibliographie des biographies de religieuses décédées à l'Hôtel-Dieu
St-Vallier de Chicoutimi (1884-1959) Préface du Chanoine Joseph
Lalancette. Jonquière, 1961. 60 p. (Ms. Ecole de Bibl., U.L.)

2:1995 **Sainte-Marie-Odile, soeur**
Bibliographie critique: sources à consulter sur la vie et l'oeuvre de la vénérable Marguerite Bourgeoys, fondatrice de la Congrégation de Notre-Dame de Montréal. Lettre-préface de la révérende mère Saint-Ignace, c.n.d. 1945. xii, 137 p. facsim. (Ms. Ecole de Bibl., U. de M.)

2:1996 **Sainte-Marie-Rita, soeur**
Bibliographie analytique du révérend frère Marie-Maximin, é.c., directeur adjoint de la Légion de Marie. Préface de révérende soeur Marie-Alma, s.c.q. Québec, 1964. 177 p. (Ms. Ecole de Bibl., U.L.)

2:1997 **Sainte Mariette**
Bibliographie des notices biographiques et des écrits des Soeurs de la Charité de Québec décédées, 1918-1938. Québec, 1963. 161 p. (Ms. Ecole de Bibl., U.L.)

2:1998 **Sainte-Marthe-de-la-Trinité, soeur**
Bibliographie analytique de l'oeuvre du R.P. Laurent Tremblay. Préface de Mgr Victor Tremblay, p.d. Chicoutimi, 1961. 75 p. (Ms. Ecole de Bibl., U.L.)

2:1999 **Ste-Martine, soeur**
Bibliographie sur 'quelques monuments historiques de Québec (1901-1920).' Préface de Révérende Mère Marie-des-Victoires, s.s.c.m. Québec, 1963. 111 p. (Ms. Ecole de Bibl., U.L.)

2:2000 **Sainte-Monique, soeur**
Bibliographie des biographies des religieuses décédées à l'Hôtel-Dieu du Sacré-Coeur de Jésus de Québec (1879-1925) Préface de la R. Sr Supérieure générale, Mère Marie-de-l'Eucharistie, o.s.a. Québec, 1961. 84 p. (Ms. Ecole de Bibl., U.L.)

2:2001 **Sainte-Monique, soeur**
Bio-bibliographie de M. le chanoine Jean-Baptiste-Arthur Allaire. Saint-Hyacinthe, 1941. 24 p. (Ms. Ecole de Bibl., U. de M.)

2:2002 **Sainte-Octavie, soeur**
Notes bio-bibliographiques sur le Dr Jean-Baptiste Richard, préfacées par M. Harry Bernard. 1953. 49 p. (Ms. Ecole de Bibl., U. de M.)

2:2003 **Sainte-Rachel-Thérèse, soeur**
Bibliographie analytique de l'abbé Alexandre Paradis, p.m.c., précédée d'une biographie. Lettre-préface de Mgr Edgar Larochelle, p.m.c. Québec, 1964. 247 p. (Ms. Ecole de Bibl., U.L.)

2:2004  **Ste-Suzanne, soeur**
Bibliographie analytique de l'œuvre du docteur Wilfrid Leblond, précédée d'une biographie. Préface du docteur de la Broquerie Fortier. Québec, 1962. xix, 100 p. (Ms. Ecole de Bibl., U.L.)

2:2005  **Sainte-Thècle, soeur**
Bibliographie de l'abbé Henri-Raymond Casgrain. Préf. de Mgr Albert Tessier. Québec, 1955. 100 p. (Ms. Ecole de Bibl., U.L.)

2:2006  **Ste-Thérèse-de-l'Enfant-Jésus, soeur**
Bibliographie des notices biographiques et des écrits des Soeurs de la charité de Québec décédées de 1939 à 1958 incl. Lettre-préface de Mgr Gingras, p.d. Québec, 1964. 220 p. (Ms. Ecole de Bibl., U.L.)

2:2007  **Sainte-Véronique, soeur**
Bibliographie analytique de l'œuvre du Dr Roland Desmeules, précédée d'une biographie. Préface de Sr Saint-Ferdinand, s.c.q. Québec, 1964. 161 p. (Ms. Ecole de Bibl., U.L.)

2:2008  **Salisbury, Dorothy**
Bibliography of French-Canadian poetry. Montreal, 1932. 14 *l.* (Ms. McGill Univ. Libr. School)

2:2009  **Samuel, Sigmund**
A catalogue of the Sigmund Samuel collection, Canadiana and Americana. Comp. and annotated by Charles W. Jefferys. Toronto, Ryerson, 1948. xxxii, 180 p.

2:2010  **Sansfaçon, Jacques**
Bibliographie des titres des documents sériés ayant [été] publiés sur les poissons, la pêche, les pêcheries du Canada. Préf. de Vianney Legendre. Montréal, 1957. xx, 107 p. (Ms. Ecole de Bibl., U. de M.)

2:2011  **Sansfaçon, Jacques**
Bibliography of the titles of serial documents having been published on the fishes and fisheries of Canada; preliminary edition. Montreal, Office de Biologie, Ministère de la Chasse et Pêcheries, Université de Montréal, 1957. 107 p.

2:2012  **Sansfaçon, Jacques**
La documentation scientifique: cadre, problèmes, bibliographie à l'usage des étudiants de l'Ecole de Bibliothéconomie de l'Université de Montréal 1967-1968. 1967. 52 f. (Ms. Ecole de Bibl., U. de M.)

2:2013  **Sansfaçon, Jacques**
Liste sélective de périodiques à l'intention des bibliothèques de

collèges du Canada français. Traduction d'André Contant. Montréal, Fédération des Collèges Classiques, 1967. 126 p.

2:2014 **Sarrasin, René**
Bio-bibliographie de Gérard Malchelosse. 1940. 32 p. (Ms. Ecole de Bibl., U. de M.)

2:2015 **Saskatchewan. Department of Mineral Resources**
Catalogue of maps and publications, April 1, 1965. Regina [Queen's Printer] 1965. 122 p. illus., maps.
Supersedes all previous issues.

2:2016 **Saskatchewan. Legislative Library**
List of Royal Commissions, special reports, etc., pertaining to the province of Saskatchewan. [Regina, 1947] 3, 74 (i.e., 76), 3, 2 numb. *l.*

2:2017 **Saskatchewan. Legislative Library**
The medicare crisis in Saskatchewan (January 1, 1960-July 31, 1962); a bibliography prepared in the Legislative Library, by Heather Meagher. Regina, 1963. 201 p.
Indexes all Saskatchewan newspapers, important Canadian dailies, some Commonwealth and foreign newspapers and magazines.

2:2018 **Saskatchewan. Legislative Library**
Newspaper index, covering in general the period 1949-1954. [Regina, 1959] 3 v. (1158 *l.*)
Index of daily newspapers published in the province of Saskatchewan. Previous issues: 1952. For the period 1930-1935, 68 p.; 1954. For the period 1935-Aug. 1949. 317 p.

2:2019 **Saskatchewan. Legislative Library.** Archives Division
Catalogue of newspapers on microfilm in the Legislative Library (Archives Division) and Provincial Archives of Saskatchewan. [Regina, Amon, Printer to the Queen, 1958] 15 p.
Mostly Saskatchewan papers.

2:2020 **Saskatchewan. University**
Arthur Silver Morton, M.A., B.D., D.D., LL.D., F.R.S.C., professor of history and librarian in the University of Saskatchewan, 1914-1940. Saskatoon, University of Saskatchewan, 1943. 23 p. facsim.
'List of publications [of Arthur Silver Morton]': p. 21-23.

2:2021 **Saskatchewan. University**
University of Saskatchewan postgraduate theses, 1912-1966. Saskatoon, 1967.
iii, 93 p.

2:2022 **Saskatchewan. University.** Library
Recent acquisitions. v. 1– Nov. 1967– [Saskatoon]
v. monthly

2:2023 **Saskatchewan Teachers' Federation.** Library
Catalogue of books. Saskatoon, Saskatchewan Teachers' Federation,
1968.
2 v.

2:2024 **Saucier, Camille**
Bio-bibliographie de Thomas Taggart Smyth. Lettre-préface de Son
Honneur le maire Camilien Houde. 1952. 51 p. (Ms. Ecole de Bibl.,
U. de M.)

2:2025 **Savard, Léo**
Bibliographie analytique du Rév. F. Eloi Gérard. Québec, 1955.
112 p. (Ms. Ecole de Bibl., U.L.)

2:2026 **Savard, Marcelle**
Bio-bibliographie analytique de l'abbé Félix-Antoine Savard,
professeur à la Faculté des Lettres de l'Université Laval, Québec.
Québec, 1947. 18 p. (Ms. Ecole de Bibl., U.L.)

2:2027 **Savard, René**
Bio-bibliographie de Ernest Myrand. Préface de M. Avila Bédard.
[Québec] 1947. 25 p. (Ms. Ecole de Bibl., U. de M.)

2:2028 **Savic, Edward**
Changes in Canada's Northern Atlantic Treaty Organization. 1967.
[9] 1. (Ms. U. of O. Libr. School)

2:2029 **Savoie, Michèle**
Essai de bio-bibliographie sur M. Marcel Clément, écrivain, sociologue,
journaliste. 1953. vi, 34 p. (Mf. Ecole de Bibl., U. de M.)

2:2030 **Savoie, Odette**
Essai de bio-bibliographie: R.P. Julien Péghaire, c.s.sp., en philosophie
et en théologie. Montréal, 1954. vii, 24 p. (Ms. Ecole de Bibl., U. de M.)

2:2031 **Savoie, Suzanne (Chabot)**
Essai bio-bibliographique sur M. Pierre Demers. Préf. de Mlle Juliette
Chabot. Montréal, 1961. viii, 40 p. (Ms. Ecole de Bibl., U. de M.)

2:2032 **Scantland, Jean-Marie**
Le drapeau canadien; bibliographie. Ottawa, Université d'Ottawa,
Ecole de Bibliothécaires, 1954. xi, 27 p. (Ms. U. d'O. Ecole de Bibl.)

2:2033 **Schlesinger, Benjamin**
The multi-problem family; a review and annotated bibliography.
[Toronto] University of Toronto Press [c1963] xiv, 173 p. tables.

2:2034 **Schlesinger, Benjamin**
Poverty in Canada and the United States; overview and annotated
bibliography. Editorial consultant: Florence Strakhovsky. [Toronto]
University of Toronto Press [c1966]
xiii, 211 p.

2:2035 **Schmelz, Oskar**
Jewish demography and statistics: bibliography for 1920-1960,
compiled and edited by O. Schmelz with the assistance of R. Shebath.
Jerusalem, 1961.
1 v. (various pagings)

2:2036 **Scott, Doris**
Young Canada's choice. [Ottawa, Canadian Library Association.
1963?] 4 p.

2:2037 **Scott, Doris**
Books and exhibits; a bibliography of books in Boys and Girls House
[of the Toronto Public Library] relating to activities in the Royal
Ontario Museum ... [Toronto] 1948. 34 *l.* (Ms. Toronto Univ. Libr.
School)

2:2038 **Scott, Francis Reginald**
Bibliography on constitutional law. [Montreal, McGill University,
1948] 6 p. *l.*, 2-27, 5 numb. *l.*

2:2039 **Scott, Michael M.**
A bibliography of Western Canadian studies relating to Manitoba.
Winnipeg, 1967.
79 *l.*

2:2040 **Sealock, Richard Burl**
Bibliography of place name literature: United States, Canada, Alaska,
and Newfoundland. Comp. by Richard Burl Sealock and Paulin
Augusta Seely. Chicago, American Library Association, 1948. 331 p.
2d ed. Chicago, American Library Association, 1967. x, 352 p.

2:2041 **Séguin, Claire**
Bibliographie de Roland Vinette. 1953. 24 p. (Ms. Ecole de Bibl.,
U. de M.)

2:2042  [Severance, Frank Hayward]
... Contributions towards a bibliography of the Niagara region.
Pamphlets and books printed in Buffalo prior to 1850. Being an
appendix to volume six, Buffalo Historical Society publications.
Buffalo, N.Y., 1903. [58] p.
(In Buffalo historical society, *Publications.* Buffalo, *1903.* V. 6, p. [547]-605)

2:2043  [Severance, Frank Hayward]
Contributions towards a bibliography of the Niagara region. The
Upper Canada rebellion of 1837-38. Being an appendix to volume
five, Buffalo Historical Society publications. Buffalo, N.Y., 1902.
69 p.
(In Buffalo historical society, *Publications.* Buffalo, *1902.* V. 5, p. [427]-495)

2:2044  Severance, Henry Ormal
A guide to the current periodicals and serials of the United States
and Canada, 1907. Ann Arbor, Mich., Wahr, 1907. 330 p.

2nd edition: *1908.* 435 p.
Supplement: Sept. 1, 1910. 72 p.
3rd edition: *1914.* 462 p.
4th edition: *1920.* 564 p.
Supplement: December, 1920 to January, 1923 ... 123 p.
5th edition: *1931.* 432 p.

2:2045  Sévérien, frère
Bio-bibliographie analytique de Rodolphe Laplante. Préface de
Albert Rioux. Québec, 1955. 344 p. (Ms. Ecole de Bibl., U.L.)

2:2046  Sévigny, Françoise
Notes bio-bibliographiques sur Claude Melançon. 1948. v, 10 p.
(Ms. Ecole de Bibl., U. de M.)

2:2047  Shaffer, Emilienne
Bio-bibliographie de Damase Potvin. 1941. 62 p. (Mf. Ecole de Bibl.,
U. de M.)

2:2048  Sham, Irene
Wildlife conservation in Canada. 1965. vii, 6 1. (Ms. U. of O. Libr.
School)

2:2049  Shanahan, Mary B.R.
A bibliography; the aeroplane in Canada. [Toronto, 1933] [14] *l.*
(Ms. Toronto Univ. Libr. School)

2:2050  Sharp, Donald James
An annotated bibliography of Irving Layton. [Toronto, 1962] ii, 8 *l.*
(Ms. Toronto Univ. Libr. School)

2:2051 **[Sharp, Hugh Frederick Bower]**
Books of American & Canadian interest. [Edinburgh, Clark, 1932]
35 p., 2 *l.*

2:2052 **Shea, John Dawson Gilmary**
Bibliography of Hennepin's works. New York, Shea, 1880. 13 p.

2:2053 **Sheffield, Edward F.**
Educational and vocational guidance materials; a Canadian bibliography. Compiled by Edward F. Sheffield and Nora Morrison Sheffield.
Ottawa, Canadian Council of Education for Citizenship, 1946. 49 p.

2:2054 **Shepard, Odell**
Bliss Carman. Toronto, McClelland and Stewart [1923]. 184 p.
Includes 'A checklist of first editions of the works of Bliss Carman, comp. by Frederic F. Sherman, with revisions and additions by R.H. Hathaway.'

2:2055 **Shepherd, Eleanor V.**
A bibliography of Women's Institutes in Canada ... [Toronto, 1933]
[2] , 4 *l.* (Ms. Toronto Univ. Libr. School)

2:2056 **Shepherd, Mary**
Coburg, 1798-1900. [Toronto, 1963] 10 *l.* (Ms. Toronto Univ. Libr.
School)

2:2057 **Shepp, Mary**
Canadian literature (English and French); a bibliography of reference
sources. Montreal, 1954. 10 *l.* (Ms. McGill Univ. Libr. School)

2:2058 **Sherbrooke. Université.** Bibliothèque
Sens national, 1965; bibliographie de 400 articles et livres pour mieux
comprendre les orientations nouvelles du sens national au Canada
français, compilée par la bibliothèque de l'Université de Sherbrooke,
pour la session d'études patriotiques, 19 et 20 mars 1965 (Université
de Sherbrooke, Québec) [Sherbrooke] Association canadienne des
éducateurs de langue française, 1965. 20 f.

2:2059 **Sherlock, Marjorie**
Bibliography of material in the Reference Department, Toronto Public
Library, on transportation in Upper Canada before the railways, to
1860. [Toronto, 1932] 2 pts. (Ms. Toronto Univ. Libr. School)
Contents: Pt. 1, By water, by M. Sherlock; Pt. 2, By land, by R.I. McKenzie.

2:2060 **Shortt, Adam**
Canada and its provinces; a history of the Canadian people and their
institutions by one hundred associates. Adam Shortt, Arthur G.

Doughty, general editors. [Archives ed.] Toronto, Glasgow, Brook; [etc., etc.] 1914-1917. 23 v.

V. 23. General index; manuscript sources; bibliography; chronological outlines; historical tables.

2:2061   **Siddall, James N.**
Mechanical design; reference sources [compiled by] James N. Siddall. [Toronto] University of Toronto Press [c1967]

ix, 156 p.

2:2062   **Simard, Diane**
Expo 67. 1966. [3] 8 1. (Ms. U. of O. Libr. School)

2:2063   **Simard, Gisèle**
Notes bio-bibliographiques sur Madame Emma-Adèle Bourgeois Lacerte. 1950. 14 p. (Mf. Ecole de Bibl., U. de M.)

2:2064   **Simard, Rita**
Bio-bibliographie d'Emile Coderre. Préface de Mlle Marie-Claire Daveluy. 1942. 42, [15] p. (Mf. Ecole de Bibl., U. de M.)

2:2065   **Sinclair, Donald Michael**
Reading reference to Social Credit; a bibliography. [Victoria, B.C., 1964?] 26, 16 *l*.

First 26 *l*. originally published Vancouver, 1963.

2:2066   **Singh, Kuldip**
Library Schools in Canada since 1938. 1964. [v] 5 1. (Ms. U. of O. Libr. School)

2:2067   **Sir George Williams College**, Montreal
Bibliography of Canadiana, 1944. Compiled and arranged by the Librarians, Jean Breakell Crombie and Margaret Alice Webb. Montreal, Sir George Williams College, 1945. 322 *l*.

Supplement 1944-1946. Montreal, Sir George Williams College, 1946. 55 *l*.

2:2068   **Sirko, Hlib**
Essai de bio-bibliographie du R.P. Thomas-André Audet, o.p. Préface par le R.P. Benoît Lacroix, o.p. [Montréal] 1959. xxvii, 68 p. (Ms. Ecole de Bibl., U. de M.)

2:2069   **Skelton, Raleigh Ashlin**
The marine surveys of James Cook in North America, 1758-1768, particularly the survey of Newfoundland; a bibliography of printed charts and sailing directions, by R.A. Skelton and R.V. Tooley. London, Map Collectors' Circle, 1967.

32 p. illus., maps.

2:2070  **Slavica canadiana.** 1951—. Winnipeg, Ukrainian Free Academy of Sciences, (*Slavistica, Proceedings of the institute of Slavistics of the Ukrainian free academy of sciences*) Annual.

Title varies.

Selected bibliography of Slavic books and pamphlets published in or relating to Canada.

Ukrainian titles in this list are also listed separately as Ukrainica Canadiana, 1953—.

2:2071  **Slon, Eugene**

Role of Canadian libraries in adult education. 1964. vi, 5 l. (Ms. U. of O. Libr. School)

2:2072  **Smith, Albert H.**

A bibliography of Canadian education. Compiled and annotated by Albert H. Smith and others. Toronto, Department of Educational Research, University of Toronto [1938]. 302 p.

2:2073  **Smith, Anne Marie**

Canadian theses in forestry and related subject fields 1913-1962, compiled by Anne M. Smith, Robert W. Wellwood and Leonid Valg. [N.p., 1962] [375]-400 p.

'Reprinted from the *Forestry chronicle,* September, 1962, vol. 38, no. 3.'

2:2074  **Smith, Charles Wesley**

Pacific northwest Americana; a checklist of books and pamphlets relating to the history of the Pacific northwest. Edition 3, revised and extended by Isabel Mayhew. Portland, Ore., Binfords & Mort, 1950. 381 p.

First ed.: Checklist of books and pamphlets relating to the history of the Pacific northwest ... Olympia, Wash., Boardman, 1909. 191 p.
Second ed.: New York, Wilson; [etc., etc.] 1921. xi, 329 p.
Includes a substantial number of titles relating to British Columbia.

2:2075  **Smith, Cliff**

Social Credit and its application in Canada. 1963. vi, 12 l. (Ms. U. of O. Libr. School)

2:2076  **Smith, Harlan Ingersoll**

Bibliography [of writings of Harlan I. Smith on the archeology of] Canada. Ottawa, 1932. 20 p.

2:2077  **Smith, Jean**

A bibliography of books and periodical articles on the Royal Commission on National Development in the Arts, Letters and Sciences. Montreal, 1954. 9 l. (Ms. McGill Univ. Libr. School)

2:2078 **Smith, Olive I.**
Bibliography of the Red River settlement, 1812-1870. Toronto, 1934. [2], 12 *l.* (Ms. Toronto Univ. Libr. School)

2:2079 **Smith, Robert Dennis Hilton**
Alice one hundred; being a catalogue in celebration of the 100th birthday of Alice's adventures in Wonderland. Victoria, B.C., Adelphi Book Shop, 1966.
77 p. illus.
Annotated catalogue of books, pamphlets, leaflets and recordings, dating from 1858-1965, of works by and about C.L. Dodgson, purchased for the Library of the University of British Columbia by the graduating class of 1925.

2:2080 **Smith, Robert Dennis Hilton**
Crusoe 250; being a catalogue in celebration of the 250th anniversary of Robinson Crusoe. Victoria, B.C., Canada, The Adelphi Book Shop Ltd., 1970.
119 p. illus.
A comprehensive listing of many editions, translations, imitations and parodies of the Defoe classic; based on a collection of 700 titles offered for sale by the Adelphi Book Shop.

2:2081 **Smith, Rosemary Jean**
Clarke and Darlington Townships; a bibliography including Bowmanville and Newcastle as found in Toronto area libraries. Toronto, 1965. iii, 10 *l.* (Ms. Toronto Univ. Libr. School)

2:2082 **Smith, Shirley**
Royal Canadian Mounted Police: Schooner St Roch. 1967. vii, 12 1. maps. (Ms. U. of O. Libr School)

2:2083 **Société canadienne de criminologie**
... Littérature criminologique publiée au Canada au cours des cinq dernières années et disponible pour les autres pays. [Ottawa, 1964–] semestriel.

2:2084 **Société canadienne d'histoire de l'Eglise catholique. Rapport. (Index)**
Index des mémoires de la Société canadienne d'histoire de l'Eglise catholique, dressé par Lucien Brault. Ottawa [1960] 248 p.
Index par sujets des v. 1-25, 1933/34-1958.

2:2085 **Société des écrivains canadiens**
Bulletin bibliographique. Montréal, 1937. 1959.
23 no. Annuel.

2:2086 **Société des écrivains canadiens**
Répertoire bio-bibliographique de la Société des écrivains canadiens,

1954. Montréal, Editions de la Société des écrivains canadiens [1955, c.1954]. 248 p.

2:2087 **Société royale du Canada**
Index général, mémoires et comptes rendus de la Société royale du Canada; première et deuxième séries, 1882-1906. Toronto, Copp, Clark, 1908. 133 p.

*Mémoires de la Société royale du Canada,* sections I et II, 1882-1943. Index dressé par Lucien Brault. [Ottawa] Editions de l'Universit]e d'Ottawa, 1944. 4 f., [11]-112 p.

Table des noms d'auteurs, comptes rendus de la Société royale du Canada, sections I-V troisième série: tomes I-XXXV, 1907-1941. [Toronto, University of Toronto Press, 1942?] 90 p.

2:2088 **Sotheby & Co.**
Catalogue of the highly important papers of Louis Antoine de Bougainville, F.R.S. (1729-1811) relating to the Seven Years' War in Canada, the foundation of the first colony on the Falkland Islands, his voyage round the world and the American War of Independence ... [London, 1957]

45 p. illus.
Catalogue of items sold by auction by Sotheby & Co., June 24, 1957.

2:2089 **Sotnick, Vivian Joyce**
Donald Grant Creighton; a bibliography of his writings, 1931-1956. [Toronto] 1965. ii, 8 *l.* (Ms. Toronto Univ. Libr. School)

2:2090 **Soucy, Lorette**
Notes bio-bibliographiques sur Antoine Gérin-Lajoie. 1948. 18 p. (Mf. Ecole de Bibl., U. de M.)

2:2091 **Soucy, Réjane**
Bio-bibliographie de Sir Louis-Hippolyte Lafontaine. Préface de M. Casimir Hébert. 1947. 162 p. (Mf. Ecole de Bibl., U. de M.)

2:2092 **Special Libraries Association.** Special Committee on Municipal Documents
Basic list of current municipal documents; a checklist of official publications issued periodically since 1927 by the larger cities of the United States and Canada. New York, Special Libraries Association, 1932. 71 p.

2:2093 **Spencer, Loraine**
Northern Ontario; a bibliography, compiled by Loraine Spencer and Susan Holland. [Toronto] University of Toronto Press [c1968]
x, 120 p.

2:2094 **Spicer, Erik John**
The Graphic publishers limited, Ottawa, Ontario, Canada, 1924-1932. (Ms. Univ. of Mich. Dept. of Libr. Sci., 1959) [49 p.]

2:2095 **Spiridonakis, Basile G.**
Mémoires et documents du Ministère des affaires étrangères de France sur la Russie. [2e éd.] Sherbrooke, Faculté des arts, Université de Sherbrooke [1965]
148 f.

2:2096 **Stakenas, Elaine**
Ecology of North American alpine flora: a bibliography. [Toronto] 1967. v, 24 *l*. (Ms. Toronto Univ. Libr. School)

2:2097 **Stefansson Collection**
Dictionary catalog of the Stefansson Collection on the Polar regions in the Dartmouth College Library. Boston, G.K. Hall, 1967.
8 v.
Represents the Stefansson Collection as of 1962. Cf. v. 1, p. iv.

2:2098 **Stephens, Mary C.**
Bibliography of books, pamphlets and periodical articles on the history of Canadian art ... [Toronto, 1933] [1], 11, [1] *l*. (Ms. Toronto Univ. Libr. School)

2:2099 **Stevens, Henry**
Catalogue of Canadian books in the Library of the British Museum, Christmas 1856; including those printed in the other British North American provinces. London, 1859. 14 p.
Later included in his *Catalogue of American books in the Library of the British Museum* ... London, Whittingham, 1866, as pt. 2.

2:2100 **Stewart, Alice Rose**
The Atlantic Provinces of Canada; union lists of materials in the larger libraries of Maine. Orono, Me., University of Maine Press, 1965. vi, 85 p. (*University of Maine studies*, Ser. 2, no. 82)
Published as v. 68, no. 23, June 1, 1965, of the *University of Maine bulletin*. First published 1963.

2:2101 **Stewart, Charles H.**
The Eastern Townships of the province of Quebec: a bibliography of historical, geographical and descriptive material. Montreal, 1940. [14] *l*. (Ms. McGill Univ. Libr. School)

2:2102 **Storey, Dorothy S.**
A bibliography of treaties with the Indians of Canada included in

government documents from earliest times to 1933. Montreal, 1934. 6 *l.* (Ms. McGill Univ. Libr. School)

2:2103 **Storoshchuk, Roman**
Federal social security legislation in Canada. 1963. vii, 10 1. (Ms. U. of O. Libr. School)

2:2104 **Stott, Margaret M.**
A trial bibliography of research pertaining to adult education, by Margaret M. Stott and Coolie Verner. Vancouver, Extension Dept., University of British Columbia, 1963.
ii, 29 *l.*

2:2105 **Strathern, Mrs Gloria**
A bibliography of British Columbia, 1774-1848. Victoria, B.C. (In progress)
This volume, on the period of exploration and discovery includes the years before the era covered by the first volume of this set – *Laying the foundations, 1849-99,* published by the University of Victoria in 1968. *See* Lowther, Barbara J.

2:2106 **Stuart-Stubbs, B.**
Maps relating to Alexander Mackenzie [compiled by] B. Stuart-Stubbs. [n.p., 1968?]
[36] *l.* maps.
'A keepsake distributed at a meeting of the Bibliographical Society of Canada – Société bibliographique du Canada, Jasper Park, June, 1968.' Also distributed with v. 7 of the *Papers of the Bibliographical Society of Canada,* 1970.

2:2107 **Stuntz, Stephen Conrad**
List of the agricultural periodicals of the United States and Canada published during the century July 1810 to July 1910. Edited by Emma B. Hawks. Washington, G.P.O., 1941. viii, 190 p. (U.S. Dept. of Agriculture, Miscellaneous publications no. 398)

2:2108 **Sumner, Elsie G.**
The newspaper press in Oxford County, 1840-1940 ... [Toronto] 1940. [1], ix, 57 *l.* (Ms. Toronto Univ. Libr. School.)
Revised and printed without notes as *Western Ontario history nuggets,* no. 2.

2:2109 **Surprenant, Denise**
Bio-bibliographie du R.P. Guillaume Lavallée, o.f.m. 1953. 27 p. (Ms. Ecole de Bibl., U. de M.)

2:2110 **Sutherland, Betty**
Canadian Rockies; a short bibliography. (In *Public libraries,* v. 20, p. 220-221, May 1915)

2:2111  **Swoger, Donald**
Criticism of Canadian literature; an annotated bibliography. Montreal, [1954]. 6 *l.* (Ms. McGill Univ. Libr. School)

2:2112  **Tabisz, Rosemary M.**
A bibliography of the limestone and marble industries of Canada. Toronto, 1964. v, 9 *l.* (Ms. Toronto Univ. Libr. School)

2:2113  **Tai, Daniel W.P.**
Which way to go for today's Canadian foreign trade. 1963. [ii] 9 1. (Ms. U. of O. Libr. School)

2:2114  **Taillefer, Louise**
Essai de bio-bibliographie de Mgr Emile Dubois. [Montréal] 1950. vii, 12 p. (Ms. Ecole de Bibl., U. de M.)

2:2115  **Talbot, Alice**
Bibliographie du docteur Hubert Larue. Précédée d'une notice biographique. 1943. 15 p. (Mf. Ecole de Bibl., U. de M.)

2:2116  **Talbot, Bernadette**
Bibliographique analytique de Renée des Ormes [Marie Ferland-Turgeon]. Québec, 1947. 31 p. (Ms. Ecole de Bibl., U.L.)

2:2117  **Tanghe, Raymond**
Bibliography of Canadian bibliographies. Toronto, Published in association with the Bibliographical Society of Canada by University of Toronto Press, 1960.
206 p.
Supplement, 1960 & 1961. Toronto, Bibliographical Society of Canada, 1962. 24 p.
Supplement, 1962 & 1963, compiled by Madeleine Pellerin. Toronto, Bibliographical Society of Canada, 1964.
27 p.
Supplement, 1964 & 1965, compiled by Madeleine Pellerin. Toronto, Bibliographical Society of Canada, 1966.
32 p.

2:2118  **Tanghe, Raymond**
L'Ecole de bibliothécaires de l'Université de Montréal, 1937-1962. Montréal, Fides, 1962.
69 p. illus.
En appendice: liste des fondateurs, des administrateurs, des professeurs, des diplomés et des travaux bibliographiques compilée par Jean-Bernard Léveillé et Jeanne Chéné.

2:2119  **Tangri, Om P.**
Transportation in Canada and the United States; a bibliography of

selected references, 1945-1967 [by] Om P. Tangri. Winnipeg, Center for Transportation Studies, University of Manitoba, 1968. viii, 218 p.

2:2120 **Tanguay, Marthe**

Bio-bibliographie analytique de l'œuvre de Paul-Antoine Giguère, directeur du département de chimie à l'Université Laval. Lettre-préface de Henri Demers. Québec, 1959. 40 p. (Ms. Ecole de Bibl., U.L.)

2:2121 **Tanner, Väinö**

A bibliography of Labrador (specially Newfoundland-Labrador). Helsingfors, 1942. 83 p.

'Reprinted from *Acta geographica fenninæ*, vol. 8, no. 1.'

2:2122 **Tarbox, George E.**

Bibliography of graduate theses on geophysics in U.S. and Canadian institutions. Golden, Colo., Colorado School of Mines, 1958. vi, 55 p. (*Quarterly of the Colorado School of Mines*, v. 53, no. 1)

2:2123 **Taylor, John Culbert**

A short bibliography of Henry Marshall Tory, 1864-1947. [Toronto, 1957] iii, 12 *l.* (Ms. Toronto Univ. Libr. School)

2:2124 **Taylor, Nina Ruth**

Farley Mowat, the writer and his work; a bibliography. Toronto, 1966. 25 *l.* (Ms. Toronto Univ. Libr. School)

2:2125 **Telmon, sœur**

Bibliographie analytique de R.S. Gabriel-Lalement, s.g.c., précédée d'une biographie. Préface par R.S. Paul-Emile, s.g.c. Buckingham, 1962. 52 p. (Ms. Ecole de Bibl., U.L.)

2:2126 **Ternaux-Compans, Henri**

Bibliothèque américaine, ou Catalogue des ouvrages relatifs à l'Amérique qui ont paru depuis sa découverte jusqu'à l'an 1700, par H. Ternaux. Amsterdam, B.R. Grüner, 1968. viii, 191 p.

'Réimpression de l'édition de Paris, 1837.'–verso de la p. de t.

2:2127 **Tessier, Antoinette (Roy)**

Bio-bibliographie sur Cécile Rouleau éducatrice, précédée d'une biographie. (Préface de Yves Tessier) Québec, 1964. 49 p. (Ms. Ecole de Bibl., U.L.)

2:2128  **Tessier, Germaine**
Bibliographie des publications françaises du comité provincial de défense contre la tuberculose. [s.d.] 14 p. (Ms. Ecole de Bibl., U. de M.)

2:2129  **Tessier, Monique**
Les publications du Conseil de la Vie française en Amérique (depuis sa fondation en 1937). Préface par Mgr Paul-Emile Gosselin. [Montréal] 1959. xliii, 39 p. (Ms. Ecole de Bibl., U. de M.)

2:2130  **Tessier, Rachel**
Bio-bibliographie de M. Arthur Buies. Préface de M. Arthur Buies, fils. 1943. xxviii, 36, [24] p. (Mf. Ecole de Bibl., U. de M.)

2:2131  **Tessier, Thérèse**
Bibliographie d'auteur (livres seulement): Laure Conan (pseudonyme de Félicité Angers) membre de la Société historique de Montréal, 1845-1924. Montréal, 1931. 3 *l.* (Ms. McGill Univ. Libr. School)

2:2132  **Tétreault, Madeleine**
Bio-bibliographie de Eugène Achard. Préface de Mlle Juliette Chabot. 1947. xviii, 10 p. (Mf. Ecole de Bibl., U. de M.)

2:2133  **Tétreault, Ruth**
Bio-bibliographie de Mgr Antonio Camirand, p.d., v.g. Préface de Mgr Robert Charland, p.d. 1951. xvii, 102 p. (Ms. Ecole de Bibl., U. de M.)

2:2134  **Têtu, Horace**
Historique des journaux de Québec ... Québec, Brousseau, 1875. 51 p.
Nouvelle édition, revue, augmentée et annotée. Québec, 1889. 107 p.

2:2135  **Têtu, Horace**
Journaux de Lévis. Québec, 1890. 12 p.
2e édition: Revue et augmentée. Québec, 1894. 21 p. 'Tirage: Deux cents exemplaires.'
3e édition: Revue et augmentée. Québec, 1898. 29 p.

2:2136  **Têtu, Horace**
Journaux et revues de Montréal, par ordre chronologique. Québec, 1881. 16 p.

2:2137  **Têtu, Horace**
Journaux et revues de Québec, par ordre chronologique. Québec, 1881. 16 p.
3e édition: 1883. 26 p.

2:2138  **Théoret, Germaine**
Bibliographie de Mlle Hélène Charbonneau. 1938. 20 p. (Mf. Ecole de Bibl., U. de M.)

2:2139  **Thérèse-de-l'Immaculée, soeur**
Notes bio-bibliographiques: le Père Polyeucte Guissard, a.a. 1951. 15 p. (Ms. Ecole de Bibl., U. de M.)

2:2140  **Thérèse-de-Lisieux, soeur**
Essai de bio-bibliographie de Rév. soeur Anger, s.g.s.h. 1951-52. xi, 23 p. (Ms. Ecole de Bibl., U. de M.)

2:2141  **Thérèse-du-Carmel, soeur**
Bibliographie analytique de l'oeuvre de Félix-Antoine Savard. Préf. de Luc Lacourcière. Montréal, Fides [c1967]
229 p. portr.

2:2142  **Thériault, Adrien**
Jules Fournier, journaliste de combat [par] Adrien Thério [pseud.]. Montréal, Fides [1954] 244, [1] p.
Bibliographie de Jules Fournier p. [11]-22.

2:2143  **Thériault, Normand**
Bio-bibliographie d'Adrien Thério (Thériault) Préf. du Lt-Colonel Charles-A. Chabot. Saint-Jean (Québec) 1961. ix, 43 p. (Ms. Ecole de Bibl., U. de M.)

2:2144  **Thèses canadiennes.** 1960/61– Ottawa [Imprimeur de la Reine] 1962– annuel.
Première liste publiée en 1953 sous le titre: Thèses canadiennes, une liste des thèses acceptées par les universités canadiennes en 1952. 50 p.
Compilé par la Bibliothèque nationale du Canada.

2:2145  **Thibault, Huguette**
Notes bio-bibliographiques sur M. Adolphe Poisson. 1948. 9 p. (Ms. Ecole de Bibl., U. de M.)

2:2146  **Thibault, Lucile**
Notes bio-bibliographiques sur Monsieur le docteur Ernest Choquette. 1948. [10] p. (Mf. Ecole de Bibl., U. de M.)

2:2147  **Thibault, Priscille**
Bibliographie de l'oeuvre de Mgr Arthur Maheux, p.d., précédée d'une notice biographique. Préface de M. Maurice Lebel, directeur du département des études anciennes de l'Université Laval. Québec, 1964. 109 p. (Ms. Ecole de Bibl., U.L.)

2:2148  **Thierman, Lois Mary**
Index to Vernon Blair Rhodenizer's *Canadian literature in English.*
Edmonton, Printed by La Survivance Print. [1968]
ix, 469 p.

2:2149  **Thomas, Clara Eileen (McCandless)**
Canadian novelists, 1920-1945. Toronto, Longmans, 1946. 6 p. *l.,*
129, [12] p.

2:2150  **Thomas, Morley K.**
... A bibliography of Canadian climate, 1763-1957. Ottawa [Queen's
Printer] 1961 [i.e. 1962] 114 p. (NRC 6521)

2:2151  **Thomas, Paule Rolland**
Documents audio-visuels. 1967-68. 27 f. (Ms. Ecole de Bibl., U. de M.)

2:2152  **Thomas, Paule Rolland**
Services internes de la bibliothèque: classification et catalogage.
1967-68. 27 f. (Ms. Ecole de Bibl., U. de M.)

2:2153  **Thompson, Laura Amelia**
... Government annuities in Canada and New Zealand; a list of
references. [Washington, 1934] 5 *l.*

2:2154  **Thompson, Laura Amelia**
A list of references: old-age pensions in Canada ... Washington, G.P.O.,
1929. [1] , 212-217 p.
'From the *Monthly labor review* (February, 1929) of the Bureau of labor
statistics, United States Department of labor.'

2:2155  **Thomson, Murray McCheyne**
A bibliography of Canadian writings in adult education, compiled by
Murray Thomson and Diana J. Ironside. Toronto, Canadian Associa-
tion for Adult Education, 1956. 56 p.

2:2156  **Times Book Company**
Canadian printed books, 1752-1961; an exhibition. [Catalogue.
London, 1961] 27 p.
Exhibition held in the Antiquarian Dept., the Times Bookshop, July 11-22,
1961.

2:2157  **Tirol, Marcel and D.M. Hayne**
Bibliographie critique des Anciens Canadiens (1863) de Philippe-
Joseph Aubert de Gaspé. (In *Bibliographical society of Canada.
Papers. v. 3, 1964: p. 38-60*)

2:2158 **Toan, Tran Van**
Bio-bibliographie du T.R.P. Louis-Marie Régis, o.p. Préface du R.P.
Hoang Kim Thao, o.p. 1955. xix, 37 p. (Ms. Ecole de Bibl., U. de M.)

2:2159 **Tod, Dorothea Douglas**
A bibliography of Canadian literary periodicals, 1789-1900. Com-
piled by Dorothea Tod and Audrey Cordingley. Ottawa, The Society,
1932. 87-96.
'From the *Royal society of Canada, Transactions,* 3d ser., v. 26, sec. 2, 1932.'
Pt. I (p. 87-92) previously submitted to Toronto University Library School.
Pt. II (p. 90-96), French-Canadian literary periodicals, compiled by A.
Cordingley.

2:2160 **Tod, Dorothea Douglas**
... Catalogue d'ouvrages imprimés au Canada [1900-1925]. Compilé
par Dorothea D. Tod & Audrey Cordingley ... Liste à vérifier. Ottawa
[Imprimeur du roi] 1950. 370 f.

2:2161 **Tod, Dorothea Douglas**
A checklist of Canadian imprints 1900-1925 ... Compiled by Dorothea
D. Tod & Audrey Cordingley. Preliminary checking edition ... Ottawa,
King's Printer, 1950. 370 *l.*

2:2162 **Tolmie, Ruth H.**
Bibliography of personal accounts of travel in Upper Canada from
the earliest years to 1833. [Toronto, 1967] v, 25 *l.* (Ms. Toronto
Univ. Libr. School)

2:2163 **Toronto. Public Library**
A bibliography of Canadiana; being items in the Public Library of
Toronto, Canada, relating to the early history and development of
Canada; edited by Frances M. Staton and Marie Tremaine, with an
introduction by George H. Locke. Toronto, The Public Library,
1934. 828 p.
Caption title: *A bibliography of Canadiana, 1534-1867.*
... First supplement ... Edited by Gertrude M. Boyle, assisted by Marjorie
Colbeck, with an introduction by Henry C. Campbell. Toronto, The Public
Library, 1959. 352 p.

2:2164 **Toronto. Public Library**
Books and pamphlets published in Canada up to the year eighteen
hundred and thirty-seven, copies of which are in the Public Reference
Library, Toronto, Canada. Toronto, Public Library, 1916. 76 p.
'Compiled by Miss Frances Staton.'—Pref.
Supplement. Toronto, Public Library, 1919. 8 p.
Supplement. Toronto, Public Library, 1926. 8 p.

2:2165 **Toronto. Public Library**
Canada; a reading guide for children and young people, 1941-1946.
Toronto, King's Printer, 1946. 7 p.
Reprinted from the *Ontario library review,* Nov. 1946.

... 1951-1958. Supplement, prepared by the Boys and Girls and Circulation
Divisions of the Toronto Public Libraries. (In *Ontario library review,* v. XLIII,
no. 1, p. 40-46)

2:2166 **Toronto. Public Library**
Canadian books; a study outline for the people, compiled by the
Reference Division, Toronto Public Library. [Toronto] Department
of Education, Public Libraries Branch [1923]. 20 p.

2:2167 **Toronto. Public Library**
The Canadian catalogue of books published in Canada, about Canada,
as well as those written by Canadians, with imprint 1921-1949.
(Consolidated English language reprint edition) with cumulated
author index. [Toronto] Toronto Public Libraries, 1959. 2 v.

2:2168 **Toronto. Public Library**
The Canadian North West; a bibliography of the sources of information in the Public Reference Library of the city of Toronto, Canada,
in regard to the Hudson's Bay Company, the fur trade and the early
history of the Canadian North West. Toronto, Public Library, 1931.
52 p.
Compiled by Miss Frances Staton.

2:2169 **Toronto. Public Library**
Catalogue of Canadian books [English section], British Empire
Exhibition, Wembley Park, London, 1924. Toronto, 1924. 57 p.
Second and revised edition, 1925. 63 p.

2:2170 **Toronto. Public Library**
Guide to the manuscript collection in the Toronto Public Libraries.
[Enl. ed. Toronto] 1954. iv, 116 p.
'The ... collection ... consists mainly of Canadian, and more particularly of
Upper Canadian historical manuscripts, with a few British and American
items ... This guide includes all the manuscripts in the collection with the
exception of non-Canadian material ...'
Prepared by Donalda Putnam and Edith Firth.

2:2171 **Toronto. Public Library**
Map collection of the Public Reference Library of the city of Toronto.
Toronto, Public Library, 1923. 111 p.
Compiled by Miss May MacLachlan.

2:2172  **Toronto. Public Library**
The North West Passage, 1534-1859; a catalogue of an exhibition of books and manuscripts in the Toronto Public Library, compiled by Edith G. Firth. With an introd. by H.C. Campbell. Toronto, Published by Baxter Pub. Co. in co-operation with the Toronto Public Library, 1963. 26 p. illus., ports., maps (on cover p. [2-3]) facsims.

2:2173  **Toronto. Public Library**
Preliminary guide to the manuscript collection in the Toronto public libraries, prepared by Florence B. Murray and Elsie McLeod Murray; under the direction of Charles R. Sanderson. [Toronto] Toronto public libraries, 1940. iv, 60 p.
Second edition (1954) has title: *Guide to the manuscript collection ...*

2:2174  **Toronto. Public Library**
The rebellion of 1837-38; a bibliography of the sources of information in the Public Reference Library of the city of Toronto, Canada. [Toronto] Public Library of Toronto, 1924. 81 p.
Compiled by Miss Frances Staton.

2:2175  **Toronto. Public Library**
Recent Canadian books ... Compiled by the Toronto Public Library for the Minister of Education in the interest of the Canadian book week of 1922. Toronto, Department of Education, 1922. 12 p.

2:2176  **Toronto. Public Library**
A subject catalogue, or finding list of books in the Reference Library, with an index of subjects and personal names. 1889. Including additions made up to February 1st, 1889. Toronto, Murray [1889]. 381 p.
Canada and Newfoundland: p. [267]-321.

2:2177  **Toronto. Royal Ontario Museum.** Art and Archaeology Division
... Brief bibliography of Ontario anthropology, by Kenneth F. Kidd, Edward S. Rogers [and] Walter A. Kenyon. [Toronto, University of Toronto Press, c1964] 2 p. *l.,* 20 p.

2:2178  **Toronto. University.** Library
Ontario New Universities Library Project author-title catalogue. Final cumulation, 1964-1967. [Toronto] 1967.
5 v.
'This final issue is a cumulation of all previous issues, which were originally published in monthly, quarterly, semi-annual, and annual editions.'–Pref.

Catalogue compiled by computer of the collections of Brock University, St Catharines, Ont., Erindale College, University of Toronto, Guelph University, Guelph, Ont., Scarborough College, University of Toronto, and Trent University, Peterborough, Ont.
Project sponsored by the Ontario government and administered by the University of Toronto Library.
Contents: v. 1. A-Compt.–v. 2. Compu-Halc.–v. 3. Hald-Mayh.–v. 4. Mayn-Sanf.–v. 5. Sang-Z.

Scarborough & Erindale College libraries: author-title catalogue; supplement, 1968. [Toronto] 1968.
440 p.
Continuation of the project on an experimental basis as a joint venture of the two college libraries. Cf. Pref.

2:2179 **Toronto. University**. Ontario College of Education. Dept. of Educational Research
Theses in education, Ontario College of Education, University of Toronto, since 1898 (including theses in pedagogy from Queen's University, 1911-1925) ... Toronto [1949-1952?] 2 v. (Educational research series)
Pt. 2 includes 1950-52 theses.

2:2180 **Tougas, Gérard**
A checklist of printed materials relating to French-Canadian literature ... Vancouver, University of British Columbia Library, 1958. 1 *l.*, 93 p.

2:2181 **Tougas, Gérard**
... Liste de référence d'imprimés relatifs à la littérature canadienne-française. Vancouver, University of British Columbia Library, 1958. 1 f., 93 p.

2:2182 **Toupin, Juanita**
Essai de bio-bibliographie sur Marcelle Gauvreau, M.Sc. Montréal, 1956. xiv, 81 p. (Ms. Ecole de Bibl., U. de M.)
éd. précédente. 1947. iv, 46 p. (Ms. Ecole de Bibl., U. de M.)

2:2183 **Toupin, Madeleine**
Bio-bibliographie de Lucille Desparois. 1950. ii, 25 p. (Ms. Ecole de Bibl., U. de M.)

2:2184 **Toussaint, Alice, soeur**
Bibliographie analytique de l'oeuvre du R.P. Ubald Villeneuve, o.m.i., précédée d'une biographie. Préface de M. Roland Lelièvre. Edmundston, N.-B., 1962. 105 p. (Ms. Ecole de Bibl., U.L.)

2:2185 **Toutant, Thomas, frère**
Bibliographie de l'oeuvre du R.P. Joseph François Richard, s.j., avec notice biographique. Québec, 1963. 89 p. (Ms. Ecole de Bibl., U.L.)

2:2186 **Towle, Edward L.**
Bibliography on the economic history and geography of the Great Lakes–St Lawrence drainage basin. Prelim. draft. Rochester, N.Y., 1964. 41 *l.*
Supplementary list no. 1. Rochester, N.Y., 1964. 34 *l.*

2:2187 **Towner, Madeleine**
Bio-bibliographie de Marjolaine [Justa Leclerc]. Préface par Monique [pseud.]. 1946. 60 p. (Mf. Ecole de Bibl., U. de M.)

2:2188 **Traversy, Paul**
Bibliographie de l'oeuvre musicale du révérend Frère Barnabé, s.c., précédée d'une biographie. Préface du Frère Charles, s.c. Trois-Rivières, 1963. 44 p. (Ms. Ecole de Bibl., U.L.)

2:2189 **Treffry, Philippe**
Bio-bibliographie de Damase Potvin. Québec, 1947. 44 p. (Ms. Ecole de Bibl., U.L.)

2:2190 **Tremaine, Marie**
A bibliography of Canadian imprints, 1751-1800. Toronto, University of Toronto Press, 1952. 705 p.

2:2191 **Tremblay, Louis-Marie**
Bibliographie des relations du travail au Canada, 1940-1967, par Louis-Marie Tremblay, avec la collaboration de Francine Panet-Raymond. Montréal, Presses de l'Université de Montréal, 1969. ix, 242 p.

2:2192 **Trépanier, Jacqueline**
Bio-bibliographie de Philippe Aubert de Gaspé. 1943. 26 p. (Mf. Ecole de Bibl., U. de M.)

2:2193 **Trépanier, Rosa**
Bio-bibliographie de Soeur Mondoux, r.h. Préf. de Mlle Marie-Claire Daveluy. [Montréal] 1947. xvii, 37 p. (Ms. Ecole de Bibl., U. de M.)

2:2194 **Trépanier, Thérèse**
Essai de bio-bibliographie de l'oeuvre de l'honorable Elzéar Gérin. 1949. v, 161 p. (Ms. Ecole de Bibl., U. de M.)

2:2195 **Trépanier, Yvette**
Bio-bibliographie de M. Ivanhoë Caron. Lettre-préface de M. l'abbé Irenée Tardif. 1945. 54 p. (Ms. Ecole de Bibl., U. de M.)

2:2196 **Triquet, Florence**
Bio-bibliographie du T.R.P. Forest, o.p., doyen de la Faculté de

Philosophie de l'Université de Montréal. 1945. 49 p. (Mf. Ecole de Bibl., U. de M.)

2:2197 **Trott, Margaret**
Canadian religious art; bibliography of publications between 1955 and Feb. 1967. [Toronto] 1967. i, 13 *l.* (Ms. Toronto Univ. Libr. School)

2:2198 **Trotter, Reginald George**
The bibliography of Canadian constitutional history. Chicago, University Press, 1929. 12 p. (In *Bibliographical society of America, Papers*, v. 22, pt. 1, 1928)

2:2199 **Trotter, Reginald George**
Canadian history, a syllabus and guide to reading. Toronto, Macmillan, 1926. 162 p.
New and enl. ed.: Toronto, Macmillan, 1934. 193 p.

2:2200 **Trottier, Aimé**
Essai de bibliographie sur Saint Joseph. 4e éd. Montréal, Centre de recherche et de documentation, Oratoire Saint-Joseph, 1968.
463 p.
Première éd. en 1953; 2e éd. publiée dans les Cahiers de Joséphologie, 1953-55; 3e éd. en 1962.

2:2201 **Trottier, Guy-N.**
Bibliographie analytique de Mgr Arthur Robert, p.a., v.g. Québec, 1955. 215 p. (Ms. Ecole de Bibl., U.L.)

2:2202 **Trottier, Irénée**
Bibliographie analytique de l'œuvre de Mgr Joseph-Clovis K. Laflamme (1849-1910) Préface de M. René Bureau. Québec, 1961. 80 p. (Ms. Ecole de Bibl., U.L.)

2:2203 **Truax, Keitha Lynne**
George Brown; a bibliography of materials from 1856-1963. [Toronto] 1966. 12 *l.* (Ms. Toronto Univ. Libr. School)

2:2204 **Trudeau, Claude-Bernard**
Bio-bibliographie de Cécile Chabot. 1948. 109 p. (Mf. Ecole de Bibl., U. de M.)

2:2205 **Trudeau, Paul-Albert, père**
Bibliographie viatorienne. 1939. 22 p. (Ms. Ecole de Bibl., U. de M.)

2:2206 **Trudeau, R.**
Bibliographie d'Edmond de Nevers [Edmond Boisvert]. 1944. 21 p. (Mf. Ecole de Bibl., U. de M.)

2:2207  **Trudeau, Yvan**
Essai de bio-bibliographie de Pierre Dagenais. Montréal, 1956. viii,
55 p. (Ms. Ecole de Bibl., U. de M.)

2:2208  **Trudel, Marcel**
Chiniquy. [Trois-Rivières], Editions du Bien public, 1955. xxxviii,
[1], 339 p.
Bibliographie: p. [xv]-xxxvi.

2:2209  **Tung, Chang Yiu**
A selected bibliography on Chinese in Canada. 1964. vi, 6 1.
(Ms. U. of O. Libr. School)

2:2210  **Turbide, Jean-Louis**
Notes bio-bibliographiques sur Me Damien Jasmin conservateur de la
bibliothèque St-Sulpice. 1948. 13 p. (Mf. Ecole de Bibl., U. de M.)

2:2211  **Turcotte, Fernande**
Les bibliothèques paroissiales; bibliographie analytique de la
littérature française parue sur le sujet dans la province de Québec.
Préf. du R.P. Gilles-Marie Bélanger, o.p. Québec, 1952. 75 p. (Ms.
Ecole de Bibl., U.L.)

2:2212  **Turcotte, Monique**
Essai de bio-bibliographie: R.S. Marie Stéphane, d.m. 1953. 19 p.
(Ms. Ecole de Bibl., U. de M.)

2:2213  **Turek, Victor**
... The Polish-language press in Canada: its history and a bibliographi-
cal list. Foreword by John W. Holmes. Toronto, Printed by Polish
Alliance Press, 1962. 248 p. illus., map. (Polish Research Institute
in Canada. Studies, 4)
'Second supplement to Polinica canadiana, 1848-1957': p. [217]-229.

2:2214  **Turek, Victor**
Polonica canadiana; a bibliographical list of the Canadian Polish
imprints, 1848-1957. Foreword by Robert H. Blackburn. Toronto,
Polish Alliance Press, 1958. 138 p. (*Polish Research Institute in
Canada. Studies, 2*)

2:2215  **Turgeon, Marguerite**
Bio-bibliographie de Roger Lemelin. Québec, 1949. 56 p. (Ms.
Ecole de Bibl., U.L.)

2:2216  **Turmel, Yvon**
Relevé des périodiques de langue française (non quotidiens) publiés
à Montréal. [Montréal] 1959. ix, 52 p. (Ms. Ecole de Bibl., U. de M.)

2:2217 **Turnbull, Jean**
Periodical articles, pamphlets, government publications and books
relating to the West Kootenay Region of British Columbia in the
Selkirk College Library, Castlegar, B.C. Castlegar, B.C., Selkirk College,
1968.
36 *l.*

2:2218 **Turpin, Marguerite**
... The life and work of Emily Carr (1871-1945) A selected bibliography. Vancouver, University of British Columbia School of Librarianship [1965]. 20 p.

2:2219 **Tyszkiewicz, Alexandra**
La ville de Québec vue par le voyageur (1776-1960) Bibliographie
analytique des imprimés. Préface de M. Pierre Savard. Québec,
1964. 52 p. (Ms. Ecole de Bibl., U.L.)

2:2220 **Ubald, frère**
Bio-bibliographie du T.R.P. Georges-Henri Lévesque, doyen de la
Faculté des Sciences sociales de l'Université Laval. Québec, 1947.
38 p. (Ms. Ecole de Bibl., U.L.)

2:2221 **Ukrainian Free Academy of Sciences**
List of publications of Ukrainian Free Academy of Sciences–UVAN
of Canada, inc. Winnipeg, 1965. 15 p.
First ed. 1961.

2:2222 **Ukrainica canadiana.** Winnipeg, Ukrainian Free Academy of
Sciences, 1951–. (*Ukrainian Free Academy of Sciences. Series:
Bibliography, no. 1–* ) Annual.
Books and pamphlets also listed in *Slavica canadiana,* 1951–.
Ukrainica canadiana, 1951-52, published in *Ukrainian year book,* 1952/53-
1953/54. 1953– published separately.

2:2223 **Uldéric, frère**
Bibliographie du R.F. Patrice, s.c. Préface du R.F. Claude, s.c.
Québec, 1961. 60 p. (Ms. Ecole de Bibl., U:L.)

2:2224 **Ullman, Solomon Baruch**
Bibliography. Toronto [1961?] 15 *l.*
Bibliography of author's publications.

2:2225 **United States. Department of Agriculture.** Library
... A classified list of soil publications of the United States and
Canada. Washington, 1927. xi, 549 p. (Bibliographical contributions.
no. 13)

2:2226 **United States. Geological Survey**
Annotated bibliography on hydrology and sedimentation, United
States and Canada, 1955-58. Compiled by H.C. Riggs. Washington,
Govt. Print. Off., 1962.
iv, 236 p. (*Its* Water-supply paper, 1546)
Prepared in cooperation with the Subcommittees on Hydrology and Sedimen-
tation, Inter-Agency Committee on Water Resources.
Supersedes Annotated bibliography on hydrology, 1941-1950: United States
and Canada; Annotated bibliography on hydrology (1951-54) and sedimenta-
tion (1950-54): United States and Canada, both compiled by the American
Geophysical Union; and Annotated bibliography on sedimentation.

2:2227 **United States. Geological Survey**
Bibliography of North American geology, 1906– Washington, U.S.
Government Printing Office, [1908?–] annual.

2:2228 **United States. Information Service.** Ottawa
A list of selected publications and sources of information on
Canadian-American relations. Ottawa, [1966]
75, viii p.

2:2229 **United States. Library of Congress.** Division of Bibliography
Brief list of references on Canadians in the United States.
[Washington], 1925. 5 *l*.

2:2230 **United States. Library of Congress.** Division of Bibliography
List of references on Canada, with special reference to present-day
problems. Washington, 1920. 5 *l*.

2:2231 **United States. Library of Congress.** Division of Bibliography
List of references on Canadian independence. Washington, 1915. 2 *l*.

2:2232 **United States. Library of Congress.** Division of Bibliography
List of references on question of annexation of Canada to the United
States. Washington, 1904. 4 *l*.
Another edition: 1907. 8 *l*.

2:2233 **United States. Library of Congress.** Division of Bibliography
... List of references on reciprocity; comp. under the direction of the
chief bibliographer; 1st ed.: Appleton Prentiss Clark Griffin; 2d ed.,
with additions: H.H.B. Meyer. Washington, G.P.O., 1910. 1 p. *l.*, 137 p.
Additional references relating to reciprocity with Canada, Washington, G.P.O.,
1911. 1 p. *l.*, 44 p.
Other lists issued in 1902, 1907.

2:2234 **United States. Library of Congress.** Division of Bibliography
List of references on the constitutional history of Canada.
[Washington] 1920. 3 *l*.

2:2235 **United States. Library of Congress.** Division of Bibliography
... The St Lawrence navigation and power project, a list of recent references. Washington, 1940. 11 p.
Compiled by Ann Duncan Brown.

2:2236 **United States. Library of Congress.** Division of Bibliography
... The St Lawrence navigation and power project, a list of recent references (supplementing previous lists). Compiled by Ann Duncan Brown under the direction of Florence S. Hellman, chief bibliographer. [Washington] 1942. 28 p.

2:2237 **United States. Library of Congress.** Division of Bibliography
Select list of references on the commercial and treaty relations of the United States and Canada, with special reference to the Great Lakes. Washington [1910]. 4 *l.*

2:2238 **United States. Library of Congress.** Division of Bibliography
... Selected list of recent books and pamphlets on Canada. Compiled by Ann Duncan Brown, under the direction of Florence S. Hellman, chief bibliographer. [Washington] 1941. 145 p.

2:2239 **United States and Canadian publications on Africa**
1964. Compiled by Liselotte Hofmann. [Stanford] Hoover Institution on War, Revolution and Peace, Stanford University, 1966.
ix, 180 p. (*Hoover Institution bibliographical series,* 25) annual.
Books, pamphlets and articles relating to all of Africa except Morocco, Algeria, Tunisia, Libya and Egypt.
First published for 1960, Washington, African Section, U.S. Library of Congress, 1962.

2:2240 **United States and Canadian publications on Africa**
1965. [Stanford, Calif.] Hoover Institution on War, Revolution and Peace, Stanford University, 1967.
ix, 227 p. (*Hoover Institution bibliographical series,* 34) annual.
Cover title: United States and Canadian publications and theses on Africa in 1965.
Compiled by Liselotte Hofmann.
Books, pamphlets, theses and articles relating to all of Africa except Morocco, Algeria, Tunisia, Libya and Egypt.
First published for 1960, Washington, African Section, U.S. Library of Congress, 1962.

2:2241 **Université Laval. Centre de documentation**
Index des projets de recherche en cours dans les universités du Québec. Index of research projects being carried out in Quebec universities. 2d ed.; 1968. Quebec, 1969.
1 v. (unpaged)

2:2242 **Université McGill. Centre d'études canadiennes-françaises.**
Bibliothèque
Bibliographie préliminaire de poésie canadienne-française. [Montréal]
1968.
26 f.

2:2243 **University of Western Ontario. School of Library and Information**
Science
Book catalog. [no.] 2; fall 1968. London [Ont.] 1968.
363 p.
Began with no. 1, winter 1968 [i.e. 1967/68]

2:2244 **Vachon, Madeleine E.**
Bibliographie analytique de l'œuvre de Jacques de Monléon, précédée
d'une biographie. Préface de Emmanuel Trépanier. Québec, 1963.
15 p. (Ms. Ecole de Bibl., U.L.)

2:2245 **Vaillancourt, Emilienne**
Bio-bibliographie de Eddy Boudreau. Québec, 1954. 84 p. (Ms.
Ecole de Bibl., U.L.)

2:2246 **Vaillancourt, Jacqueline**
Bio-bibliographie de Louis-Joseph Doucet. 1945. 27 p. (Mf. Ecole
de Bibl., U. de M.)

2:2247 **Vaillancourt, Madeleine**
Bio-bibliographie de Simone Routier. 1948. 21 p. (Mf. Ecole de Bibl.,
U. de M.)

2:2248 **Vaillancourt, Thérèse**
Notes bio-bibliographiques sur Jacques Hébert. 1950. x, 21 p.
(Mf. Ecole de Bibl., U. de M.)

2:2249 **Vallée, Camille**
Bibliographie de Joseph Belleau, professeur de langues à la faculté
des lettres de Laval. Préf. de M. Jean-C. Falardeau. Québec, 1951.
47 p. (Ms. Ecole de Bibl., U.L.)

2:2250 **Valley, Jeannine**
Essai de bio-bibliographie de M. Joseph-Antoine Brunet. Préface de
M. Trefflé Boulanger. 1954. xii, 55 p. (Ms. Ecole de Bibl., U. de M.)

2:2251 **Valois, Robert**
Bio-bibliographie du R.P. Gustave Lamarche, c.s.v. Préface de M.
Léo-Paul Desrosiers. 1942. xii, 81 p. (Mf. Ecole de Bibl., U. de M.)

2:2252 **Vandal, Claude**
Bio-bibliographie de Joseph Marmette. Préface de M. Maurice Brière.
Granby, 1944. 30 p. (Mf. Ecole de Bibl., U. de M.)

2:2253 **Vandandaigne, Osias, père**
Bibliographie du R.P. Bonaventure Péloquin, o.f.m. Préface par le
T.R.P. Georges-Albert Laplante, o.f.m. 1943. 57 p. (Ms. Ecole de
Bibl., U. de M.)

2:2254 **Vanier Institute of the Family**
An inventory of family research and studies in Canada, 1963-1967.
Un inventaire des recherches et des études sur la famille au Canada.
Ottawa, 1967.
xiv, 161 p.

2:2255 **Van Patten, Nathan**
Arthur Machen, a bibliographical note. Kingston, Queen's University
Library, 1926. 4 p.

2:2256 **Veilleux, Bertrand**
Bibliographie sur les relations entre l'Eglise et l'état au Canada
français, 1791-1914. Montréal, Bibliothèque, Centre d'études
canadiennes-françaises, Université McGill, 1969.
92 f.

2:2257 **Véronique-Marie, sœur**
M. Adélard Breton, i.e.; essai de bio-bibliographie. 1953. 35 p.
(Ms. Ecole de Bibl., U. de M.)

2:2258 **Verret, Madeleine**
Bibliographie de Joseph-Edmond Roy. Québec, 1947. 28 p. (Ms.
Ecole de Bibl., U.L.)

2:2259 **Vézina, Claire**
Bio-bibliographie du T.R.P. Paul-Emile Farley, c.s.v. Préface du R.P.
Gustave Lamarche, c.s.v. 1945. xv, 15 p. (Ms. Ecole de Bibl., U. de M.)

2:2260 **Vézina, Germain**
Québec métropolitain; répertoire bibliographique. [Québec] Université
Laval, Faculté de théologie, Centre de recherches en socioloreligieuse,
1968.
64 p.

2:2261 **Vézina, Jacqueline**
Bio-bibliographie de M. Joseph-Charles Taché. 1945. v, 28 p. (Mf.
Ecole de Bibl., U. de M.)

2:2262  **Videbech, Bent**
Kanadiske biblioteker; indtryk fra en rejse i Kanada. Viborg, Denmark, The Author, 1932. 15 p.
[Canadian libraries; impressions from a journey in Canada.]

2:2263  **Vient de paraître**; bulletin du livre au Canada français. v. 1, no 1; janv. 1965— Montréal, Librairie Beauchemin, 1965— mensuel.
Remplace un bulletin du même titre, publié 1963-64 par l'Association des éditeurs canadiens.

2:2264  **Villemaire, Fernande**
Bio-bibliographie: N.-E. Dionne, historien et bibliothécaire. Préface du colonel G.-E. Marquis. 1945. x, 87 p. (Mf. Ecole de Bibl., U. de M.)

2:2265  **Villeneuve, Jocelyne**
Le Révérend Père Auguste-M. Morisset. 1964. iv, 6 1. (Ms. U. of O. Libr. School)

2:2266  **Vincent, Emile**
Notes bio-bibliographiques sur le T.R.P. Marc-Antonio Lamarche, o.p. 1947. 31 p. (Mf. Ecole de Bibl., U. de M.)

2:2267  **Vinet, Bernard**
Bio-bibliographie de Elzéar Labelle. Préface de Marie-Claire Daveluy. 1946. 45 p. (Mf. Ecole de Bibl., U. de M.)

2:2268  **Virginie-Marie, soeur**
Bibliographie analytique de l'abbé Herman Plante, précédée d'une biographie. Trois-Rivières, 1964. 42 p. (Ms. Ecole de Bibl., U.L.)

2:2269  **Vleminckx, Gérard**
L'oeuvre de M. l'abbé Lionel Groulx; petit essai bio-bibliographique. 1939. 55 p. (Mf. Ecole de Bibl., U. de M.)

2:2270  **Voisine, Nive**
Bio-bibliographie analytique de l'oeuvre de Marcel Trudel. Préface du chanoine A. Fortin. Québec, 1959. 90 p. (Ms. Ecole de Bibl., U.L.)

2:2271  **Wagner, Monique**
Bio-bibliographie du R.F. Antoine Bernard, c.s.v. Montréal, 1961. xv, 67 p. (Ms. Ecole de Bibl., U. de M.)

2:2272  **Wagner, Rosemarie E.**
Manitoba in fiction. Montreal, 1957. iii, 6 *l*. (Ms. McGill Univ. Libr. School)

2:2273  **Walcott, M. Alena**
A selective bibliography on the Indians of Eastern Canada. Montreal, 1938. 4 *l*. (Ms. McGill Univ. Libr. School)

2:2274 **Waldon, Freda F.**
Canadiana published in Great Britain 1519-1763. A list of books, pamphlets, broadsides, etc.
Manuscript deposited with the Canadian Bibliographic Centre (National Library) July, 1950.

2:2275 **Walker, Sir Byron Edmund**
List of the published writings of Elkanah Billings, palaeontologist to the Geological Survey of Canada, 1856-1876. Reprinted from the *Canadian record of science,* v. VIII, no. 6, for July 1901, issued 10th August, 1901. [n.p. 1901] [366]-387 p.

2:2276 **Wallace, William Stewart**
The periodical literature of Upper Canada. Toronto, The Author, 1931. 22 p.
Reprinted from *Canadian historical review,* v. 12, 1931.

2:2277 **Wallace, William Stewart**
The Ryerson imprint, a checklist of the books and pamphlets published by the Ryerson Press since the foundation of the House in 1829. Toronto, Ryerson Press [1954]. 141 p.

2:2278 **Wallbridge, Allan**
Air services in northern Canada. 1957. [4] 8 1. 1957. (Ms. U. of O. Libr. School)

2:2279 **Walters, John**
An annotated bibliography of reports, theses, and publications pertaining to the Campus and Research Forests of the University of British Columbia. Vancouver, Faculty of Forestry, University of British Columbia, 1968.
viii, 71 p.

2:2280 **Walters, John**
An annotated bibliography of western hemlock (Tsuga heterophylla (Raf.) Sarg.) Vancouver, Faculty of Forestry, University of British Columbia, 1963. 86 p.

2:2281 **Wang, Jung-Kuang**
Labour supply and labour relations in Canada, 1960-1962. 1963. vi, 5 1. (Ms. U. of O. Libr. School)

2:2282 **Ward, Dederick C.**
Bibliography of theses in geology, 1965-1966, by Dederick C. Ward and T.C. O'Callaghan. [Washington, D.B.] American Geological Institute in cooperation with the Geoscience Information Society [c1969]

v, 255 p.

Continues Bibliography of theses written for advanced degrees in geology and related sciences at universities and colleges in the United States and Canada through 1957, by John and Halka Chronic (Boulder, Colo., Pruett Press, 1958); Bibliography of theses in geology, 1958-1963, by John and Halka Chronic, (Washington, American Geological Institute, 1964); Bibliography of theses in geology, 1964, by Dederick C. Ward (Published as a supplement to v. 7, no. 12 of Geoscience Abstracts, 1965). Cf. Pref., p. v.

2:2283  **Waterloo. Ont. University.** Engineering, Mathematics & Science Library Reference list[s] Waterloo, Ont., 1967.

14 v.

Includes only representative titles of periodicals, reference books, important series, etc.; monographs are excluded.

2:2284  **Watson, Albert Durant**

Robert Norwood. Toronto, Ryerson [1923]. 124 p. (Makers of Canadian literature ...)

Bibliography: p. 117-118.

2:2285  **Watson, Dorothy**

Duncan Campbell Scott; a bibliography. Toronto, 1945. [3], xiv, 11 *l.* (Ms. Toronto Univ. Libr. School)

2:2286  **Watters, Reginald Eyre**

A checklist of Canadian literature and background materials, 1628-1950. In two parts. Being a comprehensive list of the books which constitute Canadian literature written in English, together with a selective list of other books by Canadian authors which reveal the backgrounds of that literature. Compiled for the Humanities Research Council of Canada. [Toronto] University of Toronto Press [1959]. xx, 789 p.

2:2287  **Watters, Reginald Eyre**

On Canadian literature, 1806-1960; a checklist of articles, books, and theses on English-Canadian literature, its authors, and language, compiled by Reginald Eyre Watters [and] Inglis Freeman Bell. [Toronto] University of Toronto Press [c1966]

ix, 165 p.

2:2288  **Webber, Mildred G.E.**

Canadian wild flowers; a bibliography. [Toronto, 1932] [2], 7 *l.* (Ms. Toronto Univ. Libr. School)

2:2289  **Webster, John Clarence**

Those crowded years, 1863-1944. An octogenarian's record of work. Privately printed for his family. Shediac, N.B., 1944. 51 p.

Bibliography: p. 42-51.

2:2290 **Webster, John Clarence**
William Frances Ganong memorial, edited with an introduction by
Dr J.C. Webster. Saint John, N.B., New Brunswick Museum, 1942.
31 p.
Bibliography: p. 19-31.

2:2291 **Wells, Angéline**
Notes bio-bibliographiques sur M. J.-Ernest Laforce et la colonisation.
[Montréal] 1947. 13 p. (Ms. Ecole de Bibl., U. de M.)

2:2292 **Wen, Shu**
Monetary policy of the Bank of Canada in the last three years
(1957-1959) An annotated bibliography. Ottawa, University of
Ottawa, Library School, 1961. 14 p. (Ms. U. of O. Libr. School)

2:2293 **Westman, William**
Factors affecting Quebec separatism. 1963. [2] 8 l. (Ms. U. of O.
Libr. School)

2:2294 **Weston, Sydney Moss**
Publications of the Government of British Columbia, 1871-1937;
a checklist. Victoria, B.C., Banfield, Printer to the King, 1939. 167 p.
A revised and enlarged edition, compiled by Marjorie C. Holmes, was published
in 1950.

2:2295 **Whiffin, Jean Iris**
Percé and Bonaventure Island, Quebec; a bibliography. [Toronto]
1963. 13 l. (Ms. Toronto Univ. Libr. School)

2:2296 **White, Arthur V.**
Bibliography [of British Columbia] (In Canada, Commission of
Conservation, Water powers of British Columbia, Ottawa, 1919.
p. 602-620.)
A representative list of books, government reports, etc., relating to British
Columbia and the Northwest.

2:2297 **White, Meredith Allison**
The Canadian little theatre; a bibliography. Montreal, 1932. 14 l.
(Ms. McGill Univ. Libr. School)

2:2298 **Whiteside, Margaret Susan**
Upper Canada from the woman's viewpoint; a bibliography of jour-
nals, letters and books written by women travellers and settlers in
Upper Canada, 1767-1900. Toronto, 1966. vi, 13 l. (Ms. Toronto
Univ. Libr. School)

2:2299 **Whitworth, Fred E.**
Teaching aids obtainable from departments of the government at Ottawa. Ottawa, Canadian Council of Education for Citizenship, 1944. 20 p.
New edition: 1946. 17 p.

2:2300 **Wickett, Samuel Morley**
Bibliography of Canadian municipal government ... (In Toronto, University, *University of Toronto studies, History and economics.* [Toronto] 1903. v. 2, no. 2, p. [63]-70.)
Supplementary bibliography of Canadian municipal government. (In Toronto, University, *University of Toronto studies, History and economics.* [Toronto] 1904. v. 2, no. 3, p. [63].)

2:2301 **Wiedrick, L.G.**
Selection sources for print and non-print school library materials, by L.G. Wiedrick. Edmonton, School Library Council, Alberta Teachers' Association, 1968.
iii, 14 p.

2:2302 **Wigmore, Shirley K.**
An annotated guide to publications related to educational research, by Shirley K. Wigmore, with the assistance of W. Brehaut, J.F. Flowers [and] H.W. Savage. [Toronto] Department of Educational Research, Ontario College of Education, University of Toronto, 1960. v. 26 p. (*Educational research series,* no. 32)

2:2303 **Wigney, Trevor John**
The education of women and girls in a changing society; a selected bibliography with annotations. [Toronto] Department of Educational Research, Ontario College of Education, University of Toronto, 1965. v, 76 p. (*Educational research series,* no. 36)

2:2304 **Wildgoose, Nancy M.**
Leonard Cohen: a bibliography of his published volumes of poetry, 1956-1966; with critical and biographical works about Cohen the poet and Cohen the man. [Toronto] 1967. iii, 14 *l.* (Ms. Toronto Univ. Libr. School)

2:2305 **Wiles, Valerie**
The Canada Council—promoting Canadian culture in the arts. 1964. [v] 7 *l.* (Ms. U. of O. Libr. School)

2:2306 **Wilkinson, Susan**
The Development of regional library systems in the Maritime provinces. 1966. iv, 12 *l.* (Ms. U. of O. Libr. School)

2:2307  **Williams, C. Brian**
Manpower management in Canada; a selected bibliography, by C.
Brian Williams. Kingston, Ont., Industrial Relations Centre, Queen's
University, 1968.
121 p.

2:2308  **Williamson, Elizabeth J.**
A bibliography of the history of Essex County. Toronto, 1938. 24 *l.*
(Ms. Toronto Univ. Libr. School)

2:2309  **Williamson, Mary Frances**
Bibliography of hand-books for emigrants to Ontario, printed in
Canada from 1860 to 1890. [Toronto] 1960. 14 *l.* (Ms. Toronto
Univ. Libr. School)

2:2310  **Wilson, Lucy Roberta**
Regional and county library service in Canada; a bibliography.
Ottawa, Canadian Library Association, 1949. 13 *l.*

2:2311  **Wilson, Roma M.H.**
Bibliography; Charles William Gordon (Ralph Connor, pseud.).
[Toronto] 1933. [16] *l.* (Ms. Toronto Univ. Libr. School)

2:2312  **Windsor, N.S. University of King's College.** The Haliburton Club
Haliburton; a centenary chaplet. With a bibliography by John Parker
Anderson ... Toronto, Briggs, 1897. 116 p.
Published for the Haliburton Club, King's College, Windsor, N.S.

2:2313  **Windsor, Ont. Public Library**
Bibliography of Windsor and Essex County, prepared by Edith Jarvi.
[Rev. ed., Windsor] 1955. 35 *l.*

2:2314  **Winnipeg. Public Library**
A selective bibliography of Canadiana of the Prairie Provinces;
publications relating to Western Canada by English, French, Icelandic,
Mennonite and Ukrainian authors. Winnipeg, Public Library, 1949.
33 p.
A.F. Jamieson, editor.

2:2315  **Winship, George Parker**
Cabot bibliography; with an introductory essay on the careers of the
Cabots based upon an independent examination of the sources of
information. London, Stevens; New York, Dodd, Mead, 1900. 180 p.

2:2316  **Woeller, Richard**
Stratford festival—History and growth. 1967. v, 10 1. (Ms. U. of O.
Libr. School)

2:2317 **Wolfe, Rosemarie**
Edward John Chapman, 1821-1904; an essay in bibliography.
Toronto, 1966. 21 *l*. (Ms. Toronto Univ. Libr. School)

2:2318 **Wood (T.F.) and Co.**
T.F. Wood & Co's. Canadian newspaper directory, containing accurate
lists of all the newspapers and periodicals published in the Dominion
of Canada and province of Newfoundland. Montreal, Wood, 1876.
79 p.
'We purpose continuing the publication annually ...' cf. 'To the public' p. [4]

2:2319 **Woodward, Frances**
'Bibliography of British Columbia.' Appears in *BC Studies*, No. 1—,
Winter, 1968-69— Published three times yearly; includes books and
articles published in the province in the period covered by each issue.

2:2320 **Woycenko, Olha**
... Frankiana in Canada. A selective annotated bibliography (1910-
1956) Winnipeg, Published by Shevchenko Foundation, 1957. 64 p.
Reprinted from *Ukrainica occidentalia* IV (2), 1957.

2:2321 **Writings of Benjamin Sulte.** Milwaukee, Keogh, 1898. 13 p.
Attributed to Henry J. Morgan, by Fraser, I.F., in his *Bibliography of French-
Canadian poetry (q.v.).*

2:2322 **Würtele, Frederick Christian**
Index of the lectures, papers, and historical documents published by
the Literary and Historical Society of Quebec; also the names of
their authors, together with a list of the unpublished papers read
before the Society, 1829 to 1891. Quebec, Morning Chronicle, 1891.
xlix p.
(In *Literary and Historical Society of Quebec, Transactions,* no. 18. 1883-
1886)

2:2323 **Wyczynski, Paul**
Emile Nelligan; bio-bibliographie. (In *Lectures,* octobre 1959)

2:2324 **Young, Beatrice L.**
Dr John Rolph, 1793-1870; a bibliography. Toronto, 1936. 20 *l*.
(Ms. Toronto Univ. Libr. School)

2:2325 **Young Women's Christian Associations.** Montreal. Roles of Women
Study Committee
Bibliography. Rev. ed. Montreal [1966]
47 *l*.

# Index

Subjects of bibliographies appear in UPPER CASE. Emphasis has been placed on geographical classification where applicable. Names of compilers and editors appear in lower case.

Abbott, D., 2:1625
Abbott, Maude Elizabeth Seymour, 2:1; 2:2; 2:529
ABBOTT, MAUDE ELIZABETH SEYMOUR, 2:2
Abernethy, George Lawrence, 2:3
L'ACADEMIE CANADIENNE-FRANÇAISE
  bio-bibliographies des membres, 2:4; 2:92
  publications, 2:92
Acadia, see NOVA SCOTIA
ACADIA UNIVERSITY, WOLFVILLE, N.S. LIBRARY
  ERIC R. DENNIS COLLECTION, 2:6
  MARITIME BAPTIST HISTORICAL COLLECTION, 2:7
  WILLIAM INGLIS MORSE COLLECTION, 2:5
Acadie, voir NOVA SCOTIA
ACHARD, EUGENE, 2:862; 2:2132
Achille, frère, 2:8
ACHILLE, FRERE, 2:892; 2:1537
ACTE DE QUEBEC, 1774, 2:1302
Adam, Margaret Isabella, 2:9
Adams, Charles Joseph, 2:10
Adams, Dorothy S., 2:11
Adams, Ethel M., 2:12
Adams, J., 2:189
Adams, Margaret B., 2:13
Adams, R.D., 2:14
ADDISON, ROBERT
  library, 2:334
ADDRESSES, 2:656
Adelmus, frère, 2:15
ADOLESCENCE, 2:1069
ADULT EDUCATION, see also EDUCATION; ENSEIGNEMENT, ADULTES, 2:305; 2:479; 2:1889; 2:2104; 2:2155
  libraries and, 2:2071

ADVERTISING, 2:477
Aedy, Lenora Gladys, 2:16
AERONAUTICS
  bush flying, 2:981
AEROPLANES, 2:2049
AFRICA, 2:2239; 2:2240
Agnès-de-Marie, soeur, 2:17
AGRICULTURE, 2:372; 2:373;
  Dept. of Agriculture (Alta.) publications, 2:21
  Dept. of Agriculture (B.C.) publications, 2:280
  economics, 2:371
  histoire, 2:1738
  Ministère de l'Agriculture (Can.). Division de l'économie, publications, 2:433
  Ministère de l'Agriculture (Can.). Division de l'économie rurale, publications, 2:434
  Ministère de l'Agriculture (Can.). Division de l'information, publications, 2:435
  Ministère de l'Agriculture (Can.). Service de l'information, publications, 2:436
  publications, 2:436
  periodicals, 2:817; 2:2107
  United Farmers of Ontario, 2:823
AIGLE, JEANNE D', 2:1451
Aitken, Barbara Boyd, 2:18
AKINS COLLECTION
  Public Archives (N.S.), 2:1641
Alarie, Maurice, 2:19
Albert, Thérèse, 2:20
ALBERTA
  imprints, 2:1717
Alberta Library Association, 2:27
Alberta-Marie, soeur, 2:28
Alberta Society of Petroleum Geologists, 2:29

Dept. of Mines and Resources (Can.).
Surveys and Engineering Branch, 2:385
Dept. of Mines and Technical Surveys
(Can.), *see also* Ministère des Mines
et des Relevés techniques (Can.), 2:386;
2:387
Dept. of Mines and Technical Surveys
(Can.). Geographical Branch, 2:388; 2:389;
2:390; 2:391; 2:392; 2:393; 2:395; 2:396;
2:397; 2:398; 2:399; 2:400; 2:401; 2:402;
2:403
DEPT. OF MINES AND TECHNICAL
SURVEYS (CAN.). GEOGRAPHICAL
BRANCH
publications, 2:394
Dept. of Mines and Technical Survey
(Can.). Geological Survey, 2:988
Dept. of Mines and Technical Surveys
(Can.). Mines Branch, 2:404
DEPT. OF MINES AND TECHNICAL
SURVEYS (CAN.). MINES BRANCH
publications, 2:410
DEPT. OF NORTHERN AFFAIRS AND
NATIONAL RESOURCES (CAN.), *see
also* MINISTERE DU NORD CANADIEN
ET RESSOURCES NATURELLES (CAN.)
publications, 2:411
Dept. of Northern Affairs and National
Resources (Can.). Northern Administra-
tion Branch, 2:1638
Dept. of Northern Affairs and National
Resources (Can.). Northern Co-ordination
and Research Centre, 2:1353
Dept. of Public Printing and Stationery
(Can.), *see also* Dépt. des impressions et
papeterie publiques (Can.), 2:405; 2:406;
2:407; 2:408; 2:409
Dept. of Public Printing and Stationery
(Can.). Documents Library, 2:410; 2:411
DEPT. OF THE INTERIOR (CAN.)
geographical publications, 2:412
DEPT. OF THE INTERIOR (CAN.).
NATURAL RESOURCES INTELLIGENCE
BRANCH
publications, 2:413
DEPT. OF THE INTERIOR (CAN.).
SURVEYS BRANCH
maps, 2:414; 2:415; 2:416
publications, 2:414; 2:415; 2:416
Dept. of Trade and Commerce (Que.),
*see also* Ministère de l'Industrie et du
Commerce (Qué.)

Dept. of Trade and Commerce (Que.).
Geographical Service, 2:1793
DEPT. OF TRANSPORT (CAN.). LIBRARY
Canadian Pacific Railway, 2:1374
Depatie, Lise, 2:745
Déry, Claire, 2:746
Desaulniers, François Lesieur, *voir*
LESIEUR-DESAULNIERS, FRANÇOIS
DESAULNIERS, GONZALVE, 2:1267
Desaulniers, Hélène-L., 2:747
Desaulniers, Jacqueline, *voir* Pelletier,
Jacqueline (Desaulniers)
Desautels, Adrien, 2:748
Desbarats Advertising Agency, 2:749
Descarries, Andrée, 2:750
DESCHAMP, PHILIPPE, 2:619
Deschene, Jean-Claude, 2:751
Des Chérubins, Marie, *voir* Marie des
Chérubins
De Serres, Clorinde, 2:752
De Serres, Françoise, *voir* Grégoire,
Françoise (De Serres)
DESILETS, ALPHONSE, 2:1294
Desjardins, sœur, 2:753
Desjardins, Claire, 2:754
Desjardins, Jeanette, 2:755
Desjardins, Lucienne, 2:756
Desjardins, Simone, 2:757
Desjardins, Suzanne, 2:758
Deslandes, Germain, 2:759
DesLauriers, Françoise, 2:760
DESMARAIS, MARCEL-MARIE, 2:818;
2:1283
DESMARCHAIS, REX, 2:278; 2:1310
DESMEULES, ROLAND, 2:2007
Desnoyers, Paul-Henri, 2:761
Des Ormes, Renée, *voir* FERLAND-
TURGEON, MARIE
DESPAROIS, LUCILLE, 2:2183
Després, Azaile-Etienne Couillard, *voir*
COUILLARD-DESPRES, AZARLIE-
ETIENNE
DESROCHERS, ALFRED, 2:991
Desrochers, Edmond, 2:762
Desrochers, Guy, 2:763
Desrochers, Lucienne, *voir* Leduc,
Lucienne (Desrochers)
Desrochers, Marthe, 2:764
DESROCHERS, RENE, 2:137
Desroches, Denyse, 2:765
DESROCHES, FRANCIS, 2:765; 2:1773
Desrosiers, Elphège, père, 2:766